WACO

WACO

A Survivor's Story

DAVID THIBODEAU
and LEON WHITESON

with AVIVA LAYTON

hachette
BOOKS

NEW YORK   BOSTON

Hachette Books
Hachette Book Group
1290 Avenue of the Americas, New York, NY 10104
hachettebooks.com
twitter.com/hachettebooks

Original hardcover edition published September 1999 by PublicAffairs as *A Place Called Waco*

First Paperback Edition: January 2018

Hachette Books is a division of Hachette Book Group, Inc. The Hachette Books name and logo are trademarks of Hachette Book Group, Inc.

The publisher is not responsible for websites (or their content) that are not owned by the publisher.

The Hachette Speakers Bureau provides a wide range of authors for speaking events. To find out more, go to www.hachettespeakersbureau.com or call (866) 376-6591.

All photographs in the insert are courtesy of the author with the exception of the following: David Koresh, leader of the Branch Davidian community: Copyright © *Waco Tribune-Herald/SYGMA*; David Koresh on a trip to Australia: Copyright © Elizabeth Baranyai/*SYGMA*; Marc Breault and Steve Schneider: Copyright © Elizabeth Baranyai/*SYGMA*; ATF agents attacking: Copyright © *KWTX-TV/SYGMA*; The ATF retrieves its wounded agents: Copyright © Rod Aydelotte/*Waco Tribune Herald/SYGMA*; Six hours after federal tanks: Copyright © *CORBIS/Reuters*.

Print book interior design by Jack Lenzo.

Library of Congress Cataloging-in-Publication Data has been applied for.
ISBNs: 978-1-60286-573-0 (paperback), 978-1-60286-576-1 (e-book)

Printed in the United States of America

LSC-C

10 9 8 7 6 5 4 3 2 1

CONTENTS

BOOK III: LIFE AS A SURVIVOR

PROLOGUE
This Could Be the Day That I Die

It is hell. Day and night booming speakers blast us with wild sounds—blaring sirens, shrieking seagulls, howling coyotes, wailing bagpipes, crying babies, the screams of strangled rabbits, crowing roosters, buzzing dental drills, off-the-hook telephone signals. The cacophony of speeding trains and hovering helicopters alternates with amplified recordings of Christmas carols, Islamic prayer calls, Buddhist chants, and repeated renderings of whiny Alice Cooper and Nancy Sinatra's pounding, clunky lyric, "These Boots Were Made for Walking." Through the night the glare of brilliant stadium lights turns our property into a giant fishbowl. The young children and babies in our care, most under eight years old, are terrified.

The dismal racket and the blinding lights are tortures invented by the small army of law enforcement officers armed with tanks, armored vehicles, and automatic weapons who've surrounded the complex we call Mount Carmel for the past seven weeks. These torments are intended to sap our wills and compel us to surrender to an authority that refuses to accept that we are a valid religious community with deeply held beliefs. All our attempts to explain our commitment to what we believe have been dismissed as mere "Bible babble."

As the days drift by, we've begun to fear that, in their disregard for our faith and their frustration at our refusal to submit to naked force, the seven hundred or so agents of the Federal Bureau of Investigation (FBI) and the Bureau of Alcohol, Tobacco, and Firearms (ATF), plus the officers of several state and local police forces besieging us, may be edging toward an action that will end up wiping our small community right off the map.

In here, we're all hungry and exhausted. For fifty days we've existed on two military Meals Ready-to-Eat (MREs) per day. The prepackaged rations of spaghetti and meatballs or tuna casserole taste like mud when eaten cold, slime when warmed over our lanterns. I've lost thirty pounds during the siege. We have no heat or electricity and little water. We use buckets for toilets, and we freeze in the chilly winter prairie wind that rattles our broken windows and whistles through the building's thin sheetrock walls.

Huddling in the cold inside Mount Carmel are sixty-two adults and twenty-one children. Originally, there were some 130 of us in here, but many left voluntarily during the long siege. Six of our people were shot to death when armed ATF agents stormed our property without warning on February 28. The agents had fired at us, and we fired back. Four of them died and sixteen were injured as we drove them off.

The people who chose to leave Mount Carmel after the ATF attack, and the parents who stayed in Mount Carmel but sent out some or all of their children, made an agonizing decision to trust the solemn word of the FBI that all would be treated with respect. The feds guaranteed that the children would be allowed to remain with their parents or be reunited with relatives waiting in Waco. But the feds promptly betrayed their word. They separated children from their parents, some of whom were arrested, and placed the kids in public care; they shackled the adults, even some of the elderly women, and threatened to indict them all for attempted murder. These broken promises and hostile actions on the part of the federal government certainly don't inspire the rest of us to leave the fragile security of our collective home.

The ones who've stayed inside Mount Carmel are a core group of our leader David Koresh's extended family, plus some others. My close friend, Julie Martinez, and her five children decided to remain after hearing how the FBI treated those who'd gone out. The rest of us who have elected to stick it out with David to the end are an international group of men and women of various ages and nationalities, including Americans, Mexicans, Australians, Canadians, British, and one Israeli.

We have no formal name for our community. If anyone asks, we just say we're students of the Bible. "Branch Davidians," the name by which we've become known to an amazed world, really belongs to the splinter group of Seventh-day Adventists who lived in the Waco area for fifty years or so before David Koresh arrived on the scene and reorganized Mount Carmel. We are not, as the FBI and the fevered media claim, a crazy "sect" or "cult" led by a man they've dubbed the "sinful Messiah"; rather we are a continuity in more than half a century of serious religious faith. We've long lived in peace with our neighbors. Above all, we have never threatened anyone.

It's now 2:00 A.M. on a cold Monday morning, April 19, 1993. I stand guard at the window over the front door to our building. A blanket covers the window to keep out the scouring winds and the dazzle of the lights. Lifting a corner to peer out, I see the bulky silhouettes of a pair of M60 tanks. With their bulldozer scoops and thirty-foot-long booms, these "combat engineering vehicles," as the feds call them, seem like prehistoric raptors in the dark, eager to chew our bones. Knowing that the function of their long snouts is to help the tanks snort tear gas into our home makes me shudder. My sense of dread is sharpened by glimpses of several Bradley Fighting Vehicles, small combat tanks, scurrying in the shadows beyond the glare.

In the interval of silence between one hi-amp speaker-blast and another, an owl hoots. It's the first natural sound I've heard in weeks. Then I realize that the night birds are human. The agents besieging us are exchanging birdcalls, signaling one another in the night.

In these moments I'm all too aware of the vulnerability of the stark, spare structure we dub the "Anthill."

A rambling two- and three-story complex cobbled together out of salvaged lumber and cheap siding, Mount Carmel sits on a naked, flat plain ten miles southeast of Waco. With unpainted walls and rooms without doors, the raw structure shudders whenever icy gusts sweep through.

The FBI knows how flammable our wood-framed building is. It knows we've stacked bales of hay against some of the outside walls to protect us against gunfire. It knows that we've used Coleman lanterns, kerosene, and propane for light and heat since they cut off our electricity. It is aware that we're low on water, down to a couple of eight-ounce ladles per person per day. At one point an FBI negotiator asked us if we had fire extinguishers, adding jokingly, "Somebody ought to buy some fire insurance."

A child cries somewhere in the dark bowels of the building. It's one of the loneliest sounds I've ever heard. I think of my little stepdaughter, Serenity, sleeping beside her mother, Michele, in the women's quarters on the second floor. Serenity and I are good pals; we love spending time together, chattering about everything under the sun. We're both Aquarians, and this past February we celebrated our birthdays—her fourth, my twenty-fourth.

Alone at my post over the front door, I ask myself yet again: *Can the authorities really intend to endanger the lives of so many women and children in a violent assault?* Another signal from the hostile darkness seems to whisper back—*Yes, we can.*

Steve Schneider, David Koresh's deputy, comes to check on me. "How's it goin'?" he asks.

"Scary," I reply in understatement.

"I have a feeling the feds will jump us tomorrow," Steve mutters. "They're making those weird birdcalls. And all day long we've been hearing snatches of conversation on the FBI radio wave band we're monitoring. It's hairy, Thibodeau. Stay sharp." He shivers and walks away, leaving me even more nervous than before. I huddle by the window, peeking out from behind the blanket, ears cocked for the ominous owl calls.

This is a strange scene for me to be in. A rock drummer by trade, a kid from Bangor, Maine, from the same French-Canadian New England stock as Jack Kerouac, I'm no religious fanatic, just a dreamer looking for answers in a place called Waco. The two years I've been here have been tough, but they've tempered my body and my spirit. I've quietened my life, reduced my needs, made great leaps in my heart and mind. Being in Mount Carmel has given me a rare inner surety. Put simply, this hard place has made a man of me.

Is that a reason to kill me?

I ask this question of the air on this dark Monday morning, knowing it may be answered all too soon. A refrain from the old seventies Don McLean song, "American Pie," repeats over and over in my head: *This'll be the day that I die.*

Still, I can't quite believe that the responsible officials and politicians in Washington will allow this atrocity to happen. After all, this isn't Iraq or Somalia, Bosnia or Tiananmen Square. It's the goddamm middle of Texas!

And a host of press photographers and TV cameras are watching us, even at a distance. Though the FBI has held the reporters a mile away from our place, and the agents have cut off our electricity, leaving us without TV, we know that the images of our long siege have been broadcast across the nation and around the world. True, the government spin doctors have put an evil slant on our character, casting us as child abusers, drug users, gun nuts, demonizing our community as a bunch of Bible-crazed loonies. They claim the women and children living here are hostages. This blatant deceit is a rotten strategy, and I have a stubbornly naive faith that the FBI will not be allowed to get away with it.

The FBI tanks fly white pennants slashed with red diagonals, reversed Dixie colors. We interpret these aggressive standards as the promise of a bloody end to our confrontation, a determination not to allow us to surrender peacefully. At one point during the siege we hung out a bedsheet banner: "RODNEY KING WE UNDERSTAND."

A few nights back we gathered in the upstairs hallway where David Koresh lay on blankets, propped up against the wall. He wanted to talk to us about our situation, how it might come out. Once or twice I notice him wincing from the wound in his side, made by a bullet that struck him in the lower torso during the February onslaught. The shot passed right through him, but the lesion hasn't healed, since he has never been allowed to get medical attention. The wound is still seeping, and he suffers spasms of intense pain and dizziness.

David's a skinny, casual kind of guy, not charismatic or physically compelling. He's of medium height, dressing mainly in rumpled jeans and sweatshirt, sometimes a black leather biker jacket. His curly brown hair is untidy, and his pale, dimpled face is framed with a scraggly beard. He seems fragile yet radiates a quiet kind of sincerity and strength. If the spirit moves him, his brown eyes sparkle, and his usually low-key voice vibrates with power. When we play music—him on guitar, me on drums, someone on bass—he really gets into it, jiving with the best.

"Any questions?" David asks us solemnly.

"Have we brought this Armageddon upon ourselves, in a spiritual way?" someone says.

David's expression is hard to read. "If we die here it's because our purpose in this life has been served," he says quietly. "In that sense, the feds are instruments of fate."

"You mean, our attackers are also our deliverers?" I query, startled.

"You could say that. But," he adds with a wry grin, "that doesn't mean we have to love 'em."

Now, keeping my lonely vigil at the window as the dawn sky begins to lighten, I tell myself that, if our end comes, I'll be ready. But I can't say I'm eager for it. My skin crawls, and that refrain keeps nagging at my mind: *This could be the day that I die.*

Before six o'clock, just as dawn breaks, I'm awakened from a doze by the ringing of the one telephone the FBI has left us. It's the line they've used in a series of surreal conversations, mainly with David and Steve Schneider, trying to coax us out. Now the sound is ghostly.

"I want to speak to Steve," a rough voice says as I put the receiver to my ear.

"He's asleep," I reply curtly.

"We have to speak to Steve right now," the voice insists.

Shivering, I stumble along the corridor to the room where Steve is sleeping. While I'm shaking him awake, my roommate, Jaime Castillo, appears. He looks alarmed. "Something's going on," he mumbles as we haul an irritable Steve to his feet. Looking out the window, we see a formation of the demolition tanks closing in on us in the cold, gray light. "Shit!" Steve exclaims.

Just then, the amplified speakers, which have fallen momentarily silent, start up again. A metallic voice shouts at us: "The siege is over. We're going to put tear gas into the building. David and Steven, lead your people out of there!"

A pause. We stare at one another, stunned.

"This is not an assault," the loud voice continues. "The tear gas is harmless. But it will make your environment uninhabitable. Eventually, it will soak into your food and clothing." The tone of fake concern switches to an abrupt: "You are under arrest. Come out with your hands up!"

"Get your gas masks," Steve orders. "Now!"

Gas masks had been issued to everyone at the start of the siege; they were part of a job lot we'd bought at a gun show when we were starting to buy and sell firearms to earn some income for the community. Until the siege began, we never imagined we'd end up needing them for our own protection.

Racing through the long building, I wake people up, alerting them to the attack, urging them to put on the masks. Startled from sleep, people bump into one another, and the kids whimper anxiously. One young woman, Jennifer Andrade, can't locate her mask, so I hurry to find her one. Meanwhile, the loudspeakers continue their hectoring. "The siege is over," brassy voices shout. "We will be entering the building. Come out with your hands up. Carry nothing. There will be no shooting." One phrase is repeated over and over. "This is not an assault, this is not an assault."

Not an assault? With helicopters buzzing our building like giant hornets sent to sting us to death? With tanks coming at us, their long trunks filled with tear gas, nosing the air?

Suddenly, a sickening, crashing sound reverberates through the entire structure, as if the building has been struck by a giant metal fist. My dazed ears make out the rumble of heavy engines and raw squeals from the tank tracks biting dirt. This heart-stopping racket crescendos as the steel claws of two tanks bite chunks from the flanks of the long dormitory block. Another punches a hole through the middle of the block, ripping out a section of wall and roof, shaking the place stem to stern.

In the shock and confusion I run up and down the second-floor corridor, checking to see if there are any women who haven't yet taken shelter in the concrete walk-in cooler at the base of the residential tower. My heart's pounding enough to jump right out my mouth. *This can't be happening!* a voice shrieks in my head. But it *is* happening.

All at once I see a powdery cloud billowing into the building, and I hear the sinister hiss of tear gas. Windows shatter as small canisters, like miniature rockets, shoot through the glass and explode, adding fumes to those spewing from the nozzles attached to the tank booms. A hail of broken shards flies toward me as I hurry to the ground-floor chapel at the east end of the building, my brain hammering with worry for the children. About three days before the assault I tried to fit Serenity with a mask, tightening it to see if it worked, but it only made her cry. Since the masks are too big for the kids' small heads, the women have prepared buckets of water to soak rags and towels to cover the children's faces. I hope some of the women and children have taken shelter in the old school bus we buried underground at the west end of the property months ago, before the siege began. It was meant as a refuge against tornadoes, but now it might protect the little ones.

In the chapel I again find Jaime Castillo. Tears are streaming down his cheeks. His mask isn't working properly and he begs me to fetch the spare one he keeps under his bed. Usually quiet and soft-spoken, Jaime's close to screaming. I run down the corridor, and when I get to the room I find that the entire corner's been torn out, leaving a gaping wound in the side of the building. Shaken by such a crude scene of destruction, I'm startled by the clear view to the world outside. Out there, military vehicles churn in mud under the overcast sky.

A strong wind blows into my face, and I'm tempted to remove my mask to take a deep gulp of clean air, to be a normal, breathing person again—if only for an instant. Wearing a gas mask makes you feel smothered, as if a hand is squeezing your face. Only the certainty that the air is poisonous keeps me from ripping it off.

Climbing over the piled debris of timber and sheetrock, I find Jaime's mask. When I try to return with it to the chapel, however, the corridor is blocked. The tanks have pushed in the side of the building so far that the internal walls have collapsed. I manage to stumble around the mess and make my way toward the chapel. A moment after I get there I see the piano we had moved to reinforce the front door being shoved deep down the hallway by a tank, blocking the entryway.

People are sheltering in the chapel, which is now directly under attack. A tank batters the east wall, poking its snout through the gap its boom has opened. When it releases gas we move in a crowd to the far end of the room. From time to time I remove my mask to judge the quality of the air. Sometimes the gas cloud has dissipated, other times it instantly stings my eyes, forcing tears down my cheeks.

All this time the speakers are blaring: "Do not shoot at us or we will shoot at you. The siege is over. This is not an assault." Then the voice challenges David directly: "Come out now, David. You're the leader, come out now." At any moment I expect agents to burst in, spraying bullets. Yet a strange calm fills the chapel, between the screeching tank strikes. It's as if we're in a bubble of silence amid the uproar—a silence punctuated by the sinister popping sounds of gas-filled rocket shells.

In a moment of curiosity, I examine an unexploded rocket that embedded into a wall. It's the size of a soda can with tiny fins at one end, a devilish toy filled with poison but somehow touching, like a child's plaything. But the skin-scarring blisters my Australian friend, Clive Doyle, shows me on his hands are no joke. "Burns like battery acid, mate," he says, face screwed up in pain. So far my black leather jacket has protected me from such injuries.

(Later I learn that the FBI Bradleys projected in excess of four hundred explosive rocket rounds into our building, boosting the effect of the sprayed tear gas. Both methods of delivery use noxious CS gas; whereas the sprayed gas is suspended in nontoxic carbon dioxide, the CS in the rocket rounds is mixed at a concentration of one part in ten with deadlier methylene chloride, a petroleum derivative. Methylene chloride is an eye, skin, and respiratory tract irritant. It's flammable when mixed with air and can become explosive in confined spaces. When it burns it produces hydrogen chloride and the poisonous gas phosgene, which crippled many soldiers during World War I.)

Along with the popping sounds, I make out the near-distant squeal of a tank turning on its tracks. This monstrous machine is getting set to come at us yet again, and the relentless grind of its engines rattles my bones.

Despite the uproar and confusion, people are sitting in the pews facing the raised stage, quietly reading their Bibles, half-listening to the crackle of a battery-powered transistor radio.

About 9:30 A.M., more than three hours into the assault, David comes to check on us. "Hold tight," he says. "We're trying to establish communication, maybe we can still work this out." His hand is pressed against his wounded side and he holds himself awkwardly, but he's amazingly calm, eyes sharp behind his glasses. Somehow he's managed to summon the strength to overcome the injury and tour the battered building to bolster our courage. I truly fear for my life, yet David's reassurance gives me hope that we can make a deal with the authorities for a safe surrender. One problem is that our contact with the FBI is cut off because Steve threw the phone out the window in outrage as soon as we were attacked. Apparently, a tank ran over the cord, severing our phone link with the agents.

In between another wave of poisonous gas and yet another, in the timeless bubble that holds those of us huddling in the chapel in suspension, my thoughts drift to my mother, Balenda Ganem. For the past month she's been living in a Waco motel, unable to contact me. I know she must be scared, really scared. As I'm thinking of her, a wave of intense longing washes over me. I want to be a kid once more, cuddled in her arms, and I'm terrified I might never again get close to her comforting warmth.

My spirits rise when I listen to Ron Engelman's radio show at 10:30 A.M., broadcast on station KGBS out of Dallas. Engelman, the one media source steadfastly sympathetic to our plight during the siege, is saying he can't believe the U.S. government is actually attacking us with such violence. He implores us to come out, fearing we'll all be killed if we don't. But I can't shake off the fear that if we do walk out we might be shot down like dogs.

A network news flash interrupts Engelman's show—an update from Waco. "Up to this point no one has come out," the announcer rattles off breathlessly. "The FBI claims that eighty to one hundred gunshots have been directed against its agents."

This stuns me. It makes us seem as if we're acting like the guys in the Alamo, making a suicidal last stand. My heart sinks, the last trace of hope drains from my body.

I can't swear that some of us aren't responding to the assault with firearms at the other end of the building, but I've heard no gunfire in the chapel or anywhere nearby. In my despair I begin to believe that we are truly doomed, that the FBI may be setting the American public up for a massacre, and the possibility that I really could die today hits me full-force.

The tank comes at us again, the gaseous nostrils at the tip of its boom poking blindly through the shattered wall. The machine sniffs air, searching, before spewing its foul stuff into our faces; I imagine it can actually smell our terror. We're trapped here, debris blocks the exits. As the tank attacks, people scream and back away. There's no way out and we cower wherever we can. I try to hide among a tall stack of amplifiers, squeezing into the middle of them, but when the tank crashes into the wall nearby I back away onto the stage.

————

By noon, the building is a tinderbox. A thick layer of methylene chloride dust deposited by the CS gas coats the walls, floors, and ceilings, mingling with kerosene and propane vapors from our spilled lanterns and crushed heaters. To make things worse, a brisk, thirty-knot Texas wind whips through the holes ripped in the building's sides and roof. The whole place is primed like a pot-bellied stove with its damper flung open.

Suddenly, someone yells—*Fire!*

Frantically, I look around for an escape route. The gym beyond the chapel is destroyed, a huge timber beam blocks my way. Working on gut instinct, crawling on hands and knees, I back up to the stairway leading to the overhead catwalk. On the upper level there's debris everywhere, as if the building has been hit by an aerial bomb. Trying not to get cut by the shattered glass, I inch along the catwalk that crosses the length of the chapel ceiling, hoping to find a way to reach the children.

The opening at the end of the catwalk is covered by a blanket. When I tentatively lift its edge a blast of smoke staggers me. Gingerly, I poke my head out. A fireball shoots down the corridor before my eyes—a red-and-yellow flash whose heat scorches my cheeks and deafens my ears with its roaring.

Since I can't go forward, I have to retreat down the catwalk to the stairs. When I get to the lower level I find that the chapel is on fire. Another fireball, from the gym area, races across the ceiling. The tank has knocked a hole in the wall at the edge of the stage and I see people huddled there, trying to get away from the thick smoke. The air's heat causes me to remove my black leather jacket; it's covered with white spots from the gas. My gas mask's filter has run out; feeling suffocated, I tear it off.

Ray Friesen, an elderly Canadian, says he can't take it anymore—he's going to jump out the window. I warn him they might shoot us, and he hesitates. Derek Lovelock, a black man from Britain, tells us he saw the women and kids in the concrete storage room. They haven't made it to the underground bus because the way is blocked by rubble, he says, and my heart sinks lower. When Jimmy Riddle, a thirty-two-year-old Southerner, goes out the back door to the cafeteria, a tank rolls over the top of him, ripping off the right side of his torso. Stephen Henry, another young black man from Britain, is also run down, his left leg sheared off at the hip.

Amid these horrors, a mutt puppy, one of the children's pets, comes trotting toward me out of the smoke. I toss him out the window, shooing him away into the open air, but the terrified dog keeps coming back. In the distance I hear the mocking cries from the FBI speakers: "David, you've had your fifteen minutes of fame! Now bring your people out, the siege is over."

Now I'm down on my hands and knees, praying, *God, if I'm going to die just make it quick.* Just then, the wall of the stage catches fire, scorching the side of my face. The sharp smell of singed hair fills my nose and I scream from the depths of my gut. Seeing Jaime and Derek run out of the hole in the wall at the edge of the stage, I follow, preferring a swift death by the agents' bullets to being roasted by fire.

Time slows down as I stumble through the mud. There's a Red Cross sign fifty yards away, its symbol a small ray of hope in the dark clouds of smoke.

As Clive Doyle staggers through the same gap that I've just used to escape, flames follow. His arms are smoking, blistered skin peels from his hands, his coat is melting against his back. He thought he was the only survivor, he says, until he saw us. Marjorie Thomas, a black woman from Britain, is trapped on the second story. She puts her hands over her head, jumps out a window, then does a slow, 180-degree, midair turn, thumping on the ground, hideous burns all over her body. Graeme Craddock, a friend of Doyle's from Australia, is lying inside the base of the tower, paralyzed, barely alive. Most of the nine people who escape the fire come out of the east wall of the chapel, like me, or through a crack in the front wall.

FBI agents force us to lie in a row on the ground, face-down, and they tie our hands behind our backs with plastic straps. "Where are the women and children?" an agent demands, his face close to mine. When I tell him I still hope they're in the buried school bus, I hear another agent say, "We teargassed that bus." Oh no, I cry silently, imagining the kids being suffocated in that underground tomb. It turns out that six women died near the trapdoor, suffocated in the blocked passageway.

One agent, a burly guy with a mustache, says grimly: "Hell, I knew this wasn't going to work. We should've gone to Plan B." *What's Plan B?* I want to ask, but I keep my mouth shut; these men are scary.

Abruptly, the whole building explodes. The wind from the pyrotechnic blast tugs at my exposed back, the din stuns my ears. I lift my head and see a sight that burns deep into my soul—a gigantic funeral pyre, black smoke and red-yellow flames filling the sky, incinerating my friends, Michele, my stepchildren, my life.

BOOK ONE

A Sense of Community

1

A GALAXY FAR AWAY

The journey that brought me to Waco began twenty-four years earlier, in a galaxy far away. The psychological and emotional voyage between my life in Maine and my life on Planet Koresh would baffle any astronaut's navigational skills. As my mother later told an interviewer, "I can't imagine the Davey I know and love finding the answers to his questions in quotes from the Bible."

Born in 1969, I grew up during an unsettled time in which everything was up for question, even in quiet, Bangor. My mother, Balenda Ganem, was sixteen and pregnant when she married my father, David, only nineteen himself. It was, as she said, "the famous Summer of Love." My mother wanted to name me Aaron, but a few days after I was born my father, who was in the Navy at the time, shipped out for active duty and, feeling sentimental, she named me after him.

Theirs was truly an attraction of opposites. Balenda's father's family came from Lebanon, and her ebullient, emotional nature, always spilling over the edge, contrasted vividly with my dad's French-Canadian–New Englander reserve. However, they shared a tremendous sense of humor, and my mom says my dad first took notice of her when she was the only one to laugh at his jokes at a high-school party.

Balenda had another talent: She was a singer. When she was young she sang in cabarets, and her warm, strong voice charmed many audiences. My very first memory is of lying in my crib scared of the dark, until she came and sang me a lullaby about lambs. The melody was so beautiful it overwhelmed my fears and I began to cry, no longer with fright but with joy.

The emotional pattern of my childhood was laid down early: my mom, a deeply comforting presence, the bedrock of my security, yet as vulnerable and nervous as I was; my dad, quiet, funny, brainy, introverted, and remote. He shared my mom's love of music, though, and especially loved Chuck Berry's "Little Queenie," encouraging me to dance around the living room while it played on our stereo. He never took me to play ball or go fishing; he wasn't that kind of dad. Instead, he was happiest reading, spending whole weekends with his nose in a book.

My mom raised me on her hip, carrying me to protest marches and music and theater festivals even before I could walk. She brought me up to be very open, to discuss anything I might want to ask her about: politics, sex, society. Her mantra was, "Question authority." She took me to folk festivals with political themes and to demonstrations against Maine Yankee, the nuclear power plant. When I was eight or nine we went to a Holly Near concert in Portland to hear her sing about suffering people in Chile and Nicaragua.

We lived in a small apartment in Bangor's east side, we were poor, and tensions were relentless. My father had a quick tongue, was always quick with the quip or a funny story; but all too often he used his sarcastic wit to keep people at a distance, including my mom and me. And he drank a lot. Their spats were scary, and even at four years old I felt that this was not how people ought to be with one another, especially two people I loved. Balenda and David separated when I was four, got together again six months later for a year, then, mercifully, divorced. Lots of kids I knew came from divorced families, so it was no big deal. My mom was involved with the experimental Shoestring Theatre in Portland, and those people were fun to be around because they were all passionate about life—very creative. It was a great environment to grow up in, very tolerant of personal lifestyles.

When I was with my dad, in the various places his uneasy spirit led him, my scene was much narrower. In his curt Mainer's way, he was impatient with what he perceived to be "weakness" or "self-indulgence." For instance, one day after a real bad hazing at school, I moaned to him that kids were evil and mean. "Wait till you grow up into the world of men," he curtly replied.

After my parents split up Balenda and I moved into the home of my maternal grandmother, Gloria, in a middle-class neighborhood. For the first time I was in a calm place, and my dad receded into the middle distance. He went through yet another divorce before settling down with his present wife in Isleboro, an island off the coast of Maine. My mother's brother, Bob, was the only male figure in my childhood who did fatherly things with me, like fishing and camping. I guess the lack of a real father figure, a supportive male role model, skewed my view of things.

I loved Gloria and admired her. She worked three jobs to keep her family going after she divorced her husband. The Scottish strain in her inheritance inhibited her from being demonstrative, but she was always offering food, her way of showing affection. Maybe that's why I could never say no to a snack. We watched old movies together, the roly-poly kid and the quiet old woman, alone in the house while my mom was working.

My father's family was Catholic, but he was never a churchgoer; on the contrary, he despised religion. Under the urging of Mim, my paternal grandmother, I attended Sunday school and midnight mass at Easter, but organized religion and the holy rollers on TV disgusted me with their hypocrisies. Mim insisted that I mumble my prayers before bed. Grandma Gloria never went to church, but she was the most Christian person, in the true sense, I've ever met. From Gloria I learned strong notions of right and wrong, and though she never spanked me, her quiet rebukes cut me to pieces. Both women were a vivid contrast to my mother, a typical, easygoing parent of the sixties—the fierce rebel against old moralities.

Although I had little formal religion in my life, I often felt as
if I had an angel looking out for me. When I really needed something it always seemed to be there. I didn't see myself going out in
search of God, whoever or whatever he, she, or it was. If there was
something momentous out there, I had to learn it through music.

I can hardly remember a time when drumming wasn't the focus of
my dreams. I had always loved music, ever since I was very young.
I'd dance around the house, a rocker from the get go.

My cousin, Marty, was my mentor. I was up in Marty's room one
day when he was packing to move out. I picked up his drumsticks
and started to play, "I Want You to Want Me," by the Midwest four-
some Cheap Trick. It was the first song I ever learned, and it was
the beginning of a long, enduring love affair.

When I was twelve, Marty got a new drum set and handed
down his old one, a five-piece, red-glitter kit. I played every day, im-
itating Led Zeppelin, the Beatles, the Doors, Rush, Iron Maiden,
and my two favorite drummers, Englishman John Bonham (whose
rhythms helped Led Zep invent the genre of heavy metal) and Neil
Peart (whose technical wizardry supplied the backbone of Canada's Rush), crazily mimicking fills and licks. I was into every style—
folk, cabaret, classical, heavy metal, big band, and Motown—but
the driving rhythms of rock energized me most, especially from
metal icons like Zeppelin, Iron Maiden, Rush, and Judas Priest.
I read all the rock magazines like *Circus*, *Metal Edge*, and *Rolling
Stone*, fantasizing about leaving for Hollywood to create my own
future. I was going to be a world-class drummer and no one was
going to stop me!

From then on, I lived in my imagination, dreaming of stage
performances I'd have, of drums coming out of the floor on risers,
of money and fame. When I was flashing the sticks, it didn't matter
that I was a fat boy (reaching 250 pounds in high school) the other
kids razzed. I was going to be a rock-and-roll drummer! In ninth
grade, when my mother moved to South Portland's Willard Beach

in search of a better job, I bounced around between her place, my dad's homes in Bangor and Maryland, and my grandmothers' houses. During those nomadic years drums became my true country. I spent many hours learning from albums, playing and memorizing lyrics, feeling the musicians' passion. The fire in it drove me wild, and when I shut my eyes I could visualize the audience right out there, a-rockin' and a-rollin'.

Since my mom worked two jobs to support us, much of the time I was a latchkey kid, left alone to follow my own obsessions. I was usually allowed to do whatever I wanted. Balenda did try to make time for me on weekends, to take in a movie and have dinner, and I appreciated that, knowing how hard she worked. But for me, coming home from school to an empty house meant I could grab a snack from the fridge and immediately get into the drums.

School was a bust. Though I could drum away for hours, concentrating intently on the rhythms, during class my hyperactive mind skipped around like a cricket on a hotplate. My penmanship was horrible, my math was in the crapper, and my mind was absent. I lacked discipline in my life, and no one was consistently there to get on me to study. In the end I graduated high school as a solid "C" student, with a "B" here and there.

The role that suited me best during school was class clown. In the school band, I was the chief cutup, cracking wise, telling jokes, upsetting the bandleader. I was the big fool, the fat kid who got the giggles going. But under the clownishness I was really a goody-goody. At the time I didn't drink or do dope. I just wanted to play the skins and make people laugh, and despite my impatience to get out of high school, grow up, take charge of my life, I felt I never wanted to lose touch with being a kid. I had an instinct that if I ever became too wise to the world I might lose the belief that special things would happen to me.

My Bangor High senior yearbook entry says it all. The photo showed a neat, overweight boy with a soft mouth and yearning eyes wearing a jacket and tie. However, the quote I chose, from Blackie Lawless, leader of the band WASP, gave the game away:

I want shiny cars, dirty money, and lots of rock and roll.
I will live in fame and die in flames; I'm never getting old.

———•—•———

After my high-school graduation in the summer of 1987, I applied for
the one-year drumming course at the Musicians Institute of Technology in Hollywood, a school I read about in rock magazines favored
by hard rock bands. I sent the school a tape and they accepted it—a
boost to my ego, even though I sensed they probably took in anyone
who could pay the tuition. My mom was now living in Greece, and
no one in my family had the cash to help me out, so I found a job
at a German car company in Bangor, working on the paint line and
deburring metal shavings from gearing rods under a microscope. It
was monotonous work, but the pay was better than delivering pizzas.

Freed from the tight world of the classroom, I could take a
deeper breath and ask myself some basic questions.

What were my talents? Dreaming and drumming. *What were my
prospects?* Vague to nonexistent. *What were my hopes—apart from shiny
cars, dirty money, and lots of rock and roll?* Infinite.

Concerned for my future, my grandmothers and Uncle Bob
urged me to think about going to college to get the education
I'd so skillfully managed to avoid in school. But I had an instinct
against it, a feeling I'd never learn what I needed to know about
life from books. Or rather, that books would never give me those
vital clues to myself I so obviously lacked.

I'd learned that the purely emotional life had its costs; I saw
that in my mother's bafflement, her displaced angers aimed at "authority," and I feared I might be caught in the same mesh of frustrations. I loved her a lot, but I didn't want to share her anxious,
unanchored kind of life. Drumming was a power in me, but I knew
my gifts as an artist were still untried. Was my talent strong enough
to carry all my hopes? Would it really tell me who I was? And if it
failed me, what was left, apart from a terrifying emptiness?

Drifting through that interval between school and Hollywood,
I hung out at bars, played a gig or two with some friends in clubs,

pounding out riffs against a crowd of shouting, half-drunk patrons grooving more on sheer noise than any rhythms I might conjure up. I was friends with a couple of girls, trying to find out how to be with women. My personality always seemed to work out with people if they got to know me, but my initial awkwardness, covered by fake charm, was often unappealing. Finally, I accumulated enough funds to leave Bangor. The next semester's class schedule at the Musicians Institute began in February 1989, and I registered. It was the depths of the New England winter and I itched for California sunshine and everything it promised.

My mother came home for Christmas, as she usually did, and we had a conversation about my future. Or rather, she revealed, consciously and unconsciously, how terribly worried she was about my vulnerabilities and how much she feared for my safety in a world she clearly felt would likely prove too much for me. She knew my tendency toward emotional overspill all too well; it was so much like her own.

A few days before I left Bangor behind, Uncle Bob took me to ride snowmobiles out on Pushaw Lake. We raced over frozen snowdrifts at sixty miles per hour, slicing through the bitter cold, shouting with sheer exhilaration as our eyeballs froze. It was my last, pure moment as a Mainer, made all the more poignant by the knowledge that I'd soon be baking in the golden Los Angeles sun.

------·------

It had been raining the morning I landed at Los Angeles Airport, and by the time I arrived the skies—wider than any I'd ever seen in Maine—were brilliant. I was picked up at the airport by Joe, a Los Angeles musician my mom had met on the plane coming back from Greece; she'd asked him to protect her boy in his first encounter with Hollywood, and I was glad she had. The sheer size of Los Angeles knocked me out. How would I make my mark in all that geography and humanity?

But the rainwashed palm trees along Hollywood Boulevard glistening in the sunshine lifted my heart. This, I quickly concluded, was a magical place, despite the grunge I saw on the sidewalks, the desperate, dirty kids panhandling tourists outside Mann's Chinese, the obvious air of decay in the street facades. But that was big-city life in all its glory—a limitless, wide-open landscape that jibed with my own desire to live on the edge. All the same, I was well aware that I was a real rube, a pigeon for the plucking. As Joe dropped me and my one battered suitcase outside the music school on Mc-Cadden Place, just off the boulevard of dreams, my feathers shivered at the presence of hidden predators.

The Musicians Institute was bursting with a cacophony of wild drumming, electronic guitar plucking, pounding pianos. I toured the three stories of sleek classrooms and recording studios, production rooms, computer and study labs, and a five-hundred-seat performance space with large-screen video projectors. Everything, from the colored linoleum tiles to the glass-walled practice rooms, told me I was in a place where music was a *profession*, not just an amateur fantasy. I felt I was home, plunged into a pure universe of music. I was *in*. Hollywood had opened her arms and embraced *me*, little Dave Thibodeau from Bangor.

Suddenly, it struck me—*Where was I going to live?* I'd made no plans, and I guess my mom hoped Joe would help me out, but he'd vanished. Bewildered, I looked around to ask someone how I might go about finding a room, but everybody was rushing somewhere, late for class or too busy to stop and talk. Then I caught sight of a noticeboard filled with cards. One card advertised for a roommate to share an apartment with three musicians named Artie, John, and T-bone. I phoned, and John said come on up, giving me directions to a stretch of Yucca and Whitley that he cheerfully dubbed "Crack Alley." The guys offered me a room doubling up with T-bone, whose real name was Tommy, for $200 a month. The place was part of a big apartment complex, including a swimming pool and a whirlpool. There was a sauna on the roof with a panoramic view of the fabled Hollywood sign. I was in heaven. My real life was finally beginning.

Those first few months in L.A. were heady. At school, I reveled in the percussion classes, soaking up every nuance of the instructors' teachings. I learned the history of jazz, from Dixieland to bebop, picking up the ride patterns and brush techniques, studying song soloing and cymbal turnarounds. I shared a cubbyhole with another student and could practice anytime I liked, night and day. Since I'm a night bird by temperament, I was quite happy hitting the skins at three or four in the morning, when the place was empty.

The classes were amazing: Latin drum class, odd meter class, big band drumming class, how to read swing charts. Most of the students were from out of town, young guys from all over the States and some from Europe, all looking to make it big. Many of them were, like me, kids fresh out of home. Ten to fifteen of us stickmen jammed together in performers' sessions accompanied by a bass player, and every Wednesday was Rock Performance, a stage show where we'd form small bands, rehearse one song, and play it on stage in front of the others. Night and day I was doing what I loved most, even in the rudimentary classes where we sat at tables with pads, five drummers to a row, knocking out sixteen-note paradiddles, flams, triple ratamacues, double drag taps, and four-stroke riffs. For a few hours once a week I worked one-on-one with Doane Perry, the drummer for Jethro Tull.

It wasn't until I had to look out for myself that I began to realize how spoiled I'd been at home, with my mother or grandmother taking care of the laundry, shopping, cooking. I had to learn how to be self-reliant, to do the chores needed to get by, even in our postadolescent mess.

To supplement my savings, I got a job in a telemarketing "boiler room" off Sunset, doing telephone surveys about movies. It was boring as hell, but it paid seven bucks an hour. Since I was still under twenty-one, I grew a mustache to look older, to get into clubs like the Frolic Room. My whole focus was drumming, perfecting my technique, trying to get a sense of how I measured up with the best. Virtually every waking hour was for practicing, even in the street, where I walked along, whacking a little pad I strapped to my thigh. At times I was homesick, but my one visit back to Bangor made me realize I could never return to my old life. After Hollywood, the place seemed the size of a pinhead; I couldn't wait to leave.

Back in California, I all but kissed the soiled sidewalk. If any place in the world was home for me, this was it. I walked the streets late at night, breathing in air charged with fame and failure. I hung out on the Sunset Strip, dipping into dives like the Rainbow and the Whisky, lost in the crowd, grabbing flyers from bands trying to make it. After the clubs closed, we rockers gravitated to the "rock and roll" Denny's, on Sunset between Fairfax and La Brea, or cruised the shelves of the Ralphs supermarket a few blocks down, where all the weirdos congregated, sipping orange juice and snacking on groceries they never paid for. The strippers from the local clubs joined us, their faces tired and gray under streaks of the gaudy makeup they were too pooped to remove.

After school, I'd often drift down to the Guitar Center on Sunset. In the glassed-in soundproof electronic drum room, I pounded beats on incredible kits only rich musicians could afford. Famous rockers frequented the place, and often I caught glimpses of faces I'd only seen on album covers, magically translated into flesh.

By now I was working for Roadway Package Service, loading trucks four nights a week, ten to two in the morning. One night I met a guy named Scott who was looking for someone to play drums for his band. When he heard I was a drummer, he invited me to come to a studio to make a demo tape of a band they were forming. We chose some weird names for the band, like Joyride and Powerhouse, and we got a few gigs around town, playing the Gaslight and the Whisky. Trouble was, these guys got high on pot all the time and fooled around too much. I wanted to get serious, begin to build a career, but they were into the rock life for its kicks rather than its ambitions.

As the year went on, I began to have problems with one of my instructors at the Institute. My instinct that I must stick with playing passionately rather than technically was getting stronger the more the school thrust me toward the discipline of the metronome. I was hyper, my foot forever tapping out its own rhythms. I felt that if I played with feeling I could fuck the timing. One time I played Zeppelin's version of "In My Time of Dying," one of Bonham's greatest rhythm tracks, and demonstrated that it was all over the place.

"This doesn't follow a metronome," I pointed out. "It switches and changes, the key is pure heart. If there's a groove, you can fluctuate." My instructor was unimpressed, but I was more determined than ever to go my own sweet way.

All the same, I feared I might be screwing up yet again, heading toward the kind of failure that had dogged my heels in Bangor. It seemed I couldn't carry things through, that maybe I had some kind of fatal flaw. All I knew was, when I was behind a drum set, I was happy.

All too soon, my year at the Institute was over. Those months had taught me what I could and couldn't learn about music—indeed, what I should and shouldn't learn. Most of the students knew they'd end up in cover bands, making a steady living playing other people's songs. That was the sensible view of the average rock musician's prospects in a fiercely competitive market. But I wasn't yet ready to be sensible; there was something in me that ached for a deeper level of satisfaction than a lifetime just knocking out the riffs. I was twenty-one years old. Playtime was over.

To mark the change, I moved to Franklin and Orange, behind the Hollywood Holiday Inn. I made new friends, like Bam Bam, a drummer from Connecticut, a sweet, Harley-Davidson kind of guy. We lived off the Holiday Inn happy-hour buffet, gorging on chicken wings and Swedish meatballs, pigging out for three bucks. I met a singer named Ryan, a warm, mischievous person who liked to party. We hung out a lot at Denny's, joking and giggling. Ryan claimed I had a weird light around me, something he couldn't quite describe. "Nothing that could happen to you would ever surprise me," he said.

By the spring of 1990, not much in my life was going right. The other guys in the band were still more concerned with getting high than getting serious. At the lowest point, later on that summer, I was working in the gift shop at Mann's Chinese, selling junk souvenirs to gullible tourists, wearing a uniform, looking like an organ grinder's monkey in my short, brass-buttoned, scarlet jacket. I was totally at a loss.

One Saturday, during a lull, I gazed up at the sky and addressed a God I'd seldom given thought to. *What are you saving me for?* I demanded. *Can I please meet the people I'm supposed to meet! Come on! Deliver me from this, show me the way.* Although I hoped no one was around to hear my pleas, I was too desperate to feel foolish. *Come* on*!* I repeated passionately.

A couple of nights later, while driving with the band to rehearsal, I insisted we drop by the Guitar Center on Sunset so I could pick up a pair of Promark drumsticks. Ryan and Scott protested that we were late, that I could get by with my old sticks, but I ignored them.

After I bought the sticks, I had to try them out in the sound-proof drum room. There were two men in the room, examining a brand-new kit called D-Drums, electronic drums that use real drumheads; you hit them, and you get an electronic trigger-sound that shivers your spine. Seeing the sticks in my hand, one of the strangers said, "Are you a drummer?" When I replied that I was, he asked me to hit a few fast licks.

While I was playing, showing off a little, I stole glances at the pair. The one who'd spoken to me was blond, athletic, probably in his late thirties. A serious type with a neat beard, he wore a business suit, unusual for that informal scene. The other man wore jeans and a T-shirt and had long, wavy hair and a dimpled chin covered by a two-day beard. His liquid-brown eyes were hidden behind gold-rimmed, aviator-style shades, but I could feel them following me intently, even though he was silent.

"Are you playing in a band right now?" Suit asked. I told him I was on my way to a rehearsal, that my friends were waiting out on Sunset. "I'm in a band but still I'm looking around," I said.

Suit introduced himself as Steve Schneider. "This," he said, indicating his companion, "is David Koresh."

2

THE MAN AND
THE MUSIC

I didn't have much time to talk, since Ryan and Scott were waiting for me, but something about this pair, especially the silent guy, intrigued me.

"David's a guitarist," Steve said. "I'm his manager. We're looking around for a drummer for our band."

"Sounds interesting," I said, playing cool.

The card Steve Schneider handed me had the words "Messiah Productions" printed in gold letters. Turning the card over, I saw excerpts from the Bible and promptly handed it back. "You guys are a Christian band," I shrugged.

Steve just smiled at me. "Surely you have some kind of spiritual curiosity?" he said.

"Sure," I replied. "Who hasn't?"

At that, Steve began to talk. His voice was quiet but compelling. He told me about a trip to Israel he and Koresh had taken. They weren't conventional Christians, Steve assured me, but they wanted their music to have a sacred meaning. "Our band is great, it's going to be huge," he said, coming off like a salesman. All the while his partner kept his own counsel.

15

When Steve wound down, I looked at David. I liked his smile, and when he spoke I detected a soft, down-to-earth Texas twang.

"Look, it's like this," he began. "I've been all over the world, talked to a lot of people. I have a knowledge of the Scriptures other people don't have, though I don't want to sound arrogant or anything. There's a lot of stuff in the Scriptures that has to do with music. I feel that, basically, if you're spiritual that's all you need. I'm not out to convert anyone. I'd like to play some music with you and see where we can go from there."

At that moment, Scott and Ryan came racing up the stairs to get me. They were in a sweat, so I grabbed Steve's card and left. My residual feeling was, *Don't call me, I'll call you.* At that moment in my life the idea of getting involved with a bunch of religious nuts didn't grab me.

The card stayed in my pocket for a couple of days. I wanted to throw it away, but for some reason I thought I ought to call Steve and David. When I did call, Steve seemed surprised but friendly. "I'll pick you up, take you to our place in Pomona, show you our setup," he said.

During the forty-five-minute drive out to Pomona a few days later, I listened to Steve talk. He told me his home was Madison, Wisconsin, that his family was very close-knit. I noticed he sprinkled his speech with folksy midwestern sayings, like his greeting to me that afternoon: "How's yourself?" When he said, "I was always looking out at the stars and wondering how I got here," I caught a glimpse of an earnest boy troubled by the mysteries of the universe, just as I had been.

Steve's mother was a Seventh-day Adventist, and he had followed in her faith, enrolling in the Adventist Newbold College near Nottingham, England. "I was expelled for a bout of drunkenness," he said, jaunty but apologetic for having shamed his mother. "I went from England to Hawaii, changed into a heathen, lived a swinging life of booze and broads, partying with the fast crowd, the likes of Pat Boone and Clint Eastwood." In 1981 he married

Judy Peterson, an attractive blonde he'd met at a Madison dance hall when he was in his early twenties. He enrolled in the University of Hawaii and worked toward a Ph.D. in comparative religion.

In 1986, a friend he knew through the Diamond Head Adventist Church in Honolulu introduced him to the teachings of David Koresh. The way Steve said this, I realized he revered Koresh, that the man was far more than a guitarist he was managing. This made me wonder, but I was too fascinated by his quick-talker story to stop him right there.

"To start off, I doubted David," Steve confided. "I plagued the man with questions, argued the hell out of him, trying to catch him out. Both the academic and the spiritual seeker in me took him through a fine wringer to detect flaws and inconsistencies in his scriptural system. It took many transpacific phone calls before I was ready to come to California to meet Koresh. Even then, I was still a doubter. Hell, I even took David to dispute Scripture with a professor!"

(Later, I heard someone say of Steve, "This guy could sell you smog." Echoing this, someone else said, "It's like I sold them a toothbrush and he comes along and sells the house that goes where the toothbrush hangs." He boasted that, during a trip to England in 1988, he'd made more than twenty converts to David's teachings.)

In the rush of his story, Steve mentioned Mount Carmel, which he described as "a spread we own near Waco, Texas—a hellhole in the prairie!" That was the first time I heard the name that was to take on such significance. "We just think of ourselves as 'students of Scripture,'" he said cheerfully.

In an abrupt shift of mood, Steve suddenly exclaimed: "To tell the truth, I really don't like this world!" Startled, I asked him what he meant. In a quiet voice, he continued. "Solomon, the wisest man who ever lived, once said, 'It's better to spend your time at a funeral than a party.'"

Steve paused, his profile grim. "I know what he meant. If you're at a party, the next day you wake up with a hangover, haunted by the sense that everything passes away, leaving hardly a memory. A funeral, on the other hand, brings the issues of life and death before you." He was silent for a moment, staring through the windshield at the freeway rolling under our thrumming tires. "I look for absolute truth," he murmured. "But where is absolute truth? Only one thing's absolute, as far as I can see, and that's death."

His tone chilled me, and I was glad when the conversation switched to music. Instantly professional, Steve filled me in about Messiah Productions. The outfit was more than just the music, though that was the heart of it, he explained. They had an artist, Cliff Sellors, who customized Koresh's guitars, airbrushing biblical scenes onto the wood. Steve spoke about getting into the guitar business and said that they also had a landscape company called the Yardbirds. He talked about their goals for the band, David's ambitions for the music, and I had the sense that this was a bunch of guys who could make things happen, maybe lift me out of my rut. I began to think that this might be the answer to my appeal to the heavens that day in Mann's Chinese gift shop.

Since it was built of stone, the Pomona place was referred to as the Rock House. The group also owned another suburban residence in nearby La Verne. I couldn't quite make out who was living in Pomona, but I was introduced to several people, including Jaime Castillo, Greg Summers, Mike Schroeder, Scott Sonobe, and Paul Fatta. The living room was a music studio complete with drum set, and soon after I arrived David got us together and we started jamming.

David played electronic guitar and sang his own songs with a scriptural slant, including the psalms as well as snatches of the prophets. At times, he switched to a classical-influenced hard rock that was more upscale and orchestrated than I was used to, but we clicked at once. He seemed to groove off my energy and told me my hot style inspired him to play better. When I asked who taught him the guitar, he said he'd learned on his own. "I had a vision of the way I wanted to play and I tried to achieve that."

I could see he was the sort of musician driven as much by ideas as instinct, and that intrigued me. We didn't talk Bible, and David just seemed to be a guy who had money and some talent and wanted to rock. But he could play, and he had good people around him. Messiah Productions seemed like a professional outfit with a real business plan, unlike my own past projects.

That night, after jamming, we sat out on the neat lawn in the cool summer night and downed a few beers while rapping about rock and the bands we dug. David was just one of the guys, but there was something else about him, a kind of quiet gentleness and sincerity that drew me. As yet, no one in the group had asked me to believe in Jesus or tried to con me out of the money I didn't have. In fact, they didn't come off at all like a religious bunch, and I appreciated that. I didn't know exactly how David's mix of music and gospel shook down, but I liked him and we played well together, and that was good enough for me. On the drive home I told Steve I'd be interested in jamming with the group again.

The next time Steve drove me to Pomona he began to talk about David's scriptural message. I only half-listened, watching the landscape go by, my inner ear focused on the rolling thumpety-thump of rubber on road, imagining how I might work that rhythm up into a melodic line.

Steve mentioned that he wanted to have a study of Scripture at my place and that I should invite my roommates and any other friends. I told him outright that I'd never been able to come to grips with the Bible, but he just nodded and insisted that he wanted to come over and give us a study session; being my usual easygoing self, I consented.

At the time, I was sharing an apartment with some other musicians behind the Roosevelt Hotel. "Hey, guess what," I said. "I got some friends coming over for a Bible study." Their faces fell, and they reached for their coats when Steve knocked.

Opening the door, I was surprised to see a whole delegation—Steve, Jaime, Paul, and a couple of others. "You guys want some brews?" Steve said, brandishing six-packs. Easily seduced, my friends and roommates squatted on the floor around Steve. He got out the biggest Bible I'd ever seen, with wide margins filled with color-coded notes. The size of that tome, and the obvious diligence with which it had been studied, impressed me.

Steve talked about Isaiah, describing a kingdom to be set up during the earth's last days. In his voice the rhythm of the King James verses lulled my ear, seeming somehow very American, like the flowing passages from *Leaves of Grass* that I'd heard in school. My fingers began to tap on my thighs as I listened: *The Lord shall go forth as a mighty man, he shall stir up jealousy like a man of war: he shall cry, yea, roar; he shall prevail*. Steve's delivery was not like the Bible-thumpers I came across while channel-surfing on TV; he was clearly not a Jimmy Swaggart type, drunk with fakery and false potency. His voice offered a quieter and more thoughtful music.

The Bible was put together like a puzzle book, Steve said, a coded manual for the human race. The image caught my fancy, and I could see that, two hours later, all my friends were still sitting there, rapt. For the first time the Bible came alive for me; I sensed its innate force. "These people might have something," I said to one of my roommates after Steve and the others had gone.

During the next few weeks, Steve and the others came over for more Bible studies, and I went to Pomona to jam a couple of times. I slowly began to take in some of what they referred to as the "message," but it was the music that kept me coming. The more I played and talked to David, always about music, the more I liked him. And I respected Steve; he was an educated, intelligent man, a little like my father in his gravity and his reverence for learning. David, I sensed, was watching me covertly, wondering, perhaps, if my passions as a drummer echoed something deeper in my heart.

———————

In September I was finally invited to Waco to celebrate the Hebrew Day of Atonement and the Feast of Tabernacles that followed. The group followed some of the Jewish rituals, I was told, and kept Saturday as the Sabbath. "I want you to be the drummer in this band, but you have to understand where I'm coming from and what my message is," David said, laying it out for me clearly for the first time. "Two hundred people, from all over the world, will be in

Mount Carmel next month. We'll study, but we'll also have some fun, play music. After that, you'll have to make a decision." Implicit in this statement was the fact that the music and the message went together, and I would have to be in both or neither.

This was the first moment I had to face the prospect of becoming David's disciple. During those early days of our acquaintance, my grasp of his teachings was extremely vague, my understanding of its implications even vaguer.

Looking back, I ask myself a tough question that never quite occurred to me with any clarity during the early days of my connection with David, perhaps because I was so young and so unconscious: *How could someone like me, who'd shown little previous interest in belief or Scripture, who had almost no religious background, later become so entranced by the Bible?*

The key was David himself. He first touched me as a fellow musician and a warm friend, and I was taken by his deep sincerity and natural authority. I soon realized that he was an extraordinary personality, but his unique interpretation of the Old and New Testaments only gradually came to fascinate me, when the music and the man had already opened my mind and heart.

In David, the music, the man, and the message were all of a piece; without his Bible, he had no purpose and his music had no focus. Following his example, I came to appreciate Scripture as a way to make sense of myself and the world.

If, back then, he'd said right out that I had to embrace Scripture totally or cut loose from Messiah Productions, I might well have taken a walk. At the time, though, my gut instinct said: *Go with it, what've you got to lose?* A couple of weeks, maybe? A trip to Texas? My habit of going with the flow, if it feels right, softened the edge of my reservations.

Anyway, I didn't have a lot of options. I could see David's band really taking off, and it could be a great opportunity to crack the tough nut of the rock world. My only real reluctance boiled down to a concern about losing my job and my apartment if I was away for two weeks or more, but David countered that with a promise to cover my expenses.

"You're going to come back as Father Dave," my friend Ryan and the other guys in my band protested. "You of all people—a holy roller!"

"I'm sick of the old Hollywood routine, jammin' for no money, no respect, not going anyplace," I replied. "I'm off to Mount Carmel. Wish me luck."

3

COMING TO THE MOUNTAIN

'On a bright September morning, the Messiah Productions tour bus, the Silver Eagle, rolled eastward through the Mojave Desert, bound for Texas. After cresting steep, spectacular Cajon Pass, we were already in a stark, spare landscape that would continue for the next 1,500 miles, to a semimythical place named Mount Carmel—the Anthill, as Jaime called it. "Fire ants, chiggers, and rednecks," he grimaced.

Jaime and Paul Fatta were on the bus with me. It turned out that I was the only one who'd never been to Waco, and Paul spent a lot of time talking to me as he drove.

Paul, who came from a wealthy family in Hawaii, was one of Steve Schneider's converts. Accepting David's teachings, he'd sold his share of the family business to his father and moved to Mount Carmel with his son, Kalani, then about twelve years old. I gathered that he ran some of the group's business ventures, like souping up classic American cars, to generate income to keep the community going. He was a bright guy with a quick wit, and we took to each other immediately. Paul was the one who gave me the nickname

23

"Baby Gorilla," mocking my restless, rambunctious way of swinging from the overhead grab bars to pass the tedious hours of travel.

From time to time, Paul pulled the bus over and stopped on the side of the road. We squatted down in the Silver Eagle's shadow, and Paul took out his Bible and gave us a study. One of them was about King Cyrus, the ancient Persian king who conquered Babylon in 539 B.C. Cyrus freed the Jews, allowed them to return to Israel, and helped them rebuild the temple the Babylonians had destroyed. "According to Isaiah," Paul said, "Cyrus was a 'messiah,' a word which means 'anointed one' in Hebrew. And in Hebrew, 'Cyrus' is 'Koresh,' the name David took last year."

"You mean, 'Koresh' isn't David's real name?" I asked.

"That's exactly what it is," Paul said cryptically, and I saw from his expression that he didn't invite further questions on this point. However, he did add that David was the reincarnation of King Cyrus, the man who would confront "Babylon" in its modern form, which I gathered included the political and military powers that ruled the world.

"So what are you saying?" I queried. He shrugged, and I let it go at that. To be honest, none of it struck me as totally outlandish. Maybe I'd lived in Hollywood too long, had heard too many strange tales, some of which had actually turned out to be true.

During the long ride I grew close to Jaime. He was my age, dark, soft-spoken, with soft brown eyes. He told me he was born in Texas but grew up in various suburbs east of L.A. His father, a *ranchera* musician, moved out, and the family had to survive on welfare. His mother was a devout Jehovah's Witness, but his childhood was very difficult. "Where I grew up, dope was everywhere," he said. "I was expelled from school for having poor grades, then worked as a courier, playing drums and guitar at night, fucking groupies," Jaime said.

In 1988, feeling he'd lost his way, Jaime put an ad in a newspaper about wanting to play in a Christian band. David answered his ad, and later that year Jaime moved to Mount Carmel, shuttling between Waco and Pomona to play in the band. He loved and respected David, but as a musician he had a certain beef with him.

"He likes to set us drummers against each other, maybe to keep us on our toes. David made me feel I was part of the band, then he auditioned other drummers for my spot, like Mike Schroeder and you. He told me he was 'just trying the guys out,' but I got the impression he was going to leave me hanging, that maybe I wasn't quite good enough. He told me he was going to use Mike for 'a while,' and I threatened to go and find myself another situation. I wanted to pack up and hit the road; I didn't need to take that kind of shit from anyone."

He shrugged. "Maybe David's testing each of us musicians to see if our main commitment is to the message or to the music." After I'd joined the band, Jaime began playing the bass. He felt it was a lesser role, and there was an edge of resentment toward me that his better nature tried to set aside as we rolled on toward Waco.

He made one particular remark that stuck in my mind.

"Mount Carmel is the one true, stable family I've ever really had," he said. "And that is David's doing. He's been more of a loving father to me than any man I've ever known."

———

Waco is the navel of the Texan plains, the Brazos Valley sinkhole in the belly of that vast aridity. Its main claim to fame is that it's the birthplace of Dr. Pepper cola, an achievement the town celebrates with the Dr. Pepper Museum, along with the Texas Ranger Museum and Hall of Fame. My first glimpse of Waco, as we skirted downtown's squat cotton warehouses and turned southeast along the mud banks of the Brazos, reminded me of *The Last Picture Show*, a desolate movie about a desolate place. Arizona and New Mexico had been hot and bright, but the sunlight in East Texas was like an iron fist.

How the hell did I come to be here? I wondered as we headed into the barren countryside pocked with disconsolate cattle giving off a stink of dung methane in the frying-pan heat. These stupefied oxen were not the same species as the happy, milk-heavy Holsteins I'd seen in Maine. That how-in-hell-did-I-get-here refrain would be repeated often during the coming years.

The sight of Mount Carmel didn't thrill me either, to put it mildly. A narrow dirt track led through a gateway off the winding farm road we'd been following for the last few miles, running from the study house or "church" at the entrance to the property, past a row of shabby, clapboard cottages straggling up the rise to the barn at the back.

At the top of the rise—the Anthill, where the new building was just beginning to be constructed—was the concrete storage room the FBI later referred to as the "bunker." This squat, gray box, with its foot-thick reinforced concrete walls, served as a vault for the community's records and as a walk-in cooler for supplies. Beside it was the first, almost completed section of the main building, intended as the cafeteria, but at the moment still without a roof. Behind the vault was a recently built plywood chapel building and a rusting, circular steel water tower about forty feet tall. Up on the hill the earth was gouged to make foundations for the main building, and some of the cottages had been stripped to their framing so their timber could be recycled in the new building. The whole scene was a cross between a makeshift encampment and a construction site.

My heart sank. Was this cockeyed shambles David's idea of the Promised Land? Or was it his re-creation of the Sinai Desert in which the Children of Israel wandered for forty miserable years? The second guess was accurate, I later learned; we were meant to spend time in the wilderness, in what David called a "withering experience," meant to purify our spirits. "I want to keep the place kind of rough and unfinished," David said. "That way people that come here, they're coming for one reason. They're coming to learn something." The crudity of the conditions was a deliberate "stumbling block" on the path to virtue, to use his vernacular.

Back then I was appalled as I grabbed my duffel bag, stepped down on that dusty soil, and took a sniff of baked earth and dried grass, a smell that was to become all too familiar. Jaime showed me to a room with bunk beds we were to share in one of the cottages, and my worst fears were confirmed. Desperate for a shower, I discovered that only a few of the houses had running water, and ours wasn't one of them. To wash, one had to gather water in a bucket from a neighbor's faucet. There wasn't even sufficient water pressure to flush the toilets; it was necessary to empty a bucket into the pan and hope it did the job. The only water supply, Jaime told me, was an artesian well with a tricky pump, connected to a row of 1,500-gallon tanks. The air was hot and humid, and fire ants attacked our legs the moment we stepped outdoors. At night, mosquitoes with vicious tempers sprang out of the scrub and attacked every inch of bare flesh. On rainy days, I was told, when the clouds burst, the dirt turned to a sea of mud.

Wandering around Mount Carmel during those first days gathering information and collecting impressions, I began to get a sense of the community. It seemed very open and friendly. Some of the hundred or so people living there had been in residence even before David's time, others were relative newcomers, and I was amazed by the diversity of nationalities and races. Apart from Americans from the mainland and Hawaii, there were many black people from Britain, as well as citizens of Australia, Mexico, the Caribbean, New Zealand, the Philippines, and Canada. Clive Doyle was Australian, Margarida Vaega was a Chinese New Zealander, Mark Wendell was Asian American, Juliet Santoyo Martinez was Mexican American, and so on. There were rich people, like Paul Fatta, poor people who had nothing, and highly educated people, like Wayne Martin, a Harvard-trained lawyer, and Alrick ("Rick") Bennett, an architect, a big, tall black guy from Britain. Mount Carmel was a miniature democracy where everyone was equal under David, and even he was just one of the guys when he wasn't leading a Bible study.

Many members of the community were old Adventist holy rollers, including Perry Jones and Catherine Matteson. In fact, apart from a few people like Jaime and me, most of the Mount Carmelites had a Seventh-day Adventist background. I was even more removed from this core religious body than Jaime, having had no churchgoing experience at all. Up to then my only contact with

Adventists had been the earnest folk who rang doorbells and tried to press pamphlets into my hands. I didn't know that mainstream Adventism was a highly organized, well-established international faith with around 10 million members. Anyway, I soon gathered that the Mount Carmel community had split from the mainstream decades earlier, well before David became its leader.

The older single people, like Catherine Matteson, shared residences; so did the young men and women who were living at Mount Carmel or just visiting, like me. David and his wife, Rachel, and their children had a modest home next door to the study house. Everyone used the kitchen in the house of Perry Jones, David's father-in-law, who'd lived at Mount Carmel for most of his life. Many of our meals were taken there.

I was struck by how people shared things with their neighbors and helped one another out. If you were short of something or needed someone to mind the kids or look after a sick person, you only had to ask. Everyone seemed cheerful, not earnest or glum like some religious groups can be. More than anything, the easy ambiance at Mount Carmel was reminiscent of hippie communes as my mom had described them to me. But Mount Carmel wasn't totally communal; for instance, bank accounts weren't pooled, and possessions weren't held in common.

The community's rituals were simple. Twice a day, at the third and ninth hour from sunrise, according to Old Testament prescription, the residents gathered for brief religious observances, usually including a simple communion service of bread and wine. When David was around, he usually followed the service with a Scripture study. The rest of the time people went about their chores, the women taking care of the kids, cooking, sewing and making garments for sale, the men busy with the construction of the new building, working in the auto shop or the landscaping business, or going off to jobs in Waco. Idleness, I discovered, was not encouraged; but as a visitor, I could take it easy.

I was disappointed that David didn't seem to have time for music during the Day of Atonement gathering. However, with another hundred people arriving from as far away as Britain and

Australia, I wasn't surprised that he was busy. The cottages were bursting at the seams, Jaime and I had to cram extra couches into our small room for visitors to crash, and tents sprang up in the scrub around the chapel.

I spent some time with Mike Schroeder, my fellow drummer. A temperamental guy from Florida, slightly built, a few years older than me, he was given to strange, sullen moods and outbursts of rage. It was rumored that he'd had a bad time with drugs a while back. He told me he'd run through a bunch of churches, Lutheran, Baptist, the Church of God, and others before Adventism and, eventually, David. When he was wasn't drumming, he worked as a mechanic in the community's auto shop four miles away, where he was known for hurling his wrenches in a fury if the machinery didn't respond to his touch.

There were a lot of kids around, many of them babies, but I couldn't figure out who the fathers were. My first impression was that David had some of his former girlfriends living there with their children and that his wife, Rachel, didn't seem to mind. That was really broadminded of her, I thought. I learned that a few years back married couples and their children, like Mark and Jaydean Wendell, Wayne and Sheila Martin, Neal and Margarida Vaega, Scott "Snow Flea" Sonobe and his wife, Floracita, occupied their own homes. Again I was reminded of the hippie communes where men and women made love to whomever they chose and sexual jealousy of any kind was considered uncool. When I asked questions about all this the answers were vague and I let it go, not wanting to seem too nosy.

Michele Jones, the woman who later became my wife, was one of the young women I talked to. She seemed much more mature compared to girls I knew in Hollywood. She was quiet and reserved, amiable but not flirtatious, nothing like the young women I knew. All of the women at Mount Carmel wore very sober clothes, long skirts and tops, and no makeup. Their only female extravagance was their long hair, worn, in Michele's case, loose and unadorned. To tell the truth, I wasn't much attracted to her, perhaps because she didn't put out the flirty signals I was used to.

Serenity, her two-year-old, was as self-contained as her mother, a shy girl with a touch of mischief in her eyes. We immediately set up a sly game of hide-and-seek; I'd see her peeking out at me from behind her mother's skirts and pretend to be surprised.

———— · ————

To discover more about the community and why it attracted such a mixture of people, I talked to many of the visitors who'd come for the festival. There was Zilla Henry, a black woman from England. Zilla told me that when David visited her school of theology in Nottingham, she and many others who heard him felt they'd learned more about the inner meaning of the Scriptures in a few hours than in years of previous study. Zilla told me she was thinking of moving herself and five other members of her family, including her grownup children, to Mount Carmel to continue learning David's teachings. "He has the answers to my questions," she said simply.

One of the most devout and learned visitors was Livingston Fagan, a slight black man from England. He was a serious student, even a little stuffy. His usual greeting, delivered in an educated, very deliberate British accent, was, "Hello, Livingston Fagan here. Shall we study?"

Fagan arrived with his wife, Evette, his children, Renea and Neharah, and his sixty-year-old mother, Doris. Livingston had been an Adventist lay minister, studying for a master's degree in theology at Nottingham's Newbold College, when, like Zilla Henry, he attended a talk David gave during his 1988 trip to the United Kingdom.

"David visited the campus to conduct some unscheduled lectures on the nature of God and salvation," Livingston told me. "I heard a couple of his studies, and in three hours I perceived more biblical truths than I had done the entire eight years I'd been involved with organized religion. It was clear to me that David offered a highly intelligent, systematic inquiry into the nature of Scripture. I visited Mount Carmel later that year for the first time, and I'm thinking of settling here permanently."

Evette was a charming woman who favored African dress and braids. She was devoted to her husband, whom she seemed to admire enormously. But it was Livingston who impressed me. If such a deeply serious, extremely thoughtful man held David in such high repute, clearly I wasn't in the presence of a religious charlatan.

I questioned Livingston closely, and though my queries must have seemed elementary, he listened patiently, his head cocked, alert as a little black sparrow, as if trying to divine my underlying intention. "Mount Carmel is fashioned for purposes of holistically transcending our present artificial and sensory-based conscious-ness," he said, speaking, as he always did, in rounded sentences, as if he were reading from a private and carefully composed book. "The transcendence of the sensory-based human perceptions opens the mind to a higher truth." His conviction was honest, and his quiet passion infectious. Even the words themselves—"tran-scendence," "sensory," "holistically," spoken with Livingston's grave intonation, had a pleasant musical vibration in my ear.

One of the most extraordinary men I came across was Wayne Martin. The son of a transit-authority worker from Queens, New York, Wayne had risen through hard study and intelligence to be-come an attorney with a law degree from Harvard. His grandfather was an Adventist minister, and his wife, Sheila, was a member of the Branch Davidian sect that had split from the Adventist main-stream during the 1930s. After a few years of practice in Boston, Wayne found that the formalities and rough-and-tumble tactics of lawyering didn't really appeal to him. For a while he took a job as a lecturer and law librarian at North Carolina Central University, an African American college in Durham. Along the way he became unhappy with traditional Adventism and stopped attending the church. He was a quiet man, very civilized, known in the commu-nity for going out of his way to help people.

Wayne went through a spiritual crisis during the mid-1980s when his son, Jamie, fell ill with meningitis that blinded and crip-pled him and stunted his growth. "I felt it was a judgment," Wayne told me. Sheila tried to comfort him by offering her husband some of David's biblical tapes, but it was many months before he'd listen. "Then, one day, I opened my ears and I was hooked," he said, with a wry-serious smile.

The family moved to the Waco area and Wayne opened an office in the town, handling personal injury, criminal, and domestic cases. He was, as a state judge remarked later, "a moral kind of guy." Even so, Wayne was convinced that his application to be admitted to the federal bar was blocked because he was a member of the Mount Carmel community.

Wayne had an amazing talent for astrology. In fact, he successfully played the stock market on astrological predictions, but only as a game, never in reality. His virtual "profits" were staggering. More seriously, he told me he'd predicted that Jamie would contract meningitis. I asked him to do my horoscope but he refused, saying only that I was on the verge of a major life change that he didn't want to influence.

———•·•———

One evening Steve told me something about Mount Carmel's history. He explained that the community had been founded on a patch of prairie in 1934 by Victor Houteff, a Bulgarian-born former Maytag washer salesman. Houteff was a follower of the visionary nineteenth-century Seventh-day Adventist leader Ellen G. White. Mount Carmel was named for the biblical place where the prophet Elijah battled the worshippers of the pagan god Baal. Houteff's prophetic doctrines were rejected by mainstream Adventism, so Houteff named his community the Davidian Seventh-day Adventist Association, signaling that he was the latter-day Elijah who would prepare King David's throne for the Messiah, as prophesied in the Old Testament. When that glorious moment came, it was believed, the entire community would travel to Jerusalem to welcome the Advent.

In ten years, Houteff's Davidians grew in number from a handful to more than a hundred. The community was a spartan, self-enclosed, miniature society with its own school and communal kitchen, but with deliberately primitive living conditions: just a collection of cheaply built clapboard cottages. The life was designed to test its members, to discover whether they were willing to suffer the hardships of the "withering experience"—the conquest of the flesh in the name of the spirit—to prove they were servants of

God rather than Baal, Houteff created the Mount Carmel Training Center, offering, in its catalog, "a survey of history from the divine point of view."

According to the older folk I talked to, like Perry Jones, Brother Houteff was a benign and honest leader. He refused to celebrate Christmas and Easter, regarding them as Roman festivals in origin. These views surprised the local people, to say the least. Waco, after all, is the seat of Southern Baptist Baylor University, the stronghold of a puritanical denomination whose strict doctrines frown on such frivolities as drinking and dancing. But the Davidians paid their bills on time and bothered no one.

Unfortunately, Houteff did not clearly name his successor. During the 1950s, when he got ill, his followers split into factions. Perry Jones, David's future father-in-law, chose the group led by Ben Roden, an oilfield hand who named his adherents the Living Waters Branch, based on a revelation he'd received and on Christ's words to his disciples: *I am the vine and you are the branches.* Native to Texas, Ben and his wife, Lois, came to live permanently in Mount Carmel in 1955, just after Houteff died. Their rival for the succession was Houteff's young widow, Florence.

At this time, the community was in a geographic as well as a spiritual transition. The booming town of Waco was reaching its suburban tentacles out toward the community's sanctuary, and the Davidians sold off their property. In 1957 they moved to a large ranch on a prairie rise ten miles or so southeast of the town. They named this New Mount Carmel, but later the "New" was dropped. Over the years parcels of the ranch were sold off, leaving the seventy-seven acres I was visiting.

Before he died, Houteff had been obsessed by prophesies that his church would be purified by persecution leading to the End of Days. His widow and his followers decided that this biblical End Time would occur on April 22, 1959. On that day around nine hundred Davidians from all over the United States gathered at Mount Carmel, expecting Armageddon, the final battle between the forces of good and evil, in which they would die the glorious death of martyrs and ascend to heaven. However, the appointed day passed uneventfully and the deeply disappointed crowd dispersed. After this, Ben and Lois Roden's "branch" was in the ascendancy.

Following standard Adventist practice, the Rodens observed Jewish festivals such as Passover, Pentacles, the Feast of Tabernacles, and the Day of Atonement. They encouraged their followers to go and live in Israel to await the still-expected fulfillment of Houteff's apocalyptic prophecy. In 1978, when Ben died, Lois Roden buried her husband on Jerusalem's Mount of Olives. Three years later, David Koresh appeared on her doorstep.

———————

I was sitting in the chapel with Jaime one afternoon a week or so into my visit, when David walked in. "Hey, Thibodeau," he said, using my surname, as everyone came to do at Mount Carmel, liking the Frenchy ring of it. "You want to get into it a little? Have a study?"

"Yeah. Sure," I replied, surprised, but willing to go along.

David opened his big Bible, which always seemed close at hand. As if on signal, people immediately started gathering. The eager, expectant looks on their faces revealed that having a study with David was the highlight of their lives.

David began with a dramatic passage from the Book of Revelation, the last book in the New Testament, plunging immediately into the midst of what I could see was a running stream of inspiration. *And there appeared a great wonder in heaven; a woman clothed with the sun, and the moon under her feet, and upon her head a crown of twelve stars. . . .* The woman was struggling with the pain of childbirth, David went on, when a great red dragon with seven crowned heads and ten horns threatened to devour her. *And she brought forth a man child, who was to rule all nations with a rod of iron.* The holy child, David asserted, would "prevail in the final battle between Good and Evil at the end of time."

The text David intoned was like a comic book, all lurid colors and sharply defined heroes and villains. Its vivid simplicity entranced me, but I was more impressed by another phenomenon: the shuddering bolts of thunder that rattled the windows out of a clear sky each time he emphasized a phrase or word.

My skin crawled. Rationally, I knew that the Texan plain was given to abrupt, sky-cracking thunderstorms. But the timing was awesome, as if David were literally conjuring up these heavenly responses. Stealing glances at the people around me, I saw that they were as startled as I was by this sound and light show. Some were hugging their neighbors and muttering, "Whoa, there! Whoa!" David himself smiled from time to time, as if simultaneously discounting the lightning's literalness while accepting it as his due.

"That was somethin' else," Jaime said as we filtered out of the chapel. I could see that he was shaken. "Each time I begin to doubt David, something like this happens to wow me."

Being impressionable, dramatic events always impressed me, until my more sober mind sifted out the grit. But seeing David in action for the first time made me begin to take him more seriously as a religious figure.

The next day David took me for a drive in his '68 Camaro with the 400-plus-c.c. turbocharged engine. He talked about his life, how, as he put, "I always saw things differently from other people." This remark resonated with me; I also considered myself to be the odd man out in any group. As a child, he heard voices, he told me, and I immediately thought "psycho," then rejected this glib diagnosis as obscuring more than it explained.

"No one understood me; I knew I was on a special path," he said. He tried to tell me that he was given some kind of insight, but his description of this experience was too vague and oblique for me to grasp. In truth, I wasn't really getting it, and I could see his mouth draw down when I countered with, "Yeah, no one's really understood me, either." Yet I appreciated his straightforward manner, his soft-sell approach, the opposite of Steve's driven style. David was more laid-back, he was modest, he spoke from the heart and didn't try to overwhelm me.

Sometimes, late at night, after a long day of Bible study, we stayed in the cafeteria after the others left and jammed a little to cool out. Sheer exhaustion put us into a deep daze, kind of peaceful, way beyond tiredness, David easy on the strings, me barely tapping the skins, moving together in a shared zone that was like a trance.

Between licks, David talked about his life, reverting to a working-class Texan twang. He told me his original name was Vernon Howell, that his mother, Bonnie, was only fourteen or fifteen when he was born in 1959, ten years before me. His father, Bobby, split when he was a baby, after nicknaming him "Sputnik." "Because I was so rackety and restless, just like you, Thibodeau," he added with a grin.

Bonnie moved from Houston to Dallas and got hitched to a shady guy named Roy Haldeman, known as Rocky, who often beat young Vernon so bad "he made me fly like a kite." David was slightly dyslexic, couldn't keep up in school, and the other kids, with typical cruelty, dubbed him "Mr. Retardo." He tended to stutter when stressed, which didn't help him in the classroom, and he was painfully skinny. I was given a hard time in school because I was too fat, but it came to the same thing: being an object of fun and derision.

"I failed the first grade twice and failed the second grade, too," David said, a kind of pained pride still vibrating in his voice. In third grade he was sent to a "special" school for backward kids. The first day, at recess, he said, the children in the regular classes shouted, "Here come the retards!"

"I just stopped dead in my tracks, like the sun went down, instant night. When my mom came to pick me up after school I bust out howling, 'I'm a retard!' She tried to reassure me that I just had a 'learning disability,' but the polite phrase didn't snow me. I was a retard, plain and simple. In a year of special school I finally learned the alphabet and some reading, but writing was a bummer. Words like 'angel' came out 'angle,' and such."

I remembered that my father, worried about my weight problem, had sent me to a counselor specializing in "eating disorders." But that strategy didn't take, any more than Vernon's "special" schooling. Oddballs like us just had to take our chances.

"I could understand machines, like cars, engines, radios, anything I could put my hands on and take apart to see how they worked," David told me. "But reading and writing was a foreign language. It's still a bit of a problem for me," he admitted, with a hint of shame. He was totally self-taught, and it showed in his misuse of "convicted" for "convinced," "bizarrity" for "bizarre," and "globular" for "global."

The experience of being a bright child who couldn't express himself still caused him pain. Such hurts run deep, I knew, from my own hard time in school. I'd hung in till I graduated, but Vernon had dropped out in the eleventh grade, unable to bear the constant humiliation. My heart went out to that lonely, lost kid desperate to make a place for himself in the hard scheme of things.

His family life was no fun either, he said sardonically. Apart from his maternal grandpa, who took him fishing and hunting on weekends, his relatives were heavy. "At my thirteenth birthday party my mom beat me black and blue in front of everybody. My stepdad was a cruel, cold man and my half-brother, Roger, ended up in the slammer on burglary and drug charges. My cousins tried to rape me so I started pumping iron, toughening my body, to defend myself. For sheer survival I became a fitness freak.

"I was lousy at school, but I was good with guns, four-ten shotguns and twenty-two rifles, bagging rabbits, doves, and squirrels around the lake. Like every Texan kid of my background, a gun was a friend and protector, as loyal and obedient to my wishes as my dog, Jet Fuel." His other friend was music. He found a guitar in an old barn, took some lessons, and picked up the local country-and-western style of singing and playing. He put together some garage bands, just as I had, but his partners often got sucked into the Dallas drug culture. Our common experience of finding refuge in music made me feel very close to David in these intimate moments of quiet talk. Like me, he'd been a kid with an intense inner world; a dreamer whose life was lived within the boundaries of his very private soul. For him and for me, music, our most personal avenue of self-expression, was also the main means of communicating our deepest feelings. Paradoxically, performance made the private world bearable in public.

But young Vernon had a powerful extra dimension: a natural gift for the spiritual. His mother was raised in the Adventist Church, and his maternal grandmother, Earline, often took him to worship in the local congregation—"a bunch of folks dyed, fried, and tied to the side," he joked, mocking their conventional propriety. "But I was fascinated by the service, and even by the hokey evangelists I watched on TV and heard on the radio. I learned huge swatches of Scripture by heart and bored other kids at school with Bible lectures. I was thrilled by holy writ and knew that the great book was a puzzle of the truth I just had to decode in my very own way.

"One time I played hooky from school and went to the church to put the question to the Man Himself. On my knees, I prayed: 'Dear Father, I know I'm stupid, but please talk to me 'cause I want to serve you.' A while later I heard His word in my heart, as if we were discussing things directly."

Vernon's conversations with the Lord intensified when he was eighteen. While working as a nonunion carpenter in an oilfield, he met Linda Campion, a girl he'd once hung out with, in a North Dallas arcade. He had a bankroll in his jeans and owned a new pickup, and for the first time in his life his self-confidence was high. "I was shy, still a virgin, kind of straitlaced on account of my church life, and she was beautiful. At first, I didn't want nothing to do with her, she was too gorgeous, a real temptation. Lustful thoughts . . . ," he murmured, a strange look on his face, wistful, yearning, and sad. "She had the beauty to make good men fall," he added primly.

Despite his scruples, he ended up making love to Linda.

"She was jailbait, just sixteen, but you know how humanity is," he shrugged ruefully. After the second time they made love, he tried to escape temptation by moving away. But escape wasn't that easy. One night she called to tell him she was pregnant.

Vernon was staggered. "Me, Mr. Retardo, going to be a daddy! I blurted out a lie, that it was impossible, because I was 'sterile'—a word I'd heard in a movie or something. She hung up on me and that seemed to be that. But that holy voice in my heart reminded me that, according to Scripture, since I'd been with her, had entered her body with mine, we were married in His eyes. I went back to Dallas intending to marry her, but she told me she'd had an abortion. I was shaken, reckoning she must hate me. But to my amazement she said she was still drawn to me, because I was different, didn't smoke dope like the other guys she knew, never hit the six-packs. 'You don't have to do what everybody else does to have a good time,' she said."

Vernon moved in with Linda and her family. The girl's father thought his daughter, who was still in school, was too young to marry. For religious reasons—as Vernon interpreted them—they didn't use condoms, and a few months later she was pregnant a second time. In a fit of rage, her father kicked him out of the house and forbade him to see Linda again. Troubled and confused, Vernon bedded down in his truck, praying that God would help him understand why he wasn't allowed to bond with the woman he loved, a marriage he'd thought ordained by heaven.

"One night, in the midst of my pain, I was enshrouded by the 'presence.' I was shaking, scared out of my wits. I was looking up at the sky, seeing those bright stars in the black night, with nowhere to run. There's this voice in my head, not words but a speaking image. 'You're really hurt, aren't you? You love her and she's turned her back on you, rejected you.' In my mind I ran a review of all the strange experiences I'd had in my young life.

"God said to me, 'Don't you know that for nineteen years I've loved you and for nineteen years you've turned your back and rejected me?' And all of a sudden, everything is like, bang!—how I'd forgotten the purpose of my life, to be true to His word. It was a marvelous moment of self-affirmation. Best of all, God said he would give my first love back to me in time."

His voice trailed off, and I thought he'd forgotten I was there. "But He never did," he went on. "I lost contact with her and our child, my firstborn."

For a few years after that he drifted, obsessed with his lost first love. "I came to God because of her," he said, tears in his eyes. "I couldn't make sense of the failure of our connection. It wrenched my gut. I had to find my way back to my true fate. It was waiting for me, I knew, out there, somewhere," he said, giving me one of his sappy, appealing grins.

During the late 1970s, while living with his aunt in Dallas and working in the construction industry, Vernon had another startling spiritual experience. One evening he was on his knees, saying his prayers before bed, desperate and in tears because nothing seemed to be going right for him. Suddenly, he had the sensation he was rising up an elevator shaft.

"My vision was limited, like I was seeing things through a dark-tinted welder's mask," he said. "I saw a gigantic wall, like the front of a skyscraper. On this wall was a huge inscription cut into the stonework: 'THE LAW.' And there was an even bigger wall beyond that with another inscription: 'PROPEHCY.' The light was so intense it would have blinded me if not for the tinted glass shielding my eyes. I saw God the Father with a book in one hand. His other hand was held out to me, and I took hold of it."

David paused to catch his breath. "When I came down to earth, I ran to the kitchen and asked my aunt: 'Why aren't there any more prophets?' She told me she'd heard somewhere that there was one in Waco, at a place called Mount Carmel. 'Take me there, now!' I cried, but she didn't."

David shrugged and was silent for a while, recalling what must have been an amazing moment. By the way he told it, straight and simple, I knew he was recounting something very real. To me, it sounded like an acid trip, yet I knew he'd always hated drugs. Listening to him, watching the play of expression in his eyes, I was fascinated by a mind that took such extraordinary journeys.

Though this vision was staggering, it didn't really connect him to anything, David explained. In 1981, when he was twenty-two—around my age at the time we were speaking—he was still floating, looking for a place to settle, waiting for great things to happen. Unlike me, he had a powerful spiritual push, a strong hand at his back urging him onward. His need to know was focused, whereas mine was fuzzy. Then and now, it was this sincere and passionate concentration that gave David his rare force, his influence over those who, like me, didn't know how much they needed to know.

"Anyway," he said, "I finally made my own way to Mount Carmel."

4

EDGING TOWARD BELIEF

On the summer afternoon in 1981 when David first came to Mount Carmel he was a confused twenty-two-year-old beset by visions and still deeply hurt by the disappointment of his first love affair. Two years earlier he'd been baptized in his mother's Seventh-day Adventist Church, but he'd soon come to feel that mainstream Adventism offered a corrupted doctrine that betrayed its original purpose—to prophesy and prepare for the End Time and the coming of a Messiah. From his aunt and others, he'd heard that Lois Roden had been given revelations, and his hungry soul was ready to serve her.

"I drove my flashy yellow Buick up to the front door and knocked," David recalled. "Just a bonehead coming to see what was going on." Perry Jones told me he remembered "a scruffy, wild-eyed kid with a straggly beard, looking for the light in a fog."

At the time, Lois was in her sixties. Her son, George, was a big, hulking guy in his forties who hoped to take over the community when his mother died; but to most of the community he was known simply as Poor George, an overgrown boy plagued by twitches. "Sometimes he'd just spit in your face, or make the table jump and

41

the soup fly by slamming down his fist for no reason," David said. "He was a mess."

Gradually, David replaced George as Lois's heir, and George was furious. David was also Lois's lover for a time. He said he hoped a miracle would occur; that the old prophetess, past her menopause, would conceive a son, just as the ninety-year-old Sarah had done for Abraham in Genesis. Accusing David of raping his mother, George denounced him as Lucifer.

Lois Roden had added a vital new idea to the Davidians: the revelation that the Holy Spirit was feminine. In her teaching, *Shekinah*, the ancient Hebrew term for the Bride of the Sabbath, the earthly presence of the divine spirit, was integrated within the traditional concept of the Messiah. Some of her followers found this hard to swallow, but others welcomed it as a deeper and more expansive insight into the divine nature. Lois renamed the community the Living Waters Branch, based on a holy Trinity in which the Spirit was feminine. Later, when David became the Davidian leader, he embraced the female aspect of divinity wholeheartedly.

"It floored me when I first heard this and grasped its implication," he murmured. "That the womanly *Shekinah* was the Holy Spirit—female! And that her symbol, the downward triangle in the Star of David, was locked with the upward triangle of God's male aspect." For David, the divine character was as much female as male, a notion that connected directly with the female presences of my own childhood, my loving grandmothers, my close ties to my mother.

In the spring of 1984, to ease the tense situation with George, David and the core of those who believed he was Lois's true successor moved away, relocating to a smaller camp at Palestine, a hundred miles or so east of Waco. The Palestine place was primitive, hardly more than a bunch of old school buses, tents, and crude plywood shacks with outhouses whose buckets had to be emptied into the fields. But it was the first place where David was the undisputed leader of his community.

This gave David fresh confidence in his destiny. Just before leaving Mount Carmel, he married Rachel Jones, Perry Jones's fourteen-year-old daughter. He had her parents' blessing, and under Texas law the marriage was legal. Besides, there were biblical precedents, such as the young Virgin Mary wedding Joseph at an age younger than Rachel's.

In 1986, after Lois died, George, isolated and increasingly crazy in the empty Mount Carmel, dug up the twenty-year-old cadaver of one his mother's followers and challenged David to raise her from the dead. David refused the challenge with a laconic "Not today, George," and reported George to the McLennan County sheriff.

"We got some pictures of the coffin draped in an Israeli flag, but the sheriff wanted a photo of the bones," David told me. "So, on a cold day in November 1987, a bunch of us, armed with shotguns and rifles, snuck onto the property and tried to get a shot of the body, but it was gone. The dogs were yowling and George came out, firing his Uzi, so we hunkered down for the night. Next day we had a shootout with George and the deputies grabbed us. When we were in jail they played on the news that PLO terrorists had assaulted Mount Carmel!"

David and seven of his comrades were acquitted at the trial after the disturbed George took the stand and admitted that he himself had tried to resurrect the woman's decayed corpse. George was banned from Mount Carmel, and David paid the huge backlog of taxes due on the property with the help of some of his wealthier disciples. In April 1988, he took over Mount Carmel, which had been badly neglected.

"Sometimes, when you're living through things, you can't see the woods for the trees," David said. "But slowly I came to realize that all these events, good and bad, were part of a plan, the fulfillment of a vision I had in Jerusalem."

David's essential message derived from his vision that the entire Bible, from Genesis to Revelation, was an integrated, coded narrative describing humanity's spiritual history. He claimed he'd been given the key to unlocking this coded story, thereby making the events prophesied in Scripture about the end of human history actually happen.

"I've been sent to explain and do the Scriptures," he said.

David believed he was the incarnation of the sacrificed Lamb spoken of in Revelation—*the Lamb that was slain to receive power*—who took the mysterious book from God's hand and proceeded to unlock the Seven Seals described in Revelation, one by one. He made it clear that he was not a resurrected Jesus but an "anointed one," a Hebrew term referring to the biblical ceremony in which oil is poured over the head of a priest or king.

David said he followed Jesus and his predecessor, Melchizedek, a priest who was a contemporary of Abraham, *made like unto the Son of God*. David argued that, since the messianic Melchizedek had lived 2,000 years before Jesus, another prophet could appear 2,000 years after.

Being totally ignorant of the Book of Revelation, I was amazed by the progression of images and metaphors as David unfolded them for me. The opening of the First Seal, the biblical narrative recounted, was accompanied by a clap of thunder heralding a conqueror riding a white horse. The Second Seal spoke of a red horse whose armed rider spread death and war. The Third Seal's horse was black, carrying a man holding a pair of balances, and the Fourth Seal's ashen horse carried Death, a pale rider followed by Hell, given the power to kill and spread hunger over a large part of the earth.

These Four Horsemen of the Apocalypse ruled the world while, in the Fifth Seal, the souls of the dead huddled under the altar crying out for justice. They were told to rest for a "little season" before their fate was fulfilled. Things turn truly black in the Sixth Seal, when the earth is shaken by quakes, the sun turns black, the moon is an eye of blood, stars fall to the ground, and the temporal rulers tremble from heaven's rage. Angels appear, holding the winds in their power, pleading with God not to destroy the world until his faithful ones, numbering 144,000, 12,000 for each of the twelve tribes of Israel, are marked with a special sign for salvation. The Lamb who unlocked the Seals offers them protection and promises them relief from suffering.

The Seventh Seal is heralded by a silence, followed by seven angels blowing trumpets in turn. One apocalyptic catastrophe after another follows each trumpet blast, and the angels pour out seven bowls of wrath upon the earth. The world's time ends forever, giving way, after a cosmic war between good and evil, Jerusalem and Babylon, to a dimension of eternity ruled by twenty-four elders seated at God's feet. A victorious Jerusalem, the Bride of Heaven, gathers all splendor into her arms.

The text of Revelation is filled with amazing figures out of some biblical *Star Wars* epic. There are seven-headed beasts, winged creatures with the faces of lions, calves, eagles, and human beings, a false horned prophet, Satan in the form of a dragon, a harlot on beast-back, one woman drunk with the blood of saints, another covered in a garment of stars. Frogs come out of the dragon's mouth and angels hurl millstones big enough to destroy a mighty city.

What kind of mind could dream up such an incredible scenario? I wondered. Either a genius or a loony. And what kind of man must David be if he could claim to have the key to unraveling these magnificent obscurities?

Either inspired or nuts. . . .

David's study sessions, held before a large crowd under the airless chapel's open-raftered ceiling, often ran on for twelve hours at a stretch.

As a teacher, David's style was all his own. He was not charismatic in the manner of a Jim Jones or some television preachers. Neither was he formal or dignified, like a robed priest or a rabbi in his prayer shawl. In fact, his whole style was a kind of debunking of such expectations. He spoke fluently but he was never preachy, which for me would've been an instant turnoff.

In his teaching mode, David Koresh was a Texas good ol' boy transformed by the spirit. He shuffled up to the podium in jeans and T-shirt, wearing sneakers, sometimes still sweaty from jogging or biking, other times with mechanic's grease on his fingers or streaking his cheeks, hurrying in from the auto shop where he loved to tinker. Much of the time he hadn't even bothered to shave, signaling to us that studying the Scripture was just part of everyday life, not something removed from the mundane but woven into its texture.

When he began to speak his voice was low, casual, almost chatty. One of his favorite similes was comparing the puzzle of Scripture to the workings of a car engine. "To fire it up, get the wheels moving, you have to have the plugs, pistons, gears, transmission, and all operating in sync, otherwise all you have is a junker. Our souls are junkers, stuck in neutral, until we get our spirits in sync."

Holding the Bible pressed to his brow, he said: "I have these pictures in my head. Most people see this book as two pieces of leather with pages in between. I hold the book to my head and see it instantaneously, panoramically, all the events happening now. The written Word of God and the Mind of God are harmonized in my brain, and all I can do is show it to you." This notion that he was living in a movie that had begun thousands of years ago, way back in the origins of the human imagination, caught my fancy. If it were true, what an experience it must be!

David spoke of being "in the message" or "coming into the message." When he read Scripture it was as if he were actually there taking part in the events, striding back and forth, gesturing expressively. If God was cursing his flock, David's voice would rise dramatically. As he warmed up he took fire, his wiry, six-foot frame twisting with the intensity of his deliverance, his glasses smudged with the heat of his feelings, his words stuttering as his larynx struggled to keep pace with his racing brain. But he was no hell-fire Pentecostal minister. When he spoke of the grace of God his voice was loving and compassionate. Altogether, his stamina was amazing; he could talk for up to twenty or thirty hours at a stretch, barely pausing to sip a glass of water while his listeners took notes and the kids played at their parents' feet.

At times, though, his metaphors could be downright disgusting, like his comparison of sin with a sticky booger hanging on your finger. "You're pickin' away, and it gets on your other finger, even when you're goin' fifty down the road and you're tryin' to flick it off." We chuckled at these images, sometimes with embarrassment, but they caught our attention.

He disarmed doubters by jokingly dismissing the Bible as "just a game the Jews made up." Scripture, he told us, was a way to escape "the guy in the mirror. We want to go from here to a place of freedom where we're no longer in bondage to the flesh, our stupidity, our vanity." He likened the prophets to a bunch of journalists "giving you a hot scoop on the future." He compared the biblical texts he quoted to a series of movie previews, "fast, action-packed pictures to grab your eye." Other times, describing God's harsh judgments, he commented: "The Lord is beating some butt, right?" He was always honest with us about the consequences of his theology. "It ain't going to be pretty," he warned.

There were moments when David seemed exhausted by his own intensities. "I'm tired of giving Bible studies to you guys," he'd say wearily. "Leave me be." Occasionally he dozed off from exhaustion in the middle of a study. When that happened, people just sat and waited, often for an hour or more, for him to wake and pick up the thread of his discourse exactly where he'd left off.

Sometimes he'd deliberately provoke us, to jar us out of a trance. "You know, I hate black people," he said once, out of the blue. I cringed reflexively. The crowd, which was around one-third black, was shocked. You could cut the hush with an axe. "And I hate yellow people," David went on after a pause. "And I hate white people. The people I value are people of light."

Suddenly, the audience let out a huge sigh of collective relief. "Are you people of light?" David challenged harshly, and the brief moment of complacency evaporated.

Listening to him, I ran through a whole catalogue of emotions, from fascination to frustration. Sometimes the study really took off like a good jam session, David and the crowd right there in the groove, flying on the wings of his words. Then there seemed to be a powerful energy in the room, everyone attuned to the same soul rhythms. David was inspired, feeding off the power of the response, like I would when the riffs were rolling. On other occasions, exhausted by his energy, I fell asleep or left the room to stretch my legs, so choked by all the talk I just had to go outside and kick the dirt for the hell of it.

"How long is this going to friggin' go on?" I cried out one time when I was outside and was startled to hear Steve chuckling behind me. I challenged him: "How do you go through this, sitting still for hours on end, living in this hellhole?" He laughed grimly. "You wouldn't believe the things I've been through to be here." There was an edge of resentment in his voice, and he broke off abruptly, afraid of seeming disloyal.

That night I had a surprising dream. In the dream, Michele Jones and I were down by the lake at night. I knew I wasn't supposed to have this assignation, but the warm black night and the big Texas moon, the crickets and the fireflies, softened my guilt. I was about to kiss Michele when, looking over my shoulder, I saw David watching us, smiling knowingly.

I woke up abruptly. *What does that mean?* I wondered. *Am I already trapped here? Is there no way of getting away from this guy?*

Though I was strongly drawn to David and fascinated by his ideas, I often had difficulty believing everything he said. I didn't doubt that he believed, but my natural skepticism got in the way of my own credulity.

For example, I had a hard time with David's account of his vision on Mount Zion, received during his second visit to Israel, in 1985. He said that Russian cosmonauts had reported the presence of seven angelic beings flying toward earth with wings the size of jumbo jets!

"Okay, so what happened was, while I was standing on Mount Zion," he said, "I met up with these angels, these presences made of pure light. They were warriors surrounding the Merkabah, the heavenly throne, riding on fiery horses, armed with flaming swords. They only allow those who can reveal the Seals into the higher realm, into those innumerable worlds that exist alongside our own.

"I was taken up past Orion, to meet God. He spoke to me, and I saw that he was made of unblemished flesh. In a flash I received a complete key to the Scriptures, how the puzzle fitted together. I knew then it was my destiny to unlock the Seals and open the way for our community."

Clive Doyle told me that David's visionary experience in Jerusalem was so concentrated and so charged he could barely stutter afterward. "As he described it, the way he saw the Bible was like a video, and at first he couldn't speak it as fast as he could see it. He told us that he would bring us the Seventh Angel's message, predicting that the End Time would happen in 1995, ten years after that amazing moment on Mount Zion. He was truly inspired."

After this, David began to speak of the "Cyrus message." Cyrus is the anointed king mentioned in Isaiah 45. *And I will give thee the treasures of darkness, and the hidden riches of secret places.* In this view, the people living at Mount Carmel were the "wave sheaf," the core group leading the way for the 144,000 souls chosen to follow, and David was the Lamb who would open the Seals.

As David's grasp of his role in the fulfillment of prophecy evolved, he had a further series of revelations. One of the most important and startling of these was his "New Light" experience during the summer of 1989, in which he foresaw the crucial role of sex and procreation in what he called the coming New World Order—a phrase later echoed by President George Bush around the time of the 1991 Gulf War.

The New Light revelation was so radical it shocked some of his people and shook their faith. Simply put, it mandated celibacy for everyone except David. Single men in the community had to give up sex. Married men, such as Steve Schneider and Livingston Fagan, had to separate from their wives and cease making love altogether. Sex was a distraction, David told his people, an untamed power seducing the spirit away from its focus. Only David was given the right to procreate with any of the women, married or single, to generate the inner circle of children who would rule the coming kingdom to be established in Israel.

In David's spiritual logic, he saw himself assuming the burden of sexuality for the entire community, both male and female. The children David would have with these women, married and single, ranging in ages from fourteen to forty, would represent the most sacred core of the community. "They are our hope and our future," he said simply.

David's children were intended to be the twenty-four wise ones or Elders surrounding the divine throne, as described in Revelation 4, *clothed in white raiment; and they had on their heads crowns of gold.* These Elders would rule the earthly kingdom to be set up in Israel in the last days, as Isaiah predicted. In Psalm 45, the Messiah fathers children meant to be princes under the Lamb. It was a bold, astounding, even incredible notion; but, for David, it was crucial to his entire belief in his calling.

"It was a tough thing to sell," David admitted. "Some of the guys and some of the women chomped at the bit. But I told them that Jesus himself spoke about becoming celibate for the kingdom's sake, and most finally accepted the New Light."

"You mean—?" I began, slowly grasping the implications of this notion.

"Yes," David cut in bluntly. "If you join us, you'll have to be celibate. Can you cut it, a randy guy like you?"

"No way," I retorted instantly. Then, considering it, I modified this reaction. "I'd have to think about it, you know? I mean, if it's part of the deal, if I understand its purpose in the whole scheme. . . ."

"It's a toughie," David conceded, "but I hope you will come to understand its purpose. Some of the people didn't, like Marc Breault, the man who was then closest to my heart. He'd just married this girl, Elizabeth, and couldn't give her up. They left us."

In Marc Breault, David had his Judas—a favorite disciple who abandoned and betrayed him. Whenever he spoke of Breault, a veil of baffled sadness fell over his face.

David met Marc in early 1986 through Perry Jones, who'd struck up a conversation with him in a bookstore in Southern California. Again the common bond was music, and Marc joined the band, playing the keyboards. Born in Hawaii, he was a computer whiz and had a master's degree in religious studies from a Seventh-day Adventist college.

"He was bright as a penny, like a brother to me," David said. "I trusted him with my life."

Along with Steve Schneider, whom Marc had recruited, he was David's most loyal and articulate ally. But he broke away a year or so before I first met up with David. As an apostate, he became David's bitter and vindictive enemy. Hiding out in Australia, he hired a detective to investigate Mount Carmel and "expose" the community. Later, Marc played a diabolical role in provoking the government's assault on Mount Carmel.

———————

One of the appealing things about David was that when he wasn't giving a study period he became just one of the guys. He liked to hang out with other musicians when he was relaxing, and after a particularly intense Bible session he'd come down off the podium and invite a bunch of us to go into town, "kick back, swallow some suds, play some tunes." On these occasions David, Jaime, Mike Schroeder, and I piled into the Camaro and headed for town, to the Chelsea Street Pub, a popular West Waco eatery. While downing a few beers, we mingled with the crowd and chatted to the band playing in the din.

During our expeditions among the Wacoans, David was like a chameleon. He had many different modes, telling strangers what he sensed they needed to hear. His manner was easy, his twang broader, and people opened up to him. When he was around there was a quiet energy in the room. But it was clear that those who decided to hate David really loathed him. Within minutes of walking into a bar or after talking to him for a short while, some men and women became his immediate adversaries. When that happened, he'd simply walk away, deflecting confrontation. Or he'd buy the person a beer and say, "Well, let's just be best enemies, okay?"

Once or twice during these bar busts we took over the stage to bang out a couple of songs, me on the drums, David singing and plucking a borrowed guitar. We did hard rock, no religion, just the music I grew up with, like Peter Frampton and Ted Nugent. In a way that maybe only fellow musicians can truly understand, by performing together I recognized that David had an intuitive understanding of where I was at and what I yearned to be.

Despite his easy ways, I couldn't avoid the slow realization that there appeared to be a very dark side to David's "truth." It seemed that he expected to be destroyed, along with anyone who followed him. The possibility that the forces loose in the world would reject and kill him was always on David's mind; and if the world rejected his message, his death was inevitable and terrible. *For wherever the carcass is, there eagles will be gathered together,* he quoted. "I am the one whose body will be mutilated and left to rot in the open field." As he explained it, the opening of the Fifth Seal includes the prediction that the community will suffer a violent death. *I saw under the altar the souls of them that were slain for the word of God,* Revelation writes, portraying a terrible confrontation between the temporal powers and the Lamb, between "Babylon" and the "Peculiar People," like the Mount Carmel community. In the pivotal events of the Sixth Seal, Mount Carmel and society at large would be hit by terrifying natural disasters. "I knew then that we had to live through the 'little season' spoken of in Revelation Five, before being killed," David said. "It's a hard fate, but inevitable, and somehow magnificent."

His words scared me. I simultaneously absorbed them and buried them in my subconscious: This cataclysmic scenario was too tough to swallow whole. My old habit was to live day by day, chewing on morsels of experience and information as they came. Like many of the people at Mount Carmel, and maybe David himself, I kind of hoped the prophecies would be modified somehow, and his followers wouldn't have to suffer the total annihilation predicted in Scripture. But the words of Revelation 6:12, that on the opening of the Sixth Seal, *there was a great earthquake; and the sun became black as sackcloth of hair, and the moon became as blood,* echoed in my mind. In other words, the place was primed for martyrdom.

David represented himself as the intercessor between humanity and a wrathful deity. Sometimes he compared himself to Noah, warning of the flood to come and being scoffed at by everyone except his own family.

When David spoke like that my nape hairs prickled and my palms got clammy. Was I really ready to accept an inevitable, possibly violent death? Was what I was learning from David really worth such a risk? These questions hovered in the air, never really answered until the final period of the siege of Mount Carmel.

In David's view, every one of us was connected to his body, physically as well as spiritually. The community was, he said, one collective entity, and he could be in great pain, even get ulcers, because someone was doing something wrong, like giving way to lustful thoughts or sneaking a hamburger in defiance of the dietary rule that forbade eating meat—lapses I tended to indulge in. When Marc broke away, for instance, David had been stricken with a high fever, his body racked by sweat and chills. We were his family, his body, members of his heart, David said, and his vulnerability to our derelictions touched me deeply. "I'm suffering this pain because of the sins you've committed," he told us. "Don't fret, it's my role."

Though David was only ten years older than me, I respected his voice. Maybe I didn't immediately understand all the implications of his message, but there was something about him that seemed very genuine, very human. If I hadn't liked him so much as a person I most likely wouldn't have listened to him.

Following David wasn't the result of lengthy deliberation. To be sure, I'm not someone who thinks everything through logically in advance. I'm more instinctive, following through on things that seem intuitively right for me at any given time without too much critical examination. For instance, I never really stopped dead in my tracks and said to myself, "Holy shit, I'm living with the Messiah!" People in the community rarely spoke of David as the Messiah; when they did, he corrected them sharply.

"You people may claim I'm something special," he'd say. "But thank heaven you guys don't bow down and worship me. That's the last thing I want. I don't want you to worship the person but the teaching. I'm just a messenger of the truth. I'm like a Dixie cup that God will crumple up and throw away when he's done with it."

Sometimes David half-jokingly referred to himself as the "sinful" Messiah of the Psalms, a conquering figure "anointed with the oil of gladness," one who marries virgins and has children who become "princes in all the earth." Jesus, he said, was the saintly Messiah who had never, like himself, lived out the life of a fallible human being, warts and all.

All the same, it troubled me a whole lot that I'd be sacrificing my sex life if I committed myself to David's teachings. Sure, the sacrifice was for some higher purpose, something I might come to believe was more valuable to me, but it was a tough call. I thought long and hard about this, but in the end it came down to whether I trusted my instincts. I could not, like Steve or Wayne, come to accept David's way through a searching, intellectual self-scrutiny. Compared to them, I was sloppy-minded, but I did honor my intuitions. Then and now, they're all I have, when it comes right down to it. If I ever lost faith in my feelings, I'd be totally at sea.

David was a lot like me in this respect, I recognized. He'd found his way intuitively, fumbling through the dark of his unhappy childhood and adolescence, following his feelings without the benefit—or hindrance—of a good formal education or abstract mental discipline. The evidence that his native instincts had led him to such profundities was a great example to me.

In a way, perhaps, I suspended disbelief. Maybe it was the old habit of tolerance I learned growing up around my mom and her friends, where no one was ever condemned for being different or "deviant," whatever the mainstream might say. This applied particularly to sexual preferences. I'd been brought up in a seventies atmosphere of erotic liberation, everyone doing his or her own thing without moral judgment, so long as nobody laid a bad trip on anyone else and nobody got hurt.

As I listened to David, in the public studies and the private moments we had, I began to connect the more deep-rooted part of myself that David had begun to open up for me to the high I had as an artist. It struck me that there was a kind of kinship between spiritual excitement and the surge in my soul when I was really on a roll with the sticks. David was showing me how to make a pathway for my raw, instinctive energies—for what Jack Kerouac called the "crazy dumb-saint of the mind."

However, I still had a hell of a lot more questions than answers about his religion. I couldn't quite accept that David was the Lamb. And if he was, he was in for a very bad time, as he himself explained. He made a point of emphasizing that the messianic figure mentioned in Revelation would provoke some terrible reactions. "The entire world will hate him," David said, quoting the Bible, "and all his followers." It troubled me that David seemed to have elected or been elected to play out a terrible fate. When I was a kid, listening to Grandma Mim go on about Jesus, I'd think that if Christ ever did come back to earth he'd be crucified all over again. No one would ever believe his claim to be "anointed of God." It seemed to me that if a man actually chose this scary scenario—especially a down-home man like David—it must mean that he had a very interesting soul.

Either way, I thought, maybe I should get out of here right now, before I'm hooked. But my innate curiosity countered with, *Let's just hang around for a while and see how things work out.*

"I'm really glad your mother raised you the way she did, no religion, no preconceived ideas," David told me. "Your openness makes it easier for you to listen to what I'm saying without having to shove your way through a web of religious half-truths and hypocrisies."

I was flattered, but also wary. A little signal went off in my head, reminding me that I could be very gullible as well as open, so I'd better go slow with this man.

Being shrewd, David intuited my reservations. "Faith isn't so easy, Thibodeau," he murmured. "We're supposed to struggle to understand. Give yourself time. I'm not trying to con you into believing anything you find incredible. But if you begin to glimpse the outlines of a powerful plan developing here, maybe you'd like to stick around and find out what it's all about."

My sensible side said: *You've grown up questioning everything, and here's a guy giving you a bunch of weird stuff.* Was he subtly twisting

my mind, using his skill in adapting his style to different tempera-
ments? Were David's extraordinary stories turning my head, like a
missionary in Africa bamboozling a heathen with Bible anecdotes?

Reflexively, I wanted to surrender to my fundamental doubts.
But I had to ask myself if my old habit of disbelief had served me all
that well and if there was something in this man that could help me
root my life in a deeper ground than any I'd yet discovered in myself.

Certainly, during the last few years—maybe always—I'd been
skating on the surface of things, trying to find a way into my true
nature. My weeks at Mount Carmel had shown me that I was ac-
quainted with hardly more than a fraction of myself; that my sense
of the world and my own true character was that of a creature
barely clinging to reality. Would letting go, dropping off into space
under David's guidance, really be so stupid?

Actually, I had no problem with the concept of a spiritual force
guiding humanity, a powerful dynamic driving destiny. However,
the notion that David was imbued with that force, that he claimed
to be its direct instrument, was hard to swallow. His low-key, unbul-
lying style worked both for and against him. If he'd come on gang-
busters like the TV holy rollers, I'd have dismissed him instantly.
At the same time, he was so *ordinary*, so much one of the guys, it
was hard to see him as *holy*. Yet I felt he was utterly genuine.

David was outlining a destiny meant for a select group of people, and despite doubts and apprehensions I found his message
fascinating. *Would I be cheating myself if I didn't go along with it?* I wondered. Was I capable of the kind of commitment it required? And
did I really want to have my life wrenched from its previous mean-
dering path?

If it took me a while to grasp the intricacies of David's theology, I trusted my connection with the human being. I'd never met
anyone like David in my life. The people I'd come to respect at
Mount Carmel, like Steve Schneider, Wayne Martin, and Livingston Fagan, were convinced his inspiration was genuine, so who
was I to dismiss him offhand as a phony?

In Texas, like the song says, the stars are incredibly bright.
Looking up at them after hours of Bible study, I sensed eternity

and could easily imagine flying up there on David's energy. All the while, though, I could hear my mother's concerned voice whispering in my ear: "Davey, is this really you?" I knew that if I ever did decide to stick with Koresh, I'd never be able to explain my motives to her, and that made me sad.

David didn't push it. After my first two weeks or so at Mount Carmel, when the festival period was over and the other visitors had departed, he told me to return to Bangor and think about all this before I made a decision whether or not to come back.

"Speak to priests, rabbis, scholars, whoever," he urged. "Ask them what they think about what you've heard here. If you feel, after all, that Mount Carmel is your place, I'll be happy to have you back."

He paused, cocking his head at me, and his tone toughened. "But if you do decide to be here, your commitment must be total. The more you learn, the more you'll be responsible for that knowledge. There's no room for tourists at Mount Carmel."

Then he smiled. *With much wisdom increaseth much sorrow,* he said, quoting Solomon. "It may be already too late for you. Maybe you'll never see things the same way again, even if you don't come back."

The moment he said it, I knew it was true. I'd begun to view the world differently, and that both gladdened me and made me melancholy.

"Don't be put off when people you talk to think you've gone goofy with all this 'Seals' stuff," David said. "That's the way of the world, Thibodeau, and you'll have to make up your mind which side of the fence you want to live."

Apart from the theology David was offering, I sensed that what I required right then was a male counterpoint to the powerful feminine presences in my background: the kind of close, intimate father figure and teacher my own dad never was. I was strong on intuition and feeling but weak on self-discipline, a structure to shape my character. But I wasn't going to accept just any structure or discipline. It had to be a very special person, someone I would have to feel I could trust with my life.

Knowing myself, however, I wasn't sure I'd be capable of following the path that David offered me all the way through. When it came right down to it, could I actually walk the walk?

The last night before I was due to leave, I had a disturbing dream. I saw David sitting on a throne, hovering above ground, giving a study, just me and him. I resented his instruction, my mind fatigued by all the complex and challenging information I'd absorbed in the past few weeks. *Gimme a break*, I thought, as I felt the earth roll in on its constant rotation and David's image began to vanish with it toward the horizon. I rejoiced that I was getting my wish, until I heard his voice grow louder as the earth came full circle.

When I awoke, I felt the dream was telling me that, like it or not, I was already caught up in the character of Mount Carmel. It gave me a strange feeling—part elation, part apprehension— and I nervously began to mumble the words to the Eagles song "Hotel California": *You can check out any time you like, but you can never leave. . . .*

5

SLIPPING THROUGH THE FENCE

After the intensities of the past few weeks, it was a relief to get on the bus in Waco and just drive away. Mount Carmel and David had disrupted my old continuity, and I felt like a displaced person, especially in that rough area of Texas.

My generally positive feelings about the Mount Carmel community were jolted by something Catherine Matteson said to me as I was leaving. "Keep the faith," she called out, and somehow this friendly phrase, with its ring of old-time religion, jarred me.

On the bus, heading through Texas and Louisiana, listening to the radio, I was happy, thinking about seeing my family and old friends in Bangor. The heaviness of Mount Carmel was set aside by my innate tendency to take things as they come, to delight in things both serious and silly.

Along the way, a long-haired freak around my age got on the bus and sat down beside me. We immediately started talking rock and roll. In a burst of enthusiasm, I began to tell him about Mount Carmel. Suddenly, it all poured out of me in a jumbled rush: the proverbs, the Seals, the feminine Holy Spirit, the Mother, King

Solomon. "'The angels carve out our paths every day,'" I quoted, excited by memories of the fascination I'd felt listening to David.

As I ran on, I saw that my companion was getting angry.

"I'm a Christian, and I don't like what you're saying about the Holy Spirit, especially, 'She was daily his delight,'" as he pointed to Proverbs 8 in the book we had open. "You don't like what I'm saying, or you don't like what we just read for ourselves out of the book?" I questioned him. He burst out: "You don't need to read that book. Faith is simple, just believe in Jesus Christ." I was amazed at this Christian hypocrisy. "You believe in Christ," I started to argue, "but you don't need to know His word you claim you believe?"

But he just turned his back on me, then went to the toilet at the back of the bus to cool out with a joint, leaving me upset and shaken. David had warned me that people might react to me this way if I tried to tell them about "the message," but this was the first time I'd actually experienced such a thing. It was a caution, I reflected, warning me to say as little as possible about Mount Carmel when I got back to Bangor.

Right then, I decided not to tell my mother or my family anything essential about my experience in Texas. I knew that whenever I went home I automatically reverted, in my own and my family's eyes, to the clown with nothing going for him but drums and dreams. Any talk of my recent discovery of a desire to be "spiritual" would be taken as a confirmation that I was an unredeemable fantasist.

My mother was my main hurdle. She knew me so well, read every nuance of my moods, shared the same nerves and hectic energies. When she hugged me and looked deep into my eyes, her anxious voice asking, "What's *up*, Davey?" I countered with a casual, "Hey, Mom, I just met this cool guy who has a band in Texas. Don't worry about it."

But, of course, she did. As the days went by, and I got back into my old Bangor ways, my mother kept probing. "Is Mount Carmel a commune?" she asked. "Like that place in New Mexico I lived in for a while, a few years back? I know that life," she said, rushing on to delay a possibly dangerous answer. "Fun for a month or so, but not for restless characters like us, eh?"

I answered vaguely, avoiding any talk of religion to deflect her reaction against "Bible stuff." She was a feminist, opposed to any version of what she might consider a patriarchal authority. Mount Carmel, under David, had a structure that would surely have raised her hackles.

Finally, though, she wore me down, and I had to tell her about David and why I'd grown to respect and admire him.

I tried to explain that I was drawn to David's disciplined yet affectionate authority. "He's teaching me things I need to know," I said, aware that I was fumbling. "He's an awesome guy, but not a bully." Balenda was skeptical, so I just kept repeating my stubborn, he's-an-awesome-guy mantra, hoping to fudge the awkwardness between us.

"I know you've been having a tough time in Hollywood," my mother ran on. "It's hard dealing with the streets, the brutal music business." Then, in an outburst that was typical of my mother's tendency to let her tongue run away with her, she added, "You've always had one foot in reality, the other in pie-in-the-sky!"

"Get off my back, Balenda," I growled.

She flinched, and I felt like shit, but I couldn't bear her close scrutiny. Not then, when my own feelings about David were still so new, so unformed, essentially inexplicable.

My father's questions were, typically, more guarded and more oblique. Knowing his vehement antireligious views, I just told him I was playing in David's band. "Mount Carmel's a fun place to be, Dad," I said, leaving it at that. I sensed that he preferred not to know too much about something that might be "messy," something that might upset the equilibrium of his life in nearby Isleboro with his new wife and his safe teaching job. About five years earlier he had finally gone on the wagon, and he still struggled to maintain his fragile balance. Since he and my mother didn't communicate much, I knew they'd never put their heads together about me.

In quiet moments I thought over what I'd learned at Mount Carmel. Before I left, David remarked that I had more information
than I realized about his teachings, that I'd taken a deep plunge
into Scripture. "You're already beginning to view the Scriptures as
a key to history and the future, as words and wisdom from God,"
David said. However, in Bangor there was no one, apart from my
Uncle Bob, who'd gone through a born-again phase in his past, to
comfortably talk with about all this. But remembering the reaction
of the freak on the bus, I wondered if that very fact might prejudice
even my Uncle Bob.

A part of me said I should walk away from the biblical thing, just
go back to being a drummer, a regular rocker. But a powerful attraction drew me, rooted in an instinctive quest for self-knowledge
and a recognition that I needed some discipline in my life. Maybe,
as my mother implied, I was simply looking for a structure; but I
wasn't going to accept just any structure. It had to be provided by
a very special person, like David, a man I was beginning to feel I
could trust with my life. Still, I feared I might disappoint both of
us. Perhaps he and I might discover that my spirit had no unre-
vealed depths; that maybe I was as shallow and immature as my
family and friends seemed to think.

Oddly enough, I had a premonition that David wasn't going
to be around too long, that the dark fate described for the Lamb
in Revelation would soon catch up with him. He wasn't harming
anyone that I could see, but the biblical predictions were scary. If I
turned my back on him I might miss out on something extraordinary and I'd be forever haunted by my refusal to pursue a rare and
exceptional path that might give me a key to my deeper nature.

And what were my real alternatives? To fall back into that aim-
less, competitive Hollywood rock scene, struggling against the inertia of my old musician pals who couldn't focus on making it in that
tough business? Or maybe stay in Bangor, get some joe job, settle
into the rut my lack of education fitted me for? At the very least,
Messiah Productions offered me a place in a really professional outfit backed by David's talent and Steve's management. And because

the Messiah Productions band was still based in Los Angeles, I wouldn't immediately have to commit to living in Mount Carmel.

In those floating Maine days, I found myself slipping through a hole in the rickety fence dividing my old, easy disbelief from a new and difficult faith. My instincts urged me on, but I still had to shed my protective sheath of skepticism. During the transition I felt naked and vulnerable, and my dreams were filled with visions of hungry wolves and circling birds of prey. All the same, I had a surge of certainty, a quiet excitement. The word "apocalypse," David had told me, was Greek for "revelation," literally "uncovering," and I felt I was on the edge of my own private discovery.

David called me one night from Los Angeles. "Hey, Thibodeau, how're you doing?" he asked amiably, his twangy tone capturing my ear. "Are you going forward with us?"

"I'm with you," I said at once, and my heart sank. In that instant I knew that life would never be the same for me, that I was giving up my old, light ways for a heavy new reality. My spirit was lumbered with a guilty reluctance I couldn't shake off. I *wanted* to pass the point of no return, drawn by a sense of mystery I felt compelled to explore, yet the lazy part of me resented the tug implicit in David's cheery, "Are you going forward with us?"

"I'll be on a plane to L.A. next week," I promised, and he rang off happy—happier than I was, in truth. I knew what I had to do, but I wanted to have just one more party, sleep with a girl one last time, before committing myself to the existence of a monk.

———

A few hours after I got off the plane in Los Angeles, David gave a study session in the house he rented in Hollywood just off Melrose Avenue. We sat in a circle on the floor while David talked, and as he was speaking I fell asleep. His voice droned on in my dreams, and suddenly I was surrounded by all the women of my past, like zombies from the grave, a night of the living not-yet-quite-dead. They backed me into a corner, threatening, and I had to talk fast, putting on the old charm to save my newfound chastity.

Suddenly, one girl I'd once played around with was kissing me passionately. I bent her over and began to make love to her. All this was so graphic and so absolutely real I had a hot, rushing wet dream, right there in the middle of the study.

I woke up with a start and, horribly embarrassed, hurried off to the upstairs bathroom to wash up. In that single, shameful moment, staring into the mirror, I knew I had to learn to discipline my feelings, to deny or delay gratification, not remain the passive victim of my sensuality. This aspiration had nothing to do with religion, though the spiritual path could be the way I might have to go to achieve self-control. Rather, it was a deep urge to be better than I was. I needed David's tough drill for both my body and my soul.

Once I came to that conclusion, everything seemed clear. I left the bathroom and rejoined the circle downstairs. David gave me that sappy grin of his, continuing his flow of talk, linking me back to the community. In the guilty act of dreaming, I'd slipped farther through that hole in the fence.

For the next few months David remained in Los Angeles to deal with some business affairs, and a group of us camped out in the Melrose Avenue house.

I tried to explain to my Hollywood friends why I'd committed myself to David Koresh as a musician and a Bible student. In their laconic way, Ryan and Scott were upset with me. Their "Father Dave" mockeries sharpened, but I knew that they were concerned for me. *Why? Why? Why?* they asked over and over as we partied one last time. "I never figured you for a Bible junkie," Ryan said. "What's the angle?"

I had no clear answer. I knew I would never be able to explain myself in the language of faith, a tongue I was still fumbling with. And as we would learn during the siege of Mount Carmel, one man's spiritual discourse is another man's Bible babble.

"I feel it's right for me," I said lamely.

I could see from Ryan's dubious scowl that he wasn't convinced, but we lifted a few more beers and passed on to more pleasant things.

Along with Steve Schneider, Paul Fatta, Jaime, Greg Summers, and Pablo Cohen, an Argentine-Israeli bass player recently arrived from Tel Aviv, the group living in the Melrose house included a few women, like Kathy Andrade and Nicole Gent, a nineteen-year-old Australian whose brother, Peter, I'd met at Mount Carmel. Back home, Peter had dabbled in drugs, booze, and gangs, but he'd reformed in Mount Carmel and had, like his sister, stayed in the community even though his parents had turned against David and left after the 1989 New Light revelation.

Nicole, a beautiful young woman with strawberry-red hair and gentle eyes, had a baby son named Dayland, fathered by David. He'd taken her as his "sacred wife" on a visit to Australia during 1988, with the consent of her parents, who were at that time David's disciples. "David wants me to be his teddy bear for the night," she'd told her father and mother. "I want to have a baby for God." Her son was born a year or so later. To me, it was obvious that she adored David.

"Nicole's so lovely, I wanted to just run off with her and forget everything else, Mount Carmel, the message, everything," David confided to us in a study session. In the near distance was the hum of people, traffic, and loud music from Melrose, a street lined with trendy boutiques for the young, hip crowd. As he described his momentary yearning for a "normal" life, maybe somewhere in the Australian Outback, his eyes filled with tears and his face seemed about to melt. I had a glimpse, then, of the penalties David suffered in being this apostle of "truth." It was clear he had no choice but to follow the inner voice that drove him, whatever the cost to his happiness as a man.

At that moment he seemed very open, and I had an impulse to question him more thoroughly about his relationships with the women in the community. At Mount Carmel I'd learned that there was a group of ten or so women and their children known as the "House of David." They were the nucleus of the group that would inherit the future. "It's like winning in the bedroom," David joked when I asked him about his children. "If you don't win in the bedroom, son, you're not going to win on the battlefield."

Despite my doubts about this notion, I didn't probe farther. Actually, I was more concerned with my own struggles to accept not being close to a woman, physically and emotionally. For those first few months, desire prickled me continually, an itch I longed to scratch—but managed not to.

Most evenings we hung out in Hollywood, scoping out the clubs on Sunset Strip. For me, it was like living in a college dormitory, sleeping casually on a couch or on the floor, getting an education, playing drums, all expenses paid. I knew this was a kind of interval between my old life and my new life, that Mount Carmel and Texas loomed in the future, but at the moment it was pleasant enough.

I was impatient to perform in public, though, needing the energy rush that only a live audience can give you. But David said the band wasn't ready. He was forever tinkering with the meters and the melodies, aiming for a perfect marriage of music and message, and sometimes I was irritated with him, suspecting he was on a head trip that might squeeze out the spontaneity essential to my way of playing.

The music was vital to me; it provided a continuity between my old life and my new one. If, back then, David had said that giving up the drums as well as sex was a condition of joining his community, I would definitely have turned him down. Not having sex was one thing, not drumming quite another.

In quiet moments I strolled around the neighborhood, thinking as I went. I told myself I still had a lot of friends outside the community; so if I decided, in the end, that David's message was way too much for me or if he turned out to be someone other than I thought he was, I could just travel a few blocks to Hollywood Boulevard and resume my previous existence.

"I'm not burning all my bridges," I mused, excusing my lingering reluctance with the argument that, even if you totally believe in something, there's always an element of doubt. "Keep a way out, Davey," my mother had said as I kissed her goodbye in Bangor. "Don't put all your eggs in one basket." I was irritated with her caution then, but the thought that I could walk away any time eased my concern that I might be in the grip of an inexorable process.

Before I first bumped into David that fateful evening at the Guitar Center, I wasn't a conscious seeker. But in listening to David, and by visiting Mount Carmel, I'd begun to realize that a whole other dimension of being existed within me—a deeper level of my own soul. Though many of my friends told me I'd flipped out, I knew I was still the same old Dave Thibodeau, but more so. I felt I was growing, maybe in a way my friends and family hadn't expected, yet true to myself all the same. However, I still had a hard time accepting David's claim that he was the Lamb from Revelation. And some of David's prejudices bothered me. For example, his classification of gays as "sinful" jarred me when I first heard it. When I was a child my mother had many gay friends, and his implication that homosexuality was an aberration provoked a sharp objection. David tried to counter with a story about his father-in-law, Perry Jones. Though Perry had been married his whole life and had fathered children, he'd long been troubled by "tendencies," as he called them, that ran counter to his deep religious beliefs. As a young man, Perry had made the decision to suppress his homosexuality. He was, David said, an example of a man who resisted his tendencies because of his belief in Scripture; his devotion was charged by a denial of his natural inclinations, amounting to his own personal kind of "withering experience."

"But I notice you hold back certain studies from some of the people here who are gay, who can't or won't deny themselves," I accused. "Isn't that pure prejudice?"

"I don't condemn people for what there are," David replied. "I have friends who are prostitutes, for example. Some of them are the way they are because they've been abused or brutalized. The bottom line is, mankind is sick. Promiscuity, perversion, and prostitution are forms of that sickness."

I didn't push it any farther. But David's views on homosexuality as a perversion rather than just another way of being human did give me pause. It revealed that, under the skin, he was still the child of his Texas redneck upbringing, still the old Mr. Retardo who'd suffered so much humiliation at the hands of others. I hoped he and my mom never got into an argument over this issue, or the sparks would really fly.

During those early months, the strongest challenge to my growing commitment to David came from my old friend, John. We'd been roommates while I was at the Institute, two struggling musicians, always broke, forever hopeful. He was a serious guy, very intelligent, a true searcher who'd rejected the Christianity of his upbringing. "I've got a lot of questions for God," he told me. "Hard questions."

Back in the summer of 1990, when Steve came around to my Hollywood apartment to give his first studies to my friends, I'd invited John to join us, thinking maybe he might find something of value in the teaching. After visiting Pomona a couple of times, I told John about Messiah Productions. "Forget it," he told me. "Religious bands never go anywhere." I tried to say that David's band was different, but John wasn't convinced.

While I was in Mount Carmel that autumn I phoned John, excited by a study David had given about the Temple and its priests. David had described the breastplate the high priest once wore, studded with green and red jewels. When he was asked a question, the jewels lit up, red for no, green for yes.

When I finally ran out of steam, I heard an echoing silence in the receiver pressed to my ear.

"Dave, are you okay?" John said finally.

I laughed. "You think I'm being brainwashed, eh? My mind turning to mush?"

"Is it?" he asked pointedly.

When I returned to Los Angeles, John grilled me about David. "Does he believe he's the Messiah? What's this 'truth' he claims to reveal? If we're living in the 'Final Days' or 'End Time,' why mess about with music?" He asked to meet David in person, for what he mockingly called an "audience."

For reasons he wouldn't reveal, David resisted meeting John, despite my urging. "John really wants to meet you," I said several times. Even Steve and Paul were puzzled by David's reluctance; usually, he wanted to talk to anyone who might like to join the community, and I'd told him John was a very serious guy.

"I suspect that John is crippled in his spirit as well as in his body," he said finally. "But I'll talk to him."

We arranged a meeting at the Denny's on Sunset. David, Steve, and I tooled up to the restaurant, riding a pair of David's beloved Harley-Davidson motorbikes. All three of us proudly sported Messiah Productions T-shirts, inscribed "David Koresh/God Rocks." On the bike I clung to David's back, the wind whipping my hair, my arms locked around his middle. As David skillfully bent the bike into a curve, I had the sensation that we were about to fly off the surface of Earth.

John was late, and I went to his nearby apartment to fetch him. While I was waiting for him to get his jacket I sneaked a chocolate bar I found on his table. "Don't tell David," I begged John when he caught me. "Chocolate is banned; it's an aphrodisiac, David says." John gave me a funny look.

"I'm glad to see you're still a sinner," he laughed, watching me wipe brown smudges from my chin.

David began by deliberately challenging John. He liked to open people up with outrageous questions. "Would you die for the truth, if you encountered it?"

John hesitated a moment, suspecting a trick question.

"Yeah, I guess so," he murmured finally.

David came back at him fast. "Would you kill for it?"

"What?"

"Would you kill for the truth?"

"No way. Life is sacred."

David turned to me, smiling. "Looks like you brought me another weak Christian," he said sardonically. "If you can't kill for the truth you can't die for it."

"But what about 'Thou shalt not kill'?" John protested.

"And what about the passage in Matthew that has Christ saying, *Think not that I am come to send peace on earth: I come not to send peace but a sword?*"

They tossed biblical quotations back and forth, until David called it quits and settled down to explain the Seals. John listened intently, and when we said goodbye I wondered if John had changed his mind about David. I talked with John a couple of days later when we met at Denny's on Sunset Blvd. and I got my answer.

"I think David might be the real deal, that he has the truth, but I'm not going to go with it. I just want to do my thing. I have a lot of questions for God. If God can't answer my questions in the judgement then I'll just flip him off and jump in the lake of fire." I was stunned.

"This whole experience was for you," David said, when I told him about John's response. "To help you understand that not everyone is ready to listen to something you consider vital, even those you love. I had that experience with Marc Breault, and it still hurts. God showed me something about John's character. I didn't want to show John this truth because I was shown that he wouldn't accept it, that his spirit was at odds with what John considers to be God. This experience was for you, not for John."

John's rejection of David hurt me a lot, but it didn't shake my feelings. John chose his way, and I felt I'd chosen mine.

6

THE WITHERING
EXPERIENCE

In the spring of 1991 we all returned to Mount Carmel for Passover. Along with the Day of Atonement, Passover was one of two major festivals celebrated by the community, a time when all of those attracted to David Koresh's teachings gathered in Waco to hold a series of intense scriptural studies. There was no traditional Passover service, however. David was against all such rituals. "If we have the truth, why do we need a performance?" he said.

I went back to Texas with mixed feelings. Although I was eager to learn more from David and knew I must fully commit myself to the "withering experience"—the hard routine of Mount Carmel and its discipline—I was reluctant to leave Los Angeles and sever my last connection to my old life. In Hollywood, I'd been able to maintain the illusion that my options were still open, that I could, if I chose, just walk away from David and all he offered and demanded. It was an illusion, I knew, because in my heart I'd accepted his message; but I preferred to leave the full consequences of that acceptance up in the air.

My heart sank as the Silver Eagle approached Mount Carmel. The place was as stark and makeshift as I'd remembered it, a squatter's camp stuck out in the middle of the flattest landscape I'd ever seen. In Maine and in Los Angeles, there were the ever-present hills and mountains, a rise and fall in the horizon to enliven the eye. Here there was nothing but straightness, like a flatline on a heart monitor signifying that the patient has died.

During the five months or so since my first visit, most of the remaining clapboard cottages had been stripped of their timber for reuse in the Anthill. The new building's skeleton had expanded, growing two-story wings out from the core chapel and cafeteria. When fully finished, these wings would be the dormitories where all of us would live.

I was assigned a room in the part that was completed, just a bare cell with uninsulated, unplastered sheetrock walls, no door, and a rough plywood floor. Four wooden bunk beds crowded the space, and we had to keep our gear in suitcases tucked under the bunks. I shared the room with Peter Gent and Peter Hipsman, a guy my age from Upstate New York, and a Passover visitor from London whose name I never got. After Passover, I moved to another, similar room shared with Jaime and Paul Fatta.

The living conditions were even more primitive than I recalled. Only the cafeteria kitchen had running water. For a bathroom, we had a shower rigged beneath a tree with a screen wrapped around it. For toilets, the men used an outhouse connected to the old septic tank, whereas the women and children were allowed chamber pots in their rooms. In late March it was still cold at night, and we shivered around a few electric space heaters plugged into outlets or overhead ceramic light fixtures. "Think of it as camping indoors," Steve told me cheerfully when I complained. "That way it may seem like fun."

At times it was fun, especially during nights when we lit the camping lantern and chewed the fat about the good old days before Mount Carmel. Greg amused us with stories about his job at Westlake Video on the outskirts of Los Angeles. One of his clients was pop star Michael Jackson. "A sweet guy, very pretty," Greg said. On occasion, Steve dropped by to talk about David, giving us the more intimate view of the man that he was privileged to know.

If we were lucky, David himself would visit us; sometimes he invited us to join a select group for dinner in town. The trick, it seemed, was to try to be around David as much as possible, hoping he might launch into an impromptu study. I discovered that he often sat in the kitchen late at night eating a bowl of soup, and I started hanging around there when most people were asleep, hoping he'd come in.

With few of us around, these late-night talks were intimate and intense. Our group energy was more focused, and that seemed to pull deep material out of David. I remember the night he told us that, in the midst of a vision, he'd levitated a few feet off the bed. "Like in *The Exorcist*," he said. Sometimes he seemed almost speechless, dazed by his inner force, and his face had a haunted look that twisted my heart. "God gave me some light," he'd murmur, and I imagined it had taken several days for him to integrate such an experience and pass it on to us.

During Passover week, when Mount Carmel filled with visitors, I lost even the minimal comforts of my shared cubicle and had to camp out in the chapel with nothing but a thin sleeping bag between me and the hard floor. I shivered all night, dreaming of my happy Hollywood days, cursing the impulse that had led me here. It was even too cold and uncomfortable to think about sex—and maybe that was the point. The women in the community were too busy with mothering to be flirtatious, and several were carrying David's babies, including Michele. Her twins, Chica and Little One, were born during the summer.

A special excitement seized Mount Carmel during the festival period. After each study, people discussed the teaching David had given them with a kind of eagerness, especially those who were visiting. It was as if they had to top off their tank of spirituality before returning to their ordinary lives.

However, not everyone was happy. Some visitors had family members who were there for the studies but who thought the whole thing was totally crazy. In some cases, like the Henry clan from

England, dedication to David's message ended up dividing families. Some people sincerely wanted to come and live at Mount Carmel but felt they wouldn't be able to hack it, whereas others went away cursing us as a bunch of charlatans. But no one I talked to was untouched by the experience.

After the visitors departed, the community reverted to its settled routine. While the others went to communion and then to work on construction, I was allowed to rise at nine or ten o'clock, have breakfast, then practice drumming all day until the ranch bell rang for supper. David wanted me to concentrate on the music, and he seemed to recognize that I was used to going to bed late and needed a good eight or nine hours' rest or else I'd be yawning all day. My sleep rhythm was dictated by David; when he went to bed, so did I.

My days were punctuated by the ringing of the food bell as well as by the jam sessions we had after supper, before the evening Bible study. After dinner we'd play for an hour or so on the chapel stage while men, women, and children assembled for the evening Scripture sessions, which sometimes lasted into the early hours of the following morning.

Life at Mount Carmel revolved around meals and study periods. However, the meals were basic. Breakfast was oatmeal, bread, bananas, sometimes eggs, and millet. I hated millet! Lunch was usually a simple salad, maybe some soup and beans; but when Julie Martinez and her mother, Ofelia Santoyo, were preparing lunch, they treated us to delicious burritos, maybe roast chicken or grilled fish. Supper, served around six o'clock, was nothing but popcorn and a banana or two, with some leftovers from lunch. A lot of the food we ate was scavenged cheap from restaurants and supermarkets by Perry Jones: day-old pizzas and groceries that had passed their sell-by dates. The women did the cooking while the men worked on the building, a patriarchal division of labor that would have horrified my mom.

On Friday nights, to welcome the Sabbath, the women dressed up a little, wore their best sweaters with maybe a bow in their hair and pretty earrings. No work was done on Saturday, and we were left to study on our own. That evening we got to watch a movie on a screen in the chapel, sometimes a war movie such as *Apocalypse Now* or a fascinating film like *Lawnmower Man*. During lighter moments, we had movies that appealed to the kids, like *Ernest Goes to Jail*, and we all gorged on usually desired treats such as ice cream and hamburgers.

Everyone was responsible for doing his own laundry; we used buckets and hung the clothes on lines to dry. Accustomed to my convenient neighborhood laundromat, I found cleaning clothes a tedious, time-wasting task. Before Mount Carmel, I'd thought my wardrobe was basic: just a few pairs of jeans, some T-shirts, and sweaters along with underwear and socks; but when it came to having to hand wash every item, I found I had far too many clothes, and so I soon cut my wardrobe in half. I also did without my daily shower. I was a bit ashamed of this, since everyone around me always seemed clean and neat, the women's long hair brushed and shiny, the men scrubbed after their day's labor.

No one chose to live at Mount Carmel for its luxurious lifestyle. People were there for a purpose, and the simplicity of the living conditions emphasized that, much as it did in the early Israeli kibbutzim I'd read about. Like on a kibbutz, the community not only endured discomforts but also took pride in doing so, gratified by the withering away of the endless excrescences of a materialistic lifestyle.

At first, I found the deprivation and rigors hard to stomach. But Mount Carmel's challenge was bracing, and gradually I began to enjoy it. Extreme by temperament, I tend to respond to anything that's thrown at me with total revulsion or attraction. Since the hard life at Mount Carmel was part of the deal I'd accepted, my only choice was to embrace it wholeheartedly. After some early moments of revulsion, I began to actually enjoy scrubbing dirty laundry.

Although I was at first allowed to dress as I wished, I finally had to conform to the dress code. For example, my shorts left my knees bare, and Steve told me to make them longer, so as not to distract the women. I must admit I hadn't realized my knees were so sexy.

One thing I did resist was cutting my long hair. (At one point toward the end David and all the other men got trimmed, but I stubbornly refused, even though short hair was cooler in that heat, and David let me off.) It was my lone refusal to be withered.

"God is like a rock," David said. "Those that fall upon Him are going to be broken. Those who avoid the rock will have it fall on them." David's message rode a rough roller coaster. Having just hopped aboard and strapped in, I had to go along for the ride.

————·——

When David felt I'd made my basic adjustment to life at Mount Carmel, he shifted me to the construction crew. His general message was, "Time to get down and dirty, Thibodeau. We may be living on an anthill, but that doesn't mean we can't spruce it up a little, tear all those ugly houses down, build a pool maybe, and a sandbox for the kids. Don't you want to be part of that?" Frankly, I felt I could take it or leave it; but when David made a suggestion, people generally went along. His command style was casual, but few questioned it, and it helped that he got down and dirty with the rest of us.

On a darker level, David said during several study sessions that he could sense the "waters rising around us." The new, more compact, perhaps more defensible building was meant to house all those who might decide to join us at Mount Carmel for the coming confrontation with adverse forces. We had to create a solidarity against the dangers David felt were mounting in Babylon.

At the time, our perception of these dangers was vague. Before the ATF and FBI focused their devastating attentions on Mount Carmel, there was no specific antagonism against the federal government as such in the community. Our wariness of this Babylon boiled down to a feeling that we were surrounded by a society that largely lacked a spiritual dimension and might easily turn on us because we held values different from the mainstream. In practice, however, David always tried to cooperate with state and local authorities, appreciating that Mount Carmel had enjoyed a mostly peaceful coexistence with its Waco neighbors for more than a half-century.

Working outdoors was no fun. With spring came the monsoons—warm, moist air moving up from the Gulf of Mexico—bringing thunderstorms and steady rains, sometimes five or six inches in twenty-four hours, turning dust to mud. Whether it was raining or not, I felt I was toiling in a sauna, passing the days swimming in sweat with fire ants feasting on my calves.

My job was to help demolish the few remaining cottages, stripping them to the foundations. I had the task of pulling rusty nails out of the framing and clapboard—a backbreaking, unglamorous, repetitious chore. I'd never in my life handled any tools, not even a hammer, and my palms broke out in blisters. The only construction job less skilled than mine, the gathering and piling of recovered lumber, was assigned to women and children.

It was hot, hard labor, but after a while I perceived its deeper purpose. Working together molded and confirmed a group identity, a sense of communal achievement. We came from many different places, had many different pasts, belonged to a variety of races and nationalities; but under the boiling summer sun, when shade temperatures often reached the century mark, the heat beating our backs like hammers until I felt like a nail myself, we were brothers sharing sweat, building our own Jerusalem in a desolate place. And David was there alongside us, skilled in construction, sharing our hardships. "Everyone has to get stuck in," he said, when people suggested he should save his often frail strength for teaching rather than toiling.

David loved working with his hands. Besides being a fine carpenter, he was an expert auto mechanic. He also maintained our musical equipment, keeping the power amplifiers and mixing boards in prime condition. He had a very American feel for machinery and gadgets, and he loved to drive the hired tractor we used to haul materials around the site. At times, irritated by our incompetence, David would complete a task by himself, busily sawing and nailing until the work was done to his satisfaction. For a man with such a spiritual dimension, he was very much at home in the physical world.

"We don't need no extravagant church to worship God," he said, urging us on. "All we need is a roof over our heads to keep the elements out, and walls to keep the world at bay."

The construction of the new building was supervised by Rick Bennett, an English architect who'd recently joined the community. He sketched out the overall shape of the place and directed the work, but I doubt if any of it was to code. The general attitude was that this is our property and that we could do whatever we wanted—a sentiment that likely sprang from a combination of Texas individuality and a presumption that our divine mandate superseded any temporal authority.

Perhaps Rick was the only person with a clear concept of what the building would look like when completed. As he described it, the exterior had low-pitched, tar-paper roofs and a plywood exterior painted beige with white trim around the windows. The interiors, like the room I occupied, were finished in raw sheetrock. The double front door, facing southwest, had a core of plastic foam covered in sheet metal, painted white and stamped to look like wood.

The front door was on an axis with the aisle of the chapel. Flanking the entry was a telephone room and Wayne Martin's law office. To the left of the entry was a stairway linking the dormitory's first- and second-floor quarters, the lower level for men, the upper for women and children. Above the original concrete vault, now used as a walk-in cooler adjacent to the kitchen and cafeteria, was a three-story residential tower for some of the older women who had no children, with a room for David under the roof. David had another room over the chapel, opposite a second-floor room that was later used for storing the firearms Paul Fatta took to sell at gun shows.

A walkway running over the chapel connected the second-floor dormitory with the gymnasium at the rear, the last section of the building to be completed. Beside it was the pool we built with a rented backhoe. Between the tornado shelter, still under construction when the ATF attacked, and the water tower were pens for chickens and a well house. A cement block building two hundred yards east of the main structure housed our motorbikes.

A trapdoor in the floor at the west end of the men's living quarters led to a short underground passage intended to connect to an old school bus that we planned to bury as a temporary tornado shelter. I'd seen tornadoes only on TV or at the movies; David, however, had experienced several while growing up. He'd learned, too, that a tornado had ripped through the town of Waco in May 1953, killing 114 people, and that was more than enough reason for him to think about shelter.

Water-supply and sewage connections remained problems that were never resolved before the siege. There were a couple of small ponds on the property, filled with fish, but their water wasn't fit to drink. Our main water storage was three white vinyl tanks situated outside the backdoor of the cafeteria. As late as autumn 1992 we were still trying to get the well pump to function again. To replace the old septic system, we bought a big septic tank and installed the inside toilets, but we didn't have a chance to dig the sewers and link them up before the ATF onslaught.

As the months went by I slowly got to find out more about the erotic tensions within the community. At first, busy with my own struggles to get adjusted to Mount Carmel, I hadn't probed much on this score. Trying to live a celibate life was hard enough for me without bothering about other people's sexual scenarios.

At the time, all I knew for sure was that David was the only male who was allowed a sex life and that he had a number of "wives," some of whom were legally married to other men. I didn't know the details of how the couples felt about this bizarre arrangement or how hard it had been for them to accept it. At times I suspected David might just have conned everyone into allowing him an exclusive harem, so to speak. Still, I knew there was more to it than that.

By the summer of 1991, I hadn't had sex for six or seven months, not since my last visit to Bangor. The first two months were really hard; a powerful part of me definitely didn't want to accept this prohibition. Sometimes I wondered if I was capable of staying celibate; but I was increasingly aware of a spirit within me, trapped in my flesh, yearning to be free. When I looked in the mirror I could see a fresh clarity in my eyes, a kind of glowing sixth sense. But the transition to chastity wasn't smooth. Sometimes I felt as if I were pulling a knotted rope out of my gut, knot by knot, gagging all the way.

Occasionally, I discussed sex with the other guys, especially Jaime and Greg Summers. They claimed that being celibate was "restful," that they'd had a hard time getting on with women. Greg said he'd been popular in high school, had a lot of girls, but all the same he was glad to be "out of the game." It seemed that reconciling myself to being a monk was harder for me than for them. They all claimed that they had come across something greater than sex, a kind of spiritual orgasm. They no longer even masturbated, they confessed. "It's not good to spill your seed," Jaime said solemnly.

To avoid temptation, the men were generally discouraged from getting close to any of the women. I was attracted to Lisa Farris, a rocker from Hollywood, and Julie Martinez, who was still fighting a bad drug habit. These two women were hip and streetwise and had shared some of the same L.A. experiences as I, but we all took care not to get sexually entangled.

My curiosity about the larger sexual picture was aroused by a surprising outburst from Steve Schneider. Late one night he and I were alone in the kitchen foraging for a snack. I was a night bird by nature and he was an insomniac, so we often ran into each other while the others slumbered. All I said to Steve was a casual, "How's Judy?" asking after his wife, because I hadn't seen her around in a while.

"You don't even know how hard it's been!" he exclaimed, tears springing to his eyes. "I love her, and giving her up—" He broke off and looked away, overcome with shame and suppressed anger. "We were lovers for close on twenty years, married for ten, and never made a baby. . . . Now, suddenly, she's having *his* child!"

"David's?"

"That's why Marc Breault split," Steve ran on. "He chose to marry Elizabeth rather than stick around." He grimaced awkwardly. "Maybe he was right."

"Do you really mean that?" I asked.

Steve shrugged. He took a loaf of bread, a jar of peanut butter, and a carton of milk out of the refrigerator, and we sat down at the table to make sandwiches.

"Why *do* you accept it?" I asked, deliberately disingenuous. "I mean, going without sex is bad enough, but having to actually give up your wife. . . ." At the time, Judy was a very attractive woman in her late thirties, a trim strawberry blonde.

"Well, Thibodeau, if your wife had a chance to marry the Lamb, would you want to hold her back?"

From his tone I couldn't tell whether he was being sarcastic or serious, or maybe both together. Before I could query him further, he put on his solemn voice, the one he used when giving scriptural studies.

"There's an upper-room experience and a lower-room experience," Steve said. "The students here fall into either category, and you're still in the lower one, the experience that can't yet comprehend the deeper message."

"Try me," I challenged.

"In 1989, when David received his New Light revelation, it divided those who were willing to go all the way with him from the others. We in the upper room understood that David's truth was progressive, always evolving, revealing more and more of itself. We understood from the New Light that the rest of us should no longer have sex or procreate because the message, and our communal withering experience, was coming to fulfillment. As David said, if you believed your days were numbered, you had to commit yourself fully. Marc and Elizabeth couldn't do that. They turned away from David, and became his enemies. Judy and I, on the other hand, finally knew we just couldn't leave Mount Carmel. But hell," he added fiercely, "for one moment back then I really wanted to kill him!"

David, Steve said, had put the issue in his usual earthy fashion. "He told us, 'You married guys have to stop fucking and put your mind one hundred percent on the message.' Everyone went through a period of great frustration. 'This is crazy.' 'Why are we doing this?' We had to ask ourselves: *Who on earth could have concocted this insane human drama?* The answer clearly was, *No one on earth.*"

A voice spoke up behind us, and we turned to see Wayne Martin in the doorway. He must have heard some of our conversation, because he said, quietly, "I had to ask myself: If I believe this message, and if David is the Lamb, it wouldn't be fair of me to keep Sheila from having this part of the truth."

"That's awesome," I murmured.

Wayne joined us at the table. His thoughtful eyes regarded me and Steve, judging our mood. "You have to understand that David himself didn't welcome the New Light. All his common sense told him it would cause massive upheavals, desertions, outrage. In the category of 'stumbling blocks,' this was a monster. But it's David's calling to do what the message dictates, as each level is revealed by his inner vision."

"It was easier for you than for me," Steve exclaimed, then bit his lip. "I mean, you had your children already, and your relationship to your wife was more, well, low-key. I mean, you're not as horny as I am. Besides, Judy and I were together for twenty years and I never got her pregnant. Then along comes David with his magic sperm— and bingo!"

Steve's tone switched abruptly, to a calmer, more apologetic mode. "Of course, there was also a practical reason for the New Light. It eliminated the natural envy the single guys felt for the men who were married. After '89, we all were put on ice."

Wayne nodded, watching Steve with great sympathy and affection. In that instant I realized that, compared to these two, my emotional and erotic sacrifices were puny. "We all have our own way in the withering," Wayne said gently.

Steve chuckled harshly. "Ain't that the truth!"

A while later, David talked about Steve and Judy in a study session. He told us that, when the New Light came, Steve and Judy had struggled hard to accept its implications for their marriage.

"Steve was very attached to Judy, had reaped her virginity, he thought," David said. "He could not imagine his life without an intimacy with her. He was real torn up about it."

I looked over to where Steve was sitting, to see his reaction at having his private pain publicly exposed. He leaned forward, chin in his hand, elbow on his knee, and his profile was etched sharp and stiff, like the face on a coin.

"It's hard for Steve not to put his darkness on people," David continued. "He carried a cloud. He wanted to leave Mount Carmel, or kill me. He felt that Judy had been given to him by God, so who the hell was I to grab her?"

A few of the younger women tittered, but most of the audience was, like me, rapt, drinking in every word.

"In a study back then, I asked Judy if Steve actually was the first man she'd been with. Being no virgin himself when he married her, Steve was fixed on the notion that she was pure. 'Steve was the first man I ever went with,' Judy said, absolutely sure of herself. 'Judy, you say that in front of God?' I asked several times, and several times she answered 'Yes.'"

David paused for dramatic effect. "Then I came back at her, hard. I told her I'd been shown a vision of Judy and her girlfriends going out one night, way back before she knew Steve. These friends teased her about still being a virgin. They got her drunk, then sent her to come on to a guy sitting at the bar. In the vision I saw Judy and this man go out to his car and get it on in the backseat. 'This guy was pumpin' away on you, Judy. Am I crazy?' I asked her.

"Judy was shocked. Maybe she'd blocked the memory of that sordid incident from her memory. Or maybe she felt it was something she could never tell Steve. Steve was devastated. In fact, everyone was floored."

David looked at Steve for the first time that evening, and Steve nodded grimly. I looked around for Judy, but she was lost in the crowd.

"I think the discovery that Judy wasn't pure when he married her made it just a little easier for Steve to accept the New Light," David said.

After a pause, David continued. "Women are walking prophecies," he declared. "You always try and speculate what each one who catches your eye might be like in bed." He shook his head. "Women are just too much energy, my friends. Just too much energy."

He recounted an incident I'd heard some of the men talking about previously, in which David had had a young woman lift her skirt above her waist, revealing her underwear. "How many of you guys felt the old instinctive urge looking at her body?" he'd demanded. "Sexuality," he told his audience, was a "huge stumbling block, a major source of pain and lies between men and women."

Now he went on to ruminate aloud about what he called the "enmity" between men and women. "When a man and a woman make love, they feel very close to each other. But as a man, I can't say I know what's going on in a woman's mind at that intimate moment. When I put my dick in her, I know I'm feeling only myself, not her reality. There's a sadness in that, don't you think? The sadness of the limitation of the flesh as against the unlimited spirit."

In the orthodox Jewish marriage ceremony, sex was elevated into a ritual, David declared. Both the man and the women were virgins, and their wedding night had a sacred quality. "Maybe the wife suffered as her husband penetrated her for the first time," David said. "Perhaps, however, her agony was his greatest joy, an acknowledgment of the pain of the body in the midst of a divine ecstasy."

I thought he'd gotten carried away at this point, elevating his own fantasies into holy mysteries. But his remarks about the anguish and confusion involved in intimate relationships rang true to me. I loved women, but being with them was often a torment. It confirmed my feeling that it was better right now for me to be chaste.

David treated me somewhat differently from the others, because, he said, I was a musician and very emotional. He liked having me around, and if he went to town he usually took me. There was some competition for David's favor, and his choosing me to accompany him on these jaunts was a coveted intimacy. All the same, David was well aware of my weaknesses.

One time he asked the assembled members what they thought of "our Baby Gorilla." Grinning hugely, he said: "Isn't Thibodeau someone you want to know because he's a good guy, never hurts anyone?" When people murmured their assent to this, he added: "Isn't that exactly the reason he often ends up hurting others, and himself?" This shrewd perception startled me, and I blushed to the roots of my hair.

On another occasion he bore down hard on me in a study session. He used as a text the passage in Revelation concerning the Third Seal, which speaks of a black horse and a rider—one of the Four Horsemen—who carries a pair of balances in his hand. He told me that his spiritual role in regard to me was as an "oppressor," the figure that forces you to refine your spirit, submit to the withering experience. "You have to toughen up, Thibodeau," he said. "Cut yourself off from women and everything they mean to you." I shivered at the severity in his tone, but I felt he was right.

Later that same night, as I was lying in bed, just falling asleep, I suddenly felt some powerful presence nailing me to the bed. I heard a strange whirling around me, like leaves rustling, but the sound was more mechanical, closer to the thumping of a helicopter's blade.

I knew I was awake, but I had no will, no power, couldn't move my arms or legs. "Oh my God, it's happening!" I thought. There were eight other people in the dormitory with me, but none seemed to notice my predicament. I tried to talk, to cry out, "Guys, I'm being pinned down!" but no sound emerged.

"Don't flip out," I told myself. "It's like that time you were high at an outdoor concert, when everything turned white. . . ." But this was very different. It was clear that my state was induced by some inner energy, not a narcotic.

For what seemed like forever I lay there, grappling with something immediate but invisible. Finally, the whirling sound started to fade and I managed to call out.

Free to move again, I woke up Jaime and told him what had happened.

"I've had that a couple of times," he said calmly. He told me that Peter Hipsman, in a similar state, had heard demonic voices that scared him shitless. "It shows you're getting in touch with your true self," Jaime said sagely, but I wondered if I was just wigging out.

As I lay in bed afterward, a kind of exhilaration washed over me. Had this really been a direct confirmation of the spiritual world? Maybe my struggles to discipline my desire had begun to open me up to another realm of being?

"Hey, I heard you had a little experience," David said, passing me in the hallway next day. "How was it?"

"Great!" I replied. "But scary."

David regarded me intently. "It won't always be wonderful," he warned. "It all depends on your state of grace."

He was right. This kind of visitation occurred four or five more times, and once or twice I thought I'd never survive such terrifyingly abstract chastisement.

Despite our special friendship, I could not bring myself to burden David with my terrors. Perhaps I was too aware that he had his own hard times, far worse than mine.

Sometimes he would plead with us because, he said, God had "cut him off." He could be in a state of darkness, deprived of the visionary light that was his psychological and spiritual energy for weeks at a stretch. During those times he was so knocked out he could hardly get out of bed. "You're my saviors because God won't listen to me," he'd tell us. "Hell is not about being punished. It's the agony of those who get to see what they might have had but never will, because they just didn't give a damn."

When I thought I might approach him to get something heavy off my chest, I'd see that he himself was visibly suffering; with David, spiritual striving was always manifest in his manner and his flesh. As he endured his own personal moments of hell, the skin on his face peeled off in scales and his eyes skittered here and there, like a wild animal lost in a strange world.

Besides, there was an unwritten code at Mount Carmel that you had to deal with your own darkness and not lay it on others. It was, Steve explained, inherent in the withering experience, which each person had to contend with in his own way. "Dave's going through his pain; leave him alone with it," Steve told my friends. He said the same thing to me when Jaime and Pete Hipsman struggled. This attitude was cold comfort during those moments when I longed to shout at the top of my voice, "Get me the fuck *outta here*!"

In the end, though, I was—as Steve put it—"just too damn horny for the truth." When it came right down to it, my desire to master and deepen my own nature always overcame my fears and my revulsions. In fact, I slowly came to understand that the fear and revulsion were vital forces propelling my attempt to evolve as a spiritual being. Like Jacob, I had to wrestle with the angel to prove I had power with God and with men.

7

TEMPTATIONS

During the summer of 1991, my life at Mount Carmel took a surprising turn: I left my home in the community and went to live in the town of Waco.

Music was the reason. After laboring at construction for a few months, I told David that my hands were coarsening and that I was losing focus on my drumming. "Without drumming, I'm nothing," I said. "It's like trying to live without oxygen, and our off-the-cuff jamming sessions here don't cut it for me."

David agreed with me, for his own reasons. "We must refocus the music on the message," he said. "That's always been my aim. And it has to happen in public."

Characteristically, David immediately set about organizing a place for us to perform in Waco. He made the acquaintance of Randall, a truck driver who'd recently owned a nightclub named Cue Stick, "nightclub" being a fancy name for a beer joint with pool tables. When we went into Waco for relaxation we hung out there, and David finally suggested to Randall that we build a stage at the back of his bar, put in sound equipment and a speaker system, and play there on weekends.

Randall liked the idea, and David constructed the stage himself in one day, working with the intense concentration and skill I admired, while Jaime and I and a few others hung around, watching. Cliff Sellors, our artist, decorated the stage with a canvas mural depicting a tongue-in-cheek rendering of two snakes, one with David's head on it, the other with Randall's. Above the mural was the title "Ranch Apocalypse," a tag some Wacoans had given Mount Carmel.

To launch the sessions, David came up with a concept he called "Boo Night." He invited bands of all types to come play at Cue Stick on Friday nights, and the audience was free to cheer or jeer. Saturday night was for established bands like ours. David played guitar, Jaime or me beat drums, and Pablo Cohen thumped along on bass. David sang some of his own biblical songs; his voice was a pretty good rock voice, better than average, and the crowd responded to the rhythms without, I suspect, bothering too much about the message.

We had put several thousand dollars into the sound system and drum set, and David was worried about security on the nights we didn't play and when the club was closed. "Thibodeau, I'm putting you in charge here," he said one evening. "You can hang around and bed down here, keep an eye on things, okay?" My heart leaped. To be free of the Anthill and spend night and day around my drums and the social scene—what a gift!

For a while, I was in heaven. On the nights the band didn't play, I tended bar. I found I was a natural as a bartender, loving to chat up people, listen to their troubles, josh with the guys, and flirt with the girls while dishing up drinks to a raucous crush of humanity. I'm a sucker for a sad story, and that crowd had plenty. Lord, it was fun! Sacrilegiously, I thought: *If this is Babylon, bring on Nebuchadnezzar.* During early-morning hours when the club shut its doors, I locked up and played the drums till four or five in the morning, before laying out my sleeping bag between the pool tables.

That summer, Cue Stick was the hottest joint in town; I jammed with kids coming for the music and felt a new energy in my drumming; it seemed to spring back with fresh force after months of low-key neglect.

Living at Cue Stick taught me a lot about human nature, particularly my own, and particularly with regard to women. Many girls were attracted to my new persona as drummer barhop. Texas girls, I found, were amazingly forward, especially the co-eds at the famously conservative Baylor University, which was actually noted for its wild shindigs. In fact, these Baylor girls were offended that I flirted but wouldn't go to bed with them.

Amid this paradise of erotic temptation and music, I had to ask myself whether or not I was glad to be out of the old male-female game. My answer was ambiguous. In quiet moments I wondered why David had allowed me to live among the kind of temptations he knew were deadly for someone as weak-willed as me. Maybe it's a test, I thought vaguely.

Could David be that diabolical? Certainly. Could I survive his test? Maybe.

In the club, I had another chance to see how David related to outsiders, especially those who were antagonistic, like Matt, a musician who played in a band called Whirling Dervish, which played on Boo Nights. That guy made it publicly plain that he didn't like what he'd heard about Mount Carmel and David. From the stage—our stage—he referred to Mount Carmel as "Rancho Raunch" and to David as "Doctor Dickhead."

One evening after the band's session, David went up to Matt and offered to buy him a beer. Matt was suspicious, but he accepted the beer—and several more. When he was quite drunk, he turned on David. "What if I stabbed you, would you resurrect?" he said, shoving his leering face into David's. "Wait and see," David replied, launching into an exposition about the Lamb opening the First Seal. "You mean, you're the Lamb?" Matt exploded. "That's blasphemy!" But after that evening he treated David with new respect and no longer slagged us on stage.

David went out of his way to maintain a good relationship with townspeople. When a deal went sour, he always preferred to take a loss rather than engage in a dispute. "No amount of gain is worth the ill will," he said wisely. David was frequently generous with people he liked. For example, he loaned the bass player from the Zeroes a new instrument and never bugged the musician to give it back. He was friendly with McLennan County Sheriff Jack Harwell (who would later act as an intermediary during the siege, arranging a milk delivery for the children). All that most Wacoans really knew about David was that he led a community that owned this farm property on the outskirts of town. I don't think they knew that a lot of the kids were his or were particularly concerned about our setup. While working at Cue Stick I seldom heard snotty remarks about Mount Carmel, apart from a few uglies like Matt. In general, Texans prefer to mind their own business, to live and let live, and Mount Carmel enjoyed a vague existence way out on the edge of Waco's consciousness.

That summer, David often visited Los Angeles to make connections with club owners and executives in record companies, hoping for an album. Nothing ever came of these visits, so far as I could see, but that didn't trouble me. I was having too much fun, drumming and slinging booze.

But as the months went by David became increasingly discontented. "The music can't go forward because we aren't one body," he declared one Sunday morning, after a long night on the stage. "Our songs lack coherence and power." He threw up his hands. "You know, in the end I have to say, who needs the world? My true purpose is to work with a small group of people, give them a chance to fulfill the Seals. This is all I want; I don't want any more."

Immediately, he contradicted himself. "We've got a great band, but we have to be even better," he said. "But to go forward we all have to have the same mind-set, you know? And that isn't happening."

Privately, I agreed with him—but for different reasons. Though David said he was trying to develop the band's spiritual qualities, he never got down to structuring our performance, to building it, from low to high. We were just jamming and jamming, not really getting anywhere. I knew Jaime was frustrated by this, and so was I. "If the music's meant to go forward, it will," David said, but none of us felt that was a really satisfactory explanation for our increasing sense of being stuck. At times David implied that the music was secondary to the message, a remark that seemed to contradict his stated intention to make the music and the message one and the same thing.

And I had another problem with David's musicianship.

His style was getting more controlled, more technically correct, and that development was totally out of sync with my wild ways. To me, raw passion was being squeezed to death by David's head trips, his prissy precisions that seemed to snag all the spontaneity out of rock. I tried hard to get in tune with him for a while, keep a straight beat, but it was hopeless. Increasingly, we were at odds, which made for some hairy onstage moments. Fortunately, for us, the Waco crowd wasn't musically sophisticated enough to notice our cross-purposes, but I did, and so did David. "Get with the message, Thibodeau," he hissed at me on several occasions. "Get with the groove," I wanted to retort.

Day by day, night by night, my excitement drained away. I felt I was doing everything I could, yet it just wasn't happening for me or the band. In reaction, I developed a resentment toward David and his message. *What kind of friggin' sick God am I worshipping?* I asked myself. Struggling for self-control, I tried to be more grounded, to let things bounce off me and not get so riled. *Man, you're cooler than this*, I chided myself, but it didn't help.

I was aware that I was spinning my wheels, that I wasn't growing and learning as I'd hoped. Maybe being away from Mount Carmel so long had loosened the bonds of my self-discipline. Maybe, as David often said, failure was built into the plan. On a larger scale, if the message contained in the Seals was true, either we were going to almost die and God would come down and save us, or we were simply going to be wiped out.

On a personal level, the slow degeneration of my artistic sensibilities might have been a reflection of this necessary failure. It was as if I had a dream foretelling the *Titanic* wreck yet bought a ticket anyway, hoping against hope the dream was false. *But if I jumped ship, where would I be?*

The Cue Stick period slowly faded out. Randall, the club owner, felt our music had lost its pizzazz—and he was right. He wanted to bring in new musicians, but he was loath to pay for the equipment we'd installed.

There was also the issue of David's increasingly ill health. As the summer passed, he got sicker and sicker, plagued with ulcers. To get going in the mornings, he needed a bowl of soup laced with cayenne, which couldn't have done his stomach much good. He told us that he was being punished because we were out of sync and nothing seemed to be moving forward. More and more, he talked of the days when Marc Breault was still around. "Back then, everyone was in harmony," he claimed. "Nothing's gone well since then." "Get over it, move on," I said, impatient with his sad stories about Marc. But he seemed unable to set his mind to anything.

At times, everything in me just wanted to say, *Fuck this!* I couldn't walk away, but I was very frustrated.

"Take it day by day," Jaime urged wisely. "That's all anyone can do."

Finally, David pulled the band out of the club, and I had to move back to Mount Carmel. It was a real downer, being back at the Anthill, away from the music and the temptations. Yet I was encouraged that I hadn't actually succumbed to any of the easy seductions. I'd discovered that I was stronger than I thought, that maybe after all I'd gained something vital from David's discipline. Maybe, finally, I was becoming a man, not just a kid indulging every impulse.

<hr>

My suspicion that David was testing my ability to resist temptation was confirmed soon after the Cue Stick scene folded. In October, David asked me to go to Los Angeles to help Julie Martinez find her eldest son, Stephen.

Julie, it seemed, had lost contact; she believed Stephen lived with her former husband somewhere in the Sacramento area. She had five other children living with her at Mount Carmel, but the loss of Stephen troubled her greatly. David suggested that I accompany Julie to Pomona, where we could rent a car and drive together to Sacramento to visit the state records office in an attempt to trace the boy's location.

"Please don't make me do this," I pleaded.

"Julie is vulnerable; she needs a chaperone," David replied.

"Why me?" I asked. "Why are you deliberately putting temptation in my way?" But David ignored my objections.

Julie had come to the community about six months after me to join her mother, Ofelia Santoyo, her grandmother, Concepcion, and the two children she'd sent to live with them because her life was a mess. She'd divorced her first husband, Stephen's father, and had then taken up with a guy she referred to as "an El Paso junkie." By the time she was thirty she'd had six children and was a druggie herself.

Julie frankly admitted that she'd sought out Mount Carmel because she was desperate. "I didn't come for the religious stuff," she told me as we flew to Los Angeles.

"I was at the end of my string. The community gave me a chance to get my act together, have all my kids together, except Stephen. Mount Carmel saved my life."

I've always had a weakness for tragic stories, and Julie, then barely thirty, was small, dark, sad, and hot. She was intriguing, and I knew she was attracted to me. Clearly, this assignment was going to push me to the limits of my shaky self-control. Thinking about it as we winged our way across New Mexico and Arizona, I came to the conclusion that David felt I had to master my sexuality before I could become a full member of the community. If I failed this test, I was probably out, and I realized that I couldn't bear that.

Whereas Julie's tension seemed to ease as we rolled up the I-5 toward Sacramento, mine increased. I was eager to get the whole thing over with as quickly as possible; after all, how long can a man hold his breath? But Julie had other ideas. "Let's have some fun, detour up to Jordan, where I used to live," she suggested. When I seemed doubtful, she told me not to be a bear.

We spent a night in San Francisco in the home of a family friend I'd known back in Maine. We had to sleep in bunk beds in the small apartment's spare room, and I was all too conscious of Julie's female warmth in the dark, the scent of her faintly jasmine perfume lingering in the air.

"You sleeping?" she asked suddenly, and I picked up a hint of tears in her voice. "I can't sleep. Please come down here and lie with me; I need cuddling."

I wanted to say no, but how could I refuse her some comforting? I climbed down from the top bunk and slid under the covers with her. She was crying softly as I embraced her, and she clung to me with a kind of erotic despair. It took all my willpower to hold her yet not get sucked into a sexual vortex.

"What's the matter? Don't I turn you on?" Julie murmured.

"Too much; that's the trouble," I said through clenched teeth, feeling the bare skin of her belly burning against mine. "Please don't—"

"What?"

"You know. 'Seduce' me. . . ."

Julie chuckled low in her throat. "Poor old Thibodeau," she said. But she drew back a little, putting a small space between our bodies, and I was grateful.

However, as we drove toward Eureka on a hot fall day, Julie invited me to join her in a naked swim in the Pacific. The water looked delicious, but I refused. Her frank desire made me nervous. I felt like a chocolate addict in a candy store who's been told that all the goodies are poisonous.

When we finally got to Sacramento and searched the records, we could not discover the whereabouts of her son. Julie was really downcast, and for a while she retreated into her shell, curling up into a small space to contain her hurt. However, during the ride back to Los Angeles she suggested we share a motel room and get it on.

"I can't do this, Julie," I insisted. "I'm real sorry."

"Don't be a drag," she countered. "What harm's a little comfort-sex going to do to your immortal soul?"

"If I take one step down that slippery slope . . . ," I replied. She was annoyed with me, I saw, but I knew I had to hang on. I had too much to lose.

At nightfall, halfway down the Central Valley, we stopped for burgers, which we ate in the car. Before I knew it, we were kissing, and Julie was trying to undo my belt.

"I just can't do this," I panted, trying to pull away. The mixture of her neediness and my horniness was almost too much to resist. I could see David's face watching me, shaking his head in despair. With a surge of determination that astonished me, I managed to disengage and push Julie gently away.

For me, that decisive act was a huge victory. I was exhilarated. I found I had a new power to resist my impulses, to fight against my carnal nature. It may sound a bit pompous, but the gut thing was, I discovered that I was no longer a totally helpless victim of every sexual urge that stirred my blood. Whether for spiritual reasons or not, it mattered to me to be able to discriminate between one kind of appetite and another, between knee-jerk self-indulgence and the power to refuse.

When I got back to Pomona—chastity preserved—I found my mother there, as we had arranged. She was making her annual visit home from Greece, and I'd asked her to meet me in Pomona. I preferred to see Balenda in Los Angeles rather than Waco, because I really did not want her nosing around Mount Carmel. I suspected she'd be appalled by the place, by its primitive conditions and its patriarchal structure. To be frank, I didn't want to subject my life to her scrutiny right then.

During the months I'd been living at Mount Carmel we'd chatted on the phone many times. Often, I had David talk to her, using him as a screen between us. David tried to explain the Seals to Balenda, but she usually cut him off. "I get uncomfortable with that stuff," she told me. "Does this man really claim to be this 'Lamb' character?"

I left such questions hanging, and when my mother pressed for a visit, I suggested she join Julie and me in Pomona. I think that, former hippie that she is, Balenda enjoyed the easygoing, music-heavy scene in the Rock House. She got on well with Julie and comforted her for the failure to find her son. If you let her, my mom can be wonderfully soothing.

In a letter I'd recently written her, while she was still on her Greek island, I'd tried to explain what was happening to me in Mount Carmel, to correct her impression that I had been captured by some weird "faith."

"There's a difference between living by 'faith' and living by 'knowledge,'" I wrote. "I much prefer the latter. The Seals are deep and much to the contrary of organized religion as we know it. It's a lot clearer than some jive-ass preacher telling me about heaven and hell.

"I've always wondered and made a pact with my heart that if I'd ever know the will of God, not a bullshit God but a real truth, I'd go with it. You are probably the only person in my entire family that ever really, I mean really, believed in me, and I want you to know that I'm now more in touch with the real David Thibodeau, the child, than ever before. I will stand up for what I believe in, at any cost!"

My mother hadn't been convinced. In a letter I later found, written to her father, my grandfather, during the siege, she said: "The mind control practice of Koresh is very skilled and he has succeeded in instilling extreme paranoia in his devotees."

"Take care, Davey, don't get in over your head," she said, hugging me hard as we said goodbye at Los Angeles Airport. "One of these days I'll definitely come to Waco and corner your Koresh in his lair!"

God, I hope not, I said silently, with a secret shudder.

Back in Waco, David asked me, with transparent casualness: "I hope everything went well?"

"Did my best," I muttered, avoiding his eye.

"You don't have to say anything about it," David said, but I sensed he already grasped how close I'd come to lapsing from virtue.

———·———

I guess David knew I was bound to finally fall to temptation, and he was right.

A few weeks after I got back from Los Angeles, I went to a bar in Waco one night with David and a few other guys. A gorgeous blonde walked in; our eyes met and locked. She came right up close to me, and I knew I was lost. Cheryl was wrapped in that fatal air of sadness tinged with madness I've alway found irresistible.

Anyway, Cheryl accompanied a group of visitors David invited back to Mount Carmel to jam. He was always very hospitable; besides, he felt it was good policy to let some of the locals see where we lived and find out for themselves that we weren't just a bunch of crazies. I thought I'd be safe from temptation on my home ground, but it turned out otherwise. Within a short time I found myself sitting in a parked car in the dark with Cheryl's tongue down my throat. I tried to stop her, but she went down on me, and my resistance melted.

It was the first orgasm I'd had in months, the first woman I'd had in more than a year, and the experience was shattering, in more ways than one; extreme pleasure and guilt in one heady cocktail. Cheryl went back inside while I sat in the dark, trying to make sense of what had happened.

I'd not only betrayed myself; I'd sold out womanhood itself, the spiritual *Shekinah*, the mother image of all females. It was this betrayal that shook me most, the sense I'd trashed one of the deepest principles of David's teaching—the feminine aspect of the message he brought us.

In the following days I tried to talk to David about my fall from grace, but I just could not bring myself to confess. He probably knew, anyway, seeing right through me with those shrewd eyes.

A few weeks later, David asked me to take Michele as my "wife." He presented it as a "sham marriage," to deflect the official investigators who were beginning to nose about Mount Carmel. Other men "married" David's women, for more or less the same reason: Greg Summers and Aisha Gyarfas; Jeff Little and Nicole Gent; Cliff Sellors and Robyn Bunds. Some of these phony liaisons were arranged to keep the Immigration and Naturalization Service (INS) at bay, as foreign men and women were overstaying their visas. Though there were no official documents, the visitors could pretend they were married if they were ever questioned.

However, I suspected that in my case David had an extra agenda. By providing me with a wife, even in name only, he was binding me into a familial structure he hoped would bolster my weak nature. But marrying Michele meant I'd have to lie to my mother and my family, pretending that the marriage was real. I hated that, and I refused at first.

David started pressuring me. "I need you to do this for me," he insisted, and I finally consented.

Our marriage was conducted without ceremony. One day, in a study session, David announced it, and that was that. In the event, I acquired an instant family. Serenity was around three years old; the twins, Chica and Little One, were barely six months old. Serenity, with her shy, quiet smile, was my favorite little girl in the community. "Tib-o-*doe*, what are you *doing*?" she'd say. I guess that, even at her age, she pegged me for a kid needing a firm maternal hand.

"Serenity, call Thibodeau 'Daddy,'" David teased her, but she refused. She knew who her father was.

I liked Michele a lot, but she didn't turn me on, and that was good. She was pleasant-faced and fair-haired like her sister, Rachel, David's legal wife. She was a great mom, which was all she ever really wanted to be, and I respected her for that. Though she was only sixteen, she had a matron's gravity. Having Serenity when she was fourteen hadn't harmed her any, so far as I could see; but we never spoke about that.

Michele took on some wifely duties, like darning my clothes, sewing on buttons, sending me a few bucks for spending money when I was away from Mount Carmel. She also wrote to my mother and my grandmother, like a real daughter-in-law. Obviously, she wanted to reinforce the fiction that we were really married, but I think she also enjoyed the idea of having a set of conventional in-laws. My mom and Gloria responded warmly, sending presents of clothes and toys for my new stepchildren. Surprisingly, they never asked who the kids' actual father was, and I never told them.

"Serenity is eager to meet you!" Michele wrote to Balenda, soon after our union. "She fell in love with the doll right away. We named it Dave's favorite name, 'Sasha.' Also the outfit fits just right, with a little room to grow. That's my kind of style. Dave really appreciated the shirts you sent. He's gonna need a whole new wardrobe after he loses all his extra weight. His pants already fall off of him! I'm looking forward to meeting you. Your daughter-in-law, Michele and Serenity."

To Gloria, Michele wrote: "So how does it feel to be a great grandmother? You'll love her [Serenity]. She's a smart one, and also big for her age. Dave and I are very happy together. I have to keep him out of mischief. You know how he is, I'm sure. 'Party Animal' hah! hah! No, I'm just kidding, he's a great husband."

Whatever David's reasons were in marrying me to Michele, it was a shrewd move. Somehow being a husband, even in name only, settled me. I felt a responsibility to live up to the title, and my raging hormones cooled considerably.

8

ON RAPE, ABUSE, AND GUNS

My link with Michele provoked me to discover more about her relationship with David and also about his sexual connection with underage girls in general. This was a tough nut to crack, for no one wanted to discuss the matter openly, not even Steve, and I had to gradually ferret out some facts for myself.

As I came to understand it, the history of David's involvement with these girls began in 1985, after he returned from Jerusalem. He claimed that the vision he received on Mount Zion included a command to have a child with Michele, his wife's eleven-year-old sister.

Far from welcoming this imperative, David told me, both he and Rachel were shaken and upset. "I was happy with Rachel," he told me, when I finally got up the courage to challenge him about this issue. "Honestly, all I ever wanted was a traditional wife and family. But the voice said, 'Take Michele as a wife,' and I felt I had to do it, though I truly didn't want to."

Rachel was devastated, David said. "Why wouldn't she be? Michele was her little sister! She was very close to her, protected her. . . ." He paused, and a sad expression seized his face as he remembered old pain, the possible disruption of his marriage. At the time, his firstborn son, Cyrus, was a baby, and he was just consolidating his position as Lois Roden's successor.

For more than a year the couple struggled with the issue. David felt he had to be true to his vision, even though it could ruin his relationship with Rachel and possibly lead him into conflict with the authorities. The ugly term "statutory rape" hovered in the air. Although Michele's parents, Perry and Mary Belle Jones, accepted that the girl had been singled out to bear a child for God, as David put it, their sense of being honored by this divine choice was undercut by a natural concern for their barely nubile daughter. They were concerned, too, that Rachel and Michele might follow their brothers and sisters and abandon the community they'd grown up in.

Perry told me that his younger daughter had been happy to become David's wife, but I heard from some of the women that Michele had been very distressed by the prospect of losing her virginity to David at such a tender age. When I asked her about it, she just smiled serenely. In effect, I gathered, Michele's feelings were secondary to the theological issue: the implication of David's God-given command to generate an inner circle of children who would form the group of "Elders" surrounding the Merkabah, the heavenly chariot or throne.

David's situation with Michele was discussed over and over during study sessions. His followers knew he could not deny his vision, which amounted to a huge stumbling block placed in his path. There were those who suspected David's motives, I was told; after all, as one man whispered, "David has a thing for young girls. His first woman, Linda, was jailbait." But in general people were sympathetic, even insistent: David had to do what he was told.

The problem was finally resolved dramatically. One night Rachel had a powerful dream in which it came to her that David might be destroyed, even die, if he refused the divine command. In early 1987, twelve-year-old Michele became David's lover. Their daughter, Serenity, was born two years later.

With Michele's induction, the doors to the House of David were opened wide. The House of David, it seemed, would require the virginities of several young girls. During that same year, 1987,

David took as his wives Clive Doyle's fourteen-year-old daughter, Karen, seventeen-year-old Robyn Bunds, and twenty-year-old Dana Okimoto. (Dana left the community later, and her sons, Sky and Scooter, are two of only three of David's children to survive the destruction of Mount Carmel; the other is Robyn's son, Shaun.) In 1988, David married Nicole Gent, then nineteen. In 1989, he took thirteen-year-old Aisha Gyarfas into his household; her daughter, Startle, was born in 1992. All of these children were born at Mount Carmel, delivered by a visiting midwife. None of the babies had birth certificates since, as David claimed, they belonged to God, not the state.

As far as I could discover, most of the women David chose were very happy to join the House of David. As Robyn Bunds later explained it: "He's perfect, and he's going to father your children. What more can you ask for?"

(The Bunds family had a complex history with David. When Robyn's brother, David Bunds, and his wife were expelled from Mount Carmel in June 1990 for violating dietary rules, they persuaded Robyn to defect. Her departure was followed by a custody battle with David over their son, Shaun, which Robyn won. She claimed that David abused the baby, spanking him until he drew blood. Her father, Donald Bunds, had been one of David's earliest supporters; he bought the Pomona and La Verne houses for David, and gave him another $10,000 to buy a van.)

Robyn's mother, Jeannine, also went to bed with David. "He wouldn't do it unless you wanted it," she said. "It wasn't about sex, but he was a very appealing, sexual person. I wanted to be in the House of David." In 1991, Jeannine left Mount Carmel when she found she was unable to become pregnant by David. Another of David's women told me, "It's considered an honor to have a baby for God. You know, not every woman is worthy of Koresh's loins."

The one doubtful addition to this list of supposedly willing underage consorts was Sherri Jewell's daughter, Kiri. During the 1995 congressional committee hearings, Kiri told a dramatic—one might say melodramatic—tale of being sexually assaulted, but not penetrated, by David in a Texas motel when she was a mere ten years of age. However, her story was not believed by her grand-mother, Ruth Mosher, who said that Kiri was living with her in Ana-heim, California, when the girl claimed she was molested. It was subsequently revealed, too, that Kiri's aunt had helped her com-pose her congressional testimony. Kiri's mother, Sherri, who died in the fire, was a much-medaled aerobics instructor and triathlon competitor. "Kiri was the apple of her eye," Sherri's mother, Ruth Mosher, recalls, "and there wasn't anything she wouldn't do for her child. So it's difficult for me to accept that Sherri would willingly allow Koresh to molest her daughter."

Kiri was the focus of a bitter 1992 custody battle between her mother and her father, in which Marc Breault testified that David planned to rape Kiri. (Breault was the source of several other lurid tidbits about the House of David. Despite these shocking al-legations, neither Kiri nor her father, Donald Jewell, ever pressed charges against David. And a separate Department of Justice inves-tigation in 1992 concluded that Kiri's story, told to Texas Depart-ment of Child Protective Services social worker Joyce Sparks, was insufficient probable cause for an indictment.)

With the 1989 New Light revelation, more women, several in their thirties and forties, were added to the House of David, including Judy Schneider, Sheila Martin, Nicole's mother, Lisa Gent, and Robyn Bunds's mother, Jeannine, Jaydean Wendell, Stan Sylvia's wife, Lorraine, and Katherine Andrade. Between them these later women produced four children: Judy's daughter, Mayanah, Katherine's daughter, Chanel, Lorraine's daughter, Hollywood, and Jaydean's son, Patron. By April 1993, David had had sexual relations with a total of fifteen women, including Rachel Jones and Linda Campion, his "first love," and had fathered seventeen chil-dren with eleven of them.[*]

---

[*] Eight of these women and twelve of the children perished in the siege of Mount Carmel. Five women left the community before the conflict with the federal agencies, including Robyn and Jeannine Bunds, Dana Okimoto, Karen Doyle, and Lisa Gent. Kathy Schroeder and Sheila Martin left during

David did not take every woman who offered herself. I heard that he'd refused several, claiming they weren't ready to enter the House of David. Others he accepted within a short time of their joining the community. It seemed that there had to be a certain quality of understanding on both sides for David to come knocking on a woman's door; she had to really want to have a baby for God. I did notice, though, that most of David's women were sexually appealing, so maybe his choices weren't entirely spiritual. "After all," he said jokingly, "shouldn't God's children be beautiful?"

For a few years after the New Light, indeed, until the new building was finished, married couples still lived together, even though they weren't having sexual relations.

Scott Sonobe told me that he sometimes tried to cheat with Sita, his beautiful dark-haired wife, but she wouldn't go along. It seemed the women enforced their husbands' abstinence. In truth, the women were the moral backbone of the community.

Frankly, I didn't envy David his harem. I'd always had a hard time keeping up a relationship with one woman, let alone two or three who know about one another, let alone have them living together. If you're the kind of man who can keep secrets, which I'm not, you might be able to handle several women at once, but only if you could preserve their ignorance. I was never able to have simultaneous affairs because I always tripped myself up. It blew me away that all these women accepted David's setup. *How does he keep these women from killing one another?* I wondered.

Maybe it was the loving way he took care of them. David was openly affectionate with all of them, very fond and caring.

the siege. Dana Okimoto, a Hawaiian of Japanese extraction, left Mount Carmel a few months before the siege, after having lived there for five years. A serious, quiet woman, she refused to speak against David after she departed, except to say that her reasons for leaving were private and that she wanted to move on and pursue her career. When the ATF questioned her before they attacked us, seeking inside information and slander, Dana told the agents she'd made a vow not to speak about Mount Carmel. All she would say was that, as regards the community, the ATF had no idea who they were dealing with. David was very upset when Dana moved out, taking two of his sons with her.

Naturally, the women competed for his attention, and he didn't have enough time during the days, weeks, and months to keep all of them happy. Nevertheless, the wives seemed friendly among themselves, sharing the chores and the care of the kids. I never imagined such an arrangement was possible, especially in today's America—with the possible exception of some Mormons.

From time to time, David publicly discussed the challenge of having many wives. "You think it's all butter and honey?" he'd ask. "Think again!" The women of the House of David had a good laugh at this, and that revealed more than anything their general camaraderie. During one study, however, Aisha Gyarfas openly stated that she was very upset because David wasn't paying her enough attention. "I spend more time with you than any of the others," David retorted, and I recognized the old male defensiveness in his tone.

Occasionally, he'd fling out taunts at the men in the community. "I got all the women, aren't you jealous?" We'd chuckle awkwardly, and David would sigh and say, "We're all God's guinea pigs here. My lot is to procreate, yours is to tolerate. I'd swap with you any day." I came close to believing him.

I was told by a psychiatrist who once questioned me about Mount Carmel that David's sexual hierarchy had a powerful point. "When a group like yours fails to channel its sex drive into some specifically approved relationships—and I have seen a few 'anything goes' communes—the results are disastrous for the individual members and for the group's viability," he said. "As far as sex goes, nobody knows who's who and what's what."

The underlying issue, he pointed out, is that in a commune the group organizes itself as a family seeking the security and discipline of childhood supports and parental controls. "Communes give up the common liberties in exchange for security and group identity. Otherwise, you might as well enjoy the freedoms along with the anarchy of the mainstream culture."

On one occasion, David confided a subtler take on his sexual relationships, especially those with underage girls. "Something can be wrong yet still necessary and true," he said. "Apart from the stumbling-block aspect—and this is one huge stumbling block, for me—being wrong can be a way to prove your faith. Sometimes it can even lead you to that faith."

He gave as an example the case of Woodrow Kendrick. Old Bob, as he was known, had slept with his own daughters in the previous Mount Carmel, before David had arrived. "I asked him, in a study, 'Bob, how can someone like you be saved?' Bob just stood there and took it, knowing he'd transgressed, that his actions revealed how sick he was, how sick humanity in general is. But the awareness of his sickness brought Bob to reconfirm his belief in a spiritual purpose. It was his stumbling block that he overcame."

I must confess that David's relationships with young girls bothered me a lot, for several reasons. Firstly, I had a hard time believing that a girl of twelve or thirteen could really know what she was doing in agreeing to have sex with a man twice her age, especially in a closed community where sleeping with the leader was considered a supreme honor. Surely, it must be a scary and painful experience, and the social pressure must have been horribly confusing.

For sure, all of the young girls I knew at Mount Carmel, particularly Michele, seemed perfectly at ease with being David's lovers; all the same, it stuck in my craw. Perhaps this predilection for virgins was a consequence of David's Texas upbringing. Girls ripen young there, and there seems to be a hokey and, to me, repellent cowboy obsession with ravished innocence.

I was puzzled, too, by David's decision to cross a line that would inevitably lead him into conflict with the civil authorities. Of all the charges leveled against him in the media and by government officials—including child abuse and gun stockpiling—the only case in which he grossly violated the law was the crime of statutory rape.

Texas law is quite clear on this. The state's age of consent is seventeen. Girls may marry at fourteen with parental permission, but they cannot legally consent to have sex outside marriage, with or without parental permission. If the parents do collude in allowing their daughter (or son) to become sexually active under this age, they are party to the criminal offense of endangering a child— placing a child at risk of physical or mental injury.

If the underage girl has a baby, the criminal charge against her seducer is elevated to aggravated sexual assault. Sex with a girl under seventeen but over fourteen is a second-degree felony; sex with a girl under fourteen is a first-degree felony punishable by a prison sentence of five to ninety-nine years. In other words, David was guilty on multiple charges that could have sent him to prison for a very long time, perhaps for life. It doesn't lessen the force of this to understand that proving such cases is often difficult, especially if the young woman won't testify.

"It is possible that the unusual nature of the sexual abuse claims, and the complex circumstances surrounding them, especially the isolated community lifestyle and parental consent within the clan, made the task of documenting these allegations difficult," Houston Assistant District Attorney Bill Hawkins told me. "It is also possible that the psychological or emotional trauma associated with premature sexual activity was mitigated somewhat by their parents' approval, or by the group's culturally specific expectations about sexual activity for young girls." Hawkins continued: "When it comes to charging someone you must have courtroom-quality proof. That's why statutory rape laws are so rarely prosecuted."

Even so, David must have known he was moving into dangerous territory when he started sleeping with Michele, Karen, and Aisha. He was no otherworldly hero unaware of the mundane consequences of his actions. On the contrary, he operated very successfully in the everyday context, including dealing with people in official positions, such as the local sheriff and the representatives of various state agencies. He'd certainly dealt with the law when he'd beaten assault charges in the raid against George Roden in 1987.

Furthermore, Mount Carmel had previously existed in relative peace with its host society for fifty years. Its members may have offended the locals with their seemingly odd beliefs, but they had never actually broken the law, with the sole exception of George Roden's mad escapades.

There's nothing in the Seals that specifically commanded David to have sex with underage girls. It was his personal vision that impelled him, not a clear biblical example. God said to "take Michele," and only David knew for sure if this order was motivated by his vision or by a devious lust. Depending on your point of view, you can consider David either a vile seducer or a man following the dictates of a divine message. In a sense, both perceptions are equally valid: One man's prophet is another man's philanderer, and many a self-proclaimed visionary has used his tongue for more than preaching. But the interesting thing is, why did David deliberately violate the law, knowing he was setting foot down a path that would inevitably provoke the authorities, especially in a place like Waco?

If he'd been in a more liberal part of the United States, such as California, say, his actions might have passed unnoticed. But there he was, deep in the heart of Texas, locked solid into the Bible Belt, where his sexual practices were bound to cause trouble. If he didn't understand that, he was an idiot. If he did understand it, he knew it would inexorably lead to a confrontation with Babylon in all its fury.

Did he have a death wish? Was he inviting his own apocalypse? The answer is unclear, unless you understand David's complex sense of his own purpose.

For his predecessors at Mount Carmel, George Houteff and Ben and Lois Roden, the End Time was an event to be expected passively. You might predict it, always incorrectly as the Rodens had in 1959, suffering a disappointment; mostly you awaited heaven's pleasure. But David saw himself as the Seventh Angel of Revelation. *But in the days of the voice of the seventh angel, when he shall begin to sound, the mystery of God should be finished.* He had a ten-year plan, starting in 1985, the year of his Jerusalem vision. By 1995, the Seals would be fully revealed and the world would end.

If the working out of that mystery included the seduction of the innocent, who was David to deny it? David was a savvy guy. He knew he could've had other women, even unofficial wives, without breaking the law. When he reached out to underage girls like Michele and Aisha, he was surely aware he was crossing a line. But David's role—his duty, maybe—was to create "eternal souls" with a range of women, including young girls. By this act, he chose to follow his own path, whatever the consequences. Maybe those very consequences were necessary to his perceived scriptural purpose.

To be honest, I'm still deeply troubled by these questions. The only rationale I can come up with is that David believed that his message to the world was meant to fail, that failure was its purpose. You can argue that, if David hadn't provoked the authorities by committing statutory rape, he might have been allowed to continue delivering his message. You can say that what followed from this deliberate violation of the law was inevitable, so the feds can't really be blamed for doing their duty. You can even say that even though the feds acted with extraordinary violence they were simply faithful to their nature, as David was faithful to his.

If the evidence for David's guilt in the crime of statutory rape is unmistakable, then the charge of child abuse that was leveled against him and the community by various antagonists—in the sense of beating babies and otherwise mistreating the kids—was totally unfounded. This fact can't be repeated too often, since in the end the children were cynically used as an excuse to destroy us.

As a consequence of the authorities' total absence of sympathy for our religious view of life, they never grasped why we regarded the children, particularly David's own, as special, the most sacred part of our community, our hope for the future of the world. "We don't expect you to understand," David said on a videotape we made of the kids during the siege, "but these children are serious business." The feds, however, simply ignored or willfully failed to grasp this fact. Bob Ricks, head of the ATF's Oklahoma City office, contemptuously told the press that "women and children to him [David] are expendable items." As a result, the feds' view of the children as hostages was totally out of whack.

The children of Mount Carmel were a vital part of our small society. They participated in all its communal activities, including the long study sessions. If they were tired during the studies, the mothers either rocked them to sleep in their laps or took them off to bed. Often, a child would sit in David's lap while he was expounding Scripture, cuddling close while he stroked the kid's hair or kissed his or her cheek. He was very touchy-feely with all the children, perhaps in reaction to his own lonely, unloved childhood. Sometimes, amid a fire and brimstone exposition, amid talk of lion-headed horses with snakes for tails, he'd pass around a bowl of popcorn to settle the young ones.

What amazed me was the way the kids could sit through a long study session without fidgeting. Their attention spans were far better than most children I've come across, certainly better than mine. They seemed to lack that restless agitation and neediness so common among the kids I've known on the outside.

The children lived with their mothers and were home-schooled in the cafeteria. (David did not trust the public school system, disliking its secular curriculum.) The adults and the older children, like the twelve-year-olds Audrey Martinez and Lisa Martin, gave the lessons, which combined Scripture and general subjects. The Bible was the core of their learning, and it's not surprising that officials who examined the children who came out during the siege were impressed by their remarkable ability to grasp abstract concepts such as "infinity" and "humanity."

Among themselves, the children formed their own little community. The older kids looked after the young ones, read stories to them, taught them the alphabet and arithmetic. Cyrus, David's oldest son, who was barely six when I came to stay at Mount Carmel, was the natural leader, being the eldest and the crown prince, as it were. But the children were all brothers and sisters to one another, playing games and studying as equals. I seldom heard them cry.

They enjoyed the freedom of living in the country, to go roaming over the seventy-seven-acre property, riding the go-carts and mini-motorbikes David bought them. Every Sunday afternoon there were go-cart races for the little ones and bike races for the older boys on a track we made behind the Anthill, with swimming contests for all of us in the pool. Cyrus was responsible for keeping order among his small tribe, which he did with an easy authority learned from his doting dad.

When, as a treat, the kids accompanied an adult during a visit to town, they were quiet and self-contained and didn't run wild around the stores, shouting and yelling for their parents to buy them toys and candy. We bought them ice cream and sometimes took them to see an animated film, and they delighted in such simple pleasures. I loved hanging out with the children, especially Michele's Serenity and Julie's sons, Isaiah and Joseph. We played cards and I showed them how to handle the drums, and sometimes we'd just run around playing tag, me the biggest kid of all.

Discipline was strict but fair. If the kids transgressed in some way, by playing close to a dangerous construction area, or if they stole, or started a fight, or acted rudely toward each other or an adult, or did anything that could get someone else hurt, the correction process was clearly set down. First, the child was asked why he or she had acted badly. If there was an acceptable reason, or if the offense was minor, he was let off with a speech about good behavior.

If spanking was ordered, by David or another adult, the child was taken into a little room and moderately swatted on the butt with a wooden paddle dubbed the "Helper." The mothers themselves did most of the spanking; they were the prime maintainers of discipline. When it was over, the child's parent rubbed his sore behind and sent him off to play, with an admonition to be good. Once, though, I saw David paddle Cyrus hard, being more severe with him because, as a leader, he was supposed to set an example. The boy took it bravely, scowling to hide his pain. He knew that, as David's firstborn, more was expected of him.

The one absolute rule in all this was that punishment should never be administered in a passion. If David ever saw a parent spanking in anger or using harsh words to a child, he'd come down very hard on the adult. The purpose of paddling, he insisted, was to show a child how to behave, not as a release for grownups' frustrations. Kids were never slapped in the face or given a casual smack over the ear. The whole chastisement was carried out coolly, with a kind of old-fashioned solemnity.

Dick DeGuerin, David's attorney, made an interesting comment about Mount Carmel's way of treating its kids when interviewed by

Newsweek after the fire. "At what point does society have a right to step in and say you have to raise your family our way? It's applying yuppie values to people who chose to live differently."

Although I saw that the physical punishment of the children was fair, I must say the whole idea of spanking appalled me. I'd never been beaten as a child—my parents were adamantly opposed to it—so it was hard for me to watch a kid being paddled and see him or her squirm in pain, even though, mentally, I understood its purpose. Maybe spanking was one more of those Texan customs: "Spare the rod and spoil the child" and all that. However, I knew I'd never bring myself to strike a child of mine, even if it meant nurturing a brat.

The false issue of child abuse first surfaced at Mount Carmel because of David's old nemesis, Marc Breault, and his fierce campaign to discredit his former mentor. Not long after his defection in 1989, Marc and other disaffected Davidians living in Australia hired a private investigator to go to Waco to try to stir up state and federal authorities, including the INS and the Internal Revenue Service. Those agencies were urged to take action about child abuse and other alleged offenses happening at Mount Carmel.

The investigator met with local and federal authorities, but none of them seemed particularly interested in Marc's allegations, despite his lurid claim that it was "highly probable" that we would murder and sacrifice one of our children on Yom Kippur—a weird variation of the blood-libel stories once used to whip up pogroms against Jews in Eastern Europe. U.S. Attorney Bill Johnston determined that no federal violations had occurred, and the local sheriff and state agencies felt the same way.

But hell hath no fury like a disappointed apostate, and Marc returned to the attack. The next year, Marc and his wife, Elizabeth, traveled to Waco to talk to Sheriff Gene Barber, without success. "Breault's complaints, along with the others, stemmed from sour grapes," Barber commented shrewdly to the local press. The lawman discovered Breault was known for "telling whoppers," and he divined that his true contention boiled down to an objection to David's supposed claim to be "the exclusive expositor of Scripture."

Back in Australia, Marc approached producer Martin King of the National Nine Network, who sent a team to Waco to film a report for its *A Current Affair* series, in early 1992. The secret agenda of the TV program was, in Breault's and King's own words, to expose David "as a cruel, maniacal, child-molesting, pistol-packing religious zealot who brainwashed his devotees into believing he was the Messiah."

When the tabloid-TV team arrived in Waco, it was clear from the producer's attitude that he was preparing a hatchet job on Mount Carmel in general, and David in particular. David knew this, but he took a calculated risk that somehow the true character of the community would come through; that, despite the sneers we saw on the TV crew's faces, we might have a chance to present our side of the story. Maybe David was just eager for any kind of media attention; or perhaps he hoped against hope that we wouldn't been seen in too bad a light.

David tried to make the Australians welcome. He arranged musical entertainment and asked me to play the drums, but I kept out of the way, being less convinced that Martin King would ever allow anything good about us to come through in the final version. I was right, as it turned out; the documentary—if it can be called that—was utterly skewed in the editing. King sent us a tape, which appalled David. The one-hour "exposé," broadcast only in Australia, accused David of beating children and forcing them to do punishing exercises, of depriving them of food and water, and of providing poor sanitary conditions.

"How could they lie like this?" David asked. This episode was our first experience of the way the media seemed prejudiced toward us, pursuing an agenda that had nothing to do with objectivity.

It's interesting to note that, during his first year at Mount Carmel, before he rebelled against the New Light revelation, Marc made no objection to David having several wives or to his sexual connection with underage girls. At the time, he appeared to believe that polygamy was sanctioned by Scripture and that sex with minors was okay if the girl and her parents willingly consented. (Later, he claimed to have been upset in the spring of 1989 when he saw "little Aisha Gyarfas" going up the wooden stairs leading to David's room and said to himself, "I hope she's not doing what I think she is.")

In fact, Marc was knocked out by David, at first. "The light became brighter and brighter until my mind could comprehend the Bible from cover to cover," he later wrote in *Inside the Cult*, a book he coauthored with Martin King. "I was beginning to perceive in the way God perceives." Marc "toyed with the idea of becoming a prophet" himself, and David encouraged him. Before Steve Schneider, Marc was Mount Carmel's number-two man.

In October 1991, Marc phoned David Jewell, Kiri's divorced father, to warn him that daughter Kiri, then living in Mount Carmel with her mother, was "in extreme danger" because she was about to become one of David's "brides." This call prompted Kiri's father to sue for custody, and Marc flew to Michigan to give supportive testimony in Jewell's custody hearing, characterizing David to the court as "power-hungry and abusive."

Back in Waco after testifying at the Jewell custody hearing, Marc kept nagging the authorities, and in early 1992 a sheriff's department official passed on his charges to the Texas Department of Child Protective Services.

Marc provided the officials with affidavits by former Davidians Ian and Allison Manning, who claimed that David spanked kids with a wooden paddle, sometimes brutally. Former Davidian Michele Tom alleged that David spanked her eight-month-old daughter for forty minutes because she would not sit still on his lap and had once threatened to kill a child if her mother gave her a pacifier. These statements may have been sincerely made, but they were totally at odds with my experience of David's treatment of the children.

In February 1992, Child Protective Services social worker Joyce Sparks visited Mount Carmel accompanied by two state human services officials and two McLellan County deputies. Over the next nine weeks, Sparks made two more visits, and David also visited her office in Waco.

Sparks was a plump, blonde, sweet-faced woman, in her mid-thirties, I'd guess. She was very maternal and spoke to the children in a gentle, caring voice. After talking to the kids and looking over the accommodations, Sparks and the deputies sat out on lawn chairs with a bunch of us, chatting and drinking sodas. It was obvious that the deputies, in particular, were uneasy about poking their noses into our business. In Texas, a person's right to privacy is basic.

Relating to the visitors in a relaxed, good-ol'-boy way, David joshed the deputies for giving him a hard time over the Roden affair. "You guys kinda screwed us over on that one," he said amiably, and the lawmen gave aw-shucks grins. "Wanna go fishing down at the lake?" David offered. "Call us anytime. No hassles." Later, one of the deputies remarked to a *Waco Tribune-Herald* reporter: "You know, the problem with those people out there is not that they're weird. The problem is that they're misunderstood."

The Child Protective Services investigation was formally closed on April 30, 1992. "None of the allegations could be verified," the official report stated. "The children denied being abused in any way by adults in the compound. They denied any knowledge of other children being abused. The adults consistently denied participation in or knowledge of any abuse to children. Examinations of children produced no indication of current or previous injuries."

Sparks later claimed that she made an objection to her supervisor about the closing of the case, feeling it should be left open for the time being. However, in an April 1992 taped phone conversation between Sparks and David about her agency's investigation of the community, the tone was very friendly.

I felt that Sparks's concern was genuine, and I knew she was horrified when so many of our kids died. And there was a certain brutal logic to the thought she later voiced, that the children might still be alive today if they'd been officially removed from Mount Carmel, even though the abuse charges were unfounded.

Though the question of our treatment of the children might seem to have been resolved in early 1992, these false allegations surfaced as a blip on the radar screen of the ATF. A few months later the blip flared up, ignited by an issue actually within the ATF's jurisdiction: guns.

The ATF's original interest in us sprang from the child abuse charges. In late March 1992—while Sparks's investigation was pending—neighbors told us they'd seen men dressed in SWAT gear practicing forced-entry assaults on an abandoned farmhouse nearby. In May, agents from the ATF's New Orleans office set up a telephoto pole camera on a rise a few miles away to spy on us. Around the same time, we noticed a couple of men in white smocks, the kind medical personnel wear, at the ranch next door. They had beepers, and they drove away in a hurry when two of our people tried to talk to them. Steve went to the Waco sheriff's office to ask about these troubling actions, but a deputy assured us that we weren't under any kind of surveillance, so far as he knew.

These incidents were ominous. Steve, for one, was troubled enough to phone Graeme Craddock in Australia to warn him that the prophecies about the End Time might soon be fulfilled and he ought to return to Mount Carmel.

The ATF really zeroed in as soon as June 1992, when a UPS driver discovered dummy grenades in a packet he was bringing to Mount Carmel. He told the Waco sheriff's department, which promptly contacted the ATF. Examining shipping and sales records, the agency learned that ninety pounds of powdered aluminum and black gunpowder had previously been delivered to Mount Carmel. Aluminum and black gunpowder can be used to make illegal grenades; or they may be legally used to reload spent rifle cartridges. The ATF also found that David and Paul Fatta had bought devices capable of converting semiautomatic rifles to fully automatic. From this incident grew the allegation that we were stockpiling illegal weapons in preparation for an armed assault on the government.

Actually, our involvement with firearms had more to do with business than self-defense. The community operated a stall at gun shows (the Mag Bag, slang for an ammo vest) to buy and sell weapons and other gear. The Mag Bag offered a catalog of military gear, including gas masks, MREs, flak jackets, dummy grenades, and ammunition magazines. The women at Mount Carmel, many of whom were skilled seamstresses, sewed custom-cut hunting vests—some of them machoed-up with dummy grenades—for an outfit called "David Koresh Survival Wear," a sexy name with more hype than substance. Paul Fatta was a shrewd businessman, and he had helped make the gun business into a good source of cash for the community. Paul and Mike Schroeder visited gun shows around the state, buying and selling weapons. Much of the time the stock of firearms used in these transactions never left the boxes they came in.

Mount Carmel's operating expenses were around $15,000 a month, or $125 per person. Some of this money came from the businesses we ran, like the gun-show booth, the auto shop, the seamstresses, and so on. Other funds were provided by members who worked outside the community, such as Wayne Martin, who ran a law practice in Waco, Jeff Little, who had a job as a computer programmer, Scott Sonobe and others involved in the Yardbirds landscaping business, and Perry Jones's son, David, who delivered mail. Another source of funds came from people who were affluent, like Paul Fatta and Donald Bunds. Members donated money and property, and I believe one elderly couple gave between $250,000 and $500,000 to the community.

Perry Jones controlled the accounts, handling the bills and doling out cash when David needed it. He and David usually decided together when some extravagance should be bought, like the kids' go-carts and minibikes. Steve, the shrewd operator, negotiated any deals we made with outsiders, and Paul ran the gun business. These four were the community's financial Mighty Men.

(The term "Mighty Men" came from King David's psalms. It was not a term for some inner core of armed guards protecting David, as some people later claimed. Actually, it could be applied to anyone who was given strength by faith, including women. To me, the name sounded silly, a play on Mighty Mouse. One time I was doing pushups near the drum set, and David laughed, saying, "Look at Thibodeau fixing to be a Mighty Man.")

David always seemed to have a roll of bills in his jeans. Whenever I needed some pocket money, I'd tap him for it; not that I had much use for cash, stuck out at the Anthill. Maybe there was a childish dependency in the monetary arrangement I had with David—"hitting up the old man for a sawbuck," as he put it cheerfully—but it didn't bother me. I never felt demeaned by any aspect of our relationship.

The fascination with guns was, in a sense, a kind of overgrown boys' game played by David, Paul, Mike, and a few others. David loved taking the weapons apart, cleaning and greasing them, reassembling them. It was a sensual pleasure, a feeling for the way things work. He had a gift for machines, knew their shapes in his fingertips, enjoying a kind of intimacy with nuts-and-bolts technology.

For the rest of us, shooting was hardly a major part of our daily lives. During the first couple weeks I was at Mount Carmel, David brought out a shotgun, and we took potshots at an old car wreck. After that, I had some intermittent, rather casual target practice in which someone tried to show me how to keep my breath steady and my trigger finger easy while firing an AR-15 rifle. The gun's rough kick startled me, and I tried to avoid any more target practice. Personally, I hadn't grown up with guns. My parents loathed them; as a kid I'd secretly played with a friend's BB gun, but shooting harmless birds and squirrels wasn't my bag. All that fascination with muzzle velocities, trigger pull weights, and upper and lower receivers went right over my head.

Actually, these shooting sessions were seldom serious, though David said that everyone should know how to handle a gun, including the women, who practiced with handguns. For most of us, weapons were something we stayed away from as much as possible.

Gun training at Mount Carmel was certainly perfunctory. After April 19, for instance, Graeme Craddock told the Texas

Rangers that his entire experience with firearms had been to fire ten rounds from a pistol and five to ten rounds from a semiautomatic rifle. Since David considered him inexperienced with guns, he was issued an AR-15 and a 9mm pistol, but no ammunition.

However, David did say we should never allow ourselves to be attacked without fighting back. Jesus may have gone meekly to the cross, but we should follow his command, according to the apostle Luke, to defend ourselves against anyone who threatened to destroy us. The time is coming, he said, and now is when he that has a cloak should sell it to buy a sword. In David's view, a powerful action against attacking forces was our right and duty as Americans. We should not start any kind of violence, but we must respond fiercely to any armed assault. He had this primal Texan response about the right to bear arms, to protect yourself and your family. "I don't care who they are. Nobody's going to come to my home, with my babies around, without a gun back in their face. That's just the American way," he said on a videotape he sent out during the siege.

David's declaration on self-defense is backed up by the Texas Penal Code, which states: "The use of force to resist an arrest or search is justified; if, before the actor offers any resistance, the peace officer uses, or attempts to use, greater force than necessary to make the arrest or search, and; when and to the degree the actor reasonably believes the force is immediately necessary to protect himself against the peace officer's use or attempted use of greater than necessary force."

Despite my aversion to guns, I unwittingly had a hand in getting David deeper into the business. In September 1990, on my first visit to Mount Carmel, I'd met a girl named Sherry at West Waco's Chelsea Street Pub. It turned out that her stepfather, Henry McMahon, was a local licensed gun dealer. When I mentioned this to David, he asked me to introduce him to McMahon.

Operating under the name Hewitt Handguns, Henry McMahon and his common-law wife, Karen, worked the Texas gun shows. Actually, they'd previously sold some handguns to people living at

Mount Carmel, and Karen's '69 Camaro had been rebuilt and re-stored in our auto shop, located about four miles west of Mount Carmel. David and McMahon did some deals, and McMahon clued David in about how to judge the quality of various firearms to buy for resale. At the time, David knew little about the more sophis-ticated kinds of weaponry, being more familiar with the simple hunting guns he'd used as a kid. "He'd buy cheap guns and shoot them and they would break," McMahon told ATF agents after the February 28 raid. But he was a quick study, and inside a couple of months, McMahon admitted, David knew more than he did.

With typical energy, David plunged into the firearms trade. Since no one at Mount Carmel had a license to trade in weapons, David made a deal with McMahon in which the gun dealer bought and sold guns with funds supplied by us.

McMahon showed David the business, telling him which guns and bullets were going to be banned, so the prices would go way up in value. The value of a converted semiautomatic AK-47, for in-stance, jumped from $500 to $2,000 when the weapon was out-lawed. David saw an opportunity to purchase AR-15 parts cheap, assemble them, and sell the semiautomatics at a big profit to legally registered buyers.

On July 30, 1992, ATF Special Agents Davy Aguilera and Jimmy Skinner visited Henry McMahon to question him about Mount Carmel's "armory." McMahon told the agents that David bought weapons to resell for profit.

While the agents were in his house, McMahon slipped away and telephoned David. "If there's a problem, tell them to come out here," David replied. "If they want to see my guns, they're more than welcome."

McMahon offered the phone to Aguilera. "I've got Koresh on the phone," he said. "If you'd like to go out there and see those guns, you're more than welcome to."

According to McMahon, Aguilera became paranoid, shaking his head and whispering, "No, no!" McMahon had to tell David that the agents refused to talk to him and wouldn't be coming out to Mount Carmel to inspect our weapons. (Aguilera finally came to

Mount Carmel on the day of the ATF's February 28 raid, riding in one of the helicopters that circled our building.)

Agent Aguilera's refusal to come and inspect our weaponry reveals the ATF's secret agenda: their search for an excuse to attack us. As one commentator later remarked, "The agency viewed this operation exclusively through strategic and political lenses, with no attempt to ascertain why this group had guns, and what they might want to do with them, and how the larger citizenry might be assured that no harm would result from the weapons that had been purchased."

Later, ATF official Philip Chojnacki discredited his own agents. There was no reason to inspect our guns, he told Congress in 1995, because "at that particular point in time, the weapons in question were completely legal firearms . . . being transferred from licensed firearms dealer to an individual."

As far as firearms were concerned, we had nothing to hide at that time, so far as I knew. However, it seems that during the summer of 1992 David bought from McMahon a load of legal semiautomatic AR-15 rifles and the devices used to turn them into the equivalent of military M-16s. He probably intended to apply for licenses to convert them, then sell the popular automatic weapons for a profit. However, the conversion of semiautomatic AR-15s to automatic M-16s is a highly specialized procedure, and I wasn't aware back then that anyone at Mount Carmel had the equipment and expertise to actually do this. McMahon got nervous after the ATF's visit and canceled the contract, leaving us with an inventory of unlicensed guns.

When it came right down to it, the only valid argument between the ATF and us was about filling out the right forms and paying the appropriate fees, not the possession of illegal firearms as such. Fully automatic weapons could be bought or converted, if the buyer or owner obtained a permit from the local police and paid a $200 registration fee. In 1993, around a quarter-million U.S. citizens owned legally registered machine guns and sawed-off shotguns.

What federal law prohibits is the "manufacture, possession, transfer, transport, or shipment in interstate commerce [of] machine-guns, machine-gun conversion parts, or explosives which are classified, by Federal law, as machine-guns, and/or destructive devices, including any combination of parts, designed and intended for use in converting any firearms into a machine-gun, or into a destructive device as defined by Federal law, and from which any destructive device may be readily assembled, *without them being lawfully registered in the National Firearms Registration and Transfer record*" (emphasis added).

In other words, even though it was possible that our technicians may have converted some semiautomatic weapons to fully automatic capacity, our punishable offense was not the actual possession of these firearms but our failure to have their conversion registered—an omission that should have cost Mount Carmel a modest fine plus suspended sentences for the people involved in the actual conversion of these rifles.

In their affidavit of probable cause, submitted to obtain their search warrant in early 1993, ATF agents deliberately and maliciously altered a key phrase in the paragraph quoted above, to read: "including any combination of parts, *either* designed *or* intended for use in converting any firearms into a machine-gun." This sleight-of-hand put a sly twist on the crucial demonstration of the intent aspect of probable cause required to authorize the ATF search. The altered language of the affidavit was included in the search warrant signed by U.S. Magistrate Dennis Green on February 25, 1993, three days before the agency's assault on Mount Carmel.

Anyway, the whole issue of weapons being stored at Mount Carmel must be considered against the background of gun ownership in the state of Texas. In 1993, Texas had 68 million registered weapons for 16 million inhabitants—an average of more than four guns for every man, woman, and child! Some people have suggested, tongue-in-cheek, that by Texas standards Mount Carmel had *too few* weapons for its self-defense. In any case, there was no state or federal law limiting the number of firearms anyone may own. We could've filled Mount Carmel with guns from floor to roof, so long as we had the right permits.*

I don't know why David tried to delay or dodge paying the registration fees. He was foolish to have bent the law in this way, and his negligence in this regard only served those who were out to get us. Though I didn't know back then that David hadn't complied with federal firearms registration procedures and that he had some forbidden items such as silencers and live grenades, I should have asked more questions, and David shouldn't have kept most of us in the dark on that score. I blame both myself and him in this regard. But, disliking guns in general, I tried to keep well away from the whole weapons business.

I did accompany Paul and Mike to a couple of gun shows around Texas, but I certainly never heard anyone say anything about stockpiling weapons. Most of the guns we had in storage were treated as inventory for the Mag Bag and remained crated up, ready for transportation and sale. At around 8:00 A.M. on the morning of February 28, 1993, an hour or so before the ATF attacked us, Paul had cleared out the Mount Carmel gun room and had driven away in his pickup to take the weapons to display at a show in Austin.

That's how eager and ready we were for battle on that brutal day.

---

* After the April fire, federal investigators claimed to have discovered around three hundred guns in the vicinity of the charred ruins, plus some illegal items, such as homemade rifle silencers and forty-eight converted, unregistered AR-15s. They said they also found dummy grenades, plus a few exploded ones, and around 500,000 rounds of ammo. I never saw any of these items, and no independent analysts have ever been allowed to examine them. However, during the siege, I did see some grenades, but I could not tell whether they were active or just dummies. In fact, while talking to FBI agents over the phone after the February attack, David sheepishly admitted that we did have some stuff we shouldn't have had. "I mean, hey, if the Vatican can have its own little country, can't I?" he joked. Dick DeGuerin confirmed this. "Koresh told me he had illegal weapons," he said, when the attorney emerged after visiting Mount Carmel during the last weeks of the siege. However, we certainly owned no .50-caliber machine guns, as the feds claimed.

BOOK TWO

Prelude to a Holocaust

9

VISIONS AND OMENS

During the second half of 1992 ominous portents were gathering in the air around Mount Carmel. The signs were internal and external, visionary and temporal, feeding off each other to create an increasing sense that we were entering the last phase of our communal life. Some powerful, unseen force generated by fate seemed to drive our story to the cataclysmic conclusion foretold in Revelation.

"What are you going to do six months from now when this is all surrounded with tanks?" David said one summer afternoon, when four or five of us were finishing off the roof of the three-story residential tower.

My hand, holding the hammer, froze in midair. "They're not going to bring tanks against us!" I exclaimed. "Not *tanks*. That's real paranoid, David."

David answered my challenge obliquely, launching into a commentary on the biblical Nahum: *the chariots shall be with flaming torches.* . . . I only half-listened to him. To me it was inconceivable that the federal government could actually use heavy armor to attack us. *Not in America,* I said silently—*surely?* At heart I'm a true patriot. As a kid I used to dream about fighting at Valley Forge, freezing alongside the rebel colonists battling the British, putting it on the line for life, liberty, and the pursuit of happiness. David's prediction, delivered in a flat, matter-of-fact tone, shocked me deeply.

My faith in America was shaken a few weeks later. On August 22, after sixteen months of armed surveillance of Randy Weaver's cabin in the mountains of northern Idaho by the ATF and the U.S. Marshal Service, Weaver's wife, Vicki, and his fourteen-year-old son, Sammy, were fatally shot by a marksman belonging to the FBI's Hostage Rescue Team. A week later a wounded Weaver was taken to a hospital under heavy guard.

Randy Weaver was not a man we admired. On the contrary, he was a member of the Christian Identity Movement, a separatist group tainted by anti-Semitic rhetoric and a connection to the violent Aryan Nation militia. His ideas were repellent, but we felt that the violent way he'd been dealt with was an ominous portent; our community also lived by beliefs that the mainstream society might not tolerate forever. Also, we were troubled by the government's use of all the machinery of military aggression—including snipers, concealed video cameras, planes, and armed helicopters—against a family with four children. That this could happen in America to Americans sent a collective chill down our spines. (Incidentally, Richard M. Rogers, the commander of the FBI's Hostage Rescue Team at Ruby Ridge in Idaho, would later be involved in the siege of Mount Carmel. And Larry Potts, assistant director of the FBI's Criminal Investigation Section, played a leading backroom role in both events.)

"Is it a dress rehearsal for an attack on Mount Carmel?" David wondered out loud. Looking into his anxious eyes, I wanted to reassure and protest, but I couldn't summon up the conviction to argue with him.

In July, when gun dealer Henry McMahon had phoned David to tell him that ATF agents were at his house asking questions about Mount Carmel, we had our first direct confirmation that the feds were actively focusing on us.

This unwelcome attention became obvious when military helicopters began a series of low-level overflights around Mount Carmel in the summer. The aerial surveillance continued on and off
through the fall and winter.

On January 6, 1993, the Texas Air National Guard sent planes
equipped with infrared radar cameras over Mount Carmel to scan
for heat sources related to a supposed methamphetamine drug lab,
in order to validate one of the trumped-up charges the ATF was
brewing against us. The angry noise of the choppers' blades slicing
the hot air became, for us, the drumbeat of doom. But the kids had
fun, pretending to shoot down the machines, *rat-tat-tat*, whooping
with joy when one of the helicopters dipped as if hit by gunfire.

Despite these ominous events, David did his best to reach out to
the authorities. He invited local deputies to fish in our lake or join
us in target practice, and he kept in contact with children's service
people, to assure them that the kids were happy and healthy. These
attempts to soothe the temporal powers sprang from the worldly
part of David's personality, the man who didn't want trouble.

On the spiritual plane, however, David expected disaster. His
Mount Zion vision had predicted that the End Time would come in
Jerusalem; but after the 1991 Gulf War, David began to speculate
that the first stage in the prophecies of Revelation, the obliteration
of the community, would occur in Waco. *And fear not them which kill
the body, but are not able to kill the soul*, he said bravely, but the look
in his eyes was stark. "The truth will be suppressed," he predicted,
and my heart sank.

During those last months he talked often about the doctrine of
"quickening," which he described as the bringing of the soul into
harmony with the divine. *Quicken thou me in thy way*, the Psalmist
says. For the truly devout, like Livingston Fagan, Mount Carmel became more and more a refuge from the threatening world, a place
where, as he told me, "You can hear God's word, while blocking out
the artificial noise of humanity."

You could say we had created a self-fulfilling prophecy. We might
possibly have weathered most of the charges made against us, including the most serious, like child abuse and gun stockpiling; yet

David was vulnerable on the charge of statutory rape. That made it impossible for him to simply hire an attorney and challenge the authorities to prosecute us or leave us alone, as a totally innocent person or group might have done. Though the charge of statutory rape was never formally made against David, it tainted his claim of innocence on all charges. In that temporal sense, he'd provoked his own persecution—and ours. In a spiritual sense, he was destined to make that provocation, for, as he told us, the Seventh Angel comes clothed with a cloud.

I found all this quite confusing. Were we meant for disaster by divine destiny? Or could we delay or avoid it by placating or bamboozling the authorities? And why was it happening so soon, in 1993, instead of 1995, as David's Jerusalem vision had prophesied?

Wayne Martin told me he believed that we were fated for destruction because we'd somehow let David down, had fallen short of the necessary discipline and harmony to honor our leader's teachings. "We've learned a truth from him that nobody else could teach us," he said, "and in spite of it all, we still couldn't follow a few simple rules that he gave us. I'm overweight, like you. We were supposed to get in shape, we try our best, and still we come up short."

He shook his head. "If disaster strikes, it's our fault. We're the weak links in the chain that leads to God."

I wondered if we'd failed David in a vital sense, by being too much ourselves. Or had David failed himself by being too much himself?

David was the "intercessor," our intermediary between God and man, and this notion was reinforced by a vision Wayne told me David had received long ago, before my time. "David was lying on a bed, crying, 'Where are you God?' Suddenly, the bed fell out from under him and he was floating through space. He came to a place with a concrete wall, miles thick. A light penetrated this wall, an illumination so brilliant it would've obliterated him if the dense wall hadn't shielded him."

Wayne paused, his eyes dazed with the memory of David's telling. "He saw the spirit of Christ, who was himself an intercessor, and a great throng of people beneath the wall, bound for hell. 'Give these people to me, Father,' David pleaded. He was on his knees, crying, 'Father, give them to me!' When David told this to us, he was actually on his knees, reliving the experience, including the tears."

"What happened?"

"The voice said, 'Only those who come to you may you have.' David pleaded for all humanity, interceding for our souls. 'You don't know what love is,' David said. 'It is simply *the finality of the Law.*'" Wayne's smile was seraphic. "I saw love that day, was touched by a dimension in myself I'd never experienced. A dimension of eternity." After a thoughtful pause, he added: "Maybe our moment of eternity is upon us. . . ."

———————

Around that time, David reinstated the ritual of morning and afternoon communions, which had lapsed while we were busy with the construction. At 9:00 A.M. and 3:00 P.M. we gathered for an hour's Bible study, followed by crackers and grape juice. David explained that the community had to strive to intensify its harmony to confront the approaching troubles. Sometimes he seemed to be saying that if we achieved a high level of harmony we might not have to suffer a drastic outcome, but I imagined he was just trying to comfort us, and maybe himself.

We hired a bulldozer to begin excavating the tornado shelter, dubbed the "pit," in the west yard, just beyond where the old yellow school bus was buried. It struck me as odd that we should spend so much energy to protect ourselves from tornadoes when it was the feds who most immediately threatened our safety. David never gave me a clear answer on this, except to say the shelter might be used as a firing range. Whatever its purpose, we broke our backs shoveling earth and pouring concrete for the shelter's walls; nevertheless, the excavation would be only partially roofed when the attack came. We also put fiberglass insulation between the studs of the main building and poured concrete into the wall around the front door to reinforce it against possible attack.

I had a break from the increasingly tense situation in Mount Carmel during a quick visit to Bangor during the late fall. Partly, I was happy to get away from Texas for a while, but also I wanted to head off my mother, who was again pressing to come visit me. I feared that if she visited Mount Carmel and picked up on our dangerous situation she'd insist that I leave the community. This had happened with other people whose relatives had come visiting, like Katherine Andrade, whose mother tried hard to get Kathy to come away with her.

In Bangor, however, Balenda and I found we had very little to say to each other. I was quiet, unwilling to talk about Mount Carmel or Scripture to people who'd be unsympathetic. The only one I could communicate with was my Uncle Bob, and he was impressed by my knowledge of Scripture. "But where's it leading you?" he asked. "To where I have to go," I replied.

I understood my family's concern, and I understood why I couldn't explain things to them. Many of my relatives looked upon me as a black sheep, or, rather, a lamb that had lost its way. There was nothing I could say or do to change that old attitude, so I just kept quiet and waited till I could get back to what I realized was now my true home.

The one person I could really be open with in Bangor was an old friend, Alisa Shaw. I'd exchanged letters with her from time to time, telling her about life in Mount Carmel and David's teachings because she seemed interested. I never saw my role as finding new recruits for Mount Carmel; proselytizing—that's not my style. But David had talked to her on the phone a few times, and Alisa told me when I saw her that she was dying to come to Waco. Knowing how gentle and impressionable she was, I tried to deter her. "That scene is heavy," I warned her. "It could change your life." Frankly, I didn't want to be responsible for Alisa; I had a hard enough time being responsible for myself.

But Alisa was eager to visit Mount Carmel. In February 1993 she came and stayed with us for a while, leaving just a couple of weeks before the ATF raid went down. David sent her home to talk to her family before she decided to come and live with us. During the siege Alisa returned to Waco and tried to get into Mount Carmel, but fortunately the authorities prevented her. Later, her family sent Alisa to a Scripture study camp, which convinced her to follow a different faith.

Back in Mount Carmel, the dark clouds were thickening. Toward the end of the year we got word through the grapevine that the ATF had contacted Marc Breault in Melbourne, Australia. For a while Marc received almost daily calls from officials of the ATF, FBI, State Department, and the Texas Rangers. Marc told it this way in his book: "When the ATF approached me (I did not approach them), they told me they believed Vernon had amassed a huge arsenal of weapons and that some of those were illegal. I strongly advised the ATF that if they were going to arrest Vernon, they do so with no force, that they somehow lure Vernon away from Mount Carmel."

Around this time the ATF approached the Special Forces Command at nearby Fort Hood, asking for help in training agents. Under federal law, the U.S. armed services can only aid law enforcement officers if narcotics are involved, so the ATF lied, saying we were operating a drug lab. This was the hidden reason for their false accusations on this score.

The Green Berets helped the agents build a mock-up of Mount Carmel, including windows that would be shattered in a "dynamic entry." However, Major Philip Lindley of the Army's Judge Advocate General office warned his superiors that the ATF's use of military personnel and equipment in training and in a possible attack violated federal law and could lead to the Army assuming criminal as well as civil liability.

The attack the ATF was planning was officially named Operation Trojan Horse, but the troops on the ground dubbed it "Showtime," and the name stuck. An ATF advance crew arrived in Waco during mid-January 1993, setting up a command post on an airstrip northeast of the town. None of these activities was publicly announced, but by then we were well aware that we were in for a bad time.

Actually, the feds were hard to miss.

At Mount Carmel's gateway, on Double EE Ranch Road directly opposite our main building, were two small houses owned by a rancher named Perry Spoon. One house was occupied, but the other had been empty for years, and Spoon told us he wasn't planning to rent it, so we were surprised to see four men move into the house on January 10, 1993.

What was suspicious about our new neighbors was that they brought with them hardly any furniture or possessions, apart from several large cases and what looked like an elaborate array of camera equipment. For the first few days they passed the time knocking golf balls around in the yard and taking potshots at a target, making their presence obvious in a ham-handed way, trying to pass themselves off as members of a regular household. The four men, in their thirties and forties, wore ritzy Stetsons, drove several spanking-new Chevy Blazers, and sported flash Serengeti sunglasses and Rolex watches—affluent accessories that seemed at odds with the bare-bones condition of the rented farmhouse.

"These guys are weird," Steve Schneider said, immediately suspicious. He sent David Jones, Greg Summers, and Neal Vaega to the house to welcome these neighbors with pizza and beer, but their reaction was startling. One man opened the door, grabbed the pizzas and beer, and slammed the door in the visitors' faces. "They don't want us to see what's going on inside," Steve concluded, when the guys reported back.

However, it soon became clear that these strangers wanted to see what was going on in Mount Carmel. A few days after the beer-and-pizza incident, a couple of them came knocking at our door. They asked to take a look at a rusty, old iron horse walker situated near the pond. Henry McMahon, the gun dealer, was visiting at the time, and a few of us went out with Henry and David to talk to the visitors. They told us they were from Dallas and were looking to buy a country property. One claimed he'd been a ranch foreman in West Texas; but when McMahon asked him how many cattle a West Texas scrub ranch could carry per acre, he got confused.

Hospitable as ever, David showed the men around the prop
erty. One of the visitors, a dark, powerfully built man who introduced himself as Robert Gonzalez, asked David what the tornado
shelter excavation was for, and he seemed doubtful when David
told him. "Boy, you really must be worried about storms," he said.
They had a lot of questions, squinting at the buildings as if sizing
them up as prospective buyers. "The place ain't for sale," Steve said,
and Gonzalez looked blank, missing the irony.

That evening, Gonzalez came around again. David invited him
in and we sat around in the foyer drinking beer. David began to talk
Scripture, and I could see that Gonzalez was uneasy. When Steve asked
him what he did for a living, Gonzalez said that he and his companions were students at Texas State Technical College (TSTC) in Waco.

"What are you studying there?" I asked.

"Philosophy," Gonzalez replied.

We tried not to laugh: Nobody went to TSTC to study philosophy.
When Perry's son, David Jones, who'd attended the college, asked
Gonzalez about the campus, his answers were suspiciously vague.

Gonzalez hung around for a couple of hours, half-listening as
David talked about the Seals, his eyes constantly darting this way
and that, taking in details. But David continued to treat the man
courteously and seriously, as if he were a prospective member of
our community. There was something he liked about Gonzalez,
sensing a troubled but earnest quality in his restless black eyes.

"You're probably with the government, Robert, but I'm not
going to let that bother me," David remarked one morning. Gonzalez opened his mouth to protest, but David waved his denials aside.
"Maybe I can show you something you don't know but might really
want to know. Perhaps you went to a Catholic school and no one
could answer your questions, and maybe I can."

"Maybe you can, Dave," Gonzalez answered, humoring him.
"Maybe so."

After several hours, one of Gonzalez's companions came to
fetch him, obviously worried for his safety. "That's not a bad person," David remarked, when we were alone. "I see something there."

But the new neighbors really worried Wayne. He went into Waco to check their car registrations, and he found they were all named to the same address in Houston, the location of the nearest ATF office. "These people mean us no good," he said.

Gonzalez—whose real name, we discovered, was Robert Rodri-guez—came to visit us frequently during the following weeks. David kept giving him scriptural studies, and I noticed Robert's re-sponse subtly shifting from barely suppressed yawns to active atten-tion. Robert confessed that, when he'd first visited us, he and his fellow agents hadn't even known that the Book of Revelation was in the Bible. "When I mentioned the Seals, one of our guys thought I was talking about a circus act!" he laughed.

We showed him a documentary put together by the Gunown-ers of America titled, *Breaking the Law in the Name of the Law*, about the ATF and its questionable methods. The film was clearly biased against the agency, but, all the same, Robert was visibly shaken.

"Look, I know what it's like to take the heat," he said. For the first time Robert implied that he was an agent. "Some of the things I've had to do—" he began, then left the sentence hanging.

David kept at him with scriptural studies, and Robert was drawn closer to the community, sharing our meals, often remain-ing while we went about our daily routine. Sometimes he stayed till midnight, and several times one or two of his colleagues came to call him away, no longer fearing for his safety as for his grow-ing sympathy for us and respect for our community. During study sessions children clustered around his feet, and he occasionally bounced a little girl he'd taken a shine to on his knee. (Later, during the siege, he said he worried about what might happen to that child; she died.) He talked about playing college football, and I could see he was proud of the power in his linebacker's body.

Despite his growing attachment to us, Robert didn't forget he had an assignment to carry out—namely, to discover how much firepower we possessed and if we were trained to use guns.

One afternoon he came over with a weapon to show David. It was an AR-15 rifle, expertly and recently machined. "Is this a good gun?" Robert asked, pretending to be ignorant about firearms. David disassembled the rifle and examined it. "This gun has a hair trigger, meant for snipers," he said, frowning. "A dangerous weapon, Robert."

Undeterred, Robert then produced a handgun he claimed to have put together from different parts. It was a scary thing, like something out of a James Bond movie, with holes in the side and a laser sight.

Robert pretended to be very surprised. He told David that the gun shop he'd taken the rifle to for machining had seared the pin too much, accidentally making it fully auto. Clearly, he was trying to provoke an admission that we also owned fully automatic weapons, but David kept his cool telling Robert, "I hope you had that taken care of, that's illegal."

Robert later revealed that he reported to his superiors that, for all his snooping, he'd found no evidence of illegal guns or explosives in Mount Carmel. But that did not deter the ATF. It soon became clear that they had an agenda that had nothing do with "probable cause." (At the 1995 congressional hearings, Robert, while testifying, made a blunt statement about his bosses: "They lied to the public.")

Wayne and Steve became concerned that Robert was getting too much inside information about us—information that might be used in a possible assault. But David kept saying he felt he was getting through to Robert, was sure he could turn him, get him to convince his superiors that we weren't a threat to anyone. Steve angrily accused him of being naive, and Wayne suggested we might go to court to try to force the feds to show probable cause for their surveillance of our property. "We can see the camera lens flashing in the sun in the windows of their house," he said. "A judge might help us force the ATF to show its hand, get it out in the open."

David grew impatient with Wayne and Steve. One morning, passing Perry's office, I heard him tell them: "It doesn't matter who the hell these people are or what they're planning. The truth is going to go forward. Maybe there's something in Robert that will respond and he'll tell his superiors that nothing illegal is going on. Perhaps Robert can act as an intermediary. In fact, I think I'll ask him to move in with us for a while, open our doors and hearts to him. What do you say?"

There was an outburst of objections, but from what I overheard David was unmoved. "That's the way I'm going to play it," he insisted. "God has sent Robert to us, and we must trust that gift."

Of course, Robert refused David's offer to come live with us. But in knowing the power of David's sincerity and the force of his mind, I could not dismiss the possibility that the agent might indeed be turned. David treated him like a friend, speaking to the human being under the law enforcement official, and Robert was very human. It was obvious that he was seeking his own kind of truth in the stresses of his life and duty.

In an interview with the *Waco Tribune-Herald* published in May 1993, Rodriguez admitted that David's scriptural studies had almost convinced him. "He was close," he told the reporter. "The thing that probably saved me is I didn't have to stay there."

———

Apart from the visits of Rodriguez and his crew, there were other incidents that showed we were being scrutinized. On January 27, a guy with long hair, wearing sloppy clothes, turned up at our door, pretending to be a UPS employee. He asked to use the bathroom, and David Jones sent him to the men's outhouse. When the man left, David called the sheriff's office to complain about being spied upon.

Around this time, Mark England of the *Waco Tribune-Herald* phoned David a couple of times. He was interviewing people for a series the paper was preparing on David and the community, and he asked David for comment. David invited England to visit Mount Carmel or to meet with him in Waco, but England persistently refused. It was obvious to me, listening to the conversation, that the reporter didn't want to hear our side of the story for fear it might sully his subjectivity.

"They're going to trash us," Steve said miserably. "We'll sue," Wayne suggested. But David merely shrugged.

To me, these omens signified that events would definitely end badly—and soon. Oddly enough, I was exhilarated by that possibility. "I've been in this for a couple of years now, just waiting for this stuff to happen," I told Jaime. "Let them come!" He looked at me askance, but I argued that, at last, the prophecies might be fulfilled, providing a kind of confirmation that we had been true to David's teachings and hadn't put up with the hardships of life on the Anthill for nothing.

At the same time, I was truly scared shitless. The thought of being blown away gave me night sweats. Yet I was in a state of mind in which I hoped for something—anything—to happen. The music had faded out of my life, I'd hardly touched the drums for months, and, apart from that one lapse, I hadn't had sex for more than two years. I'd learned a lot about myself, had established some control over my appetites and impulses, had achieved some insight into a more profound way of being. I had become capable of thinking at a level I'd never imagined possible. But now something just had to happen. That was my gut feeling in response to the clouds gathering over our heads. I imagined a dramatic lightning storm ripping the sky, offering a release for all my pent-up energy.

However, I wondered what was actually going on in David's mind. Was he loaded down with a moral as well as a spiritual responsibility in this situation? Did he feel any trepidation that his faith in Scripture might cost all of us our lives? And if he did, how might he act? Could he simply surrender to the feds, offer himself as a sacrifice to save us, especially the forty-three children in his care? Or were we all to be sacrificed? I wanted to talk to him about these thoughts, but somehow I couldn't find the right way to phrase them. Also, I feared they might show up the gaps in my understanding. For David, Revelation was the key text. And unlike many of the books of the Old Testament, Revelation is a mystical, not a moral, story. In St. John, punishments are rained down alike upon the virtuous and the vicious. For the virtuous, such pains are part of the withering experience, the process of purification; for the vicious, they are just damnation. So we, like Job, would likely suffer terrible torments on the way to becoming God's true people. For David, a surrender to temporal authority would be a betrayal of his prophetic role; a betrayal that would damn him, and all of us. In his light, since God had not forsaken him, he couldn't forsake God.

Despite my terrors, I wanted to share the community's fate, whatever David and the forces gathering against us decided it might be. However, a couple of weeks before the ATF attack, I had a disturbing hint that I might be excluded from the community's worst scenario.

On February 13, my twenty-fourth birthday, David, Steve, and I drove into Waco to have a celebratory evening meal at a Denny's. In light of what we expected to happen, the occasion was rather solemn. We spoke little, but I felt very close to David and Steve; they were like family to me, only more so.

Steve was talking about the people "across the street," when I said, out of the blue, that the one thing I wanted most was not to be left out. "I don't care what happens," I declared. "I don't care if the music goes forward or not, if we die or go to jail. I just don't want to be left without the group."

This outburst startled me, but I meant it at that moment. And in saying it, I realized how deeply I'd come to identify myself with the community—to the point of sharing a common violent end, if necessary. The fear of being left out was now greater than any fear of death. Of course, death was an abstraction, and the Mount Carmel community and my friends there were very concrete. All the same, I was utterly sincere.

David was silent. His face was stony, and my blood ran cold. He just stared at me for about thirty seconds. In that instant I realized that he believed I was going to be a survivor, whether I liked it or not. The premonition that I would not be killed in the coming confrontation with the authorities seemed more a condemnation than a reassurance.

The keystone in the ATF's attack plan was the scripting of an affidavit as the basis for a warrant to search Mount Carmel and arrest David. A corrupt document on its face, the affidavit served as the original act that brought about the obliteration of our community. The ATF affidavit was built upon deliberate deceptions concerning charges that were legitimately under ATF jurisdiction, such as firearms violations; however, it raised issues that were not the agency's concern, such as child abuse and drug trafficking. (We only got to see the sealed warrant during the siege, on March 19, weeks after the ATF attack. For the public, the warrant remained sealed until after the fire, too late for the media to examine it and question its validity.)

The most blatant lie in the ATF affidavit was the drug charge. ATF agents told Texan officials that the community was "involved in drug trafficking." In addition, the ATF involved IRS agents by dropping hints of drug "money laundering." These trumped-up allegations allowed the ATF to requisition military materiel, normally forbidden to nonmilitary agencies under the 1878 Posse Commitatus Act. (The drug charge dated back to George Roden, who had allowed speed dealers to operate in Mount Carmel during the mid-1980s. But local law officers knew that when David—who hated drugs—took over Mount Carmel in 1987, he'd kicked out the dopers and called the Waco sheriff to have the methamphetamine lab removed.)

A few weeks after the initial ATF assault, ATF spokesman David Troy blandly denied that there ever was any "suspicion of illegal drug activity" in Mount Carmel. Later, sources within the ATF quietly admitted to reporters that the drug-lab story was "a complete fabrication," concocted to deflect sharp questions from Texas officials about the deceitful use of the National Guard and other state agencies. When challenged for their "dishonesty and misrepresentation" by the then-governor of Texas, Ann Richards, Troy contradicted himself with a claim that an "infrared overflight [by] a British military aircraft brought over from England" had found evidence of a meth lab in our building. According to Bill Cryer, her former spokesman, Richards "was surprised, and she was furious about the original attack. She thought it was unnecessary."

At the 1995 congressional hearings a New Hampshire Republican congressman, Bill Zeliff, commented that "ATF agents responsible for preparing the affidavits knew or should have known that many of the statements they were making were false."

Special Agent Davy Aguilera, the mastermind behind the corrupt affidavit, had visited Henry McMahon's house in July 1992, when Aguilera refused David's invitation to come and inspect our weapons. Apart from listing the legal gun parts and explosive ingredients in Mount Carmel, Aguilera's affidavit claimed that an "informant" had seen magazines like *Shotgun News* in Mount Carmel, offering that up as evidence we were a dangerous bunch. But *Shotgun News* is an established trade magazine with close to 150,000 subscribers.

Aguilera also interviewed a number of former community members who'd turned against David, including Jeannine and Robyn Bunds, Poia Vaega, David Block, and, of course, Marc Breault. Breault told Aguilera that David might kill agents who tried to serve him with a warrant; or, if we were forewarned, we'd hide all our guns. Marc also asserted that David might order a mass suicide or start a "holy war" if agents tried to investigate Mount Carmel. The ATF's affidavit also quoted social worker Joyce Sparks as saying that David had told her that "when he 'reveals' himself the riots in Los Angeles would pale in comparison to what was going to happen in Waco." However, Sparks said she heard this on April 6, 1992, weeks before the L.A. riots broke out on April 30. Throughout the affidavit the loaded word "cult" was used to describe and damn us.

Aguilera even misrepresented an incident in which a neighbor of ours had claimed he'd heard a machine gun firing on our property. When deputies investigated the complaint, they found that the supposed machine gun was actually a perfectly legal "hellfire device," a trigger attachment that merely simulates the sound of a machine gun—nothing more than a grown-up toy that appealed to some of our more macho characters. In the affidavit, however, it was simply stated that a neighbor had reported machine-gun fire, without explaining the rest.

Also, there were gross technical inaccuracies about firearms, all in a document prepared by an agency that was supposed to regulate them. For example, the affidavit declared that David had bought devices called "upper and lower receivers" to modify AK-47 rifles to fire as full automatics. However, any gun expert could have explained that an AK-47 has a solid receiver that cannot be deconstructed.

To top things off, David was portrayed as a raving child molester and abuser. Poia Vaega claimed that she'd been "imprisoned" for three and a half months and that her sister, Doreen Saipaia, had been physically and sexually abused. But in a February 23 memo, later reported by the *Dallas Morning News*, the FBI stated that no information had been developed to verify allegations of "child abuse and neglect, tax evasion, slavery, and reports of possible mass destruction." Apart from the falsity of all these charges, the point is that none of them, except the firearms issue, were under the ATF's jurisdiction.

In fact, the ATF blatantly ignored the FBI, along with Texas authorities at every level, deeming them untrustworthy. The ATF flew Marc Breault in from Australia in January, and Kiri Jewell's father, David, an ally of Marc Breault's, revealed later that he was transported to and from Waco by the ATF "because there was a concern of [*sic*] the integrity of local law enforcement." The ATF's overall concern was to grab for itself all the glory that would result from a raid against Mount Carmel. Well in advance of the event, ATF Special Agent Sharon Wheeler planned a press conference to feature the triumphant attack on Mount Carmel immediately after it was concluded. For days before February 28, she phoned TV stations and other media to invite them to attend. And ATF representatives collaborated with the local *Tribune-Herald* for months during the time the newspaper was preparing its "Sinful Messiah" series on David. The agency told the paper's editors when it was going to mount its assault, and the *Tribune-Herald* arranged to begin publishing its articles at the same time.

In truth, the ATF was badly in need of some good press. The botched Ruby Ridge engagement had shown the agency in its worst light thus far—incompetent and trigger-happy. In addition, allegations of sexual harassment by female ATF agents were aired in a segment on CBS's *60 Minutes* during January 1993. As a consequence, the ATF seemed to many inside and outside government to have lost its coherence and perhaps its purpose. It was said that its law enforcement functions could be more efficiently handled by other agencies, such as the FBI, and its funds had long been threatened by federal budget-cutters.

Facing a congressional budget hearing on March 10, 1993, the ATF was sure that a video of a dramatic raid on Mount Carmel would mend its image. The bureau leaders seemed to envisage the attack as an episode on a reality-TV program like *Cops*, in which the cameras follow law enforcement officers on actual operations.

As I pointed out earlier, the ATF affidavit fudged the crucial issue of proof of our intent to use guns for criminal purposes. Even ATF chief Stephen Higgins later confessed that the warrant was weak in this regard. Though we were legally "ordering various parts and components and bringing them onto the premises," Higgins explained, he had no valid reason to believe we intended any illegal use whatsoever of our guns.

The issue of intent is central here, and it deserves an explanation. For example: It's illegal to own an unregistered sawed-off shotgun; but that does not mean that anyone who owns a standard shotgun and a hacksaw automatically intends to cut off its barrels. Intent must be demonstrated under law before officials are allowed to come and inspect a person's weapons, and the ATF had no real evidence of intent in our case.

There's another legal issue to consider in preparing a warrant: "staleness." In a later comment on the ATF's affidavit, Professor Edward McGlynn Gaffney Jr., a noted expert on constitutional law, declared that "the general rule is that information submitted to a magistrate must be based on recent information that supports the conclusion that the item sought in a search warrant is probably still in the place to be searched." Most of the information Aguilera and his colleagues gleaned from people like Marc Breault was years old, yet those "facts" formed the core of the document submitted to U.S. Magistrate Dennis Green. "I conclude that . . . the [ATF] raid was an improper exercise of governmental authority," Gaffney wrote.

Gaffney also concluded that "no one has yet adduced credible evidence that Koresh's community was likely to come out of their compound with guns blazing. . . . All the evidence of 'inciting or producing imminent lawless action' points to the BATF and the FBI, not to the Branch Davidians."

In any event, the warrant issued by Judge Green on February 25 was not the "no-knock" variety that allows law enforcement officers to burst into a place without warning—the infamous dynamic entry. It was, in fact, the kind of warrant that requires law officials to knock and request entry. Only if such peaceful access is denied may violent means be used. Under federal law, an officer or agent serving such a search warrant "may break open any outer or inner door or window of a house, or any part of a house, or anything therein, if, after notice of his authority and purpose, he is refused admittance." The ATF's own manual states: "Officers are required to wait a reasonable period of time to permit the occupants to respond before forcing entry." This is the Fourth Amendment's prohibition of unreasonable search and seizure in action.

Former FBI Special Agent Clinton R. Van Zandt, who was assigned to Waco three weeks after the February raid, later declared: "I believe that the initial confrontation between the ATF and the Branch Davidians should not have taken place, at least not as an armed confrontation between citizens and those sworn to protect the citizens."

Apart from all this, it was obvious that David could have been arrested outside Mount Carmel at any time during the month of February prior to the ATF raid. After all, he was the only one actually named in the affidavit, and if the ATF's main intention was to take out our leader, the agents need never have mounted their massive assault.

In January and February, many of us, including David, regularly went jogging along Double EE, right past the house where Robert Rodriguez and the other ATF agents were living. A couple of times I saw a big truck pull out of the house's driveway. The three guys with cowboy hats and Chuck Norris mustaches sitting in the front seat waved to us as we ran by. Clearly, they could've arrested David, or any of us, at any time. During this period David went into Waco on several occasions and could have been quietly taken into custody.

But that would have spoiled the ATF's dynamic-entry photo-op. As Congressmen Bill McCollum and Bill Zeliff, co-chairs of the House investigation into the Waco siege, commented: "In making this decision ATF agents exercised extremely poor judgement, made erroneous assumptions and ignored the foreseeable perils of their course of action."*

As it happened, Showtime was almost upstaged by a far more threatening occurrence. On February 26, two days before the planned attack on Mount Carmel, Islamic fundamentalists bombed New York City's World Trade Center. Six people died, and more than a thousand others were injured.

Immediately, John P. Simpson, U.S. Treasury's acting secretary for enforcement, directed that the Waco raid be called off, citing "grave reservations over the adequacy of precautions to ensure the safety of ATF agents and the Davidians." Army special forces briefing papers from that period reveal that the ATF expected casualties, including agents as well as "civilians."

---

* ATF intelligence chief David Troy would trip over his own shoelaces at the congressional hearings. First he claimed that the agents would have arrested David outside in the weeks before the raid if they had seen him, but he forgot to mention that the warrant for David's arrest was only issued three days before the attack. Then he said the trouble was that David never got personally involved in buying prohibited firearms, so there was no valid reason to charge or arrest him!

Assistant Secretary of the Treasury Ron Noble agreed with Simpson, but ATF Director Higgins insisted the raid should proceed, assuring Simpson and Noble that "those directing the raid were instructed to cancel the operation if they learned that its secrecy had been compromised." This was a surprising remark, given that the ATF agents in the Waco area had made no effort to conceal their preparations and had already alerted the media.

The subsequent Treasury Department report revealed that there was in fact no contingency plan to postpone the raid and that agents had not been instructed what to do if they "were met with either an organized ambush or scattered pockets of resistance." In the self-made disaster that was about to unfold, the ATF would bitterly regret its lack of any fall-back strategy when it came at us with guns blazing.

10

SHOWTIME

The Saturday, February 27, edition of the *Waco Tribune-Herald* was a lulu. An old photo of David, sporting long hair and a tie, accompanied a tabloid headline in bold type: "THE SINFUL MESSIAH: PART ONE."

The text ran: "If you are a Branch Davidian, Christ lives on a threadbare piece of land 10 miles east of Waco called Mount Carmel.

"He has dimples, claims a ninth-grade education, married his legal wife when she was 14, enjoys a beer now and then, plays a mean guitar, reportedly packs a 9mm Glock and keeps an arsenal of military assault rifles, and willingly admits he is a sinner without equal."

The sensational screed ran on to list all the charges against David included in the arrest warrant. In a front-page sidebar and inside editorial, the newspaper demanded to know why the authorities had allowed David to exist. "How long before they will act?" the editorial writer asked disingenuously, knowing full well that the ATF was about to launch its attack. Additional installments of a seven-part series were promised over the next week, covering such juicy topics as "Marc Breault, the faithful follower," "The grim daily life of the Davidians," and "Preying on the children."

"Well," David said, glancing up from the paper, "I guess this is it." His voice was squeezed with emotion. I gazed around the room and saw a collective, dazed expression, the look people have in that last instant at the top of the roller coaster before the car starts its sickening dive. But my main feeling was one of relief. At last the waiting period was over, and we'd soon grapple with whatever providence had in store for us.

"What do you think? . . ." a woman asked, trailing off.

She, like the rest of us, didn't want to articulate our worst fears, all the more scary because they were undefined.

That Saturday seemed to go on forever. The guys played some desultory games of football, and the women did their chores. I watched the rainy Texas sunset that evening and felt I was living in a highly symbolic moment—the end of our world, if not the end of the whole world. I was simultaneously exhilarated and terrified. I didn't want to die, but I was now so identified with the community that the prospect of sharing its biblical destiny made my heart thump with excitement. It troubled me, though, that I might never see my family again, especially my mother, who, by the light of our faith, would be damned. I wished with all my heart that it might be otherwise, but I was powerless to change fate. At the same time I felt I was going through this experience partly on my family's behalf, that my sacrifice might save them from the general damnation. I hoped they would understand this and be proud that I'd finally amounted to something.

That night, I was part of a small group that sat around discussing the firepower the feds could summon up against us. Clearly, it was awesome. We didn't know for sure how many armed agents were assembled to attack us; based on rumors we'd heard, estimates ranged from fifty to a hundred. All of them would be heavily armed, backed up by helicopters and armored vehicles, perhaps even tanks. There was some wild talk about flamethrowers and napalm—the biblical "lake of fire"—but that was too fanciful for me. Compared to the feds', our weaponry was puny. Even if we did possess some automatic weapons, our main defense comprised semiautomatic rifles and pistols. And only a fraction of our community could or would handle weapons.

Of the 130 or so people in our community, forty-three were children fifteen years of age and under, another forty-five were women. Of the men, a number were elderly; others, like me, detested guns. Though firearms had been distributed to most of the adults a few days earlier, I wasn't given a 9mm automatic until the siege began. Even then, I preferred to keep the pistol under my bunk rather than in my pocket; that way, there was less chance I might accidentally shoot myself. Besides, the idea of actually aiming a weapon at another human being utterly repelled me.

So far as I knew, Paul Fatta and his son, Kalani, planned to take a batch of guns to a show in Austin the next day, and he had no intention of changing his plans. So if it came down to a firefight, our core group of useful defenders was barely a handful, and our gun "stockpile" was far from formidable. True, we felt we had right on our side—the right to defend our property and ourselves against "unreasonable search and seizure." But that was merely a phrase; it wouldn't deflect bullets.

We didn't know exactly when the feds were coming, so they might surprise us any time, late at night or early morning. "You could wake up with a gun in your mouth," Greg said grimly. This image chilled me to the marrow. But I still could not quite believe that the U.S. government would actually mount a military-style assault on a community with women and children. Everything American in me was stunned by the possibility that *my own government* might wipe us out. *Where's Paul Revere when we need him?* I thought childishly. *Where are the Minute Men who should stand by our side?*

"Surely they won't get away with it?" someone said, and I hoped he was right. *Dammit, he had to be right!* Otherwise, everything I'd ever felt about this great country was a crock of shit.

Steve came into the room, and we talked about keeping the kids and their mothers in the concrete vault off the cafeteria. But the consensus was that such a move would scare the children and should be delayed until absolutely necessary.

"We're all in the same boat here," Steve said. "Our fate belongs to all of us. Don't be afraid. The prophecies are being fulfilled."

Steve went on to repeat David's notion of "translation"—being swept up into heaven without actually having to die, like the prophet Elijah, who was seized by a whirlwind and lifted into the blue, following God's fiery chariot. As Steve spoke, his voice trembled with a kind of exhilaration that infected the rest of us.

But after he left there was a general letdown. For most of us in that room the concept of translation was rather too abstract to apply to our actual situation. I, for one, felt I lacked the spiritual power or simple worthiness to follow Elijah's famous example.

That night, I sat for long hours staring out the window at the dark, flat, wet Texas plain, trying to imagine it as the landscape of Armageddon. *Why was I here, in this miserable place?* I wondered, not for the first time. Why had I bumped into David that day at Guitar Center? Just then, Sunset Boulevard seemed more distant than Jupiter, and I yearned for a rocket ship to carry me back there.

Why was I here?

I tried to answer the question as honestly as I could. The truth was mixed, an amalgam of the positive and negative aspects of my personality.

Positively, I'd had enough faith in my intuitions to trust David and follow him down the road of his teachings, even though it meant putting myself in harm's way. As a result, I'd discovered a valuable part of me I hadn't consciously known existed: a spiritual dimension that had expanded my soul. I'd found a structure I could accept despite its rigors and had achieved some control over my appetites. Negatively, I'd done all this in a kind of lazy dream, never really thinking anything all the way through.

So how real were the gains I'd made in the past two and a half years? Had I internalized this spiritual discipline sufficiently enough to continue it on my own if Mount Carmel were destroyed and David were imprisoned or killed? Or did I still have to have him around to guide me?

And if, as David had implied, I survived Mount Carmel's possible destruction, what then?

There were few answers to all these questions, and I ended up shivering with worry and self-doubt in the wet night.

———————

At 8:00 A.M. the next day, Agent Robert came knocking at our door, brandishing Part Two of the *Waco Tribune-Herald*'s "Sinful Messiah" series. We gathered around in the foyer while David read parts of it aloud.

The second installment featured Marc Breault, the "faithful follower" turned relentless enemy. It told about Marc's meeting with Perry Jones while he was attending Loma Linda University, a Seventh-day Adventist institution, in Southern California. He spoke about being impressed by David's sincerity in admitting he had sex with young girls. "This guy was saying it straight out," Marc told the reporter.

The article went on to give a cockeyed version of our daily routine, portraying the men in the community running obstacle courses at dawn while David slept on into the afternoon. Professor Gaffney's comments on the stale nature of the information gleaned from Marc and included in the affidavit applied equally to the article: True or false, Marc's "facts" were at least four years old.

David read aloud the conclusion of Part Two, which quoted another former member saying: "Generally in the quiet evenings, an introspective, self-absorbed malaise seemed to overshadow the place as individuals perhaps contemplated their grim future." He looked at our intent faces. "What about that?" he demanded. "'Grim future' may be truly prophetic, huh?"

Robert shuffled uneasily, trying to gauge our reaction. The day was gloomy, the sun trying to break through the foggy morning sky after the night's rain. The air was charged with tension, but David seemed amazingly cool.

Though we were unsure when the attack would come, David acted as if he knew it was imminent. "I heard that last night the ATF guys in Waco were boasting about coming out here and busting us up real good in the morning," David said, watching Robert's face. He went on to say he'd found out that the Waco hotels were filled with agents and that there was a rumor that local hospitals had been warned to prepare beds for casualties. "Probably ours," David said dryly.

Robert cleared his throat as if to respond, but nothing came out.

"Well, Robert, they're coming to get me," David said.

Flustered by the calm certainty in David's voice, the agent's protestations were feeble. Robert was nervous as a cat, his eyes skittering this way and that, and I wondered why he was with us. If an attack were in the offing, surely he would fear being caught and held hostage? My conclusion was that Robert had come to do some last-minute spying, that maybe he hoped to escape before the shit hit the fan, but without warning us.

David started talking Scripture to him, choosing as a lesson the passage in Nahum, *His fury is poured out like fire, and the rocks are thrown down by him.* Robert was sweating, and I sensed that he wanted to get the hell out. I wondered why he didn't just get up and leave, unless he was under orders to hang on until the last second. Or maybe he was simply transfixed by the tension of the moment. David had certainly gotten to Robert, and over the past few weeks he'd come to know us, so the thought of what was in store for our community must have chilled him.

In the next hour, as David talked to Robert, we were plagued by telephone calls from reporters at the *Waco Tribune-Herald.* Those eager beavers of disaster were keen to find out what we thought of their melodramatic trash. I think Steve fielded the calls, but I don't know what he said to the journalists, or whether he just told them to get lost. Since they already knew the raid was about to go down, those ghouls were obviously after a scoop. Later, the ATF tried to blame the newspaper for warning us about the attack and eliminating the "element of surprise."

Around 9:00 A.M., Perry's son, David Jones, arrived. His expression was agitated, and he seemed to be bursting with bad news. Noticing Robert, he rushed by us toward the chapel, where his father was sitting in a pew, praying. David gestured to his dad to join him in the telephone room between the foyer and the chapel. A moment later Perry came out and pretended to David that he was wanted on the phone—long-distance from England. David vanished into the telephone room, and we all waited in silence. Robert kept looking at the door, fidgeting, obviously desperate to leave yet still in the grip of whatever held him captive.

Apparently, David Jones was driving toward Mount Carmel when he bumped into a TV cameraman who asked directions to "Rodenville," a name that was once used by the locals for Mount Carmel. Because David Jones's car had the U.S. Postal Service logo on its door (he was a mail carrier) the cameraman assumed he wasn't a member of our community. But David Jones had grown up in Mount Carmel. He was David Koresh's brother-in-law and Rachel Koresh's brother.

Alerted by this encounter, David Jones sped toward Mount Carmel. On the way, he crossed a station wagon loaded with armed men in dark combat gear and riot helmets and glimpsed the yellow letters "ATF" blazoned on their backs. His ears were pricked by the sound of approaching helicopters as he hurtled along the dusty road toward our gate.

Listening at the door to the telephone room, I heard hurried whispers, David Jones's slow, country drawl alternating with his father's high-pitched rattle and David Koresh's steady response. The phrase "It's going down now" was repeated several times, and all of a sudden Koresh's voice sounded shaky. That worried the hell out of me. We all looked to him to set the tone, and if he was that disturbed by what David Jones was telling him, we were all in deep trouble.

There was a sudden pause in the conversation in the telephone room. Then Koresh said, "I'll talk to Robert. Maybe he can get them to delay it."

When David came back into the foyer, his face was gray and his hands were trembling. "They're coming," he said, confirming our fears.

Robert stood up uncertainly, stumbling over his chair. For a moment it seemed he might deny David's statement, but he said nothing, just edged a step or two closer to the front door.

"You've got to do what you've got to do, Robert," David said, repeating one of Mount Carmel's mantras.

The sentence was double-edged. What Robert had to do as an ATF agent was his dire duty; what he had to do as a man who'd seen the true nature of our community was to try and convince his superiors to resolve the coming confrontation peacefully.

David held out his hand to Robert. "Good luck," he said as they shook. Robert turned and hurried out, and I sensed from the way he hunched his shoulders that he half-expected to be shot in the back.

A second later, we heard the alarm bleeping in Robert's pickup. Perry Jones looked out the window and saw the truck roaring down the driveway, lights flashing, as if he were signaling his fellow agents in the farmhouse near our gate. As we later learned, a panicked Robert phoned the ATF raid commander, Special Agent Charles Sarabyn, from the house to warn him we knew the assault was coming. Then he sped toward the command center ten miles away, to talk to Sarabyn personally; when he arrived the place was almost empty.

"Everything was very quiet, very quiet," Robert recalled. "I went outside and sat down, and I remember I started to cry."

————

Meanwhile, the attack convoy was on its way from the assembly point at Fort Hood, fifty miles southwest of Waco. Trundling toward us were eighty vehicles, stretching out for a mile along the northbound lanes of I-35. Huddled in a couple of cattle trailers hauled by trucks in the middle of the convoy, and in the accompanying vehicles, were eighty or so ATF agents in full combat gear. To provide footage for the ATF's record of the coming glorious victory, each agent was equipped with a camera along with his weapon, his nylon handcuffs, and some flashbang grenades.

Half a dozen snipers were already in position around Mount Carmel, and three National Guard helicopters—two Apaches and one Sikorsky Blackhawk—were bearing down. Completing the scenario, a crowd of journalists and camera crews, like the lost cameraman David Jones had come across, were closing in on Mount Carmel.

After Robert left us, some of the women went upstairs, hustling the kids into their rooms. Other mothers gathered together in the base of the tower at the back of the second floor, reckoning it was probably the safest area, being farthest from the front door and protected above by two floors.

I went to fetch my pistol but thought better of it. Armed, I'd probably be more dangerous to myself than to any attacker; unarmed, I felt more innocent.

Concerned for Michele and the children, I went looking for them. Serenity regarded me with her big eyes. "Tib-o-*doe*," she whispered, glad to see me. I tried to imagine what must be going through the mind of an imaginative four-year-old at that moment. I hugged her and the twins and asked Michele if she needed anything. Self-contained as ever, she simply shook her head.

To pass the time, I went to the cafeteria and made myself breakfast. The food was comforting, and I didn't know when or if there'd be another meal. As I was eating my cereal, I heard the faint sound of chopper blades churning the air. Perry came into the cafeteria, stared at me in surprise for a moment, startled to see someone doing something as mundane as eating, and hurried out. That was the next-to-last time I saw him alive.

Though I was doing something normal, my mind was in a dreamy state. Time seemed warped, the minutes simultaneously flashing by and endlessly drawn out. I was in shock, and the world seemed extraordinarily serene.

Overhead, footsteps hurried and doors slammed. David appeared in the cafeteria, accompanied by four or five men armed with AR-15s. He seemed to have regained his cool, and that was reassuring, even as the drone of the choppers grew louder. "They're coming," David said levelly, "but I want to talk it out with these people, so don't anybody do anything stupid. We want to talk to these people, we want to work it out."

I was flooded with relief. It was clear that being mentally prepared to die was not quite the same as staring death in the face.

At 9:45 A.M. a burst of gunfire came from the direction of the front door. There was a fusillade, and I heard Perry screaming. He was shot in the stomach, poor old guy, and his agony was audible above the rattle of the weapons.

I ran into the foyer in time to see the right front door slam with the velocity of the bullets fired from the outside. The metal casing in the door had burst inward in an arc of small holes. David was staggering backward. I thought he was hit, but then I saw he was just retreating from the gunfire.

"I tried—" he gasped, holding out his hands, miming the plea he'd made to the feds. He looked absolutely shocked.

We quickly pieced together what had happened. As the agents attacked, David, unarmed, had opened the left side of the front door. "Police! Search warrant! Get down!" the agents shouted, aiming their weapons at him. (They later claimed that this outburst was all the notification required by their warrant.)

Despite this aggressive approach, David did not lie down. He stared back at the agents and was surprised to see several reporters he recognized as employees of the *Waco Tribune-Herald* standing in the roadway behind the feds.

"What's going on?" David called out. "There are women and children in here!"

But the agents kept coming, and David hastily retreated, slamming the door in their faces. That's when the bullets crashed through the front door, striking Perry. "David, I'm hit! I've been shot!" the white-haired old man cried, holding his side. He started screaming and was hit again in the leg and thigh.

When I got there, Clive Doyle was trying to help Perry, whom he'd found crawling away from the entry, still screaming in pain from his bleeding wounds. Clive carried him to a bedroom and laid him on a bunk. Perry groaned in agony for more than an hour before he died, disturbing everybody with his cries.

"They came up in the truck and it had a gooseneck trailer behind it," David told us, his voice tight. "They came all locked-and-cocked. I opened the front door as they were running up, in combat dress, guns aimed and everything, hollering. I didn't know what they were saying, it was too noisy."

He paused, eyes dazed. "They just started firing. I fell back in the door and the bullets starting coming through. I yelled, 'Go away, there's women and children here, let's talk.'" He backed away toward the stair and I watched him go with horror in my heart as the firing continued from the feds' side and, in response, from ours.

The ATF game plan, it turned out, had been to burst from the cattle trailers parked in front of the building. The agents then intended to batter down our front door with a ram and arrest David, firing if necessary. The idea was that fifty agents, including some female officers, would crash through the entry, guns blazing, to intimidate and disarm the men and take the women and children into custody. Despite being obliged by the nature of their warrant to knock first, they had practiced only the dynamic-entry approach. Clearly, that made a better movie.

I don't know for sure if David or Steve actually issued an order to return the feds' fire, or if our people started shooting in a spontaneous response to the agents' use of such deadly force. Speaking to CNN anchorman David French that evening, David said that when the bullets came through the front door "some of the young men . . . started firing on them." The general feeling among other survivors I've talked to is that several people simply returned the ATF's barrage of bullets in the shock of the moment, in a natural impulse of self-defense provoked by the unexpected brutality of the ATF's assault.

When we returned their fire, some of the agents ran for cover behind a white van while others squatted down behind our picket fence, screened by its cinder-block base. Yet others hid behind vehicles in the parking lot. The first burst of gunfire lasted fifteen minutes, followed by a twenty-minute lull. Then the shooting started up again, during which an agent was killed.

The ATF apparently supposed that some of us would be working in the tornado shelter that morning, and a team of agents went around the back to cut us off and stop us from getting back into the building. However, these agents got tangled up in the ditches we'd dug there, tripped up by the stacks of cement and sand we'd left lying around. Our hired yellow bulldozer obstructed their view, and the mess of the hen house confused them in the muddy terrain between the pit and the water tower.

The agents later claimed they were bushwhacked by "two white guys with pistols and a black male with an AR-15." One of the agents, wounded near the concrete wall of the pit, crawled into a ditch and lay there until the cease-fire while his fellows cowered behind the 'dozer. To this day, no one knows who those "two white guys with pistols and a black male" were; it's more than likely that the agents shot at one another in the confusion.

Jaime Castillo and Brad Branch were standing at the front door when David had opened it to talk to the agents. In the chaos, they wrongly believed that David had been wounded. David, for his part, claimed for a while that a two-year-old girl, one of his kids, was killed at the door. However, a few days later, while talking to an FBI negotiator, David went back on this story and tried to deny it. I guess the dead-child story was David's feeble attempt to counter-spin the media against the flood of lies put out by the feds.

Almost as soon as the action began, Wayne Martin had phoned 911. For two hours or so during attack, and for many hours afterward, Wayne talked to Deputy Lieutenant Larry Lynch, who'd just returned from the ATF's command post.

Wayne yelled hysterically into his speakerphone, telling the deputy that Mount Carmel was under attack. "Call it off!" Wayne shrieked. "There are women and children in here! We want a cease-fire!" He added: "If they don't back off we're going to fight to the last man."

"Oh, shit!" Deputy Lynch exclaimed, obviously distressed. He tried unsuccessfully to reach the ATF commanders; but for all his good intentions, Lynch was hamstrung by a momentous foul-up in his attempt to communicate with the ATF. None of the agents raiding Mount Carmel was equipped with a cellular phone or even knew Mount Carmel's number. This was not only a gross lapse of standard procedure—it showed that the ATF had no intention of allowing us to surrender peacefully.

Suddenly the shooting seemed to be happening everywhere. A host of agents were blazing away at the front, and others were climbing ladders around the east side of the chapel, trying to break into the empty gun room.

A team of agents with automatic weapons scaled the chapel roof to get to the room where they assumed David would be hiding, probably from Robert's reports. Climbing twenty-foot aluminum ladders, they smashed the windows in the gun room and tossed in their flash-bang grenades. These grenades explode with a blinding light and a terrific racket; they can mutilate an unprotected person. As the glass broke, however, someone in the room—I still don't know who—started firing. Three agents were hit; two were killed and one fell off the roof into the courtyard. A second team that attacked the roof from the south were also met with gunfire.

When the feds did get into the gun room, they found the racks were empty, since Paul Fatta and Kalani had taken our stock to the gun show. The agents spotted Scott Sonobe carrying an AK-47 in the dark hallway between the armory and the bedroom. Shots were exchanged, and both Scott and an agent were wounded. A bullet went through Scott's left hand, between the thumb and the first index finger, smashed through his wrist and struck his right leg. Meanwhile, a second agent fell off the roof, breaking his hip.

It was shockingly clear during the rooftop attack that the ATF had no intention of allowing the residents to come out quietly. "They want to kill us all, man," Scott said. The two roof assault teams had no radio communications, and no one up there announced that they were law enforcement officials, as they were obliged to do.

As the agents on the roof began to withdraw, another one on the ground was hit. We didn't know it at the time, but three agents were now dead. Meanwhile, another ATF team that had broken into the gym at the rear of the building waited to rendezvous with the rooftop raiders.

All the while the helicopters were hovering, firing down into the residential tower and the room over the chapel, targeting David. Once again, it must have been Robert's spying that made them assume he'd be in those areas.

Apparently, the National Guard had agreed that its helicopters could be used as command platforms for supervising the raid. They were not supposed to be part of the actual attack, even though they carried armed ATF agents. The strategy, it seemed, was that the choppers would arrive at Mount Carmel just as the feds burst out of the cattle trailer rigs, then hover at around five hundred feet until the ATF had secured our property.

As it turned out, the timing was off, the sequence was botched, and the helicopters ended up in the midst of the firefight. Two of them were struck by gunfire and had to land in a nearby field; the third chopper, though also hit, continued to circle overhead. Two neutral witnesses, local reporter John McLemore and cameraman Dan Muloney, took a videotape showing a chopper passing within inches of Mount Carmel's north side, apparently strafing the building.

At 10:34 A.M., forty-nine minutes into the attack, David himself called Deputy Lynch on a cellular phone. "There is a bunch of us dead, there's a bunch of you guys dead," he said. "Now, now, that's your fault." David then started talking theology to the law officer, who tried to deflect him. "All right, we can talk theology. But right now—" Lynch began.

"No, this is life," David retorted. "This is life and death! Theology is life and death."

Steve also talked to Lynch about a cease-fire, but there were arguments between Wayne and Steve over whether the agents could be armed while removing their casualties. By the time the cease-fire was seriously considered, the ATF had suffered heavy casualties: sixteen wounded and four dead officers. Having made no proper arrangements for casualties, they had to make do with makeshift ambulances to transport their wounded, some of whom were slung over truck hoods like roadkill.

Later, the Treasury Department's report made the amazing admission that the ATF had no plan to "extract any agents, including wounded agents, from their exposed positions." For our part, Wayne refused medical help for our wounded. "We don't want anything from your country!" he told the authorities. I understood his fury, but that seemed a foolish kind of pride.

—————————

Having lived in a rough section of Hollywood for a few years, where the skies were crowded with police choppers and gunfire was one of the common street sounds, I reflexively hit the deck when I heard the 'copters coming.

With my nose buried in the floorboards, I reflected that, in such situations, there are three kinds of people: those who stand in front of a tank and dare it to run over them, like the guy in Tiananmen Square; those who make brave speeches behind the barricades, like the students in Paris in 1968; and those, like me, who chew dirt.

After a while I crawled toward the cafeteria, thinking I might hide out in the vault. The double doors at the rear of the cafeteria were open, and I could see the water tanks outside. At that moment the firing all around was so fierce I was sure we were all going to be wiped out.

I saw an armed, black-suited figure coming toward me and thought, "This guy is going to come in here and kill me." He vanished, and I burst out laughing, releasing a tension of terror and fury. "You have no honor!" I shouted at the invisible assailants. I felt very betrayed, very bitter, and my laughter was harsh and hysterical.

On hands and knees, I crawled out of the cafeteria into the workout room next door, huddling among the weights and gym equipment, listening to the shooting, thinking I could die any minute. I saw Jimmy Riddle run by, carrying a gun, going toward the end room in the men's quarters. In that area was the trapdoor in the floor that led to a ladder into a tunnel connected to the buried bus. Oliver Gyarfas followed Jimmy, and I ran after them.

The three of us scurried down the ladder and along the short tunnel into the bus. Oliver handed me a flashlight, and we squatted in a circle, trying to figure out what was happening and what we should do. We heard explosions from the flashbang grenades and volley after volley of gunfire above and around us. After a while, we continued along the concrete tunnel leading to the unfinished tornado shelter. Above us, through the pit's temporary plywood roof, we could hear agents shouting and shooting. The floor was muddy with the previous night's rain, and Jimmy, who wore gumboots, waded toward the pit's far exit. I stayed back, ready to yell if I saw a fed appear.

The excavation was ten to twelve feet deep. In one of the bright puddles on the floor Jimmy saw the reflection of an agent up above. "Come on outta there, you motherfuckers!" a voice above shouted, raw with rage. Jimmy tried to get a shot at the agent but couldn't find the right angle. The attacker's shouts were so filled with hatred, we feared that if we did emerge we'd be killed on the spot. In that instant I couldn't think of anything but that I was about to die.

"Let's get outta here," Jimmy said, and we retreated back through the tunnels and the bus to the main building. Jimmy and Oliver ran off down the hallway, and I was impressed by their bravery. As for me, I was down on all fours again, keeping my head low.

Suddenly, my hands and knees felt wet. Looking around, I saw water pouring through the room to my left. The room belonged to Winston Blake, a black man from Britain. Pushing aside the blanket over the doorway, my eyes were dazzled by the light coming in from the window.

For an instant the scene was a whiteout; then I noticed that the window, which opened onto the cafeteria water tanks, was smashed. "How did the window get broken?" I asked out loud. "Why's the water pouring in?" Abruptly, I realized that the water tanks outside were riddled with bullet holes and huge spurts were spraying the room.

A dark lump lay on the floor. Focusing, I recognized a human form. I saw Winston's light blue jacket. He lay in a pool of blood, and I knew he was dead. Hastily, I retreated, shutting the curtain, trying not to throw up. Winston was the first dead man I'd ever seen, and the sight of his lifeless body turned my stomach.

Crawling up the corridor, I heard Brad Branch yelling, "Cease fire! Cease fire!"

When the cease-fire took hold, I reached a room in front, beside the stairway. Greg was there, brandishing a rifle. He was yelling at an agent who lay facedown behind the cement block base of the front fence that formed a corral for the dogs. "Get outta there. Get the hell away from the fence," Greg shouted. The dead dogs lay there. Greg had seen them shot by the ATF, and he was enraged, his face so charged with fury that it scared me.

Wandering along the upstairs hallway, I came across David, propped against the wall. He told me he'd been shot just as the cease-fire was announced, by an agent who suddenly appeared while he was making his way along the overhead walkway above the chapel.

"This fed jumped up out of the blue, firing from the hip," he said. "A bullet spun me all the way around, like a 250-pound man kicking you in the side." David pulled up his T-shirt and showed me his wounds, one in his right wrist, severing the nerve to his thumb, another low on the left side of his torso, slicing away a sliver of his hipbone.

"I was getting numb, but I managed to crawl away," he said.

<hr />

The most intense period of the firefight lasted around fifty minutes, followed by several lulls in the shooting as Wayne Martin and Deputy Lynch continued their telephone negotiations. The final cease-fire was agreed at around 11:30 A.M. During the last hour of talks, while the details were being hashed out, the ATF removed its wounded agents and retreated off our property while we took stock of our own casualties.

Looking out the window, I watched the agents retreating. Two of them went by, supporting a third man drooping between them. All three had the gray, shell-shocked look I'd noticed on the faces of Vietnam grunts in documentaries I'd seen. Another agent, a black woman with dreadlocks, slouched past with an expression of utter bewilderment. Our eyes locked for a moment, and she stared at me as if to say, "What the hell just happened here?"

"You got your asses kicked, lady," I answered silently, and she flinched, reading my response. Then she straightened her shoulders and tossed back her head, her confusion turning to arrogance. I felt sorry for her at that moment, yet I resented her haughty look after what she and her fellows had done to us.

The area was peppered with agents in their blue-black gear, wearing their signature call letters across their backs, the bold-yellow *ATF*. There were scores of them, and for the first time I had a sense of how massive the attack had been.

How had we managed to hold them off? I wondered, shivering in retrospect. Maybe if we'd known how much manpower and firepower the feds were going to throw at us, we might have been too intimidated to fight back. As it was, they were limping away, bearing their dead and their injured, sweat and anger in their eyes.

Again I wondered what might have happened if the ATF had used a less provocative strategy to arrest David; if a mere handful of agents had come to the door, showed him the warrant, and asked him to surrender himself.

Some of Mount Carmel's survivors believed he would have gone along peaceably, trusting the criminal justice system to determine his punishment for crimes that may or may not have been proven. After all, they said, he'd done that back in 1988, over the George Roden affair, and the system had worked; he was released after a fair trial. If the ATF hadn't been so hellbent on the dynamic-entry scenario, and if David had quietly given himself up, many lives would have been saved.

Frankly, I'm not so sure David would have surrendered as easily. To start with, over the six years since 1987, his understanding of the radical nature of his mission had intensified; in other words, he'd recognized that the Fifth Seal's text—*I saw under the altar the souls of them that were slain for the word of God*—was a prophecy he was convinced was about to be fulfilled—and soon. In his own mind, David was no longer simply an American citizen subject to the laws of man but an anointed one owing allegiance to a higher authority. The U.S. criminal justice system would not be the context for fulfilling his fated role on earth, so surrendering to its agents might have been seen as self-betrayal.

Yet if David's mood that Sunday morning had been more crafty, or if he'd been in one of his frequent troughs of self-doubt, he just might have submitted to a nonviolent approach by law enforcement officials, especially if some of the local police he knew and liked had been included in the posse. He was a complex man, with many sides to his personality.

But at the moment, all this was mere conjecture. We had to attend to more urgent matters, such as caring for our wounded and counting our dead.

My first thought was for Michele and the kids. Hurrying upstairs, I found the hallway filled with mothers and children huddling on the floor. The women had tucked the youngsters under their bodies to protect them from the gunfire. I found Michele and the kids where I'd left them in a corner of the room. The children seemed okay, the twins cuddling close to their mother, Serenity beside them. But the tears in Michele's eyes told me how shaken she was. In her short life she'd been through so much, and it wasn't over.

I bumped into Jaime as I was going downstairs. He told me he had a rifle but said he hadn't fired it. "The friggin' thing jammed as I was trying to out a round in the chamber," he told me. He was dressed in black and wore one of the tactical ammo vests, an item of Koresh Survival Wear.

"I look like the ATF," he joked. "Lucky one of our guys didn't off me." His eyes were stunned yet shining, shock muting the exhilaration of having lived through extreme danger.

In the next few hours I began to hear what had happened to our casualties and to some of the other people who'd lived through that terrifying morning.

I didn't know if Perry had died from his wounds, or if he'd killed himself, or if he'd gotten one of the guys to put him out of his suffering. Kathy Schroeder later claimed that Neal Vaega killed Perry as an act of mercy and that she heard David give Neal permission to do this. Perry's body was preserved from damage during the fire because we buried him beneath the dirt floor of the tornado shelter, and the official autopsy reported that Perry was killed by a single bullet wound fired point-blank into his mouth. But all those autopsies are suspect. Stored in a faulty cooler at the Fort Worth medical examiner's office, Perry's exhumed body partially decomposed before examination.

I learned more about how Winston Blake had died. A big man in his late twenties, a baker by trade, Winston, whose family came from the Caribbean, hated the cold. That damp, chilly morning he had been wearing a couple of sweaters, three pairs of pants, one of our "David Koresh/God Rocks" T-shirts, and a black ammo vest with the Koresh Survival Wear logo. Apparently, he was just sitting on his bunk, eating a breakfast of French toast, when the bullets crashed through the water tanks outside his window. One of them hit him under his right ear, and he fell forward into the water from the ruptured tanks puddling on the floor, lying in a pool of water and blood, as I'd seen him.

Later, the ATF tried to disclaim responsibility for Winston's murder. They asserted that the autopsy showed that Winston had been killed by one of us, perhaps because in his black ammo vest he'd been mistaken for a federal agent. They said his wound showed traces of powder burns, which proved he was shot at close range. However, a doctor with the Manchester, England, police who later examined Winston's body found that Winston's injury could have been covered up by a subsequent point-blank shot to make it seem as if we'd killed him. And he found no powder burns.

Apart from Perry Jones and Winston Blake, we had three other fatalities, and several wounded, inside Mount Carmel. The dead included Peter Gent, Jaydean Wendell, and Peter Hipsman. Twenty-four-year-old Peter Gent was killed in the empty water tower, hit by a bullet fired from one of the hovering helicopters, or maybe by a shot coming from the snipers hidden behind the cement block shed where our motorbikes were stored, two hundred yards to the east of the main building. (After the cease-fire, these snipers pulled back to a hay barn on the neighboring farm.) Peter was working inside the tower when the attack began, chipping away at the rust. Standing on scaffolding and ladders set up inside the tank, he'd stuck his head and upper body out of the hatch at the top of the tower to see what was going on and was hit in the chest. He was unarmed.

My friend Peter Hipsman was in David's bedroom at the top of the four-story residential tower when the gunmen in the helicopters blasted it with gunfire. He was struck in the side, the bullet passed through his body, and he fell to the floor in agony. After the cease-fire, when Steve found him, Peter begged to be put out of his misery. David and Steve refused at first; but then, seeing that Peter's wound was fatal, and that he was in terrible pain, Steve sent Neal Vaega to shoot him twice in the head. In this sad way, Peter, who loved to entertain the kids with wacky imitations of Donald Duck, ended his life. He, too, was unarmed.

In their desperate postraid media spin, the ATF tried to claim that Peter had shot at them through the roof of the tower room. But the evidence was clearly to the contrary. When I went up there I saw a series of holes in the ceiling, maybe as many as a dozen, and the dry-wall was hanging down, showing clearly that the bullets had come in from above, not the other way around. Later, several reputable Texas attorneys with military experience confirmed this fact; they stated that, in their view, the shots could only have come from the sky. And a video taken by a camera crew from station KWTX-TV clearly suggests that the trajectory of the bullets fired through the tower roof was downward.

Jaydean Wendell, our fifth fatality, had responded to the ATF assault with all the instincts of the police officer she'd once been in her native Hawaii. When the firing started Jaydean had just finished breast-feeding her ten-month-old baby, Patron. Seizing a rifle, she ran to her second-floor room, climbed onto a bunk bed, and returned the raiders' fire. After the cease-fire, Marjorie Thomas, who'd been caring for some of Jaydean's children, found her sprawled on the bunk, a bullet in her skull.

We reckoned our casualties at five dead and four wounded, including David, Judy Schneider, who was wounded in the hand and shoulder, Scott Sonobe, and David Jones, who got a bullet in his buttocks. We were amazed that with all that gunfire so few had been hurt.

David's wounds were the worst. He lay on blankets in the hallway upstairs, close to where he'd been shot. He was now shaking and semiconscious, moving in and out of pain, his eyes rolling up into his head. He was deathly pale, and his glasses were misty with fevered sweat. One of the women, a trained nurse, said his blood pressure was very low, but even in his delirium David refused any medication, including aspirin. In his lucid moments he turned down the medical attention the federal negotiators were offering, saying he was in God's hands. We all thought he was going to die, and the gloom was deep. If David died we all died—in spirit, and maybe in the flesh—fighting to the end.

Seeing David in that condition, my mind seemed to slip into an eternal rather than a temporal perspective. I felt I was living in a separate reality, ready to put my life on the line for my faith. It was a heady feeling, yet underneath this spurt of exhilaration the notion that David was dying sucked at the pit of my stomach.

To our amazement, however, David miraculously recovered. We'd thought his wound was fatal, but an hour or so later he sat proudly showing off the ugly gash in his side, asking for his guitar. "They don't kill me that easy," he whispered to me, winking. He even felt chipper enough to call his mother, Bonnie Haldeman, and leave a cheery-tragic message on her answering machine: "Hello, Mama, it's your boy. They shot me and I'm dying, all right? But I'll be back real soon, okay? I'm sorry you didn't learn the Seals, but I'll be merciful, okay? I'll see y'all in the skies."

I'll see y'all in the skies.

That phrase resonated in my head as I sat on my bunk that damp day, trying to absorb everything that had happened in the hours since Robert had arrived with the newspaper. Images

David Thibodeau with his friend, Julie Martinez. Julie and her five children were the largest single family, aside from David Koresh's own, that died in the fire which consumed Mount Carmel.

David Koresh, leader of the Branch Davidian Community living at Mount Carmel. The community was destroyed by fire on April 19, 1993, after a fifty-one-day siege by federal agents, and a final assault that led to the deaths of seventy-four people living at Mount Carmel, including twenty-one children.

David Koresh (left) on a trip to Australia in the late 1980s, to meet with the local Davidians. Clive Doyle (right), an Australian, was one of the nine survivors of the April 1993 fire, and is currently the leader of a small group of Davidians still living in the Waco area.

Jaime Castillo, one of the nine survivors of the fire at Mount Carmel, on April 19, 1993, playing music in the band room of the federal prison where he is incarcerated in Beaumont, Texas.

Marc Breault (right) and Steve Schneider at Mount Carmel in the mid-1980s. Breault and his wife, Elizabeth Baranyai, left the community in 1987 in a dispute over Koresh's New Light doctrine. Schneider, who replaced Breault as Koresh's closest associate conducted most of the negotiations with federal agents during the siege.

Michele Jones when David Thibodeau met her on his first visit to Mount Carmel in 1990.

Jennifer Andrade, aged twenty, died in the fire, suffocated by toxic fumes from lethal tear gas injected into Mount Carmel by federal agents.

Jennifer's sister, Katherine, aged twenty-four, died in the fire, along with fourteen-month-old Chanel, her daughter by Koresh.

The layout of Mount Carmel, showing the areas, such as the cafeteria, the concrete vault, and the chapel, where most people died in the ATF attack on February 28 and the final assault on April 19. David Thibodeau and several other survivors escaped the fire through the right-hand wall of the chapel.

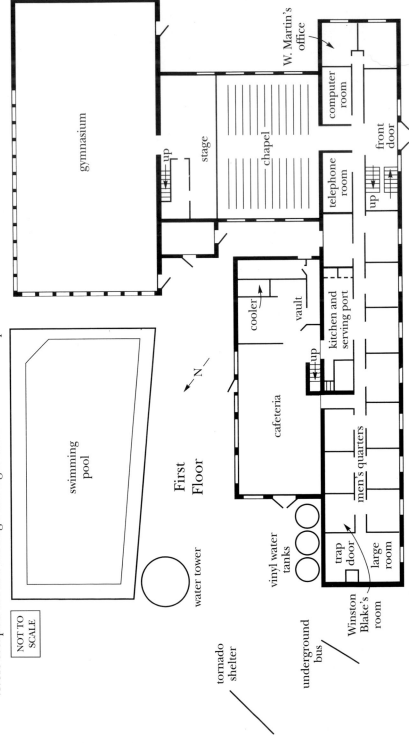

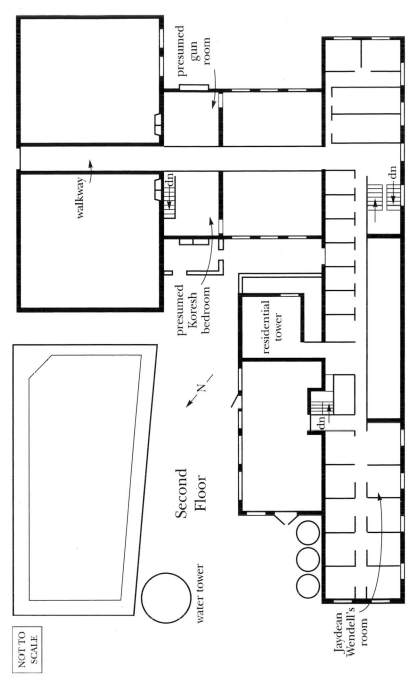

The second floor of Mount Carmel was occupied by women and children. David Koresh and some members of his family lived in the second and third floors of the residential tower, which was strafed by agents in helicopters on February 28.

ATF agents attacking the second story room above the chapel, where they believed the community stored its guns. The room was empty, but two agents were killed and another was wounded in the assault. Scott Sonobe and David Koresh were subsequently wounded by ATF agents who penetrated this area.

The ATF retrieves its wounded agents during a lull in the February 28 assault. The holes made by incoming bullet rounds are plainly seen in the right-hand metal skin panel of the front door and the adjacent wall, clear evidence that the agents fired the first shots into the building. The right-hand panel mysteriously vanished after the fire, through the left-hand panel intact.

Six hours after federal tanks ripped huge holes in
Mount Carmel's walls and filled the building with
tear gas, a brisk wind fanned the flammable chemical
residue, mixed with spilled fluid from the occupant's
heaters, into a violent blaze that finally exploded in a
fireball of smoke and flame.

Memorial quilts displayed during marches in Washington, D.C. in 1997 and 1998 to remind the public about the Waco tragedy, and to call for the release of the five Davidians still held in federal prisons. The upper quilt is dedicated to Michele and her three children, four-year-old Serenity and the twenty-two-month-old twins, Chica and Little One, all of whom died in the fire.

tumbled around my mind, colors and shapes whirling without sense and order. The scene that kept recurring was the view of Winston in his "David Koresh/God Rocks" T-shirt lying in a pool of blood and water, having lost his life while munching on French toast.

What did that last bite of toast taste like as it hit his taste buds? I wondered, trying to imagine the clotted tang of egg and the sugary sweetness of the sodden bread in my own throat. "I don't want to be eating French toast when I die," I told Steve when he stuck his head into my doorway to see if I was okay.

He looked at me solemnly for a moment, trying to gauge my state of mind. "We're all toast now, Thibodeau," he said.

11

AFTERSHOCK

When Steve moved on I wandered through the building listening to other people's accounts of their experiences during the assault. Most were still in shock, their eyes stunned with the enormity of what had just taken place. Despite our premonitions about our spiritual fate, nothing could have prepared us for the terrors of that day, those traumatic fifty minutes of gunfire.

Seventy-seven-year-old Catherine Matteson had been down-stairs when she saw the ATF cattle trailers coming down the road. As she hurried to her upstairs room, her ears were deafened by the choppers' roar. She saw three helicopters zooming toward the top of the residential tower in a V-formation, firing as they came, the yellow flashes spurting like venom. Terrified, she fell to the floor, following the same survival instinct as me—get as close as possible to the bosom of Mother Earth.

"All hell broke loose and everyone at the front of the build-ing started shooting," Catherine said. After her first panic, she and Margaret Kiyoko Hayashi Lawson, a small, elderly Japanese Hawaiian, gathered some of the children together. The windows were shattered by gunfire, and the two women tried to shield the kids with their bodies. Later, as she went down the second-floor corridor after the cease-fire, Catherine saw shot-out windows and

175

shattered blinds in every room, the razorlike glass shards scattered everywhere.

The ATF later accused farsighted Catherine and aged Margaret of using firearms "to commit the violent crimes of murder and attempted murder." Yet even the ATF affidavit described Margaret as "probably the most harmless woman around."

Like Catherine and Margaret, Victorine Hollingsworth, a middle-aged Caribbean woman from Guyana, tried to protect the children, despite her bad leg, very poor eyesight, and high blood pressure. She had the kids in her care put on their shoes and get dressed. Seeing the cattle trailers pull up to the front of the building and the armed agents jumping out, she ran into the corridor with the children and lay down on the floor while the air rocked with explosions. A simple woman, she called rifles "long guns" and pistols "short guns," and she heard plenty of both sounding off in the next ninety minutes.

Kathy Schroeder was dressing her son, Bryan, when shots came through the window of their room. Mother and son dropped to the floor and slid under a bed, both weeping and scared. They huddled there in terror for two hours, fearful of emerging even after the shooting stopped. Sita Sonobe's experience was even more scary. "My kids were in the bunk bed," she recalled. "All of a sudden these guys came out of that trailer and just start shooting. The bed is full of holes." She was still amazed at the enormity of the day's events. "If they know there are children, how come they just come out of the trailer and shoot?" she demanded.

One of Julie Martinez's daughters was fired at when, urged by a child's curiosity, she went to window to see what all the commotion was about. "They just started shooting at her," Julie said. Another daughter was almost killed. "A bullet went, like, six inches from her head," Julie told us. Other bullets came up through the floor, close to her four-year-old son, Isaiah. "I think it had to be God that kept that bullet from going through the carpet, because other bullets did go through," she said.

Wayne's wife, Sheila Martin, was in the chapel with two of her older daughters when Perry Jones warned her that the feds were on the way. Sheila took her family upstairs for safety. Standing at the window before the attack, she combed the hair of her six-year-old son, Daniel, while four-year-old Kimmie tried to dress herself. Sheila's son Jamie, stricken with meningitis, blind and crippled, lay on a loveseat under the window.

Teenager Rachel Sylvia ran into the room. "Look! They're coming!" she exclaimed, then fled. Sheila saw the agents running toward the front door, which was directly below her. Hearing gunshots, she pulled her kids down to the floor and kneeled beside them while bullets smashed the window. As glass showered the room, Jamie started screaming, but Sheila had to keep her head low under the barrage and couldn't get to him. Racked by worry, she hunkered down with Daniel and Kimmie. A pause in the gunfire gave her the chance to collect Jamie from the loveseat, only to find that the boy had been cut above the left eye by flying glass fragments.

The collective shock suffered by the children during the raid was most touchingly revealed in the crayon drawings done by the kids who were sent out of Mount Carmel after that day. Many of these sketches show hovering choppers firing bullets that made holes in the roof. With their naive, comic book–like simplicity, these crayon pictures rendered a mixture of childish excitement and deep fright. More than any one thing, they summed up the shattering experience we all went through during those few catastrophic hours.

/

The stories kept coming in, creating a crazy quilt of ragged recollections.

Graeme Craddock was washing his clothes early Sunday morning, around the time ATF agent Robert Rodriguez arrived to show us the Waco newspaper. He'd joined the group in the foyer to hear what the paper had to say about Marc Breault, his fellow Aussie. After David Jones arrived, Graeme was about to go back to his laundry when Peter Hipsman stopped him and told him the attack was coming. Graeme went to his room, collected his AR-15 rifle and 9mm pistol, donned an ammo vest, and went to the window.

He was standing there watching the roadway when David came by and told him that no one was to open fire unless he gave the signal.

Though he seemed ready for battle, Graeme was hardly a ferocious type. Skinny and short, a quiet guy, pale-skinned for an Aussie, he'd been a high-school physics teacher in his homeland. A year or so earlier, when Steve phoned him in Australia and told him to return to Mount Carmel, he'd come willingly, like the devout, obedient soul he was. Since he'd been trained as electrical engineer, he'd overseen the installation of the wiring in Mount Carmel.

Graeme remembered that David had told him that, when the attack came, one of several scenarios could occur: We'd get "translated," arrested, or killed. When the shooting started, Graeme forgot his weaponry and hit the deck until it was over.[*]

Brad Branch, in contrast, was no wimp. A big guy, an aviation mechanic from Waco, he grooved on honky-tonks and topless bars, moving back and forth between the worldly and the religious life, between sin and remorse. During the attack he ran from room to room carrying a rifle. I never saw him firing his weapon, but Victorine Hollingsworth later testified that she heard Brad boast about shooting an agent.

But in all charity, no one could claim that Victorine's mind was completely clear. She'd been brought up in poverty in the Caribbean. "My childhood was very sad and painful, only sickness and death I see," she said in her singsong, West Indian lilt. Apart from her bad leg, weak eyes, and elevated blood pressure, she was given

---

* Graeme later incriminated himself by a naive confession to the Texas Rangers after April 19. He told them he'd learned everything he knew about firearms at Mount Carmel. Though that wasn't much—Graeme had fired a weapon on only two brief occasions in an entire year—it was enough to get him indicted. In fact, David didn't much favor giving guns to poor combat prospects like Graeme and me; neither of us was allowed to have any ammunition for our weapons, except during target practice and in the kind of emergency we'd just suffered. Jaime also gave himself away by talking to police after the April 19 fire. He unwisely told the Rangers that he'd had a gun at the front door that day but hadn't fired it. At Jaime's trial, the prosecution said that this proved his intent to use the weapon, and his own confession incriminated him. But the fact was that Jaime, like Graeme, was awkward with his rifle.

to weird dreams that were almost parodies of David's visions. As a young girl she'd dreamed of a "beautiful young lady laying on the sky with all the light lying around her." The "beautiful lady," Victorine believed, was the Heavenly Mother. When she heard David speak on a visit to England, she thought he was the "King David we read about in the Word," and she followed him to Mount Carmel.

In reporting Brad's supposed boast about shooting an agent, Victorine used nearly the same words—"He nearly got me, but I got him first"—to describe what she also claimed to have heard from Livingston Fagan. Having known both men well, it's hardly plausible to me that the skinny, saintly Livingston and the beefy, raunchy Brad would use identical language to describe their actions.

An ATF agent claimed that Livingston and a couple of other men had pinned him down with gunfire, but his identification was totally suspect. I was told by several people who saw him that Livingston was kneeling in prayer in the chapel while the bullets were flying. (Despite his current forty-year sentence, Livingston himself refuses to deny or confirm any involvement in the firefight. "We were all of the same spirit in there," he told an interviewer, "so why should I talk about differences about what we did in the flesh?")

Other stories were added to the narrative of the day.

Renos Avraam, it appeared, had hidden behind a safe in Perry Jones's office. Later, he was convicted of shooting a federal agent on the testimony of a convicted dope dealer he shared a cell with after April 19. The convict claimed that Renos had bragged, "Well, I'm not a bad shot," when asked if he'd fired at any of the agents attacking us. However, there was no direct evidence whatever that Special Agent Robert Williams, killed while giving covering fire to the attackers on Mount Carmel's roof, had been shot by Renos or anyone else inside the building. Maybe Renos was showing off to his hardcase cellmate; but from everything I knew about him, he seemed more likely to huddle in a dark corner than to come out shooting.

Kevin Whitecliff, a big man who'd been a prison guard in Hawaii, was later accused of firing at the agents who were shooting at us from the helicopters. Maybe he did, and I wouldn't blame him. As his counsel later said, he did what he had to do to defend himself.

Around 1:30 P.M. a flock of choppers buzzed Mount Carmel, and we all took cover or rushed to defensive positions. Believing the helicopters were about to land on our roof, Wayne frantically phoned Lieutenant Lynch. However, the aircraft turned out to be TV choppers angling for a shot of Mount Carmel for their breaking stories. By mid-afternoon, more than sixty newspaper reporters, plus camera crews from at least seventeen TV stations and CNN, were held at a police barricade about a mile from the scene. That night the Federal Aviation Administration declared the ten-mile radius around Mount Carmel a "no-flight zone."

Later that afternoon, sometime after 4:00 P.M., I heard shots in the near distance, coming from the back, up toward the hay barn. We learned later that the gunfire was Mike Schroeder being killed as he tried to make his way back into Mount Carmel.

That morning, Mike, my friend and fellow drummer, had been in the auto shop we rented and operated four miles down the road. The auto shop, which the feds erroneously dubbed the "Mag Bag," was a couple of beige steel buildings, with partitions for an office, kitchen, and sleeping quarters. Mike lived and worked there, along with old Bob Kendrick and Norm Allison, a handsome, hip young black man from Manchester, England. They were working in the shop that morning when Bob noticed the choppers in the distance, in the direction of Mount Carmel. Mike phoned Mount Carmel and Steve told him we were under attack.

The three of them grabbed their handguns and tried to drive to Mount Carmel, but the roads were blocked so they veered off to the mobile home where Perry Jones's wife, Mary Belle, lived, two miles or so away from us. They walked down the road toward Mount Carmel, hoping to find a back way in, then turned off the road and crept through the brush to avoid detection.

Of the trio, Mike was the most determined. Sixty-two-year-old Bob's health was poor (he'd had several heart attacks), and he gradually fell behind Mike and Norm. After passing near the hay barn on our neighbor's property, Bob just missed getting caught by agents, including a couple of snipers from the Texas Department of Public Safety who'd spotted his light-blue stocking cap and assumed he'd popped out of one of the mythical escape tunnels they imagined we'd dug out from our main building. When the officers went looking for Bob, they caught sight of Mike instead, who was wearing a navy ski cap.

The agents, thirteen of them, later claimed that Mike had opened fire and that they fired back. But Bob, hugging the earth close by, heard the first shots—fired from a rifle, not a pistol like Mike's—coming from the direction of the barn where the raiders were based. Despite being heavily outnumbered and badly hurt, Mike fought off his assailants for thirty minutes or so before he was finally cut down.

The coroner's report stated that Mike was hit four times in the body and left leg, which likely happened during the firefight. However, there were also three wounds in his skull, which must have been inflicted at close range, after Mike had collapsed and was bleeding to death from his internal injuries. The fact that no powder burns were found around these bullet holes was probably due to his woolen cap, which later conveniently vanished and has never been found, not even when the Texas Rangers searched for it during their later crime-scene investigation. (The Rangers' investigations were hampered by the FBI, who blocked the officers from returning to the place where Mike was killed for ten days, giving them access only when the rain had washed away any incriminating footprints.) Mike's body had been left hanging on a fence for four days, until the Rangers released his corpse. Coyotes had chewed off one of his legs, and I could only imagine the feast the fire ants and crows must have had during that time.

Norm Allison gave himself up without firing a shot. In a later interview with Britain's *Guardian* newspaper, Norm, a former cabbie, described his experience that day: "These big Texan sheriffs, all wearing the same tartan lumber shirts and neck chockers [sic], trying to make out that we had some mission to take over the world. A big conspiracy about how we're part of David Koresh's 'mighty men.' The people at Mount Carmel were good people with faith who were trying to defend themselves."

Norm was an odd type. His mother and older brother were Adventists, but Norm, an amateur rapper and self-proclaimed swinger, had disgraced the family by spending an eighteen-month spell in the slammer in Britain for rigging poker machines. He'd come to Mount Carmel around fall the year before, to join our band, he said. David turned him down as a musician, feeling he didn't fit our style, so Norm went off to Hollywood to make his fame and fortune. But Hollywood didn't fall at Norm's feet, and the forlorn rapper returned to Waco in late January 1993, broke and broken. David didn't really want him around, but Mike, a soft touch, let him help out in the auto shop and sleep on a beat-up bus seat in the garage.

Norm told the agents who arrested him that Bob was wounded, but that wasn't so. Assuming Bob was nearby, the officers called to him to surrender, but Bob was almost deaf and wasn't wearing his hearing aid. He made his way slowly back to Mary Belle's mobile home, where he was arrested nine days later. Rather foolishly, he showed the police the two pistols he'd carried on February 28, which led to the poor old guy being charged with "aiding and abetting" a conspiracy to commit murder—a charge he only narrowly escaped.

With Mike's murder, our death toll rose to six. Along with the law enforcement casualties, the day had cost ten lives and twenty people wounded. It was the worst moment in the ATF's history up to that time—and in ours.

But our blue-and-white flag was still flying, showing the Star of David and a flying serpent with fiery wings—a symbol both of deceit and salvation, derived from God's instruction to Moses in Numbers 21:8: *Make thee a fiery serpent, and set it upon a pole: and it shall come to pass, that every one that is bitten, when he looketh upon it, shall live.*

------•·•------

As soon as the botched raid was over, ATF spokesmen scrambled to cover the agency's ass. One ATF press officer said the agency was "outgunned"! In wild swings at shifting the blame for their tragically botched operation, the ATF also claimed it was "set up" by the media and local law enforcement. They even turned on their erstwhile coconspirator, reporter Mark England of the *Waco Tribune-Herald,* accusing him of phoning David to leak news of the raid, thereby eliminating the element of surprise. At one moment, while they were retrieving their wounded, enraged ATF agents slapped a TV cameraman to the dirt while he was filming them. They seemed to have forgotten that they'd invited the media along to record their glorious enterprise.

The ATF's head honchos also seemed to have forgotten that Robert Rodriguez had warned them their surprise was blown—and that they'd ignored him. The *New York Times* later reported that "several Federal agents involved in the violent raid . . . [compared it] to the Charge of the Light Brigade, laden with missteps, miscalculations and unheeded warnings that could have averted bloodshed." The agents, the *Times* reported, "said that supervisors had realized even before they began their assault that they had lost any element of surprise but went ahead anyway." To cut the babble, the ATF belatedly issued a gag order to its agents on March 15, but by that time the damage was done to the agency's reputation.

Some seventy or eighty heavily armed, supposedly professional agents, backed by a trio of helicopters, had failed to subdue a vulnerable, unfortified community of around 130 people, three-quarters of whom were unarmed women and children.

The entire operation was graphically lambasted by no less an authority than Colonel Charlie Beckwith, founder of the U.S. Army's elite Delta Force. Writing in *Soldier of Fortune* magazine a few months after the attack, Beckwith said succinctly: "Had a similar event taken place in the U.S. Army, the responsible party would now be serving time in the correctional facility at Fort Leavenworth, Kansas."

Beckwith damned the ATF assault on several counts, including the decision to train at Fort Hood, "too close to the actual target site." Sardonically, he added: "ATF might just as well have run a flag up telling everyone something was about to happen." Beckwith criticized the agency for its failure to consider the risk to human life on both sides; for the lack of a contingency fallback when the

ATF discovered it had lost the element of surprise; for the time chosen for the attack—after 9:00 A.M., rather than at night or sunrise. "Every principle involved in mounting and conducting a successful raid/assault operation was violated," he declared.

The ATF initially responded by first suspending, then firing, Charles Sarabyn and Philip Chojnacki, two of the raid's commanders. They were charged with a failure to abort the assault after they realized we knew they were coming. However, the agents challenged their dismissal and were reinstated in December 1994. It was rumored that they threatened to reveal details from certain still-unreleased cell-phone audiotapes in which they received orders from a superior, probably ATF director Stephen Higgins, or even someone higher up the command chain, to go ahead despite losing the advantage of surprise. Higgins was eventually forced to resign, and Deputy Director Daniel Hartnett and two other ranking ATF officials were temporarily suspended. However, one of them, ATF intelligence chief David Troy, was later promoted.

Despite the dismissal of these ATF officials, the Treasury Department report, issued in September 1993, was essentially a cover-up. It concentrated on placing blame for going ahead with the assault after losing the element of surprise, but it did not bear down on the agency for attacking us in the first place on the basis of the trumped-up charges detailed in the original affidavit. Hartnett himself later told Congress that the Treasury report was deliberately distorted on the orders of Assistant Secretary of the Treasury Ron Noble.

Perhaps the ATF was bamboozled by its own corrupt affidavit into believing that raiding us would be just like any other action taken against suspected criminals, usually dope dealers and gang members. Its technique, used effectively in most cases, was to show up with massive force and terrify victims into surrender. In something like six hundred raids executed in the three years prior to the attack on Mount Carmel, the ATF had only been fired upon twice. In turn, agents had killed three suspects.

But we weren't intimidated that easily. When the agents came at us on the ground and in the air with guns blazing, we fought

back, as was our right when attacked with excessive force, even by
law enforcement officers. In short, the ATF had no idea who they
were really dealing with, even though Marc Breault, their main "expert" on Mount Carmel, had warned them we were a radical exception to their run-of-the-mill targets.

———————

Watching the sunset that Sunday, I could hardly believe that only
twenty-four hours had passed since the last one. For those of us in
Mount Carmel, the world had changed radically and forever.

I tried to think my way through to a reckoning of these changes.
On the ground, we were now no longer an obscure, unknown community in the middle of Texas but a national and international
byword. "Branch Davidians," the name we hardly ever used for ourselves, had become an easy tag for a host of talking heads and their
audiences. We were physically surrounded, cut off from the outside
world, thrown in upon ourselves even more than before.

Spiritually, the changes were more subtle. As a group, we'd
moved into the last phase of prophecy, shunted toward our own
particular End Time by the action of the authorities who had, for
their own murky reasons, focused upon us. Whatever our past tensions had been inside Mount Carmel, we were now bound tightly
together in a common and relentless fate. We'd entered our true
"soul time" and were supposedly living in a dimension that tran-
scended whatever might happen to us in the flesh.

People like Livingston and Wayne might say that our souls mattered more than our lives, but personally I felt all too human, all too
mortal, all too vulnerable to my own doubts, fears, and the furies of
the forces rallying against us. I cursed myself for this weakness, but
it was too ingrained in my nature, so I just had to live with it.

However, if I did survive the siege, I could be a witness, and I
made up my mind to remember everything that happened.

David, as usual, functioned on both levels, the worldly and the spiritual. In the first sense, he spent the evening trying to get the word

out about our situation, giving phone interviews to the media, fielding calls from news agencies as far away as Australia and Norway who wanted to know who was killed and wounded and who on earth we were.

At 7:30 P.M., David told CNN: "I had never planned to use these weapons. The problem is that people outside don't understand what we believe." Later that evening David talked for twenty minutes on Dallas radio station KRLD about his injuries. "I've been shot. I'm bleeding bad," he said while a baby cried in the background. "I begged these men to go away." Weak from his wounds, he started sobbing at one moment, telling the fake story about the child being killed. Maybe he believed the story at the time, or he was lightheaded, or he was trying to generate public compassion. However, he did offer to send out two kids each time KRLD played a short message he composed about the Seals. And when the station manager asked him if he had any sympathy for the casualties the ATF had suffered during the raid, he said vehemently: "My friend, it was *unnecessary*."

Some children did exit that evening, including six-year-old Angelica Sonobe and her little sister, Crystal, whom David requested be sent to their grandparents in Hawaii. Along with Scott and his wife, Sita, we all watched as the car sent by the feds took them away to safety. "Will I ever see my babies again?" Sita keened, and no one could answer her, not on the temporal level. Heaven, of course, was another matter.

Late Sunday afternoon, soon after we heard the shooting that ended in Mike Schroeder's death, KRLD repeatedly broadcast a message to us from the ATF. The gist of it was that the agency would not act aggressively if we were willing to give up. "Too little too late," Steve said angrily. "Why didn't they try that tack earlier?"

The first ATF negotiators who got through to us on the telephone that day struck two sour notes that were to echo through the following weeks as the government's noose tightened around our necks. One note was the tension between the negotiating-team members and their tactical commanders. The other was the feds' total lack of sympathy for our religious beliefs.

Almost immediately, the negotiators complained of pressure from their bosses. "I've got guys with scrambled eggs and gold leaves and badges like you wouldn't believe," one said, speaking on the phone from the house opposite our front gate that Robert and his colleagues had occupied. "I've got the governor, I've got the President, I've got everybody in the world—"

"You're going to smoke-bomb us or you're going to burn our building down," David countered.

"No, I'm not going to let them do it," the ATF negotiator insisted, knowing that his personal assurance carried little weight. (In fact, that Sunday evening the ATF requested the loan of ten Bradley Fighting Vehicles from the Texas National Guard.)

Yet when David tried to explain the Seals and their importance to our understanding of how the confrontation with the feds might work out, a negotiator cut him off with a curt, "I'm not a theologian, I'm just a policeman." David persisted, trying to explain the significance of the story of King Nebuchadnezzar and the three faithful men he'd tried to incinerate. "They threw those boys in the fire, didn't they? But who protected them? God did! Now we're in the fire."

During the fifty-one-day siege, 243 government tapes, some of them five hours long, were made of the negotiations we had with the authorities. We spoke with more than twenty different men and women, often around the clock, sometimes with long gaps in between. But all of these exchanges were tainted by the two factors mentioned above: the dissension between the official negotiators trying to find a common ground with us and their gung-ho, action-driven bosses; and the intractable lack of sympathy for our beliefs, dismissed as mere "Bible babble," or any realization that we were prepared to die for them.

Steve held out the hope that the federal agencies just couldn't come in and wipe us out, not after Ruby Ridge and the bad PR they'd earned there, so we did have some marginal bargaining power. But that didn't reassure me much. My old faith in America had been badly cracked by the atrocious actions of some of its official agents, and I could not build any kind of hope on it now.

Exhausted, I finally fell into bed and had an intense erotic dream. The shattering orgasm was a kind of release from the day's terrors, a reaffirmation of life in the face of death. The dream startled me, though; I hadn't had a lustful thought for quite some time and believed I'd finally mastered my sexual impulses. This sudden surge of desire shook me, but it also rescued me from my fright. "If we're meant to be toast, so be it," I thought as I lay in bed in the dark, listening to Jaime snoring. Those of us who'd been killed that day had moved on to a better place, and at that moment I had no doubt in eternity. Even as a child I'd felt there was an eternal judgment, that you just don't get away with things. Now I was about to be judged.

A childhood memory came to me, of the time I'd stolen a Matchbox toy car and Gloria had marched me right back to the store to return it. I remembered my public shame and the private little voice in me that told me I'd done wrong. Most of all, though, it bothered me that I'd hurt my granny, the woman who represented my best impulses.

During this moment I envied my friends who'd been killed. They were now safe, whereas I was stuck here, with myself.

12

NO SURRENDER, NO QUARTER

If that Sunday was dramatic and terrifying, the day that followed was a roller coaster of confused events and emotions.

During the morning most of us in Mount Carmel wandered around in a daze, unsure about what to do next. The scenario in which we found ourselves had no script and no precedent.

What were a group of Americans to do that had been assaulted by its own government with such ferocity, not because we threatened anyone, but essentially because we were different?

We ate breakfast, in silence mostly, our heads dizzy with images we could hardly believe were true. Looking at the faces around me, I saw a kind of amazement, a can-this-really-have-happened stare. Even the kids were subdued, perhaps as much by the mood of the adults as by their own memories of the previous day.

Someone suggested tentatively that we'd just experienced one of the worst moments of religious persecution in U.S. history. "Not since the Mormons . . . ," he said, and trailed off.

To me, the words "religious persecution" sounded medieval. *Wasn't this the Land of the Free? The friggin' twentieth century?* I wanted to shout that this was nonsense, that we couldn't possibly be persecuted for our scriptural beliefs. *Not in America!* But I kept coming around to an implacable question: *Why else had we been attacked so fiercely?* It just didn't make sense.

Livingston was the only one among us who really struck me as serene. For him, the prophecy was working out as David had predicted. We were in the Fifth Seal, he said, souls to be slain "for the word of God." After the "little season," we, too, would die to this world. "Freedom begins at the level of the soul," Livingston declared, and this ringing phrase lifted my spirits for a moment or two.

Outside Mount Carmel the circumstances were also very confusing. That morning, the ATF was muscled aside by its arch rival, the FBI. The ATF negotiator whom David and Steve had been talking to was bumped, much to David's annoyance, then temporarily brought back. During the day, the FBI brought in its own team of negotiators, backed by psychologists from the Austin Police Department. At the same time, a fifty-man FBI Hostage Rescue Team took over Showtime, surrounding us with a fresh demonstration of force. At 1:30 P.M. the feds cut off all our outside telephone lines, leaving only those connected to their new command post at Texas State Technical College.

At the best of times our telephones were tricky. Even before the siege the lines often went dead when it rained. During the siege, since David couldn't move about because of his wound, our sole connection to the outside world was through a hundred-foot spliced extension cord that our cats played games with and our one surviving puppy liked to chew on.

In Washington, President Bill Clinton, conferring with Acting Attorney General Stuart Gerson, stated that the FBI predicted the "standoff" would last for no more than a week to ten days. In California, Robyn Bunds gave a press conference in which she described herself as having been "brainwashed" by David. Meanwhile, David's mother, Bonnie Haldeman, and her husband, Roy, David's stepfather, came to Waco. The feds brought Bonnie to the vicinity of Mount Carmel to "talk David out," they said; but he refused to speak with her, suspicious that she was being manipulated.

"My mother . . . all my life she's been telling me she doesn't even know if I'm her kid or not," he told the feds. David's mother soon gave up on her attempts to get to see her son and went back home to Chandler, Texas. "It's hard not knowing what's going on," Bonnie said. "How many dead. How many hurt."

Meanwhile, David and Steve were discussing a possible surrender with the federal negotiators. The feds first suggested to Steve that, if we all came out, David might appear on ABC's *Nightline* and explain his beliefs to Ted Koppel and a national TV audience. They obviously felt they were playing on David's desire to get his word out.

Steve passed the phone to David, who told the negotiator that he wanted everyone in Mount Carmel to have a chance to make an individual decision.

This seemed to throw the feds for a moment, since it was their view that we were a bunch of mindless slaves of the Sinful Messiah. Between this call and the next, we heard sounds like people walking around on our roof, and David protested vigorously about this breach of our cease-fire agreement. The negotiators then offered a variant of the first proposal: that David would make a tape for a national radio network to broadcast.

After discussing this with Steve, Wayne, and several others, David agreed. Maybe he felt that the opportunity to speak his message to millions outweighed the heavy consequences—prison and public trials—that would surely follow from our surrender. Perhaps he hoped that, on national radio, the churches and their congregations would have a chance to hear his word and recognize his teachings. Maybe, like me, he still kept a basic belief in the essential fair-mindedness and decency of Americans, in their ability to hear a man's true word through the noisy distortions of our institutions.

Most of us were relieved but wary. David had appeared to accept that the little season could be prolonged, that we didn't have to live through the immediate culmination of the Fifth Seal—a reprieve from a fate we both desired and dreaded. Though by now

I was honestly prepared to die for my beliefs, I couldn't say I was eager. Surrender seemed a lot better than a shootout. However, none of us trusted the feds, having seen how they'd lied in their press conferences, denying that they'd fired first and that the helicopters had shot at us. In short, most of us feared the worst but hoped for the best.

As I wandered through Mount Carmel's rooms, viewing the shattered windows and the bullet holes, I anticipated seeing Balenda. I knew she must be tearing her hair out with worry. One negotiator told Scott Sonobe that many relatives had called in to find out how we were, and I was sure Balenda was among them. For my part, I felt I hadn't really done anything wrong, and I was prepared to defend myself in the criminal justice system, even go to jail, if that was how it worked out. Not that I was a martyr; I was just a guy who'd made his bed and was prepared to lie in it.

Despite the proposed surrender, we began to get ready for a long siege, just in case. Some of us went out to the well and filled up as many containers we could find with water. The feds had shot up our water tanks, and we feared that sheer thirst might eventually make us give up. From time to time I looked out the window, watching the FBI "secure the perimeter" with gun posts and patrolling Jeeps and Bradley Fighting Vehicles. For a while I even tinkered with the drums, knocking out a few licks, but I seemed to have lost confidence in my musical skills.

During the day we sent out more children, including Scott and Chrissie Mabb, two of Kathy Schroeder's kids. David gave the children $1,000 to give to the feds, to pay for their upkeep and various other expenses. However, David's suspicion of the FBI remained high all through the discussions about the surrender. "You are all going to kill us," he told one negotiator during the morning. Another negotiator, trying to reassure him, said that the military vehicles circling our building were there "for tactical reasons only," whatever that meant. "They took their guns off," a guy named Jim argued over the phone. "It's strictly a bullet-proof shield." We were suspicious of this jargon—rightly so, as it turned out.

And we weren't the only ones wary of the feds.

Noting the FBI's mobilization of military equipment, former McLellan County District Attorney Vic Feazell lamented the FBI's Storm Trooper tactics (his words) and the "vulgar display of power on the part of the feds." Feazell told the *Houston Chronicle* on March 1: "The Feds are preparing to kill them. That way they can bury their mistakes and won't have attorneys looking over what they did later. . . . I'd represent these boys for free if they'd surrender without bloodshed, but I'm afraid I'm going to wake up and see the headlines that say they all died."

That Monday evening, David called us all together to see how we were doing and to tell us about the deal he and Steve were in the process of working out with the feds, an arrangement to leave Mount Carmel early the next day. He lay propped up against the wall in the hallway, lying on a blanket, his face pale. If the surrender went through, this might well be the last time we would see him.

"Well, Thibodeau, what's cookin'?" he murmured, as I kneeled down beside him.

"We are," I joked, hoping to bring a smile to his lips.

He grinned at me, and I moved away, watching the people pass by David's impromptu couch. Some were weeping, especially the older women. Others voiced thoughts of suicide. "I don't want to leave here," one woman said. "Not alive. This is my *home*." Through it all, David smiled and consoled his flock. To those, like Wayne, who said he felt we'd failed him, David replied, "No matter, not now," with a certain edge of impatience. The period of the withering experience was over, and we were now into the End Time.

Afterward, in Perry Jones's office, we recorded "final messages" on audiotape, describing how each one felt about the recent events. The general atmosphere was surprisingly triumphant, a feeling that, fortified by our faith, we'd fought off a vastly superior force. "God has brought us through this," someone said. "The message is in full swing. The plan is working out."

We all wondered what had happened to Paul Fatta. Shut out of our community, he seemed to have disappeared off the face of the earth. The police were looking for him, to charge him with conspiracy to manufacture and possess unregistered firearms; but after the Austin gun show, he and Kalani had vanished.

Later, we heard Paul's story. Apparently, he'd learned about the raid on his car radio. Paul said he checked into a motel and phoned the authorities several times but was told he wasn't wanted, so he decided to hide out in northern Idaho. Angered by the feds' gross media spin, however, he contacted a reporter at the *New York Times*. "I think the talk of a fiery martyrdom is just something that's being put out by the FBI," he said. "They don't want witnesses. If they find me, they'll kill me." On March 23, however, Paul turned himself in. He is currently serving a fifteen-year sentence for aiding and abetting our resistance to the ATF's attack.

That same Monday evening, our pent-up feelings burst out in an orgy of eating and drinking. We expected to be leaving Mount Carmel the next morning, so we felt free to indulge our appetites one last time. Gathering in the cafeteria, we raided the refrigerator, opened a box of stale cakes Perry Jones had brought a few days earlier, and broke into our cache of hard liquor. For a few hours we threw restraint to the winds, drinking whiskey and smoking cigarettes, shouting and singing, making one hell of a racket, everyone blissed out in reaction to the terrors we'd experienced. We were celebrants at the court of King Nebuchadnezzar denying the writing on the wall.

The more fervent people were singing psalms and praying at the tops of their voices, like a bunch of Pentecostals. We all joined in a circle and Neal Vaega led a prayer, "Father, come down now! We're going into the arms of Babylon!" "Yeah! Yeah!" we all responded, swaying in unison, raising our arms to heaven. I knew this was crazy and I wanted to protest; but like everyone else, I got caught up in the collective high. Still, this wasn't the way we prayed and I knew it.

David disliked such overblown outbursts, and I wondered what he must be thinking about our uproar on his bed of pain upstairs. The answer came when Steve appeared and told us to shut up. "David's mad with you guys," he said. "Why are you letting down the message?" Suddenly, everyone felt like hell, and we slunk away with our tails between our legs.

Anticipating our departure, the FBI eagerly lined up buses down the road as dawn broke on Tuesday. I threw my clothes into my duffel bag ready to go. Other people made themselves sandwiches to see them through the day under the feds' care, but I felt too guilty about last night's food fest to do the same.

David had prepared his audiotape, which the FBI had arranged to have broadcast by the Waco affiliate of CBN, the Christian Broadcasting Network. He sent the tape out with Catherine Matteson and Margaret Lawson and two of Wayne's children, Kimmie and Daniel. So far, it seemed, both sides were playing their parts.

However, as we later learned, the feds treated the older ladies who exited like felons. An ATF agent drew up an affidavit alleging that Catherine and Margaret "did knowingly and willfully use weapons, including machine guns, to commit violent crimes of murder and attempted murder of federal law enforcement officers." This action enraged us when we heard about it, especially the thought of the elderly women being shackled at the wrist, waist, and ankles.

The U.S. Attorney's office was also angry over this action. "Those bozos just rushed in without talking to anybody, slapped those poor old women in leg irons and handcuffs," a federal prosecutor fumed. Catherine and Margaret were soon released, but they spunkily resisted attempts to get them to cooperate with the feds. Pressured to draw diagrams of Mount Carmel, they refused, fearing the government might use such information against us.

David's tape was broadcast several times that afternoon, but the results were disappointing. After all, how could David explain his vision of the Scriptures in under an hour?

Meanwhile, David got ready to exit. Scott Sonobe manned the phone, limping along the corridor, shouting messages back and forth between David and the FBI. Several of the women were help-ing David change out of his bloody, sweaty clothes; others got a stretcher ready to carry him out.

Greg haggled with the feds over the burial of some dead pups, tying up the phone. The rest of us hung around, waiting for the word to go.

Having no reason to trust the authorities, we asked for an in-dependent film crew—from CBS's *60 Minutes*, say—to come in and document the proceedings so the feds couldn't screw us. But the FBI wouldn't allow it, claiming that the volatile situation was too dangerous for journalists.

Everything seemed to be on track. But later that afternoon Steve came downstairs and made a stunning announcement: "We're not going. The time's not right. God has told David to wait."

We stared at him in bewildered silence. There was some mur-muring, but that last sentence killed all argument.

Generally the news was received without comment, and we began to shuffle away to rethink our personal and collective futures.

I must say, I was confused by David's abrupt change of mind. Why had he agreed to leave Mount Carmel, then reversed himself? I was not alone. Many people on both sides of the standoff were thrown by David's switch.

Some of us blamed the previous night's binge, saying we'd sinned by getting drunk and acting wildly. Kathy Schroeder later claimed that Steve had told her that, in David's view, our behavior had damned us. "Should we die then, we would not be saved," she said. The implication was that we had to rededicate ourselves be-fore we could risk annihilation.

FBI spokesman Bob Ricks had a cruder explanation. "David Koresh kissed the kids goodbye. He was going to go outside and commit suicide in front of the TV cameras, and at the last second, he chickened out."

Knowing David, I was sure his explanation that God had told him to wait was absolutely sincere. David had always followed his vision, whatever the consequences, however the world viewed him. But I knew that David's sudden change of mind would play badly beyond our building. Successfully spun by the feds' media manipulations, the American public would likely swallow the official story that David's reversal was proof that we were all his hypnotized, brainwashed hostages. In this context, we'd surely come across as a bunch of jerks, losing face with a lot of people.

But we still had little reason to trust the feds. When the surrender deal was canceled, Steve told a negotiator how we felt about the government's willingness to treat us fairly. "Frankly, I'm glad we're not coming out because, once you get into this building, you can mess with the evidence any way you want, make up any story about us. You're expert at cover-ups." Later, Steve added: "If this building stands . . . and the reporters and the press get to see the evidence, it's going to be shown clearly what happened and what these men came to do."

I had to agree with him. Yet if we had exited, independent investigators might have come in and verified that we were not guilty of all the charges the government had made against us. (As it turned out, when the place was burned to the ground, the feds were able to conceal all the evidence they chose.)

However, even if David himself didn't agree to leave Mount Carmel, most of the rest of us were free to walk out at any time, and thirty-five people actually did leave during the siege. The only exception to this general freedom to exit was David's extended family, which he and the other adults in the family felt had to stick together to share a common fate.

My prediction that David's cancellation of the surrender agreement would play badly on the outside soon proved true.

It immediately sent the feds into conniptions. The next day, ATF Deputy Director Dan Hartnett and Jeffrey Jamar, the FBI's head honcho at Mount Carmel, held a press conference damning David as a deceiver. One FBI spokesman sneered about David's claim to talk to God, and a roomful of journalists sniggered.

Even so, the feds would not allow us to tell our side of the story to the media. After cutting our communication with the outside world and keeping reporters miles away from the scene, a negotiator told Sita Sonobe that they considered it to be in our "best interest and everybody's best interest that a lot of information doesn't get out." Speaking to David, he let slip that the feds were shutting out the media "because we don't want the press to know what we are or are not doing." The *Houston Post* reported, "When enterprising reporters did seek to get closer than the three-mile limit [imposed by the FBI], they were treated harshly. . . . A number of photographers, tired of the 'lens wars' that had developed as media outlets sent stronger and stronger lenses to Mt. Carmel, violated distance limitations. . . . They were summarily arrested, thrown to the ground, handcuffed, and taken away to jail."

"The press are so far back you guys could come and blow us away [and] . . . give any story you wanted," Steve told the feds.

This, of course, was precisely the FBI's intention. The agency didn't want the media to watch as military vehicles vindictively flattened a couple of outbuildings on our property and even rammed a station wagon abandoned by the *Waco Tribune-Herald*. They didn't want video cameras to record the tanks trashing a mobile home, crushing the kids' go-carts, trikes, and bikes, flattening Paul Fatta's custom El Camino, knocking over a fishing boat and the bulldozer we'd rented to excavate the tornado shelter, and skimming the ground of our cemetery, disturbing the graves.

However, they did allow the media to film as they demolished the auto shop away from Mount Carmel, ignoring the building owner's protests. The FBI obviously hoped to publicly reveal part of our "stockpile" of firearms; but the only incriminating evidence found in the auto shop's ruins was six shotgun shells.

I talked to the FBI negotiators several times after that. An agent named Cox tried to question me about the heavy weaponry, including antitank guns and rocket launchers the ATF alleged we were hiding. I tried to tell Cox that we didn't have such armaments, but he countered with the lie that David had admitted having antitank rockets, .50-caliber rifles, and automatic weapons. His tone at the end of this exchange was openly insolent.

Despite official restrictions, or perhaps because of them, journalists by and large vigorously set about demonizing us, creating a climate in which federal agencies and their political masters were allowed, even encouraged, to wipe us out. Conjured into a bunch of maniacal weirdos by the press, we were dehumanized and made ripe for murder.

This potent, twisted contribution of the media to Mount Carmel's tragedy was later described by sociologist Constance A. Jones and public policy analyst George Baker in an essay included in the 1994 book *From the Ashes: Making Sense of Waco.*

"The deaths at Waco were caused in part by the creation of a 'media event' through the media's use of inflammatory language and images," they wrote. "The probability of a violent outcome was increased by pandering to stereotypical assumptions about non-traditional religious behavior. . . .

"Television framed the conflict in terms of good versus evil. As the . . . siege wore on, whatever violent images the camera had on file, such as the [February 28] assault, or even the last images of Jonestown, were repeatedly aired. Because of the element of suspense induced by narrative and inflamed by visual clues, viewers were prepared, and came to anticipate, that the siege would culminate in a dramatic climax. . . . The ante at Waco was upped because of the intervention of television reporting. Lives were endangered because the story line was created and embedded in a pernicious dualism which legitimated the 'authorities' and discouraged unconventional perspectives and opinions."

A prime example of this "pernicious dualism" was displayed on the March 25 episode of *Oprah.* In front of millions of viewers, and while we were in the midst of the siege, the popular host linked David's name with that of Jim Jones by inviting Jones's former attorney as a man who "understands the cult mentality." Oprah's program that day was titled "Inside Waco and Other Cults."

On the show, Oprah tried to manipulate Jeannine and Robyn Bunds into admitting that we were all under David's diabolical spell. Though Jeannine repeatedly denied this, Oprah kept pushing. "Did you, at the time, recognize that—that it was indeed a cult and that you were being brainwashed?" she persisted.

"No. I didn't feel that way at all," Jeannine replied.

"Do you believe he's evil?"

"I don't believe that he is evil," Robyn Bunds answered.

"Authorities were able to take actions against the Davidians with such immunity because they [the media] and members of the general public shared a view of Koresh and his followers and the situation that allowed, even required, such actions," stated James T. Richardson, professor of sociology and judicial studies at the University of Nevada–Reno and an expert on new religions.

Richardson and others have pointed out the crucial role the media plays in distinguishing between "worthy" and "unworthy" story subjects. People or groups that the press decides are worthy of sympathy are described in ways that predispose viewers and readers to look upon them kindly. Those whom the media choose to demonize are shown in a light that distances them from public compassion. As Richardson remarked, "The dehumanization of those inside Mt. Carmel, coupled with the thoroughgoing demonization of Koresh, made it easier for those in authority to develop tactics that seemed organized for disaster."

In general, the media treated our tragedy as a kind of TV miniseries replete with titillating issues like religion, guns, child abuse, sex, and violence. Day after day, for more than seven weeks, the audience heard lurid stories of wild sex, biblical rantings, beaten babies, and armed fanatics ready to fight and die for their crazy notions of heaven and hell at the command of a madman. On April 20, one day after the all-consuming fire and at the height of public shock over our tragedy, an ABC News special, "Waco: The Decision to Die," hosted by anchorman Peter Jennings, featured an interviewee who described David as the "spitting image of Charles Manson."

A major example of this crude characterization of David and our community was a TV movie of the week, "In the Line of Duty: Ambush at Waco," rushed into production during the siege, shown on NBC in May 1993, and rebroadcast many times since. In the film, David was shown in the most damning light as a charismatic, Jim Jones–style monster obsessed with young girls.

However, in an address given at the 1997 memorial service for the people who died in Waco, the TV movie's writer, Phil Penningroth, recanted his role in shaping the NBC film. "Within days of the ATF raid, the Davidians, and especially Koresh, were demonized as the Jews were in Germany before World War II," Penningroth said. "As we all know now, the government and the media painted a portrait of Koresh and Davidians that I now believe was insidious, malevolent, and ultimately destructive. To my everlasting shame and regret, I added to that distorted view. I pray that soon, very soon, other artists, other journalists, will recognize the truth of what happened here four years ago."

Too little, too late, Mr. Penningroth.

In an ironic twist, the FBI became a victim of its own connivance. One of the negotiators we were talking to during the siege complained of the heat the feds were getting from the press: "The bosses back in D.C. look at this thing on TV or *USA Today*, and they don't see anything happening." Having fed the media vicious tales, officials saw them amplified in a rising public pressure that eventually forced their hand.

It may well be that if the media had been allowed to come into Mount Carmel and see that we weren't a bunch of fanatical maniacs, helpless slaves to David's will, then the FBI might have found it harder to gas and burn us. Personally, though, I doubt it. In the words of linguist and political activist Noam Chomsky, groups labeled as "cults" are automatically living in a land beyond "the bounds of acceptable premises." In today's media-saturated climate, the word "cult" is an instant road sign for the audience: WARNING: WEIRDOS AHEAD. All thought is stopped, all questions skewed, as the *Oprah* episode revealed. Even the most basic question—What exactly *is* a cult?—is shoved aside.

Cult. This damning word surfaced early on in the Waco drama, and it tainted almost everything that followed.

Much of the material collected by the ATF to prop up its shaky original affidavit was based on tracts supplied by the Cult Awareness Network (CAN), the most active anticult group in the United States. Later, the FBI accepted a memorandum from CAN that characterized David as "antisocial and narcissistic" and ready to use "any ruse, pretext, trick, deception or force necessary to achieve his personal goals."

Following this formula, FBI spokesman Bob Ricks characterized David as a lying, manipulative "punk," a "con artist."

CAN's main man was a self-styled "deprogrammer" named Rick Ross. Ross first appeared on our horizon in early 1992, when he was hired by the family of David Block to stop him from quitting his job and moving to Mount Carmel. Block was a hip young guy who worked in the Hollywood film industry. I first met him at the Melrose Avenue house, before he came to visit Mount Carmel. He was drawn to David's teaching, but he had a hard time accepting the sexual setup in the community.

Block was talked into undergoing a voluntary "deprogramming," and Ross turned his head around, transforming Block into a vocal critic of Mount Carmel. Block's and Ross's claims added fuel to the complaints of Marc Breault and the other former members of our community that had sparked the original investigation by the Texas Department of Child Protective Services in early 1992.

Apart from providing the feds with his "expert" information on our "cult," Ross also thrust himself forward as a would-be TV personality. He was a guest on the March 10 *Donahue* talk show, along with Kiri Jewell and my mother. However, Ross's public career was soon cut short. He was arrested in connection with a deprogramming action in the state of Washington, charged with unlawful imprisonment and conspiracy to kidnap a young man and force him to renounce his membership in a Pentecostal sect. Ross was ordered to pay $2.5 million in damages.

During the siege a Methodist minister, Joseph Bettis, wrote to Attorney General Janet Reno that "from the beginning, members of the Cult Awareness Network have been involved in this tragedy. This organization is widely known for its use of fear to foster religious bigotry." And a consultant engaged by the government to review the FBI's performance after the fact criticized the feds for not taking into account "the numerous legal challenges to the tactics employed by Mr. Ross in extricating members from the groups he hates."

However, the use of the c-word persisted in official usage. The Treasury Department's September 1993 review of the ATF assault declared: "The Review is quite aware that 'cult' has pejorative connotations, and that outsiders—particularly those in the government—should avoid casting aspersions on those whose religious beliefs are different from their own." However, in a sly sleight-of-hand, the Treasury review offers a dictionary definition of the term "cult" as "a religion regarded as unorthodox or spurious," leading to a conclusion that "in light of the evidence of the conduct of Koresh and his followers set out in this report, the Review finds 'cult' to be an apt characterization." In other words, our community was, in the official view, declared to be "spurious."

The feds' contemptuous attitude toward us was subsequently noted by four consultants engaged after the siege was over to advise the government how to deal with "persons whose motivations and thought processes are unconventional." The consultants were brought in by Deputy Attorney General Philip Heymann and Assistant Secretary of the Treasury Ron Noble.

"During our first round of briefings, especially in our conversations with the hostage negotiators who had been involved in Waco, the most striking finding was the FBI's near total dismissal of the religious beliefs of the Branch Davidians," stated Nancy T. Ammerman, a professor of theology and one of the four consultants. "For these men, David Koresh was a sociopath, and his followers were hostages . . . everyone involved fell victim to the images inherent in the label 'cult.'"

Remarking on the general antipathy most law enforcement people bring to unorthodox religions like ours, Ammerman noted that few law enforcement officers think any clear-minded person would choose to let his life be led by Scripture. These attitudes, she added, "did not make them [the negotiators] tone-deaf so much as it made them unsympathetic." Quoting Max Weber, Ammerman dubbed the agents who'd confronted us as "religiously unmusical." She added: "But they were also blinded by the structures of their own agencies and their own standard operating procedures."

Ammerman admitted that she, too, once shared some of this attitude: "I was sufficiently influenced by this widespread assessment of Koresh as incomprehensible 'Bible babble' that I was surprised when I first began to listen to and read his teachings. They are but a variant of what could be found in many fundamentalist and millennialist churches. . . . The assessment of these beliefs as 'incomprehensible' reflects the biblical ignorance of many public officials and news reporters and the power of the term 'cult' to render all other attempts to understand as unnecessary."

Even the mainstream Seventh-day Adventist Church hurried to disown any connection with us. Concerned that fallout from our bad repute might sully their name, the Adventists rushed a public-relations damage-control team to Waco to deny that the Branch Davidians had grown from their tree. Sadly, the now-accepted, international church forgot that it, too, was once considered a mere cult.

History suggests that a cult graduates into a church if it outlasts its founders. The Romans regarded Christianity itself as a Judaic cult for several centuries, until its persistence earned official respect. The Mormons, too, have similarly evolved. David Koresh drew his direct lineage from Victor Houteff and the Rodens, and his teachings might have outlived him, despite any failed apocalyptic prophecies. After all, the Adventists survived their "Great Disappointment" (the 1844 failure of Jesus's resurrection predicted by William Miller), and several lesser disappointments, to become an organization owning its own schools, colleges, and hospitals. If things had turned out differently, the name "Branch Davidian" might one day have become as unremarkable as "Mormon" or "Adventist," and David Koresh would be just another William Miller: a patch in the crazy quilt that is American fundamentalism.

"While officially neutral about religious doctrine, the state in America has historically been involved in the most severe conflicts involving alternative and minority religions," writes sociology professor Charles L. Harper. "In the nineteenth century, officials were often helpless to intervene or looked the other way as mobs and vigilantes harassed Shakers, Roman Catholics and Mormons. . . . In the twentieth century . . . the conflicts between the state and alternative religions take the form of (sometimes primitive) investigations by regulatory agencies protecting their own interests and 'turf,' such as the rights to control taxation, licensing, and legal compliance in general."

James D. Tabor, a professor of religious studies from the University of North Carolina–Charlotte, said that "cults are 'dangerous' in American society, not merely for what they might do to an unfortunate few, but what they actually do to the uneasy many." Tabor continued: "Cults explicitly endeavor to get us to examine what we care most about and to consider unsparingly whether we are satisfied with the state of the world. . . . The eagerness to condemn 'cults' masks an unwillingness to confront ourselves and to question our society."

Having been tagged a "cult" by the government and the media, we became fair game, removed beyond the bounds of common sympathy. And the taint has stuck to us, discrediting anything we might do to help people understand the more subtle and complex reality we lived in.

We took a while to grasp this fact. Early on, after the FBI had cut us off from the world, we hung out a naive message scribbled on a banner made from a bedsheet. It said, "God Help Us, We Need Press." Trouble was, as it turned out, we had too much press—and it helped to kill us.

———

Though the FBI as a whole had contempt for our beliefs, there were nuances within the agency about how to "handle" us. To put it bluntly, the argument was this: Should we be talked out or booted out?

From the start, the FBI brass characterized the Mount Carmel standoff as a "Hostage/Barricade rescue situation." Hostage Rescue Team commander Jeff Jamar's macho style involved a constant show of force while favoring vulgar acts like allowing agents to "moon" our women, give us the finger as they circled the building in their Bradleys, and loudly and openly refer to us as "motherfuckers" and "cocksuckers."

As I mentioned earlier, it was soon apparent to us that there was tension between the negotiators and the action guys. "I've got all kinds of bosses and commanders around here," one negotiator complained, intimating that he and his colleagues resented the tactical team's pressure for "results." One negotiator later revealed that "the tactical commander said that, left to them, they would have routed the Davidians in the first week." Interviewed on television two years later, this same agent lamented the "tremendous chasm between tactical people and negotiators. I knew the dangers to those kids if we went tactical."

Kevin Clements, director of the Institute for Conflict Analysis and Resolution at George Mason University, who later conducted a review of the Mount Carmel events for the FBI, made the crucial point that the key to any conflict negotiation is to speak the language of the people you're dealing with, have personal contact, initiate a process of de-escalation and conciliatory gestures, and bring in a neutral third party. "You need to understand the logic or illogic of a group's ideas, not just draw up a menu of battle strategies," he noted. Clements is no amateur: The Institute has guided conflict resolution involving religious questions in Northern Ireland, the Soviet Union, the trans-Caucasus, and the Middle East.

Early on, experts attached to the FBI Behaviorial Science Unit had strongly advised the Bureau against an antagonistic approach toward us. "It would appear that we may unintentionally make his [David's] prophecy come true, if we take what he perceives to be a hostile or aggressive action," stated an internal FBI memo discussing the imagined possibility that we'd all commit suicide. "Do the opposite of what Koresh is expecting . . . consider moving back."

Pete Smerick, one of the FBI's behavioral experts, wrote four memos counseling restraint between March 3 and March 8. Smerick said he was "pressured from above" to alter the tenor of his fifth memo, written on March 9. "As a result, that memo contained subtle changes in tone and emphasis that amounted to an endorsement of a more aggressive approach against the Branch Davidians," he said. Frustrated, ignored by his superiors, Smerick finally removed himself from his advisory role in regard to Mount Carmel. Later, after resigning from the agency, he told the *Washington Times* that "bureau officials pressured him into changing his advice on how to resolve the situation without bloodshed."

Special Agent Clinton R. Van Zandt, another member of the FBI's Behavioral Science Unit, testified to the Senate Judiciary Committee that there was no coordination between command, tactical, and negotiation teams, which met only once during the five weeks he was in Waco.

"The negotiation team leaders were refused access to the HRT [Hostage Rescue Team] to discuss the role of negotiations in attempting to resolve the incident," Van Zandt stated. "The lack of coordination between the tactical team and the negotiators further exacerbated an already bad situation, and added emotional fuel to the physical fire that consumed the Davidians." Unfortunately, Van Zandt was an all-too-rare exception to the majority of federal cult-bashers gathered in Waco. A fundamentalist Sunday-school teacher and devoted reader of his much-thumbed King James Bible, Van Zandt lamented bitterly: "The FBI is better than this."

The Justice Department's own October 1993 report frankly acknowledged that "the negotiators felt that the efforts of the tactical personnel were directed toward intimidations and harassment. In the negotiators' judgment, those aggressive tactics undermined their own attempts to gain Koresh's trust as a prelude to peaceful surrender."

In a footnote to his evaluation of the operation, former Assistant Attorney General Edward Dennis commented: "Indeed, the 'negotiations' are characterized as 'communicating' with Koresh or 'talking' to Koresh because the Davidian situation lacked so many of the elements typically present in hostage barricade situations. Koresh made no threats, set no deadlines and made no demands. Koresh and his followers were at Mount Carmel where they wanted to be and living under conditions which were marginally more severe than they were accustomed to."

"Koresh is not delusional, not possessed by a messiah complex," chief FBI negotiator Byron Sage stated. In late March, the negotiators sent a videotape to us in which they tried to put faces to the voices we were hearing. On the tape they talked to us like human beings and showed us photos of their families. For such strategies Sage earned the slander (or compliment) written by the tactical guys on an outhouse: "Sage Is a Davidian."

In return, David tried to treat each negotiator as an individual, as a soul to be saved, not as just the faceless representative of a hostile government. Early on, when one agent suggested that a colleague was "just a voice" for the authorities, David retorted: "No, Jim is a person." On the day after the ATF attack, David expressed his regret over the four agents who had been killed and said that, had circumstances been different, they might have become his friends.

Still, we were deeply frustrated by the negotiators' lack of clout with their superiors. "They've got things being relayed all 1,000 or 1,500 miles back to D.C. It's not a simple chain of command," one FBI man told us plaintively. When David asked to speak to "one of your generals," he was told it wasn't possible. "Then why should I waste time talking to you?" he snapped. At times we thought the negotiators were pretending sympathy as a ploy, a kind of good cop–bad cop strategy. But from the exasperation in the negotiators' voices you could tell they were truly upset about the way things were developing.

Steve suggested we might exploit their frustration and turn the negotiators into our advocates. He tried this once or twice but soon bumped his head on the low ceiling of that rigid, official "culture of disbelief." Pissed off with the negotiators' powerlessness, David finally burst out with, "That's what you people are, you're professional waitresses!"

Finally, Jeff Jamar and his cohorts whipped the negotiators into line, ordering them to cut through the Bible babble and get tough with us. We now know exactly how that strategy worked out.

13

RANCH APOCALYPSE

During the first few days after the canceled capitulation, we struggled to adjust to yet another extraordinary situation. Still stunned by the recent ferocious attack, we had to get our heads around the possibility that we would again be besieged in the middle of Texas by our own government.

I'd read of ancient sieges that had gone on for months, even years, until the surrounded folk were starved into surrender. When I heard a caller on a radio show suggest that the feds should just build a razor-wire fence around our property and withdraw, leaving us alone until we were driven out by hunger, my mind froze. Could we really be treated like a kind of social cancer that had to be isolated, starved, and left to wither?

Dazed, unsure of my own feelings, I tried to gauge the general mood inside Mount Carmel, expecting a wave of despair. To my surprise I sensed a tide of triumph under the lingering shock of the assault and the bitterness of the loss of six of our people. "We're still here," Jaime said triumphantly. "We held off the feds!"

His exultant words made me realize that we had, in fact, stood up against a host of heavily armed agents representing the almighty power of the U.S. government. This buoyant feeling was tempered

211

by the realization that we now had to settle in for the long haul, cut off from the "real" world.

Psychologically, we had to begin to reconcile ourselves to the possibility that we might be confined to the Anthill indefinitely—no easy thing. "I hate this place!" Steve said, over and over. Even David, during those early siege days, blurted to a negotiator that he had no intention of "sitting here rotting and dying. I'd rather live in prison than have to live in this cold place."

Spiritually, the siege put us in a kind of limbo. Though we seemed to be in the "little season," its duration was uncertain and its outcome was out of our hands. There might be divine intervention, a sudden "translation" from earth to heaven, or the bloody end predicted in the Fifth Seal. Ironically, it was up to the feds to decide our fate, through patient negotiation, or by fencing us in and walking away, or by annihilation. All we could do was wait and stand by our beliefs.

Frankly, I had little faith in translation, and a full comprehension of the Fifth Seal was beyond me. I no longer trusted anything the government was saying, so I had no idea how things might work out. Essentially, it was up to David.

My feelings for David deepened during the siege. I saw how he suffered both physically and spiritually, his body and his soul tormenting him by turns. He had a rare kind of fortitude, it seemed to me: the courage to stick to his vision even though its consequences might be fatal for himself and the people he cared for with all his heart—not only his own children and the women who were close to him, but all of us. I'd never wanted to have that weight on my shoulders.

Whether anyone believed it or not, David felt he had to wait on God's word, and that Old Guy in the Sky takes his own, sweet time. I still didn't consider David as "Christ" or the "Messiah"—as I've said, he always vehemently rejected those terms—but as someone who had been given a special teaching I valued tremendously. My loyalty was to the message he gave me, not to any godlike being;

but I also felt a personal loyalty to a man I respected and who'd become my friend.

Now my allegiance to the teachings and the man became more and more intense. During the siege, I often deliberately sat in front of the window close to where David was lying or standing, so that if a sniper wanted to take him out he'd have to go through me. And that was no mean risk. Apparently, FBI snipers had David in their sights several times.

During the first five days of the siege, twenty-one children exited, along with some of the elderly folks, like Gladys Ottman, James Lewis Lawter, Victorine Hollingsworth, and Annetta Richards, a Jamaican nurse. All of these people were sixty-something or older. In addition, several younger women, such as Sheila Martin and Rita Fay Riddle, soon departed Mount Carmel. Eight of the adults were held as material witnesses in McLennan County Jail, then some were released to a halfway house. Victorine, ailing and shaken by her experience, was sent to the hospital.

As she saw her kids leave, one mother whispered, "See you on the other side"—a sentence than could be read several ways.

To entice David's seven-year-old son, Cyrus, to leave Mount Carmel, a negotiator spun Cyrus a yarn about his cousins, Kevin and Mark Jones: "We gave them some Coke and candy and they got to ride in that tank." The agent told Cyrus that if we all came out "moms and stuff and everybody can stay together." This was an outright lie, since many of the women were jailed.

Another negotiator discussed with Rachel, Cyrus's mother, the feeding of the children who'd exited. She suggested a healthy diet of fresh fruit, juices, and vegetables, maybe some hot dogs—but no pork, forbidden by our dietary rules. However, it soon became clear that the kids were, as Cyrus's pal said, being fed a junkload of sodas and candy, which distressed Rachel and the other mothers.

Custody hearings were held for children whose relatives had come to claim them. Grandparents, aunts, uncles, and sisters arrived from Florida and Hawaii, London and Australia. Kathy

Schroeder's former husband, U.S. Air Force Sergeant William Mabb, was given custody of the three children they had in common. When Kathy herself came out with her son, Bryan, Mike's boy, she was held as a material witness, and Bryan was put in the care of the Texas Department of Child Protective Services for "evaluation."

Balenda and my Uncle Bob had flown in from Bangor a few days after the siege began. Later I learned that she supported herself by working the desk at Waco's Brittany Hotel. She immediately began to pressure the feds to allow the families to connect with their relatives inside Mount Carmel.

"How could it hurt for our voices to come in?" Balenda insisted. "We, the families, are not going to stand back and find we waited too long. I don't want a dead son."

For all her previous activism, my mother had never experienced a situation as complex and confused as this one. After rejecting the advice of Rick Ross and his Cult Awareness Network, she had to learn on her own how to cope with both the feds and the media. A vivid, passionate person, she became the families' spokeswoman in interviews with journalists like Katie Boyle of CBS-TV's *48 Hours* and Kathleen Davis of CBS-TV's *Morning Live*.

"I am really angry because I really feel there needs to be that middle ground, a faction, a voice that is not empowered by guns, but is empowered by love," she said in an eloquent public statement. "Is there any reason that I can't say goodbye to my child if in fact I'm going to lose him?"

One of the FBI negotiators I talked to suggested that I should make a videotape and send it out to my mother. "We'll get it to her, so she can see how you're doing," he said, faking concern for Balenda. Taking the man at his word, I made a short tape and gave it to Steve to hand over to the feds. On camera, I wore my zipped leather jacket and a University of Maine T-shirt, affecting a reassuringly casual look. I told Balenda I knew she was nearby, pulling for me. "I know it's hard on you, but I have to see this through," I said. "I'm always kind of teasing you for being emotional, Mom," I added, knowing she'd understand that I appreciated her support and felt her love. (Of course the FBI lied again, my mother never got to see this tape at that time.)

Ruth Mosher, Sherri Jewell's mother, said: "When I flew to Waco on March 11, 1993, I tried to get the FBI to let me talk to Sher to see if there was any way I could talk her into coming out. The FBI refused to let me get near the scene. . . . Besides myself, there were parents who flew in from Hawaii just for that purpose, and they were also turned down. . . . My only regret is that I did not stay in Waco the entire time, like . . . Belinda [sic], David Thibodeau's mother. At least David came out and was never incarcerated."

"Sheriff Harwell was skirting the fence," Balenda told me afterward. "Being a typical live-and-let-live Texan, he felt you ought to have been left alone but had to bow to the feds. 'My hands are tied, ma'am,' he told me, but I kept at him."

I knew my mother wondered why I stayed inside Mount Carmel, risking my life. She felt that David had too much influence over me, and maybe she didn't believe any of us really had the choice to come out at any time.

She was wrong. Over the following weeks a few adults left, singly or in groups. On March 12, Kathy Schroeder and Oliver Gyarfas Jr. went out. On March 19, Brad Branch and Kevin Whitecliff departed, banished, in a way, for sneaking shots of whiskey. Two days later, seven more adults left. On March 23, David sent Livingston out as a spiritual emissary in a futile, last-ditch attempt to explain our feelings and beliefs to a deeply hostile audience.

Most of the adults who exited did so reluctantly. In some cases, especially the women, David said he wanted chaperones for the children who'd already gone out. Maybe some of the people who departed did want to leave but didn't like to admit it.

On the three main videotapes we made during the siege and sent out to the feds (who didn't show them to the media), a number of our men, women, and children explained why they had chosen to stay in Mount Carmel. The scratchy tapes, which the FBI was afraid to release, as one fed said, for fear that "Koresh would gain much sympathy," were vivid snapshots of our community:

"This is where existence is for me in the world," says Bernadette Monbelly, a young black woman from England who died in the fire.

Ofelia Santoyo, who later exited, tells her family "not to worry about me because these prophecies have to be fulfilled."

Livingston's wife, Evette, speaks of regretting her decision to send her children out in the first week of the siege. "They'd be safer [here] than being in the hands of Babylon," she declares.

David, unshaven, leans against the corridor wall wearing a white sweatshirt, obviously in pain. He talks to a number of the kids, beginning with seven-year-old Cyrus, whose long, golden hair frames his small, serious face. Flashing his Harley-Davidson sweater, Cyrus says bluntly: "They tore up my motorcycle. Makes me mad."

"You love Daddy?" David asks his shy, six-year-old daughter, Star, and she coyly nods. David's plump, sixteen-month-old girl, Bobbie, still unsteady on her pins, hugs her dad and mugs for the camera. "Our little clown," David grins, kissing the baby.

These three are Rachel's children, David's "legitimate" offspring. He goes on to introduce his other kids, the heart of the House of David, the future Elders of our faith.

"How much do you love me?" he asks three-year-old, dimpled Dayland Gent, Nicole's son. "I love you three," the boy replies, who then goes on to recite his ABCs. Nicole joins David with her baby, Paige, "my Australian baby." "We met at my mother's house," Nicole recalls, brushing back her long brown hair.

Mayanah, Judy Schneider's fair-haired two-year-old, is "my little mynah bird," David says. "She's a talker." My favorite, Serenity, waves bravely to the camera, hiding her shy face and rosebud mouth. In answer to David's question, she says, "I want to grow up to be a woman." Aisha Gyarfas, very pregnant, cradles one-year-old Startle on her lap and flicks her auburn hair.

Julie's dark-skinned son, Joe, chatters on about his 50cc motorbike and his boxing and baseball gloves. He remembers the bullets that came close to killing him on February 28. "We got on the floor, scared, praying to God," he says solemnly. David asks Joe's little brother, Isaiah, "You love your enemies?" "No," the boy retorts, provoking laughter.

Two of the older girls explain why they've chosen to remain in Mount Carmel. "I don't want to come out," says Audrey Martinez, all of thirteen. Fellow teenager Rachel Sylvia declares: "Love is here. God is here."

Confronting the inquisitive lens, David says: "This is my family. It might not be like your family, but no one's going to come in on top of my family and start pushing us around."

In a lighter vein, he compares his troubles with the ATF and the FBI to "getting into a fight with your neighbor. The little brother whips you, then big brother comes over to investigate."

An FBI negotiator's log revealed why the agency feared the tapes would create sympathy for us. "Each person on the video—male and female, young and old, spoke in a calm, assured tone of their desire to remain inside, even after the experience of the ATF raid only a few days earlier," the 1993 Justice Department report stated. "The abiding impression is not a bunch of 'lunatics,' but rather a group of people who, for whatever reason, believed so strongly in Koresh that the notion of leaving the squalid compound was unthinkable."

The FBI sent in a tape of the kids who'd gone out, and we gathered in the chapel to watch it on the VCR. Afterward, the mothers were very upset about how rackety the kids were. But I understood; it was like a party for them. Julie Martinez complained that the children out there were "hyper as heck," and many of the mothers felt the kids were being defiled by the forbidden foods they were given.

The overwrought way the children were behaving on this tape had a profound effect on Julie. Her five children—Audrey, Abigail, Joseph, Isaiah, and Crystal, ranging in age from thirteen to three—were the largest family, outside of David's twelve children, remaining in Mount Carmel.

The FBI had hoped that it would gain a psychological advantage if Julie had let her children exit, thereby leaving David and his family as the last holdouts, apart from the adult men and women, Wayne Martin's two oldest daughters, Sheila Jr. and Lisa, plus thirteen-year-old Rachel Sylvia and six-year-old Melissa Morrison. David offered to let Melissa leave if the FBI would let him talk to Robert Rodriguez; but the FBI, suspecting Robert's loyalty, refused. Melissa herself asked to stay in Mount Carmel with her mother, Rosemary, a black woman from Britain.

"You're concerned about your children, as all good mothers are," an agent told Julie. "David has repeated that you're all free to go, and that if you stay it's your choice."

Julie wavered, torn between the safety of her family and her fears that the feds would permanently separate her from her children, accusing her of being an "unfit mother," as they had accused some of the other women who'd exited with their children. If she went out with them, as the agents suggested, she feared she'd be imprisoned and her children would be taken into care.

"That should not be a concern because it's not true," the feds lied. "They always want to keep the parents with their children." Julie retorted that she knew that many of the children who'd come out were in foster homes, but the agents tried to befuddle her with veiled threats that "it's not going to get better."

Really torn up by having to make this difficult decision, Julie asked to talk to her elder brother in Arizona to see if he would take charge of her children. The feds refused; but they did get her brother to send Julie a message urging her to send her children out.

"What's best for my family?" she agonized. "To keep it together, come what may, or hand my kids over to the tender mercies of officials I really distrust?"

The night that Julie decided to keep her children with her, she was in tears. "I'm not sending my kids out there, I'm not going out," she told me. "Those feds I was talking to made me feel real cheap, saying stuff like, 'How can you be involved in this group?' Oh no, they're not taking my kids away from me. I love them. Hell, I got off drugs for them!"

Julie's fears that she'd lose her kids if they left Mount Carmel and that she would go to prison were confirmed when her mother, Ofelia, left the community and was promptly jailed for several months.

———·+·———

On a practical level, we had plenty of food to carry us through a long siege, mainly a store of MREs—our true "stockpile"—and twenty-five chickens penned up out back.

Water was scarce. Though riddled with bullets, our storage tanks could still hold a couple of hundred gallons, but that wouldn't last eighty or so people very long. Greg Summers melted down some toy solders from kids' toys and plugged some of the holes, but that makeshift repair didn't hold. To supplement our supply we went outside when it rained and collected water in buckets, even though the FBI threatened to shoot us.

After the feds first interrupted then finally disconnected our electricity supply (on March 12, the coldest night of the siege, the low dipping into the twenties), we had to rely for light and warmth on a couple of dozen Coleman and kerosene lanterns, some propane heaters, and two generators running on gasoline. We owned no personal appliances, so our power use was low anyway; but the lack of electricity immobilized the pump that drew water from the artesian well to the tanks beside the cafeteria.

Fortunately, our propane tanks were topped off. Four days or so before the ATF raid, Perry Jones had visited Star-Tex gas to fill two five-gallon tanks; in addition, we had four other tanks, three holding twenty-five gallons and one fifteen gallons. However, a thousand-gallon tank we'd installed the previous June was empty, since we'd never needed it—till now.

Milk for the children was a real predicament, and that led to our first direct challenge to the feds' humanity.

Milk was a problem for us in more ways than one. It was an Adventist tradition, dating back to the church's founder, Ellen G. White, that cow's milk was far less healthy than goat's milk and, of course, mother's milk. Now we were cut off from the supply of goat's milk we'd been buying in Waco; even worse, the mothers who were nursing babies stopped lactating because of the stress and tension caused by the raid and the continuing presence of our enemies.

David told the feds about this, and they immediately started haggling, trying to compel us to exchange kids for milk. David sent out one of David Jones's children, but the FBI reneged on its deal, perhaps to spite our canceled surrender. David, Steve, and some of the moms begged the negotiators to honor their promise, but they didn't. Instead, an FBI spokesmen told the press we'd rejected their offer.

This attitude persisted until David got to speak to Sheriff Harwell. He immediately promised to see what he could do to get us the milk. "I want those babies taken care of," the good man declared, and six gallons of milk were sent in. Cow's milk, to be sure, but we had no choice.

"We just could not understand why you all were, you know, punching at the kids," David complained to a negotiator when we finally got the milk. In his response, the agent on the line revealed again the dissension between the negotiators and the tacticians. "You know and I know who it is, and it's not us," he said.

However, the FBI once again twisted the truth, claiming to the press that Sheriff Harwell had had to beg us to accept the milk. To cap it all, the feds hid secret bugging devices in the plastic milk bottles. These bugs were the first of many the FBI managed to sneak into our building during the siege.

As a matter of hygiene, we buried Perry Jones beneath the dirt floor of the tornado shelter, along with Jaydean Wendell, Winston Blake, and Peter Hipsman. One morning, Mark Wendell, Jimmy Riddle, and Clive Doyle sneaked out to retrieve Peter Gent's body in the water tower. Peter lay where he'd been killed, on a ladder at the top of the tower. They lowered him down with a rope and zipped his body into a sleeping bag.

Peter's parents had come from Australia and wanted to get possession of his body to bury him. Steve asked the FBI to take the body to Waco for burial. Unbelievably, the feds started dickering, insisting that one of us remain with the body. We refused, knowing that Peter's escort would likely end up in jail. Nicole complained to a negotiator that her brother's corpse remained unburied, and we were finally allowed to inter him in a grave under a tree on the front lawn.

The FBI refused to give us permission to bury the dogs killed in the raid. Greg had to lay them out in a row to show the world what the ATF had done to his animals. As the days wore on the corpses had decayed, and the stench of their rotting bodies was making us sick. One afternoon three guys with shovels went outside to dig a shallow grave for Peter Gent.

Meanwhile, we settled in for the long haul. After a breakfast of nuts, applesauce, and raisin rolls, study sessions occupied us till lunch. We had a packaged MRE for lunch and another for early supper, then more study till nightfall, when most of us were too exhausted by tension and increasing hunger to do anything but fall into bed.

The FBI and, later, Janet Reno made much of the idea that we and the children were suffering from "deteriorating sanitary conditions," but things weren't nearly as bad as they made out. Everyone kept clean. Before water became scarce we took sponge baths in rainwater. I let my hair grow longer, but I shaved my face.

We soon ran out of natural food and had to fall back on cans. Assessing our grocery stores, which consisted mostly of piles of those unappetizing MREs, we reckoned we'd have to ration ourselves to two cans per day. The water ration was gradually reduced until, by early April, we were down to two eight-ounce ladles per person per day. The worst thing was the cold, especially for the kids, who shivered through some freezing nights. I battled the cold by wearing layers of sweaters, but the icy Texas winds cut me to the bone.

The gym was the most exposed area of the building, difficult to guard, and so we blocked it off, fearing that agents could penetrate it any time they liked. However, since we no longer had access to our outside toilets, we were forced to use the gym as a place to dump the waste buckets, emptying them down a plank through a hole in the back wall. We also carried the buckets through the tunnels and the underground bus into the tornado shelter, but that was more risky, since the feds could enter it easily. All that was pretty disgusting, but it was necessary to keep our living space clean.

Steve organized a roster of men to keep watch in shifts, day and night, led by guys like Neal Vaega and Brad Branch, who were most easy with guns. I was given a pistol and a rifle; I slept with them beside me as a kind of symbolic security blanket. I carried the pistol with me when I had to go into the gym at the rear of the building to collect some extra blankets. The Glock felt cool in my hand, in both senses of the word: cool to the touch and cool to be armed, like a movie hero. However, if I'd actually come across an agent back there my hands would most likely have automatically lifted in surrender. I just couldn't see myself killing anyone.

One time, though, I did want to use my gun—to shoot those damned speakers out. The noise of sirens, seagulls, bagpipes, crying babies, strangled rabbits, and crowing roosters was driving me nuts, yet I resisted the temptation. Instead, we began a kind of duel of the amps, blasting recordings of our music through our own loudspeakers, which drew a protest from the feds. Some cheek! A neighboring farmer complained that the racket of the speakers and the choppers stampeded his Brahmins, causing them to lose weight and market value. So much for the FBI's vaunted psychological operations, or "psywar."

Even though our resources were low, our spirits were high. The isolation gave me time to play cards with the children, especially Julie's sons, Joe and Isaiah. Between games we watched the tanks and Bradleys moving around Mount Carmel. "Kinda scary but kinda neat," Joe said. For many of the kids, the siege was an adventure, a real-life movie. In truth, even after the first firefight, the young boys and girls didn't appear to be shattered. They certainly weren't nearly as nervous as I was. They just went on being kids, and so hanging around with them lifted my spirits.

There were sad moments, though. A week or two into the siege we began fitting the gas masks, and I helped Serenity with hers. We had to struggle to adjust the leather mask to fit her small face; it was awkward and hurtful. After a few moments a tear escaped the mask and ran down her chin. My heart wrenched as I watched the tiny drop fall onto her dress.

All in all, though, we accepted the hard time as a test of our faith and an enhanced "withering experience," a kind of purification under duress. I didn't really miss the goodies that used to obsess me, didn't mind going without pizza and beer. On the contrary, as I felt the fat slipping from my bones, hunger became a kind of exaltation.

My body slimmed to some 150 pounds, my trimmest weight since fifth or sixth grade. Maybe it was starvation, yet I felt lighter on my feet and purer in heart than I'd been in my entire life. Even toward the end of the siege, when I got so weak I could barely walk, I was buoyed by sheer pride. As my flab dissolved, my willpower firmed up. Inside, I felt good, essentially invulnerable. For a while I was the person I'd always wanted to be.

In the seven weeks during which we were forcibly holed up, I was given a powerful taste of transcendence that will always flavor my life—a sense of going beyond the boundaries of everyday existence and my own limitations into another, more exalted realm. But a taste was all it was. During those long nights and slow days I came to realize that a glimpse of such profundities was probably all I'd ever have, all my earthbound nature would ever allow me to achieve.

"You know, Thibodeau, I just wish I had three more years with you," David told me. But fate denied me that time. Probably it would not have changed much even if I'd had the additional years of study. Day by day it became ever clearer that my destiny and David's destiny were quite different. His visionary gifts came out of who he was, his particular character. Since my personality was unlike his, I knew I'd have to find my own way forward, struggling to find how to be transcendent and earthbound together. As Steve liked to remind me, I wasn't "theologically seasoned," that is, I wasn't grounded in Adventism or any other Christian faith.

But during my best moments I hoped that lack of seasoning left me open to reaching something more personal, something more purely me: a true witness rather than a total worshipper.

———

Though the feds tried to sever all our links with the rest of humanity, they didn't quite succeed.

In an early breakthrough, a communications technician told Dallas AM station KGBS that our satellite dish could be repositioned to pick up radio transmissions, and KGBS announcer Ron Engelman sent us a message to move the dish to show we could receive his signal. For the duration of the siege, Engelman kept contact with us, speaking out on our behalf when most of the media were swallowing the official version of events or pursuing their own warped agendas.

Engelman had his own agenda, of course. He was a constitutionalist—a believer in a radical interpretation of the U.S. Constitution as a bulwark against government abuse. His sympathy for us wasn't religious but political, but at the time he seemed to be the only voice out there speaking up for our rights. However, his voice was the first indication that the events at Mount Carmel, against our will or intention, would spawn a politically charged controversy.

A totally religious community, we never had a direct interest in politics in any conventional sense. For us, the destiny of the human race would be played out on a spiritual plane, and the conflicts of the mundane arena were essentially irrelevant, except as examples of a massive Babylonian futility. But the Mount Carmel story quickly became political, much to our eventual disadvantage.

Engelman's take on our predicament attracted libertarian weirdos like Gary Hunt, publisher of a way-out tabloid, *Outpost of Freedom*. Hunt contacted Engelman, and the announcer urged us to break through the feds' communications blackout by hanging out bedsheet banners.

One day Engelman and some like-minded associates came to Waco to try to bring us a couple of "medical men"—who turned out to be podiatrists!

The FBI refused the foot men entry, but their visit did spur the feds into again offering us medical attention for the people suffering from wounds. David Jones, shot in the tailbone, was embarrassed but okay. Scott Sonobe's injuries, however, were painful. He'd treated his swollen hand, which a bullet had pierced, with a solution of Epsom salts and some of our few remaining oral antibiotics. A doctor summoned to the phone by the FBI told him his hand bones had likely been smashed and that his wound should be X-rayed and surgically cleaned. He was also limping from the bullet in his thigh. Judy Schneider's shattered right index finger was swollen and discolored, and she had resorted to rubbing it with garlic, a favorite Mount Carmel remedy that David also used on his wounds. When Judy's finger failed to heal, she suggested to Steve that he cut it off, but he rightly refused.

David was suffering the most from his injuries. He pissed blood, his stomach wound kept seeping, and it was painful for him to shit, cough, or laugh; he had spasms, tremors, and splitting headaches; his thumb was numb and his pierced wrist wasn't healing. Before she left, Annetta Richards, the Jamaican nurse, cleaned his wounds. Later, the feds sent in a suture kit, also bugged with a listening device. At times, David would fall unconscious in the middle of a sentence and awake with a startled look in his eyes, as if he'd been forced to come back to earth from a temporary heavenly translation and regretted his return.

The feds used the promise of medical attention to lure us into sending out more people, even after all those who wanted to leave Mount Carmel had departed. "Show us these signs of goodwill," a negotiator told Steve, "and we will allow those who need medical treatment to return back inside the compound if they so wish."

"A likely story," was Steve's sardonic comment.

Despite the FBI's desire to cut us off from the world, two odd guys managed to slip through the official cordon a few days after the attack.

Our first visitor was a twenty-five-year-old Pentecostal telephone operator from Houston named Louis Alaniz.

Upset by the universally bad press we were getting, Louis came to Waco to find out if we were as devilish as we were made out to be. He dodged the roadblocks and made his way through the woods to the edge of our property. Sliding around an FBI tank, he came running up to our front door and banged on the bullet-riddled metal, howling to be let in as the feds' loudspeakers screamed out dire warnings. We opened the door a crack and he slipped inside, dirty and hungry, scratched by thorns and bitten by ants. Louis stayed until April 17, studying Scripture with David, sharing our privations. When he left he was jailed by the feds.

Two days later a middle-aged hippie with a beard down to his navel appeared at our door. Jesse Amen was, he said, "a witness from God," a pilgrim bicycling across the United States on a sacred journey. He spoke fervently of "Lord Lightning Amen" and his lady "Cherry Lightning Amen" and told us a biblical army was massing on the Colorado River to rescue us from the feds. When he came in, David astonished Jesse by washing his muddy feet. This Christ-like gesture blew the man's mind, and he hung around until April 4 before giving himself up. "You get to where you just can't take no more," Jesse said. For Jesse, Mount Carmel was a spiritual feast as well as a physical famine, and that held true for the rest of us.

Jesse, the feds announced, escaped our "compound," and the constant use of that word by the feds and the press to describe Mount Carmel really annoyed us. It made us seem as if we were living in a prison camp, locked like convicts in a circle of barbed wire. "Would they refer to the Capitol in Washington as a 'compound'?" Wayne protested. "Is the Playboy Mansion in L.A. a compound?" I chimed in. The word was a clear putdown, meant to reduce our status as free men and women.

The omnipresence of the feds created an unrelenting pressure, like hands squeezing my skull. It wasn't only the loudspeakers blaring that earsplitting trash at us, or the stadium lights glaring at us all night, or even the rude shouts of the circling feds—"Get the hell outta here!" "Why don't we just kill 'em all!"—but also the frequent buzzing of the choppers swooping over our roof, prompting me to hit the floor with every pass. This protective reflex became so automatic that for months after the siege I'd hit the deck anytime I heard a helicopter—even in peaceful Bangor.

Even so, I never abandoned hope that some act of grace would rescue us. Maybe old Jesse Amen was right: Perhaps an army of biblical prophets was waiting in the wings to come marching along, banners flying, and part the Red Sea of rage with which the feds had surrounded us. But the only banners we ever spotted were Old Glory—the stars and stripes now the standard not of liberty but of our persecution—and a white flag with red diagonals, a kind of reversed Dixie banner flown by some of the tank drivers.

There were moments of humor, though. One time Sherri Jewell jokingly told an agent that the horns mentioned in Psalm 75 were symbolic penises. *Lift not up your horn on high: speak not with a stiff neck . . . the horns of the wicked also will I cut off,* she quoted, laughing as the negotiator's soft "Ouch!" came over the line in response. But Sherri was not amused by her husband's exploitation of twelve-year-old Kiri on *Donahue.* "I hate what my ex-husband has pumped into her mind," she said angrily.

There were, we heard, attempts to reach President Clinton to make him reconsider the government's aggressive attitude toward us. On March 11, two prominent Baptists, James Dunn and Dean M. Kelley, wrote the president: "Please demilitarize the confrontation in Waco, Texas. It does not call for hundreds of heavily armed federal employees and Abrams tanks waiting for a showdown. . . . It is better to let [the Branch Davidian community] alone as much as possible until it either runs down or stabilizes as a more conventional religion. If there must be a 'victory' to save face for the government, can it not be brought about in a humane way?"

That same day, Acting Attorney General Stuart Gerson left office. During his tenure, the only escalation he allowed the FBI in regard to Mount Carmel was to move more armored vehicles into the area. "I felt there was no need to force a change in the status quo. We were getting people out," Gerson declared.

However, as soon as Gerson left office, and while Janet Reno was still settling in, Agent Jamar told the FBI negotiators to treat David as if his scriptural messages were a delaying tactic. Glenn Hilburn, chairman of Baylor University's Department of Religion, warned the FBI: "It was not wise at all to do that, especially in a situation that tense."

Again, that same day, there was a flurry over an astronomical event, a neutron star sighted in our galaxy. The gases in the tail of the fast-moving star gave it a peculiar shape, so the press named it the Guitar Nebulae. At first David, the guitarist, was skeptical, suspecting an FBI attempt to con him into surrender with a heavenly "sign." For a moment, though, he got quite excited, quoting biblical prophecies about celestial chariots during a temporary delirium brought on by his wounds.

———•—•———

At times, the government appeared to be genuinely trying to work things out with us. For example, on March 16, chief negotiator Byron Sage and Sheriff Harwell arranged to meet Wayne and Steve in front of Mount Carmel. For two nights previously, Harwell talked on the phone with Steve and David, saying, in his reasonable way, that it was time for common sense to prevail. The sheriff lied a little though, pretending that most people would be set free and their property returned. Maybe the good man actually believed this. He told David that he'd talked to many of our neighbors and that none of them had anything bad to say about us.

(That, also, was a bit of a fib. Locals were surely distressed at the unpleasant reputation the "Waco wackos" were giving their town. To counter this bad rap, some of them had put "WACO PROUD" stickers on their bumpers.)

"What does the sealed warrant say?" Steve asked the sheriff over the phone, referring to the original ATF affidavit and the search-and-arrest warrant it generated. "We still don't know what David or any of us have been charged with!" The answer was vague, as the sheriff himself hadn't seen the document that initially sparked the trouble.

On March 16, while we crowded the windows to watch, Wayne, formal and nervous in his business suit, and a cool, casual Steve, snug in a windbreaker, waited in a temporary neutral zone in front of Mount Carmel for the G-man and the sheriff to arrive. Harwell and Sage, who were visibly on edge, drove up in a Bradley. For minutes that seemed like years, we watched the four of them huddle, trying to decipher their body language. The sheriff was laconic and Texan, his white hair and comfortable paunch sending a message of honest decency. Sage's tall figure was stiff, as if he expected a bullet in the back at any moment—whether from his side or ours, I couldn't tell.

Our men, too, were a contrast in attitudes. Whereas Steve kept up a steady, eyeball-to-eyeball face-off with the officers, Wayne turned away from time to time, abruptly removing himself from the tight circle before plunging back in with vehement gestures.

Wayne's intense, dark face clearly showed uncertainty about what he was hearing, and we took that as a bad sign. However, when the meeting broke up and Sage and Harwell climbed back into the Bradley, Steve walked toward our front door with a confident step. "I believe Byron is sincere," Steve announced to David. The rest of us, clustered around, nodded eagerly.

But nothing came of this meeting. In reality, FBI commander Jamar and his masters back in Washington had already lost patience. A week earlier, Jamar had apparently told the press that the "ten-day roll" standard for an FBI hostage-rescue operation had expired, and it was time to tighten the noose. It was then that he permanently cut off our electricity. A week later, on March 22, the FBI began to prepare its final assault plans for presentation to the new attorney general, Janet Reno. The following day Sage himself signed off on the decision to use tear gas against us, signaling the final triumph of the tactical team over the negotiators.

On March 25 Jamar upped the ante once more with a demand that between ten and twenty more people should leave Mount Carmel by 4:00 P.M. that day. If not, "certain actions will be taken," the negotiator warned us. "This is not a threat, Steve, this is a promise." Later the feds maliciously destroyed some of our remaining equipment, including Steve's motorcycle.

A bunch of us gathered around Steve as he talked to a negotiator about a group of us exiting, including Clive Doyle and the wounded Scott Sonobe. Judy Schneider, though in pain from her injury, refused to be separated from the daughter she'd had with David.

One of the demands Steve made for our exiting was that the ATF agents who shot at us should also be charged with criminal offenses; unfortunately, the negotiator claimed that such things were out of his hands. Meanwhile, ATF spokesman David Troy repeated his old lies that we'd been running a drug lab and that we'd been the first to shoot on February 28, and the FBI's tactical team began ripping down our fence to clear the way for the final assault.

Next day, the loudspeaker noise changed from the crying baby and the honking seagulls to howling coyotes. During the evening a Bradley dropped off nineteen pints of milk, some packets of crackers, and a fresh battery for our video camera. This was the feds' last humane gesture, for by then they had definitely decided to gas us into submission.

"Yeah, my babies, my life is over," David told an agent on the phone as we entered the last phase of the siege.

BOOK THREE

Life as a Survivor

14

"ARE YOU COMIN' TO KILL ME?"

Despite David's gloomy prediction, we began Passover celebration on April 7 with a fresh wave of hope. Some things were happening that at last seemed to open a narrow door for us to leave Mount Carmel alive—not in abject surrender but with a sense that we'd honored our beliefs and stood up for them in the face of a hugely powerful opponent. Everything hinged on the willingness of federal agents and Justice Department officials to acknowledge that our spiritual faith was genuine, not the rantings of a bunch of wackos led by a religious huckster.

For the first month of the siege FBI commanders had isolated us from all contact with the outside world in order to preserve the official view that we were dangerously weird. They'd even refused us our basic right to legal representation, preventing Dick DeGuerin and Jack Zimmerman, two highly reputable Houston criminal-defense attorneys who represented David and Steve Schneider, from talking to their clients or entering Mount Carmel. Since the feds had cut our telephone lines, confidential discussions with the attorneys were impossible.

On March 10, DeGuerin and David's mother, Bonnie Halde-man, had driven to the FBI command post and tried to talk to Jeff Jamar, the FBI special agent in charge of the siege operation. De-Guerin even filed a petition in federal district court for a writ of ha-beas corpus, which was denied by Judge Walter Smith Jr., who later played a sinister role in the trial of eleven of our members in San Antonio. DeGuerin kept pressuring Jamar. Finally, in late March, Jamar relented, perhaps to demonstrate that he was willing to try every angle before he attacked us.

Between March 29 and April 4 Dick came in five times; Jack came in twice. Their entry into our locked-down community was like a visit from an alien planet. Dick swaggered in wearing lizard cowboy boots, his tanned, boyish Texas face beaming with the kind of tough, easy confidence we'd long lost in our struggle just to survive.

Jack was plainly shocked by what he saw, and the look of sym-pathetic horror on his rugged countenance gave us a reflection of how we might seem to people living an everyday existence. I got the impression that, to the two lawyers, Mount Carmel was something like a termite mound kicked open by one of Dick's metal-toed boots, exposing a darkened world.

The attorneys talked to many of us, took a good look at the bullet holes the ATF had made in the front door, in the tower, and elsewhere, and inspected the bloodstains where Peter Gent, Peter Hipsman, and Winston Blake had died during the original ATF as-sault. They examined the wounds of Scott Sonobe and Judy Schnei-der. They saw that David's stomach wound was still giving out a pinkish ooze and that his wrist and thumb were numb; occasion-ally, David became unconscious while talking to the lawyers or was shaken by spasms and tremors. The attorneys told us to videotape all of this, especially the front door and the shattered ceiling in the tower. (We did, but the tape perished in the fire.)

Jack Zimmerman, a former combat artillery officer in Viet-nam and a colonel in the Marine Corps Reserve, later testified before Congress that the spray pattern of the bullet holes in the right front-door panel definitely indicated incoming rounds, not outgoing, as the ATF told the media, to back up its false claim that we had fired first on February 28. DeGuerin, an experienced hunter, told the Texas Rangers that in his opinion the rounds were "all punched in and they were various calibers."

After consulting Senior Texas Ranger Captain Maurice Cook, Dick worked out with David a possible way to end the standoff that was exhausting everyone. He said: "David, the world's watching. Let's have one Texas Ranger walk up to the front door and you and I will walk out and surrender to him. That'll be sending a message to the people of the world that you don't trust the ATF and the FBI, the feds that got you into this in the first place, but you trust your legal system and the Texas Rangers."

Later, in his testimony to Congress, Zimmerman explained that it was agreed that David would tell the attorneys when we'd be coming out and that they would inform the FBI. "Dick DeGuerin and David Koresh were going to exit first, to show everybody that they weren't going to get executed the minute they stepped outside. And there would be a metal detector set up outside the front door in a bus. . . . When Mr. DeGuerin and Mr. Koresh went through that metal detector, Mr. Koresh would have plastic wrist restraints placed on him, be patted down by a male FBI or ATF agent. . . . I was supposed to stay in there and see that the other adults came out, keeping a distance so that law enforcement wouldn't get nervous about people bunching up. . . . There would be a press representative there taping it [so] both sides would be protected."

After that, the FBI explosive experts would go into Mount Carmel to check for booby traps, Jack said, then hand over the site to the Texas Rangers. The wounded and others needing medical care would go to a hospital; the rest would be brought before a U.S. magistrate for arrest or release.

Passover ended on April 14, and, as Jack explained, "We told them [the FBI commanders] it would take another ten, twelve days [from April 14]. We asked them, 'Do you have that much time?' They said, 'We have all the time in the world to resolve this peacefully.'"

Jack continued: "I was supposed to be the last guy out on the surrender plan. If there had been the slightest inkling in our minds that they were going to burn up the building or blow it up, I wouldn't have agreed to be the last guy out." Jack's sharp final comment to the congressmen was this: "We wouldn't be here today if the FBI and the Department of Justice had waited ten more days."

Though, as Dick DeGuerin testified, this plan "wasn't greeted with a lot of enthusiasm" by law enforcement officials, we felt we'd at least shown that we were willing to work with the feds to find a way to end the standoff. "The holocaust is even more tragic because they were coming out peacefully," Jack wrote later. "Steve Schneider told me at every contact we had that the entire group wanted to come out. They wanted the truth about February 28 to be told."

Jack added: "The demonization of the entire religious group by our government officials is tragic. . . . The Branch Davidians included decent, loving people who were committed to a religious faith that in this country they had every right to practice."

While the attorneys' negotiations with the agents were going on, we received a communication from the outside world that really got our blood racing. On April 1 two respected theologians— James Tabor of the University of North Carolina–Charlotte, whom I quoted earlier, and Philip Arnold, director of the Reunion Institute in Houston—directed a broadcast to us on Ron Engelman's show on the Dallas AM station KGBS. On the air, Arnold and Tabor seriously discussed our core beliefs and debated the ways in which David might interpret them to allow us to emerge from our isolation without betraying our purpose.

Phil Arnold had come to Waco as early as March 7 to offer his services to the FBI. But his insistence that the feds should respect our beliefs annoyed the FBI, and he was barred from attending the briefing sessions. He returned to Houston, troubled and frustrated. "People's lives are at stake here," he said.

Tabor had first heard about us when CNN anchorman David French interviewed David Koresh by phone on the evening of the ATF assault in February. "Over the next few days," Tabor recalled, "it became clear to me that neither the officials in charge, nor the media who were sensationally reporting the sexual escapades of David Koresh, had a clue about the *biblical* world which this group inhabited. . . . I realized that in order to deal with David Koresh, and to have any chance for a peaceful resolution of the Waco situation, one would have to understand and make use of these biblical texts." He understood that the people in Mount Carmel "were willing to die for what they believed, and they would not surrender under threat of force."

Tabor and Arnold put their heads together to formulate a resolution David could accept. They talked to Livingston Fagan, whom David had sent out on March 23 as a kind of theological emissary to the feds. The FBI had promptly jailed him and turned a deaf ear to his pleas.

During several long visits, Livingston explained to Phil and Jim that, in David's view, we in Mount Carmel were living in the Fifth Seal of the Book of Revelation, the one that asked, *Sovereign Lord, holy and true, how long will it be before you judge and avenge our blood on the inhabitants of the earth?* In this passage, *the souls of those who had been slaughtered for the word of God . . .* [were] *told to wait a little season* for the final confrontation between good and evil.

Tabor and Arnold realized that this passage was crucial. They argued that because the duration of the little season was unspecified there was some leeway in its interpretation. It could be days, weeks, even years. The theologians formulated this "alternative scenario" during their April 1 radio broadcast and on a tape they sent in with Dick DeGuerin on April 4. They suggested to David that the little season could be stretched out, allowing us time to leave Mount Carmel and still be true to our beliefs.

In his account of his attempt to build a bridge between ourselves and the feds, Tabor offered his insights into something termed "biblical apocalypticism." This tradition has three dimensions, he wrote. There's the Scripture itself, the inspired teacher, and the particular time, place, and situation in which the teacher lives. The Scripture is unchangeable, but the way the teacher interprets it and the context in which he acts are flexible.

However, these subtleties were beyond the comprehension of the FBI's commanders on the ground, not to mention their masters in Washington. Impatient with our "Bible babble" and blinded by their prejudices and bureaucratic "rules of engagement," they utterly failed to grasp the opportunity these strategies offered for a humane conclusion to our confrontation.

Nancy T. Ammerman, the sociologist who served on a panel of experts that the Justice and Treasury Departments asked to evaluate the feds' role at Mount Carmel, said: "Indeed the efforts by Arnold and James Tabor represented probably the best hope for a peaceful end to the siege."

David and the rest of us joyfully welcomed Tabor and Arnold's intervention. *At last someone was listening!* And not just anyone, but a pair of reputable theologians who talked our talk, who understood that our message was not kooky weirdness but a valid part of a long tradition of apocalyptic belief. The smile on David's face as he listened to the KGBS broadcast and replayed the tape was as wide as the Grand Canyon. The black cloud hanging over Mount Carmel seemed to lift a little, letting in a few shafts of light that dazzled our eyes and fired our hearts. Weakened by hunger as I was, I even did a little jig of joy.

Phil Arnold predicted that David would decide whether to come out during Passover, which ran from April 7 to April 14. On April 4, David and Steve confirmed this prediction to DeGuerin and Zimmerman. We took it as a good sign when in early April the FBI allowed a Passover Haggadah, sent by Pablo Cohen's Israeli mother, Shulamit, into Mount Carmel.

————————

During Passover, David went into an intense spiritual mode. His intensity radiated throughout the building, warming us all with hope and faith. Even the kids picked up on this mood; I could see a new brightness in their eyes. For me, that rare quality of "holiness," of being close to a true spiritual presence, never felt more pure. It seemed that through hardship and hunger, through the pain of his wounds and the delirium of his nightmares, David had finally come into his own.

I saw him several times and was amazed by the serene look on his face. It was as if he'd arrived at the center of himself after a long journey through the wilderness of his own soul.

The impromptu Passover Bible study he gave one evening to a few of us lingering in the hallway where he lay propped up against the wall to ease his wounds was quiet in tone but very moving. His text was the opening of the 40th Psalm: *I waited patiently for the Lord; and he inclined unto me, and heard my cry. He brought me up also out of an horrible pit, out of the miry clay, and set my feet upon a rock.*

David's low voice vibrated with tenderness as he ruminated on the mercy that balances divine judgment. "The mercy is in the judgment," he said softly, "the judgment is in the mercy," and for an instant I felt I was given an insight into a dimension in which all paradoxes are illusory, a trick of the clouded eye.

In the presence of that man, who was simultaneously so ordinary and so amazing, all of my life seemed focused. For a flash of time I was given not a vision but a view of how the spiritual qualities in our lives were one and the same as the bodies and characters we carry around; how the "me" that yearned to be better than I was and the "me" that was no better than I was would always be brothers under the skin; uneasy siblings to be sure, but sharing the same blood.

As soon as Passover ended, David knew what he must do. On April 14, the day the festival was done, he sent a letter to Dick DeGuerin, informing him he'd been granted permission to write down his interpretation of the Seven Seals. He wrote:

"I am presently being permitted to document in structured form the decoded messages of the seven seals. Upon completion of this task, I will be freed of my waiting period. I hope to finish this as soon as possible and stand before man and answer any and all questions regarding my activities. . . . I am working night and day. . . . As soon as I see that people like Jim Tabor and Phil Arnold have a copy, I will come out and then you can do your thing with this beast."

The significance of this letter was huge. Until then, David had never written down his message, except for the notes he'd scribbled in the margins of his Bible, like Talmudic commentaries. He'd long believed that his message could not and should not be written down until he received permission from God. And now, at last, it was granted.

With high energy, David immediately set about writing and taping his interpretation of the Seals. Steve edited the text, knowing that David, a dropout plagued by bad grammar and poor spelling, was more at ease with the spoken than the written word. Judy Schneider tried typing the edited version, but her injured index finger had a splint, so she handed the task over to Clive Doyle and Ruth Riddle, who transcribed David's words onto a disk in the computer we powered with the last dregs of fuel for our emergency generator. At the rate he was going, David reckoned it would take him about two to three weeks to complete his exposition. In the community there was calm and joy as we dreamed of our release from the long ordeal.

To keep the lines open during those last days, David sent out a flow of letters filled with quotations from Old Testament prophets. The feds, characterizing them as "cryptic," handed the letters to a self-proclaimed cult-buster they'd retained as a consultant, who characterized the biblical quotations as "rampant, morbidly virulent paranoia." Jeff Jamar dismissed David's crucial letter to DeGuerin as "just another delaying tactic." When Dick informed the FBI that we would come out when David had finished writing his document, Special Agent Bob Ricks, second in command of the operation, was contemptuous. The agents caricatured David as Lucy from the comic strip "Peanuts," who always moves the football at the last moment before Charlie Brown is about to kick off. Even worse, it appears that Attorney General Janet Reno, still new to the office, was never shown this crucial letter lest it influence her to call off the already planned attack. The FBI continued to claim that the negotiations were "at an impasse."

David's manuscript begins with a poem:

> *Search forth for the meaning here,*
> *Hidden within these words*
> *'Tis a song that's sung of fallen tears. . . .*

David saw himself as the Lamb, the figure chosen to open the Seals and bring about the final fulfillment of prophecy. Quoting biblical chapter and verse in his complex, highly individual fashion, he explained that this Lamb, coming at the end of days, will be scorned and bad-mouthed, just as he had been. Yet those who accept the message of the Seals will be invited to the divine wedding of the spirit. It ends: "Should we not eagerly ourselves be ready to accept this truth and come out of our closet and be revealed to the world as those who love Christ in truth and in righteousness?"

On April 16 Steve told the FBI that David said the first section of the manuscript he was writing was twenty-five to twenty-eight pages long. To counter the FBI's skepticism that David's decision to write down his interpretation of the Seals was no more than a ploy to buy time, Steve, who was editing the tapes, offered to send the feds an example to show that the work was progressing quickly. He even asked for typewriter ribbons so that he could send them a sample of David's writings.

Instead of showing appreciation for this good-faith offer, the feds sent a Bradley crashing into the wall of the building right where Graeme Craddock was lying in his bunk, injuring his shoulder. David's son, Cyrus, who happened to be in the room, was terrified. To cap it all, the FBI demanded that fifty people must be sent out next day or they would have to "take action."

In an attempt to soothe the feds' impatience, David sent out a powerful drawing by our artist, Cliff Sellors, illustrating the statue from the Book of Daniel. The agents dismissed this as just more "Bible stuff," and Steve retorted that every time we did something to cooperate with the authorities their response was more destruction.

The First Seal was completed April 18, and David was deep in the draft of the Second Seal, dictating to Ruth Riddle for four solid hours the Sunday night before the FBI launched its massive final assault. Tabor later remarked that "in a short time, under most trying circumstances, Koresh produced a substantial piece of work"— the first section of a manuscript Tabor estimated would have run between fifty and seventy-five pages that "might have taken him another week or more to write." Tabor added: "There is not the slightest doubt in my mind that David Koresh would have surrendered peacefully when he finished his manuscript."

Jack Zimmerman confirmed this. "When Dick DeGuerin and I talked to them [the Davidians] on the day after Passover—April 14, 1993, they were ecstatic," he said. "The 'waiting period' described in the Bible would soon be over, and they were coming out."

———

Looking back, it's clear that the view from inside our besieged building during those last weeks was totally at odds with the way the forces facing us perceived the situation. Whereas we'd come to hope for a peaceful, spiritual resolution derived from David's explication of scriptural texts, the feds were lurching toward violence.

In late March, after four weeks' staging outside Mount Carmel, the tactical agents were getting tired and irritable. They were shivering in the cold prairie winds, eating the same cold pizzas, day after day, forced to listen to the same crazy loudspeaker racket they were blasting at us. I sympathized with their dislike of the arid Texas landscape, but at least they had heated shelters to retreat into, unlike us, who shivered when the nighttime temperatures dipped below freezing. And those pizzas would have been welcome comfort after living for weeks on bland K-rations.

"Tempers were fraying," the Justice Department report later stated. To make matters worse, the bosses in Washington were increasingly embarrassed by the agency's failure to subdue a bunch of religious nuts despite all the force and power they'd mustered.

Some seven hundred law enforcement officers were deployed around Mount Carmel. The FBI committed 250, the ATF 150, including agents and support personnel. In addition, there were officers from the Texas Rangers, the Waco police, the McLennan County Sheriff's Office, U.S. Customs, the Texas National Guard, the Texas Department of Public Safety, and the U.S. Army. The cost of maintaining this considerable force has been variously reckoned at around $500,000 per day, the final total exceeding $30 million.

Along with the feds' impatience, the Waco locals were growing restless, resenting the heavy government presence and the terrible rep their town was receiving in the global media circus, where "Waco" and "wacko" were now synonymous. Waco hotels were bursting at the seams trying to quarter more than 1,000 reporters and their crews. And though Wacoans surely welcomed the money these accidental tourists brought in, they were by nature uncomfortable with outsiders.

Meanwhile, at FBI headquarters in Washington, a diabolical final assault plan on Mount Carmel was hatching. The key concept in the so-called Jericho Plan was the use of tear gas to force us from the building. If we weren't driven out by the gas, "walls would be torn down to increase the exposure of those remaining inside," despite the stated "risk [of] harming the children." Failing that, the fallback became total demolition of our home by tanks and bulldozers.

Even the slightly more sympathetic federal negotiators were sucked into this sinister mode. For instance, FBI chief negotiator Byron Sage had agreed to get the FBI to turn off the loudspeakers to avoid a sacrilegious desecration of the Passover. But at dusk, as the festival period began, the feds rudely cut Steve off when he phoned to complain that the racket was still blaring. When Steve went outside in an attempt to talk to the FBI, they drove him back into the building with a few hurled flashbang grenades that might well have wounded him badly.

Speculating that the grenades came from the antagonistic tactical agents, Steve tried to reach Sage, screaming into the phone that he wanted to meet the negotiator to clear up the apparent confusion. But he got nowhere. When he tried to go outside again, he was greeted by more grenades. On April 15, after Passover,

several of the people inside Mount Carmel, anticipating a peaceful
end to the conflict, tried to leave the building, but they were also
driven back by grenades. So much for the feds' claim that we were
being held hostage by David.

These incidents should have shaken our optimism and warned
us that something sinister was in the works, but somehow we accepted them as part of the process. Several people were skeptical,
but nobody really wanted to listen to their deepening self-doubts.
Passing along the upstairs corridor one morning, I overheard a woman's voice: "Those guys just like to be rude. It don't mean a thing."
On April 15, we cheered when a helicopter struck a guywire on take-
off and lurched around just off the ground like a huge, drunken
dragonfly. It put a real dent in the G-men's super-macho image.

Still, we kept trying to keep the feds happy. On April 16, to
calm their doubts about our intentions, David had this conversation with an FBI negotiator named Dick, recorded on government
tapes:

> *David*: Dick, it's a real world, and that's why I'm sympathetic
> with your position. I realize you're frustrated and I agree
> with you.
> *Dick*: But—just tell me this David—are you saying that when
> you finish that manuscript—
> *David*: Then I'll be out, yes, definitely.
> *Dick*: That could mean a lot of things, David. That could
> mean—
> *David*: I'll be in custody in the jailhouse. You can come down
> there and feed me bananas if you want. . . . I'll be splitting
> out of this place. I'm so sick of MREs, Dick.
> *Dick*: I'm gonna let you go so you can get back to work because,
> David, frankly, I'm eagerly awaiting this manuscript.
> *David*: Well, I'll tell you what. It's gonna blow your socks off.

The conversation continued in a cordial fashion, and at one point
David said jokingly, "Will you take a shower for me? Thank you."
Later that day they talked again:

Dick: Well, I'm asking you . . . a simple question—

David: And I'm giving you the simple answer. Yes. Yes. Yes. I never intended to die in here.

On April 18, the day before the assault, David talked to another, unnamed, agent:

David: The general's out here, right? You have a hard time controlling them, right?

Agent: I don't control them. No.

David: Okay. Well, look, we've done everything we can to be able to communicate in a nice, passionate way. . . . We've not been your everyday kind of terrorist. . . . These [FBI] generals . . . they're not only destroying private property, they're also removing evidence. . . . Like that '68 SS El Camino that belonged to Paul Fatta . . . they're not showing good faith.

Agent: This thing has lasted way too long.

David: It should never have gotten started this way.

Agent: You're right.

David: I'm a life, too, and there's a lot of people in here that are lives. There's children in here. . . . I was at the front door. I was willing to talk to them. They shot at me first. . . . Whoever wants to go out can go out.

———————

In mid-March, Janet Reno, soon to be the leading lady in this deadly drama, took her place at center stage.

When we heard that Reno had been sworn in as U.S. Attorney General, we felt a collective surge of hope. Perhaps a woman, a prosecutor from Dade County, Florida, known for her concern for children, coming from outside the Washington political and bureaucratic circus, would stop this federal steamroller in its tracks. We prayed that Reno's cool head would prevail; that she would shake the government to its senses and compel it to realize that the feds had allowed a botched, questionable raid by the ATF to become the occasion for a macho display of official revenge.

And indeed, on April 12, when FBI Director William Sessions and Assistant Attorney General Webster Hubbell, among other Justice Department officials, presented Reno with the agency's 568-page Jericho Plan for a final assault on Mount Carmel, her instinctive reaction was, "Why now? What are the arguments for waiting?"

In her response, Reno was echoing the attitude of her immediate predecessor, Acting Attorney General Stuart Gerson. Until Gerson, a Bush appointee, left office on March 11, the only escalation he'd allowed the FBI at Waco was to move extra armored vehicles into the vicinity. "I felt there was no need to force a change in the status quo," he later testified. "We were getting people out."

However, Reno's native caution was soon undermined. In the weeks immediately following her confirmation as America's top lawyer, William Sessions and Webster Hubbell were breathing down Reno's neck, urging her to make a decision.*

Attorney General Reno also spoke with past and present commanders of Delta Force, the Army's crack assault unit, about the FBI's attack strategy. Their final solution to the Mount Carmel problem was to urge her to blitz the entire building. If they want Armageddon, the thinking went, let 'em have it!

In the end, the FBI's marginally less drastic Jericho Plan called for a "step-by-step process" in which tear gas would be pumped into our building to drive us out over forty-eight hours, but no armored

---

* A trickier Washington pair than these couldn't be found. Sessions, tight-lipped and stiff, was already under a cloud for ethical improprieties and was forced to resign as head of the FBI a few months later. Before Reno took office, Sessions, in an excess of zeal, had wanted to go to Waco to take over command of the operation, imagining himself a latter-day Patton, but Gerson refused to allow it. For his part, Hubbell showed his true colors in a series of unrelated dealings. In 1994 Hubbell, as flabby as Sessions was lean, served eighteen months in prison on charges that he defrauded clients and partners of thousands of dollars from his Little Rock, Arkansas, law firm. Four years later he was indicted on fifteen counts of attempting to obstruct a federal investigation of transactions related to Whitewater.

vehicles or gunfire would be used against us. The cocktail favored by the feds to subdue us was a mixture of a white crystalline powdered chemical called orthochloro-benzalmalononitrile (CS) in a solution of methylene chloride, a potent depressant of the human central nervous system. CS causes nausea, disorientation, dizziness, shortness of breath, tightness in the chest, burning of the skin, intense tearing, coughing, and vomiting. In January 1993 the United States and 130 other countries had signed the Chemical Weapons Convention banning the use of CS gas in warfare; apparently there is no prohibition on its use against American citizens.

The use of this chemical on civilians has been condemned by organizations across the board, from Amnesty International to the U.S. Army. The Army's manual on civil disturbances states that "excessive exposure to CS may make them incapable of vacating the area." The company that makes CS warns that when the gas burns it gives off fumes that can kill. Benjamin C. Garrett, director of the Chemical and Biological Arms Control Institute in Alexandria, Virginia, explains that CS is even deadlier for kids, because "the smaller you are, the sooner you would feel the response."

Describing the effects upon a child exposed to CS gas they had examined in an earlier incident, some pediatricians observed that immediately after exposure the child "required suctioning to relieve upper airway obstruction" and suffered from cyanosis, turning purple from lack of oxygen. The infant these doctors examined developed pneumonia and chemical first-degree burns on the skin and required four weeks of hospitalization. Harvard law professor and psychiatrist Alan Stone, who was later asked to review the FBI's actions by the Justice Department, suggested that CS made the kids vomit uncontrollably from symptoms of chemical pneumonia. "To use it with babies, I continue to believe it was like holding a gun to the parents' head," he said.

Federal Laboratories, which supplies CS to the FBI, warns in its manual: "Under no circumstances should [CS] grenades, cartridges or projectiles designed for use in riots be used in confined areas. A hazardous overdose could be created by the release of . . . even one full-sized grenade in a closed room." CS is effective at a concentration of ten milligrams per cubic meter of air. Over a six-hour period on April 19, the FBI delivered 1,900 grams of CS chemical agent into our building, creating concentrations in some rooms almost sixteen times that amount, or twice the density considered life-threatening. No greater concentration of CS has ever been sprayed by government agents at U.S. civilians.

Compounding the terrors of this gas mixture is its potential for causing fire. The Dow Chemical Company's Material Safety Data Sheet on methylene chloride states that this chemical "forms flammable vapor-air mixtures." The warning adds: "In confined or poorly ventilated areas, vapors can readily accumulate and cause unconsciousness and death." Eric R. Larsen, Ph.D., a retired Dow chemist, confirmed a later Associated Press report that "MeCl [methylene chloride] vapors will reduce the flash point of hydrocarbon fuels and thus will enhance the rate of flame spread. One might as well toss gas on a fire." Poorly ventilated areas "could have been turned into an area similar to one of the gas chambers used by the Nazis at Auschwitz," Larsen added.

This was the deadly brew the FBI brass was quietly cooking up for us while appearing to accept that we were getting ready to come out, as soon as David finished writing his interpretation of the Seals.

On Saturday, April 17, the day after David's friendly chat with Agent Dick, Reno suddenly agreed to the use of CS gas. The next day she phoned President Clinton to tell him of her decision. Clinton wondered if they should hold off a while longer, but Reno, now hot to trot, talked him around. "Well, okay," Clinton said vaguely, declaring it was her decision. (At an April 20 press conference, a Hamlet-like Clinton wondered rhetorically: "Is there some other question they [the FBI] should have asked? Is there some other question I should have asked? Can I say for sure that . . . we could have done nothing else to make the outcome different?")

Once Reno gave the go-ahead to the FBI, she was caught up in the agency's web of half-truths and outright lies. For instance,

Reno has said she was told—and believed—that David, despite his wounds, was still having sex with young girls. This information came from Kathy Schroeder, who left in mid-March. She claimed that when she went to say goodbye to David, she found him in bed with a girl. If Kathy's story was true, David was really superhuman, given his weakened state.

Reno also claimed she was told that armed groups of militiamen were converging on Mount Carmel to free us. She named the so-called Unorganized Militia of the United States as an example. However, the FBI itself had earlier declared that this "threat" consisted of an Indianapolis attorney's plan to "drive a van with other people to Waco, Texas, to stage a protest in support of the constitutional right of assembly and to have weapons."

Later, Reno added a new excuse: She said that the "first and foremost" reason for allowing the attack was that "law enforcement agents on the ground concluded that the perimeter had become unstable and posed a risk both to them and to the surrounding homes and farms." This, of course, was absolute nonsense.

Despite the FBI's proven trickiness, Reno stubbornly declared during a July 1995 interview with the *Washington Post*: "After over two years of review, nothing has given me any indication that the FBI misled me." Either she was dumber than she looked or else she was just trying to be one of the boys, a good team player.

On Sunday, the day before they struck us, the feds began clearing ground surrounding the building, preparing the terrain for armored vehicles. Their flimsy excuse was that David Jones had several times sneaked out the back door and nosed around. The agents made no attempt to conceal their movements. On the contrary, they deliberately moved Koresh's beloved, souped-up, black '68 Camaro. Believing the feds would trash his car out of sheer spite, David was very angry. That same day, the FBI demanded that fifty of us should come out as "proof of good faith," but the hostile actions of the FBI didn't encourage us to oblige.

In response to these provocations, Steve threatened the FBI negotiator, saying David would slow his work on the manuscript and thereby delay our exit from Mount Carmel. Actually, David was so caught up in the writing, so swept along with inspiration, that he couldn't have curbed his pace even if he'd wanted to. In fact, he was so juiced that he was awake at 5:00 A.M. on the morning we were attacked, having not slept the night before.

In those last moments before the final attack, sensing something terrible was about to happen, my mom and the relatives of other people in Mount Carmel pestered Reno with faxes and registered mail, pleading with her to allow family members to contact us and maybe act as intermediaries in the negotiations for a peaceful end to the siege. Reno later claimed she was never told about this.

———————

A week or so before the attack, Joyce Sparks of the Texas Department of Child Protective Services was asked by the FBI if she would work with medical staff to prepare showers and clean clothes for the children who would be coming out of Mount Carmel as a result of a gas attack. Sparks, who had led her department's investigation into charges of child abuse in our community a year earlier, was greatly disturbed by the prospect that our children would be subjected to a tear gas attack, and she let the feds know it. Their response was to tell her to "forget about it," and she assumed that the agents had sensibly decided that the use of tear gas was too dangerous for the kids.

When Sparks saw tear gas being injected into Mount Carmel on TV at 9:30 A.M. on April 19, she exclaimed: "They're going to kill them all!" It was evident to her that the use of tear gas was extremely hazardous; and from her knowledge of our community, gained over numerous visits, she knew this brutal strategy would never force us to leave the building. Disillusioned, hurt, and angry, Sparks condemned the feds for going ahead with the gas assault over her vehement objections.

It must be said that the intended use of CS gas also troubled Janet Reno. Carl Stern, director of the Justice Department's public-affairs office, sent word to Reno that he was worried that there might be a public outcry over the use of tear gas on women and children, comparing it to Saddam Hussein's gassing of the Kurds in Iraq. But a U.S. Army toxicologist she consulted unaccountably assured her that the gas would "cause temporary distress but no lasting damage." And in the rush of events climaxing during that second week of April, Reno later admitted that she hadn't known then that the United States was a signatory to the international convention banning the use of CS gas in warfare.

Despite pressure from the Beltway bureaucracy, Reno still hesitated. When she suggested waiting until the water supplies ran out, the FBI sent a plane loaded with spy equipment on April 15 and reported, falsely, that our rear water tank was full. Reno was also told that we had plenty of water and that we were rationing ourselves to a pint a day to enforce discipline. The FBI didn't tell Reno that its agents had shot the tanks full of holes and smashed the well pump outside our building. We were heading into summer, and summers in Waco are dry. Until the previous August, for instance, barely half an inch of rain had fallen in our area.

Reno didn't discover till later that the FBI had lied to her about this, as it had about many other things. "I asked the FBI to check the water supply again," Reno said at the 1995 congressional hearings, "and I was advised the supply was plentiful and it was constantly being replenished." To this day, the appendix to the Justice Department's report keeps the "Water Intelligence" entries for April 13 and 15 blacked out.

While Reno wavered, some as yet unidentified person in the FBI chain of command told her that the bugs they'd secretly smuggled into Mount Carmel revealed that David was "beating babies." "You really mean *babies*?" Reno queried. "Yes," the answer came, "he's slapping babies around."

(The bugs the FBI managed to place inside our building, by hiding them in items they sent in for us, relayed audio and visual images back to the command center at Texas State Technical College, ten miles away. These devices included tiny cameras that could record a full-color picture of a whole room from a lens measuring no more than an eighth of an inch.)

The FBI was well aware that, with Reno's background in prosecuting child-abuse cases, this charge was a hot button. On the evening of April 19, hours after our tragedy, Reno would appear on talk shows and state that the FBI had "hard intelligence" that children were being beaten.

It was bunk. Two days later the FBI denied Reno's claims, dropping her in the soup. "We did not tell the Attorney General there was evidence of abuse during the siege," an agency spokesman declared. "We passed on the 1992 reports from last year." That is, the FBI gave the Attorney General a copy of the report of the intense investigation carried out in early 1992 by the Texas Department of Child Protective Services, which had been terminated for lack of evidence. Sessions himself later admitted that the bureau had "no contemporaneous evidence" of such abuse.

In fact, Child Protective Services officials, who immediately examined the kids who came out during the siege, uncovered no evidence of child abuse. They found the children to be "surprisingly healthy, happy, well adjusted, well educated, and only wanted to return as soon as they could to their friends and relatives in the compound." In the March 8 issue of the *New York Times*, Texas correspondent Sam Howe Verhovek wrote that none of these children "show any signs of physical abuse."

On April 11, 1993, Dr. Bruce Perry, chief of psychiatry at Texas Children's Hospital in Houston, examined the Mount Carmel children in official custody and described them as being friendly, happy, and likable. He also told the Associated Press that the kids "are in very good condition and show no signs of abuse." Later, on May 5, Dr. Perry told the *Dallas Morning News*: "We have no evidence that the children released from the compound were sexually abused." On April 23, 1993, Texas child welfare executive Janice Caldwell reported, "The [surviving] children have not confirmed any of the allegations or described any other incidents which would verify our concerns about abuse."

The notion that we would mistreat our children or deprive them of food and water showed how little the outside world understood our community's values. Maybe if Reno had seen the loving, caring videotapes of our kids we sent out during the siege or heard the child say to an agent on the phone, "Are you comin' to kill me?"

she might have had second thoughts about the spurious charge of child abuse.

Reno has claimed ignorance of our videos when she was fretting about the babies. Yet just three days after we sent out the third video, on March 28, FBI spokesman Bob Ricks publicly acknowledged that David had provided a tape showing sixteen of the seventeen children and all four of the teenage girls inside, and that all of these young people were well and in fine spirits. Though the *Washington Post* reported this fact, Reno missed it. Was she lying— or just criminally careless? Did the FBI somehow screen this information from her, fearing it might provoke some honest sympathy for the children's plight? In any case, Dr. Park Dietz, another FBI "expert," claimed in a memo to Reno that David would "continue to make sexual use of any children who remain inside."

This scurrilous memo appeared to override the last remaining shreds of Reno's common sense. Together, Sessions and Hubbell bamboozled the neophyte Reno into signing off on the FBI's assault plan, tear gas and all. Fearing being labeled indecisive by a bunch of bullying males, she began to retreat from her earlier healthy skepticism.

Despite its diabolical intentions, the FBI assumed a phony tone of moral righteousness where the children's welfare was concerned. On April 3, a government negotiator criticized David for the emotional and social damage being done to kids by his refusal to surrender. David's response was cutting: "Why don't you turn the music off on the outside there?" he demanded. "You know so much about social and psychological sciences and all that, buddy, what do you think you're doing?"

A sardonic comment along these lines was made by Lawrence Lilliston, chair of the Department of Psychology at Oakland University in Rochester, Michigan. "But there was child abuse in Waco," he wrote after the fact. "Knowing there were many children inside, federal agents incessantly assaulted the building with loud music and bizarre sounds, such as rabbits being killed. Knowing there were many children inside, federal agents used tanks as battering rams, crashing into the building and punching holes in the walls. . . . Knowing there were many children inside, federal agents pumped in tear gas. . . . Certainly these children's last living moments must have been filled with unbelievable horror and agony."

During the final attack, women and children in the concrete vault huddled under wet blankets and towels in a vain attempt to escape the heat and gas. Mothers wrapped children in sleeping bags for protection, unaware that CS is denser than air and settles near the floor. "It is likely that the children received not only the doses injected after the CEV [Combat Engineering Vehicle] broke into the center of the building, but also a goodly portion of that shot into the tower and the second floor," one expert says. "Concentrations at the floor level of the bunker may have been astronomical."

Reno's decision to approve the FBI tear gas assault was severely criticized by Representatives McCollum and Zeliff, the co-chairs of the House investigation of the Mount Carmel tragedy. In their October 1996 preliminary report, the congressmen commented: "Evidence does indicate that CS insertion into the enclosed bunker . . . could have been a proximate cause of or directly resulted in some or all of the deaths attributed to asphyxiation in the autopsy reports." Labeling Reno's decision "premature, wrong and highly irresponsible," the congressmen remarked that "the attorney general should have known that the plan to end the standoff would endanger the lives of the Davidians inside the residence, including the children. The attorney general knew or should have known that there was little risk to the FBI agents, society as a whole, or to the Davidians from continuing this standoff, and that the possibility of a peaceful resolution continued to exist. . . . The final assault put the children at the greatest risk."

15

HALF-TRUTHS AND OUTRIGHT LIES

Apart from the falsehood that we were beating babies, the feds spun even bigger lies about our community. These whoppers—accepted by Reno—included the charges that we were preparing to commit mass suicide by setting fire to the building, immolating ourselves in a self-created holocaust to fulfill some horrible biblical prophecy.

After April 19, the FBI rushed to make everyone believe that we, not they, set Mount Carmel ablaze. On Monday afternoon, thirty-five minutes after Mount Carmel had been reduced to ashes, a Justice Department spokesman in Washington announced that two "cultists" had confessed to starting the fire. The very next night this totally unproven statement was retracted. In fact, these wild official fictions revealed a total lack of understanding of our community.

The FBI's reversal on the fire confession didn't stop the feds' campaign of half-truths and outright lies. The government "fire expert" appointed to head up the investigation was Paul Gray, a member of the ATF's National Arson Response Team, whose wife worked in the ATF's Houston office—hardly an impartial investigator. Gray claimed that infrared tapes made by government surveillance planes showed a "pattern of arson." According to the tapes, Gray declared, the fire broke out at 12:07:04 P.M. on the second floor. But independent witnesses who examined the tapes stated that the building burst into flames earlier, at 11:59:16 A.M., in the gym at the back. It started as a tank backed out of the room. In fact, the tapes seem to show that the conflagration erupted in three places virtually simultaneously, exactly where the tear gas–spraying tanks had broken into Mount Carmel. And when the fire reached the area where we'd stored some propane, a pall of black smoke and orange and yellow flames spurted two hundred feet into the air.

As I said previously, by noon the building was a tinderbox. A thick layer of methylene chloride dust deposited by the CS gas coated the walls, floors, and ceilings. Vapors of methyl chloride, from the four hundred–plus rocket rounds shot into our building, mingled with kerosene and propane vapors from spilled lanterns and crushed heaters. Two "pyrotechnic devices," possibly unexploded flashbang grenades, were found by the Texas Rangers in the gym and in another place where the fire started. When a flashbang explodes it creates a small fireball, which would have set the whole area alight in that charged, gas-soaked atmosphere. With powerful Texas winds whistling through the holes ripped in the building's sides and roof, Mount Carmel was primed to ignite.

According to chemistry professor George Uhlig of the College of Eastern Utah, the fire erupted so rapidly because the CS gas was diluted with acetone or ethanol, creating a liquid aerosol that "came into contact with a flame, and the flame front traveled from particle to particle to create the 'fireball' described by survivors"— like the terrifying sight that flashed before my eyes that day on the catwalk over the chapel. Professor Uhlig, a retired U.S. Air Force lieutenant colonel, compared the aerosol concept to the design of fuel-air explosive devices he worked on while in the service. He added the dreadful detail that while the CS burned it mixed "with normal fluids in the lungs of people to generate hydrogen-cyanide gas." Uhlig's comments are reinforced by an Army field manual that warns: "When using the dry agent CS-1, do not discharge indoors. Accumulating dust may explode when exposed to spark or open flame."

The fire burned for only twenty-five minutes, but it reached temperatures near 2,000 degrees Fahrenheit—"approaching cremation temperature," according to a government medical report on the disaster. The same report noted that "most of the burned bodies were unrecognizable as humans." The flames were so intense that the hotspots among the ruins took a full week to cool down.

Marjorie Thomas, who suffered third-degree burns over half her body, recalled the terror of those last moments: "The whole entire building felt warm all at once, and then, after the warmth, then a thick, black smoke, and the place became dark. I could hear—I couldn't see anything. I could hear people moving and screaming, and I still was sitting down while this was happening. Then the voices faded."

Marjorie continued: "I was making my way out of the building, because it began to get very hot, and my clothes were starting to melt on me. . . . I saw a little bit of light. I made my way towards the light, and on doing so, I could see where it—it was one of the bedrooms. I could—the window was missing. I looked out. I don't like heights, but I thought . . . 'I stay inside and—and die, or I jump out of the window,' so I put my head—my hands over my head and leapt out of the window." (Sheila Martin recalled that during the worst part of the fire Marjorie Thomas accidentally stepped on her daughter Sheila's hand while coming down the stairs in the midst of all that flame and smoke. "'Oh, I'm sorry,' she said, and young Sheila, who was close to suffocating, managed to say, 'Oh, that's all right.' It's amazing that, in all that horror, Sheila and Marjorie had enough sense of comfort and compassion for each other to say, 'I'm sorry.'")

"I saw a huge fireball," Clive Doyle remembered, "and I pretty well wrote everybody off at that point. I figured that no one was going to get out of there after that." He added: "I personally did not see where or how the fires started. . . . We were sincerely expecting to come out. We had our bags packed." ATF arson expert Paul Gray testified that Clive had "lighter fuel" on his jacket sleeves, as if that proved he was a pyromaniac. But kerosene spilled from one of our lanterns might well have been mistaken for lighter fuel.

TV footage and the FBI's own logs record that while the fire raged the tanks used bulldozer blades to push debris into the blaze.

Even during the most intense period of the fire, the air in the underground bus was still cool and breathable. Many of the children might have found refuge there and survived the conflagration. However, at the San Antonio trial, FBI agents involved in the final assault on Mount Carmel revealed that they had been ordered to spray CS gas directly into the area where the trapdoor to the bus was located to prevent anyone from escaping or seeking refuge in the underground shelter. At the congressional hearings, FBI Assistant Director Larry Potts (previously censured for authorizing his agents to shoot to kill at Ruby Ridge) told Georgia congressman Bob Barr that the feds' intention was "to move people toward the center of the compound," where we could all be rounded up.

Official lies survived the blaze intact. The day after Mount Carmel burned, FBI spokesman Bob Ricks stated that the agents in charge had not expected a fire. However, a nurse in the burn unit at Waco's Parkland Memorial Hospital reported that an FBI agent contacted her at 5:00 A.M. on April 19, an hour or so before the feds sent in the tanks to inject Mount Carmel with tear gas. The agent, said the nurse, wanted to know how many casualties the unit could handle. Two other local hospitals were also approached by the FBI early that morning. (As it turned out, the feds refused to pay for the treatment of our people in the Parkland burn unit, and the hospital administrator had to file a lawsuit against the agency to get the government to pay up. The hospital's claim was settled out of court.)

Belying Ricks's assertion that the feds hadn't anticipated a conflagration is the fact that agents engaged in the operation had been equipped with fire-retardant Nomex suits, used by assault teams in situations where a high risk of fire is expected. And on April 15, the FBI requested the use of three U.S. Army CH-47 medical evacuation helicopters from Fort Hood to ferry possible casualties from Mount Carmel. More ominously, two weeks before April 19, the FBI asked morgues in the area to arrange for a special order of around eighty body bags, enough to deal with the corpses of every man, woman, and child remaining in Mount Carmel.

Despite the obvious fire risk, intentional or accidental, no fire trucks were in place when the attack began. When smoke started to appear, the FBI waited ten minutes before calling 911. When the fire trucks did arrive, they were delayed another sixteen minutes at an FBI checkpoint. The FBI claimed that this last delay was due to a concern for the firefighters' safety—a dubious excuse, given the number of children at extreme risk inside the building.

A week or so before the attack, an agent asked Steve if we had any fire extinguishers inside. As I mentioned earlier, when he was told we had only one, the agent lightly suggested: "Somebody ought to buy some fire insurance."

As U.S. Representative Jim Traficant (R-Ohio) commented at the congressional hearings: "When you have one hundred TV crews but not one fire truck, that's not a well-thought-out plan, that's box office."

I can't swear that there may not have been a few mad moments in the thickening fog of gas and dust, of choked throats and racing hearts, that thoughts of setting off a biblical apocalypse might have seized some minds. And for a while I almost wanted to believe that someone inside *had* started the fire; it was too shocking to think that the feds had deliberately incinerated us. But the FBI chose a dry, windy day to mount its assault, prime conditions for setting a building on fire. It was the feds, not us, who created the conditions for a conflagration. For that terrible consequence, the government is completely responsible.

———————

The government's propaganda that we'd replay Jonestown—the mass suicide of James Jones's followers in Guyana in 1978—was strongly refuted by people both inside and outside Mount Carmel.

Jack Zimmerman, in his testimony to the 1995 congressional committee, stated: "They [the Departments of Treasury and

Justice] said it was a planned mass suicide. They kept putting that word out; it was a planned mass suicide. . . . Dick [DeGuerin] and I had talked to those people about a planned mass suicide, and every time we talked to them, we were assured there wasn't [any such plan]. . . .

"They [the feds] were putting out the word that the . . . Branch Davidians murdered people to prevent them from escaping. Of course, there's no truth to that at all."

In a letter written to the congressional committee, Ruth Mosher, whose daughter, Sherri Jewell, lived and died in Mount Carmel, declared: "I repeatedly asked Sher if she would ever consider suicide as the Jonestown affair had, and her repeated answer was: 'Heavens no, mom, it's a sin to commit suicide.'"

From his prison cell in Leavenworth, Livingston Fagan confirmed that "there was never any suicide pact or plan. There was, however, an expressed reaffirmation among certain individuals . . . of their willingness to die for what they believed, rather than surrender." Livingston quoted Daniel 11:33, in which it's written that in the final battle the remnant of God's true people will die *by sword and by flame, by captivity, and by spoil, many days.* But the sword and flame would be the weapons of our attackers, not our own. And Sheila Martin said: "I never heard that David had such a plan, or approved of such a plan."

In fact, after April 19 even the FBI itself discounted the mass-suicide fabrication. An agency spokesperson stated: "We went throughout the world and interviewed former cult members, associates of cult members, the number that I last checked was 61 people. The vast bulk, the substantial majority of those believed that they would not commit suicide."

On the April 20, 1993, episode of *MacNeil/Lehrer News Hour,* Sessions himself stated that "every single analysis made of his [Koresh's] writing, of what he said, of what he had said to his lawyers, of what the behavioral science people said, what the psychologists thought, what the psycholinguists thought, what the psychiatrists believed, was that this man was not suicidal, that he would not take his life."

Farris Rookstool, a member of the FBI's evidence response team, said that in his opinion the claim that the Davidians committed mass suicide was "irresponsible."

Dr. Nizam Peerwani, a medical examiner for Tarrant County, where the autopsies on the bodies of those who died at Mount Carmel were completed, declared: "A lot of these deaths were not consistent with mass suicide."

This isn't to say that there was no discussion of suicide during the siege. I, personally, never heard such talk inside Mount Carmel, but several of the survivors have stated that there was some discussion about mass suicide during those frantic last days, when the iron jaws of the federal forces began to really clamp down upon us. Kathy Schroeder, who turned government witness (at the 1994 San Antonio trial of eleven community members for attempted murder and other charges), wrote in her "confession" to the authorities that "Koresh believed . . . he was about to die . . . [his body] was to be carried from the building on a stretcher. . . . The members were to follow him and once outside they were to fire upon the FBI agents, drawing their fire, killing and being killed." Others, she said, were given hand grenades to blow themselves up, and some women, who might lack the nerve, "were told to arrange to be shot by another member, if necessary." She claimed that Neal Vaega, a sturdy Samoan from New Zealand, agreed to shoot her. Kathy did admit, though, that the idea of suicide was never formally discussed, "just spoken of . . . between people."

I liked Kathy, and I knew she was devastated by the death of her husband, Mike, in the shootout with the ATF on February 28. She and Mike had once been high-school sweethearts, and though she'd been through a bad time and a bad marriage before they finally got together, they were crazy about each other.

But the ATF had tried (and failed) to stick Kathy with a record of arrest for possession of cocaine and marijuana, so I tend to think her dramatic account of our intended mass suicide may be a little suspect, a mixture of wild rumor and her natural desire to placate the lawmen who held her fate in their hands.

But David often did say things that were contradictory, just to provoke us into a deeper understanding of some issue or another. Kathy's lurid scenario of us coming out with guns blazing, bearing the body of our dead messiah, could well be her version of one of his more sardonic provocations. Not everyone understood when David was seriously kidding us for effect, but I certainly never heard him suggest suicide as a fitting conclusion to our ordeal.

———————

On the morning of the final assault, Reno went to the FBI's Washington headquarters before dawn to watch the attack develop on a video feed from CNN. She also listened to audio from the FBI operations center in Waco, and probably heard Agent Byron Sage's voice on the phone, saying to Steve, "This is not an assault"— despite the tanks crashing into our building. Maybe the hidden FBI bugs relayed to Reno the cacophony of tank engines, clanking tracks, splintering wood, crashing walls, and roaring gas trying to terrorize us into surrender. Perhaps she heard the frantic voices of men and women desperately praying, kids crying out in fright— "Mommy!" "Daddy!"

FBI agents, breakfasting at a Waco diner before dawn that day, had drawn a detailed map of Mount Carmel on a paper napkin. The thumbnail sketch, deriving its up-to-the-minute information from the bugging devices inside our building, showed where each and every one of us was likely to be that day. A waitress in the diner found the napkin when the agents left to join the assault force. The sketch revealed that the feds chose to deliberately ram those sections of Mount Carmel where they knew people were clustered. In particular, they intended to immediately block the trapdoor leading to the buried bus to prevent any of the women and children from hiding out there to escape the tear gas.

Whatever remained of the FBI's Jericho Plan—the intention to slowly apply pressure to drive us out over a forty-eight-hour period—was abandoned within minutes of the dawn attack. Throwing aside all restraint, the tanks hacked away wildly at Mount Carmel, graphically expressing the built-up frustration of the feds.

Seen on camera, the tanks looked like huge dung beetles trying to roll the flimsy building up into a ball.

In a moment straight out of *Through the Looking Glass*, FBI spokesman Bob Ricks, in a 10:30 A.M. briefing in Waco on April 19, blithely declared: "Today's action is not an indication that our patience has run out."

Reno, it appears, was unmoved when none of us came running out of the building into the feds' arms. Apparently, it didn't occur to her that the people inside Mount Carmel were either suffocating, trapped by falling debris, or terrified that the agents would mow them down if they emerged. I never saw anyone leave until the last moments, when the building caught fire. I know I hung on to the very last, when the brutal choice came down to being burned alive or shot.

In fact, despite the obvious disaster developing in Waco, Reno, satisfied that the situation was under control, left FBI headquarters around eleven for a speaking engagement in Baltimore. However, at a hastily called Justice Department briefing at 5:00 P.M. that evening, she declared: "I think it's an extraordinarily tragic and horrible situation." At the time, Reno seemed shocked at the consequences of her decision to blast us with tear gas; but as *Washington Times* columnist Wesley Pruden dryly remarked the next day: "Any time you start the day by gassing women and children, you have to expect it to end badly."

16

IGNORANT
QUESTIONS

The final moments at Mount Carmel were eerily biblical, as if the feds had perversely conspired not to convince us how wrong we were—but how right. The tanks moved in, the fires began. With the balls of flame, gas-poisoned air, screams of children as their bones were crushed, the cries of parents as flames incinerated their bodies, it was the end of the world as we knew it.

I began this book with an account of those final moments—a nightmarish experience I can hardly bear to remember. "Nightmarish" truly is the right word, for when I emerged from the burning ruin of Mount Carmel part of me felt as if it must have been a horrible dream. In shock, I stumbled through the following hours like a sleepwalker, barely registering the sting of my own burned flesh or the stench of my scorched clothes.

I vaguely remember the FBI agents piling us into a tank and taking us to a checkpoint, where, despite our protests, they turned us over to the ATF. There were fewer than ten of us, and the ATF agents threw us on the ground, searched us, put us in a van with a bunch of tense, armed men. Without saying a word, they drove us to a second checkpoint, shoved us into a tent, stripped us and videotaped us naked, put our clothes in bags, then made us don orange McLennan County Prison overalls and sandals. At yet another checkpoint, ATF agents ordered us to remove our clothes again, searched us a second time, took our fingerprints and palm prints, and shackled our wrists and ankles. Mostly, I recalled being surrounded by a mob of men with hard, hostile eyes.

Amid all this, the ATF, to mark its terrible triumph, took time to remove the tatters of our flag and run up its own bureau's banner, along with the Texas standard and the Stars and Stripes. It seemed that rubbing these flags in our faces was more important than searching for any other survivors. Our agony was the government's triumph.

Finally, we were handed over to the Texas Rangers for incarceration and interrogation. The attitude of the Rangers was markedly different from the feds. One of them told me, "David, we're really upset about everything that's happened. A terrible thing. We just want to get to the truth. Tell me your story." Despite the Ranger's sympathetic tone, I wisely refused to speak without an attorney present. When he again asked me to tell him what happened, I said: "Sir, I've just been through a traumatic experience and I prefer to keep silent right now."

Reporters crowded in on me as I shuffled in shackles up to the entrance to the sheriff's station in Waco. "Did you kill the kids?" they shouted. "Did you burn the building?" "Those are ignorant questions," I answered curtly. Later that day I heard one TV reporter comment thoughtfully on my retort: "I guess we'll just have to wait and see what Mr. Thibodeau means."

As I was led into the station one newsman shouted out, "Your mom's here. Is there anything you want to say to her?" Seeing Balenda's familiar figure in the crowd, I called out: "I love you, Mom!"

In the jailhouse reception area I caught a glimpse of a small TV showing Mount Carmel, still burning. Reduced to that size, shut inside the glass tube, the whole scene seemed stagy, like a movie set, a fake Atlanta going up in flames, like in *Gone With the Wind*. I began to realize that what we had lived and died for was becoming a media show, an event distanced from reality.

This painful thought obsessed me as the police nurse put salve on my burned face. She tried to give me a tetanus shot but I refused. "I don't want anything put in my body," I told her sharply, unfairly shifting my anger onto her.

After I was processed, I used my one phone call to contact my dad. He'd been too distressed to actually come to Waco, but I knew that in his quiet, stiff way he was worried about me. "Jesus, I'm so fucking glad you're okay," he raged, his normally modulated voice cracked by shock and fury. Seldom had I heard him cuss and swear like that, and I had to take time to calm him down, a real role reversal. "I'm so sorry you had to go through this," he lamented over and over.

In the jail, I heard one last terrible story, the brutal coda to this workday of horrors. When the FBI mounted the final assault, just before the building burst into flames, one of the combat engineering vehicles broke into the cafeteria. Despite the fact that more than thirty women and children were crowded into the narrow concrete chamber at the base of the residential tower, the tank crashed into the ceiling, shoving chunks of broken concrete onto the people huddled below. Six women and kids were immediately crushed by falling blocks; the rest were suffocated by the dust and gas vapors as the tank injected massive doses of CS directly into their windowless, unventilated shelter. As far as I could tell, Michele, Serenity, and the twins had died in the storage room, suffocated by smoke, choked by gas, scorched by fire.

The charred corpse of six-year-old Star, David's oldest daughter, was found with her spine bent into a backward bow until her head almost touched her feet. Her muscles were contracted by the combined effect of the fire's heat and the cyanide in her body, a byproduct of CS suffocation. Cyanide contraction is so violent it can break bones, which is why prison death-chamber officials who use the gas strap their victims down.

One expert later said that the CS "would have panicked the children. Their eyes would have involuntarily shut. Their skin would have been burning. They would have been gasping for air and coughing wildly. Eventually, they would have been overcome with vomiting in a final hell." The official forensic dental report included this terrible detail: "There was a particular instance where all that remained was the arm and hand of a mother clasping a small child's hand and [the] remains of an arm. You could see how tightly the child's hand was being squeezed by the mother."

David was dead, killed by gunfire, along with more than twenty others who'd been shot, including Steve Schneider. David was found with Steve Schneider and David Jones in the telephone room. The coroner decided that David died of a self-inflicted gunshot wound to the head. All of David's women and all of his children perished in the fire. Two fetuses, one full-term, the other seven months, were reflexively stillborn as their mothers, Aisha Gyarfas and Nicole Gent, died.

I heard that Zilla Henry's husband, Sam, watched the disaster on TV in Nottingham, England, praying for his wife and four children. Wayne's four-year-old son, Daniel, watched it in his grandmother's house in New Jersey. "I saw it burning," he said in his child's voice. "How could they bear the pain and pain and pain? Burned to nothing, just bones." Edna Doyle, Clive's mother, said: "I consider I'm the living dead."

The Israeli mother of my friend Pablo Cohen, herself a survivor of the Nazi death camps, said that never in her worst nightmares did she expect her son to die by gassing and incineration in America.

Finally, I was alone in a cell. The guards offered me food, but even after weeks of semistarvation I wasn't hungry. I just needed to think. I sat on the hard cement floor, hugging my knees in the dark, and tried to calm my mind, to consider the bare facts.

Nine of us had survived; seventy-four were dead (seventy-six, if you count the two stillborn babies; eighty-two, if you include the six who died on February 28). Four of the nine survivors were in the hospital, a deputy had told me, including Clive Doyle, who needed skin grafts for the burns on his hands. Marjorie Thomas, the British woman who'd jumped off the roof in flames, was in critical condition, on a respirator. The doctors feared her face would be permanently disfigured.

Sitting in the reception area that first evening after my escape from the fire, waiting for the deputies to assign me to a cell, I watched Attorney General Reno on *Larry King Live*. She claimed the FBI had "hard evidence" that our kids were being beaten—which was the reason why she allowed the feds to burn them! The logic of this escaped me, and I wanted to throw a brick through the damn TV. "More lies!" I shouted, but no one took notice.

It made me furious that the feds were using our children, even in their deaths, as a pretext to condemn the people who'd loved them and been killed trying to protect them. The FBI even denied that David working on his manuscript, something I'd seen him do with my own eyes. The media spin was so powerful, it even began to twist my mind. Talk about brainwashing!

"Some religious fanatics murdered themselves," President Clinton declared, but he was wrong. The truth is that a religious community that threatened or harmed no one was brutally destroyed by agents of the U.S. government in broad daylight, watched by the world. The FBI assault on Mount Carmel was one of the most violent episodes of official religious persecution in U.S. history. All these official distortions of the truth were an early warning to me that the world outside had more or less made up its mind that we were merely a bunch of religious maniacs who'd murdered ourselves. I knew then that I would have an uphill fight trying to counter that perception.

In the days following the tragedy something weird happened: Reno became a heroine. Suddenly she was a media star. "STANDING TALL: THE CAPITAL IS ALL AGOG AT ATTORNEY GENERAL'S OUTSPOKEN HONESTY," *Time* magazine crowed. "RENO'S POPULARITY RISES FROM ASHES OF DISASTER," the *New York Times* reported.

Unlike Reno, McLellan County Sheriff Jack Harwell, later interviewed on PBS's *Frontline*, wept when he recalled his anguish over the tragedy. Harwell said that many FBI officials were shocked that no one came out. That included Byron Sage, who was also upset when interviewed on *Frontline*.

Sitting in my jail cell, listening to Reno being crowned Queen of the Moment, I was stunned. With the screams of my suffocating, scorched friends and the moans of the kids I knew and loved echoing in my ears, I wondered at the ways of the world. How could this woman, who had ordered her cohorts to destroy us, be hailed as Superstar? If David Koresh had been the object of such adulation, it would have been seen as a symptom of brainwashing. Instead of mourning our tragedy, Americans just seemed relieved that somebody out there had taken responsibility for the terrible decision that ended in our obliteration.

It was baffling—and saddening. Hearing paeans of praise for a high official who'd been grossly manipulated by darker minds made my heart sink. Truly, Babylon was upon us with all its monstrosities, as David had predicted.

Months later I came across an old column by Mickey Kaus in *New Republic* that made me realize that others were also puzzled by Reno's amazing post-Waco popularity. "Am I alone in thinking there's something perverse, even a bit obscene, about the current lionization of Attorney General Janet Reno?" Kaus asked plaintively. "She made a disastrous decision that resulted in the loss of more than seventy lives. In a bizarre bit of political alchemy, this somehow protected her from suffering any of the consequences that normally attend disastrously handled responsibilities. Far from restoring accountability, Reno seems to have hit on the formula for avoiding it. Make a dreadful mistake? Go immediately on 'Nightline.' Say the buck stops with you. Recount in moving terms the agony of your decision. And watch your polls rise."

Another perspective comes from attorney David B. Kopel and criminologist Paul H. Blackman, authors of *No More Wacos*. Though Kopel and Blackman are associated with the National Rifle Association, I think their comments are valid: "There is perhaps no institution in the United States government with more unchecked power than the Department of Justice. The job of attorney general is therefore one of the most difficult in the entire cabinet. It cannot be performed effectively by an attorney general who looks the other way at misconduct by her own employees. Nor can it be performed effectively by an attorney general who, having been deceived into approving a plan which directly led to the unnecessary death of seventy-six persons, fails to discipline a single one of the persons who deceived her."

After the fire, a charred copy of the Fourth Amendment was found in Mount Carmel's ashes: *The right of the people to be secure in their persons, houses, papers, and effects, against unreasonable searches and seizures, shall not be violated.* Or as Jack Zimmerman told Congress: "In America we don't kill them first then try them." Shulamit Cohen, Pablo's mother, wrote about her son in a letter to Zimmerman: "I thought he'd be safe in America." In the end, thinking about those last days, I can only echo Clive Doyle's comment: "If they thought we were a bunch of crazies, why did they drive us to the limit?"

To this day, Reno has never apologized for her horrible mistake. But to give the woman her due, she had the grace to say, a year or so later: "I will never forget Waco. The ghost of Waco will be with me all my life."

Lord, I hope so!

Those ghosts certainly haunt me, and I only lived through the experience. She made the whole thing happen.

———

My mood surprised me. I was in shock but somehow at peace. I felt the presence of those who'd died, and the kids' faces haunted me. But the growing tensions of the long siege, and all the pressure of hostile forces squeezing my soul, were at last released. Having survived, I felt that no further harm could touch me.

Gary Richardson, the attorney who offered to represent me, was amazed at my serenity when I saw him the next day. I was on my way to court to be arraigned, along with four other survivors, including my friends Jaime Castillo and Renos Avraam. Richardson told the press that "David Thibodeau's more at peace with himself than most people I know." My court visit was short, and I came out as I went in, in shackles, held as a material witness, as there was no evidence I'd ever shot at anyone. Jaime, though, was in serious trouble; he was charged with conspiracy to murder federal agents.

My mother was aching to see me, but the deputies, for reasons of their own, wouldn't let her in for several days.

Before that, however, I read about her in a newspaper. "I can't wait to be in the same room with him and hear his voice in my ears and feel his hand in mine," she told a reporter, and I could almost hear her warm, emotional voice vibrating through the newsprint. Speaking of having seen Kathy Schroeder, one of the Mount Carmel women who'd come out during the siege, being brought shackled into court, my mother said: "This lovely, petite, absolutely despondent young woman walks through the door in that hideous outfit in those chains, and I could just see my son, my tall, golden son, coming through that door. It was nightmarish."

When my mother was finally allowed a visit, her expressive blue eyes were charged with tears. "Are you sure you're okay, Davey?" she kept asking, distrusting my assurances. She touched my scorched nose and cheek and winced for me, even though I assured her it hurt no worse than a bad sunburn.

I read an account of the smoking ruin of Mount Carmel in Friday's *Waco Tribune-Herald*. The day before, reporters had been allowed to visit the site, three days after the fire. "Death paraded in front of us Thursday on Double EE Ranch Road," reporter Mark England wrote. "Two men in camouflage suits toted a black bag, bowed in the middle, down the hill that falls away from what was once Mount Carmel." England continued: "This day it was as quiet as a silent prayer. The Texas wind whipped the bright orange flags marking the bodies and carried the stench elsewhere."

England went on to describe the ruin of the concrete vault where so many children and their mothers were suffocated and burned to death; the two charred bodies found on the smashed-in roof; and the smoke that still hovered over the rubble. He described David's black '68 Camaro, still intact, "its back lifted up like a scorpion ['s tail]"; the red and purple Jet Ski resting near the lake; and the upturned white hull of our bass-fishing boat stuck up on the hill like a beached Noah's Ark. Bodies were buried in the ashes, charred into icons of human horror.

Contemplating this scene of mute devastation, England recalled meeting Koresh five years earlier, "a polite young man trying to meld rock 'n' roll and religion." When someone called him a prophet, David rebuked him, saying he just taught the Bible.

Reading this sad story, I wondered if England, who'd coauthored the sensationalist *Waco Tribune-Herald* series that ran right when the ATF attacked us, had the least twinge of conscience about the part his skewed, even vicious journalism had played in the disaster. "Memories are all that is left of Mount Carmel," he ended, and I marveled at the mentality that could be simultaneously so guilty and so sanctimonious.

One TV image I saw during those first days stuck in my mind. At daybreak on the morning of the final assault, just as the tanks were crashing into Mount Carmel, a group of black cows went on grazing peacefully in the middle distance. It reminded me of a poem I read in school, about a farmer calmly plowing his field while in the background a mythical winged man was drowning in the sea.

I was moved from cell to cell for several days, sharing space first with other prisoners. Jail was like a luxurious hotel after Mount Carmel. I'd had nothing but rainwater sponge baths for almost two months, and the prison diet was haute cuisine after those endless MREs. I got one hate letter from a Mr. Thibodeau in Springfield, Massachusetts, who accused me of disgracing the family name (no return address); otherwise, I had no personal trouble in the slammer.

For a while I was put back in my own cell. The reason for this came clear when the deputies brought in Louis Alaniz, the Pentecostal who'd sneaked into Mount Carmel during the siege. "So, did you set the fire?" Louis asked bluntly, obviously prompted by the police. "What do you think?" I retorted. "You were inside living with us for two weeks. You know what kind of people we are." "Did you kill the kids?" Louis insisted stupidly. I didn't bother to answer, and the deputies soon removed him. I guess he was just trying to save his ass by acting as a snitch.

Later, I shared a cell with Renos Avraam, who'd jumped off the burning roof to save himself, and with Derek Lovelock, who had come out of the same hole in the chapel wall I had. Derek said he was in the back with Jimmy Riddle when the tanks attacked, and they both fled into the cafeteria. Just as the fire was starting they'd tried to run out of the cafeteria but were driven back by gunfire. "You mean, the feds actually shot at people trying to escape?" I asked. Later, I looked into this possibility more closely and found that the facts were inconclusive, but Derek was certain he'd been under fire.

Derek also told me that Clive Doyle saw Wayne Martin come into the chapel amid the smoke and fire. Somebody asked Wayne: "What do we do now?" Wayne answered: "Well, I guess we wait on God." Clive escaped, but Wayne stayed and died of smoke inhalation.

Clive himself had had a terrifying experience. When the tanks attacked he was in the chapel, taking a pause after hours spent transcribing David's tape. Ferret rounds were crashing through the walls and windows. "They whizzed past my head like rockets," he said. He saw one strike Jimmy Riddle's gas mask and knock him flat.

The entry was blocked by falling debris, and Clive cowered in the chapel while the gassing continued. When the fire started he followed me into the rubble behind the stage. "If we come out, will we be shot?" he'd asked me.

It was no idle question. During the siege we had discovered that a nest of FBI snipers was hidden behind sandbags at the rear of the property. And there was a tank parked beside the boat shed, a frightening obstacle to any escape.

Now the smoke was thickening, Clive recalled. It was pitch-black where we were, the temperature so intense he fell to the floor and rolled around, trying to hide from the heat. His hands were bare, and he felt his skin begin to bubble. "I saw other adults with less clothing crying in pain as the CS gas stung their skin," he said. "Some of them were trying to wipe the gas residue off with damp rags, but that only made things worse."

Unable to stand the heat-torture any longer, Clive dived head-long through the same hole in the sheetrock where Jaime, Derek Lovelock, and I had escaped. The right side of his face and his left ankle were scorched, as were his hands. In shock and agony, think-ing he was the only survivor, he ran toward the razor-wire fence the feds had laid around the building. Then he saw me walking toward the agents with my hands in the air.

Agents shoved Clive to the ground beside Ruth Riddle, whose ankle was broken. A fed grabbed Ruth by the hair and screamed at her to tell him where the children were. Then Clive heard a voice say, "You better quit that, they're taking pictures," and the agent let go of Ruth's hair. "Soon after," Clive recalled, "I learned that my daughter Shari was dead, burned up in the building."

One of the saddest stories was the fate handed Misty Fergu-son, Rita Riddle's teenage daughter. During the fire she tried to get out the back, but the tanks had pushed the debris and the feds' razor-wire barricade toward the building, so she couldn't jump out the window. Misty ran upstairs, trying to get to the front of the building to find a way out. As the gas mask began to melt on her cheeks, she ran screaming toward a window. Just then, the floor collapsed and she was hurled down into a wall of flames. She held out her hands to stop her fall, and her fingers and thumbs were burned right off before she escaped. I was told it would take years of surgery and therapy to repair her hands, if they ever could be repaired; but I imagined that the young woman's psychological trauma would be irreparable.

Some of our people's agonies were even more horrific.

Julie Martinez's thirteen-year-old daughter, Audrey, and three other girls, raging in age from two to fourteen, were buried alive when the concrete roof of the storage room in which they were sheltering collapsed. Julie and her five children died hugging one another.

A seven-year-old boy was burned to death, along with a one-year-old child whose body was too badly burned to determine its sex. Nine children died from gunshot wounds, including Abigail Martinez, plus a six-year-old and a two-year-old. Rosemary Morrison, Jennifer and Katherine Andrade, and seventeen others died from inhaling toxic fumes. Rebecca Saipaia and a young man were also burned. Wayne died alone in the chapel. In the tower above the storage room nine men and women died in a circle, facing outward like the spokes of a wheel.

The autopsies conducted by Dr. Rodney Crow, chief medical examiner for Tarrant County, and his assistant, Dr. Nizam Peerwani, reported that, apart from those who had fatal gunshot wounds, most of the other people in Mount Carmel died of smoke and carbon monoxide inhalation. Some suffocated while buried alive or died of blunt trauma from collapsing structures. Dr. Crow said that thirty-nine of the residents in Mount Carmel expired from toxic inhalation and nine from suffocation, mostly kids. Twenty-one had gunshot wounds, some in the mouth, seemingly suicidal, some in the back of the head, mercy-killing style. Three who died from blunt force trauma were not beaten to death, as the media had previously reported, but rather had been crushed by falling masonry.

According to the coroner's autopsies, those who died from bullet wounds included David, Steve Schneider, and David Jones. James Riddle, Stephen Henry, Neal Vaega, Lisa Farris, and Abigail Martinez received gunshot wounds to the forehead. Philip Henry and Novellette Hipsman had bullet wounds in their foreheads and chests. Mary Jean Borst was shot in the back. Four adults and one child died of gunshot wounds to the head and chest. Another unidentified woman had bullet wounds in the chest and back, and one infant died of a gunshot wound to the forehead. Dr. Crow commented that the condition in Mount Carmel during the fire was so intolerable that if he'd been in there himself he might well have shot his own child as an act of compassion, rather than let him suffer.

———•———

In the years since that terrible Monday in April, I've slowly put together a more complete picture of what happened inside and outside Mount Carmel. In pursuit of a balanced view, I've talked to many of the other survivors and listened to a variety of experts and commentators. I've watched the news footage of the ATF and FBI actions over and over, and I've read the voluminous testimony of federal agents and other law enforcement officers and officials, in congressional hearings and in various reports. I've researched a mountain of newspapers, magazines, and books, scanned the Internet, and examined legal documents and transcripts. Slowly and painfully, I've developed a sense of the full dimension of the catastrophe as it was experienced by people on both sides of the fence that so fatally divided our community from the world beyond.

Despite my natural outrage and sadness over the loss of so many of my friends, I've tried to weigh the facts honestly, with a fair mind, not to generate a polemic but as a need to understand how something so horrible could happen in the heart of the United States. Given the ambiguities and confusions that will forever haunt the story of Mount Carmel, I can only offer my particular version of the truth. But I believe it to be true—as truthful as I can make it.

Take, for instance, the controversy concerning the gunfire that may or may not have occurred on April 19. Now, years after the event, questions linger unresolved: Did the feds fire on us, or did we fire on them? Was there any exchange of gunfire at all? (This is a separate issue from the mercy killings, described in the coroner's report, that may have taken place during the gassing and the fire.)

I heard no shots that fatal day, but during the morning attack one of the radios that still functioned relayed an FBI report that agents had recorded eighty to a hundred rounds of hostile gunfire. The broadcast went on to state that the FBI had refrained from returning fire for fear of endangering the women and children. At the time, my reaction was disbelief mixed with dread. Later, I was able to take a more objective view of the evidence.

The crucial documentation concerning the shooting issue comes from an infrared videotape taken by a surveillance aircraft flying two miles above Mount Carmel during the final attack on April 19. This advanced technology is known as forward-looking infrared (FLIR—pronounced "fleer"). FLIR technology was used to detect tanks and enemy installations during the Gulf War and is now included in the equipment of many U.S. airplanes.

On March 21 London's *Sunday Times* reported that two weeks earlier the FBI had requested the loan of a special British surveillance plane. Such aircraft "flying overhead can pick up conversations between cult members and pinpoint their position using infra-red devices that lock onto heat sources," the newspaper reported. However, the heat-source images on the FLIR tapes record incidents that require interpretation by highly skilled experts, and the controversy over just what these images might mean continues to this day.

Some reputable experts have claimed that the vivid flashes of light revealed on the tapes are evidence of gunfire; others, equally reputable, say that they are merely reflections of sunlight on bright objects. What charges this controversy is the fact that the flashes on the April 19 tapes are clearly shown coming from the areas controlled by the agents. So even if these flashes are, indeed, gunfire, they are proof that the feds were shooting at us, not the other way around.

Physicist Edward Allard, former supervisor of the Department of Defense's night-vision laboratory at Fort Belvoir, Virginia, worked for the Defense Department as a thermal-image consultant for more than thirty years. At the 1995 congressional hearings, and in subsequent interviews and affidavits, Allard testified that the images shown on the FLIR tapes were most definitely made by gunfire. "Nothing in nature would duplicate this kind of thermal signature," he said.

Allard concluded that the flashes on the tapes clearly showed the feds firing automatic weapons into the rear of our building, into the gymnasium and the cafeteria, at 11:24 A.M., and around ten minutes later—a total of forty-four separate incidents. He commented that the number and frequency of the flashes suggested the intensity of the FBI's fury at the people clustered in the cafeteria area, where many gunshot victims were found.

Allard's testimony to Congress was repeated in a motion in federal court, filed by former U.S. Attorney General Ramsey Clark in October 1996 on behalf of the families of those killed in the fire. Clark's motion argues that Allard's analysis "leaves no doubt the U.S. repeatedly fired gunshots into the church [Mount Carmel] and its occupants." The lawsuit accuses the government of acting recklessly, negligently, and perhaps criminally at Waco. The Justice Department says this is "outrageous and absurd" but has yet to produce expert rebuttal.

Allard's testimony was backed up by Infraspection Institute, a specialist company that was asked by the producers of CBS's *60 Minutes* to interpret the FLIR tapes for a report on Waco they were preparing in 1996.

Infraspection's analysis not only verified Allard's opinions but also claimed that the tapes revealed that several people had been deliberately run over by armored vehicles. This finding tied in with the fact that autopsies had found, in the corner of the Mount Carmel gym destroyed by a tank, five bodies with extensive mutilation, including Stephen Henry, whose leg was sheared at the hip, and Jimmy Riddle, who had the right side of his chest ripped from his body so violently that the tank that ran over him lost its tread.

However, the FBI, when approached by CBS producers, denied both Allard's and Infraspection's claims. The network never broadcast the story, claiming the FLIR evidence was deemed too "sensitive."

In an article that ran in April 1997, the *Washington Post* investigated the issue of the interpretation of the FLIR tapes and convinced the FBI to show portions of the tapes to its reporters. "John M. Hogan, Attorney General Janet Reno's chief of staff, says these bright blips are benign glints of noonday sun," the *Post* reported. It added that the "FBI says an examination of the entire FLIR tape—which runs several hours—would . . . discredit the gunfire theory. Yet the government has delayed releasing the entire tape to attorneys who filed a Freedom of Information Act suit in Arizona. The bureau also hasn't provided a full copy to the *Washington Post*, which first requested one in December 1996."

To delve deeper, the *Post* sent copies of the tape extracts to a dozen experts, some with infrared and weapons experience; others were "local defense contractors who specialize in interpreting FLIR." Four of the analysts "were convinced they saw bursts on the tape indicative of gunfire going into the compound." Others declared the evidence inconclusive. At Fort Belvoir, Allard's old base, the senior scientist said: "It looks like reflections to us." The *Post* concluded its investigation with the comment that interpreting FLIR is as much art as science.

To date, the FBI has produced no hard evidence whatsoever that we did any shooting, except for such anecdotal accounts as FBI chief negotiator Byron Sage's claim to have seen bullets ricocheting like "sparklers" from the flanks of a tank as it smashed into our front wall early that fateful Monday morning. During the 1995 congressional hearings, U.S. Representative Howard Coble revealed that his committee had asked the military for records of gunfire damage to the tanks but had received none.

No federal agents were killed or wounded on April 19, and neither is there any unambiguous evidence that the feds shot people down in cold blood. None of the Mount Carmel survivors I've talked to are absolutely sure there was any shooting at all that day. But there are several troubling details that stick in the mind, such as the FBI's order of eighty body bags. Either the FBI were victims of their own propaganda that we would commit mass suicide, or else the agency was fully aware that its dangerous tactics, including the use of firearms, might well have tragic consequences.

As anecdotal evidence, there was a phone call Clive Doyle's mother, Edna, said she received from a neighbor, who owned a house adjoining the rear of our property, the side hidden from the media's cameras. Edna lived in a trailer two miles away from Mount Carmel with Mary Belle Jones, Perry Jones's wife. The call came in around noon on April 19, at the height of the blaze. Mary Belle, who answered the phone, told Edna that the neighbor said he'd seen "twenty-five to thirty" people who ran out of the back of the building being shot down by federal agents. "He wouldn't give his name because he didn't want to be involved," Edna said. There were also rumors that another neighbor had actually videotaped this shooting; but the tape, if it ever existed, has vanished.

Apart from the fire and the gunfire questions, other issues remain for which there are, as yet, no clear answers.

These include the controversy over the amount and variety of the weaponry we supposedly "stockpiled" in Mount Carmel, and whether our armory included .50-caliber machine guns, as the government claimed. These questions have no clear answers for many reasons, not least of which is the way the feds treated the official "crime scene" that Mount Carmel became after April 19.

During the 1994 San Antonio trial of eleven members of our community for attempted murder and other charges, Texas Ranger Captain David Byrnes complained that his crime scene processing team was prevented from entering the site while the ATF was "obviously altering outside evidence." He said he was concerned that the agents had "salted" the scene with bogus evidence.

Also, Texas Ranger Fred Cummings testified that half of Mount Carmel's metal double front door was missing—the right half, which revealed the spray pattern of entry holes, confirming that the ATF had fired a burst of automatic fire at David as he tried to talk to them when the agents first attacked us on February 28. Cummings added that he'd seen "trash" being loaded into a dumpster by FBI agents before the scene was processed for evidence. The FBI also interfered with the Tarrant County Coroner's office investigation. They confiscated videotapes made by the county's photographer—then "lost" them. (The FBI also lost other relevant items, notably a steel safe containing $50,000 in cash and some gold and platinum, found in the ashes by the Texas Rangers and officially signed over to the agency.)

At San Antonio, the prosecution introduced into evidence 300 guns said to have been found "in and around" Mount Carmel, plus a bunch of dummy grenades, parts of exploded grenades, and remnants of 500,000 rounds of ammo. Prosecutors showed the court illegal homemade rifle-silencers and forty-eight illegally converted semiautomatic rifles. However, there were none of the heavy .50-caliber machine guns the feds claimed we had used against the ATF in February and threatened them with again on April 19. To add to the mystery, Byrnes, posing in the Texas Ranger evidence vault on a TV show, displayed two scorched .50-caliber guns he claimed were part of the "Davidian armory." This inventory of weapons is altogether suspect because the government has never allowed any independent examination of the guns the FBI claims to have found in the ashes of Mount Carmel.

So where does this leave our honest endeavor to evaluate the validity of the reasons the government has offered to justify its assault on Mount Carmel?

Clearly, the child-abuse excuse was nonsense, a deliberate lie designed to con Reno into allowing the Justice Department brass in Washington and the gung-ho tactical commanders on the ground to use highly dangerous tear gas on women and children. Though she was new to the wiles of Washington, Reno should have been a great deal more skeptical, of both the people pressuring her and the experts the feds produced. And she should certainly have taken the trouble to scrutinize the FBI assault plan a lot more carefully than she did. (In a footnote to the Justice Department report, Reno is quoted as acknowledging that, as far as the FBI's assault plan was concerned, she had "read only a chronology, gave the rest of the material a cursory review, and satisfied herself the documentation was there.")

Similarly, the mass-suicide line was a crock. If any of the people who died shot themselves or their children, it was a desperate response to finding themselves trapped in the gas-filled, crumbling, burning building. As Dr. Crow, the Tarrant County coroner, concluded, these would surely have been acts of compassion, not religious mania.

Although neither we nor the feds deliberately set Mount Carmel ablaze, the FBI must have been aware that the toxic brew they injected into our building in such enormous quantities would create a highly flammable condition that windy day. They obviously knew, too, that since they'd cut off our power, we were down to using kerosene lamps and propane heaters that would surely be knocked over when the tanks demolished parts of our building.

So what valid reasons, apart from frustration and impatience, did the authorities, at the highest level, truly have for wiping us out? Hardly any, it seems to me—and that is horrible.

17

AFTERLIFE

One week after the destruction of Mount Carmel I came out of jail into my mother's waiting arms. She hugged me so hard I thought my skinny ribs would crack. "Davey, Davey, Davey," she murmured over and over, as if saying my name confirmed my existence after I'd come so close to dying.

I emerged from the McLellan County lockup with bare feet. Balenda had sent me shoes to replace the ones I'd worn when I stumbled out of the burning building, but the deputies refused to give them to me. Since the ATF kept my clothes for evidence, I needed a new wardrobe to replace my orange jail suit.

After a shopping trip, my mother took me to the Brittany Hotel, where she had been staying and working. The hotel owner, Mark Domangue, had generously given rooms to all the family members who had relatives in Mount Carmel, and some of them, like Balenda and Rita Riddle, worked there as payback.

Sadly, Mark's compassion had ruined his business. Guests shunned his hotel because it had become known as a Davidian hangout.

As I sprawled on the bed, relaxing for the first time in months, I noticed that my mother was nervously looking out the window.

"Expecting someone?" I asked.

"Those feds!" she burst out. Her face was red and agitated, giving me a glimpse of the strain she must have been under for the eight long weeks of the siege and my detention.

I laughed at her fears of the feds; after what I'd just been through, what more harm could they do me? When I embraced her I found she was trembling, and for a long moment I comforted her, patting her back as if she were the child and I the parent. In a sense, it was so. My experiences, both physical and spiritual, had aged me, and I was no longer the roly-poly boy she knew and loved, no longer the delayed adolescent I'd been when David found me on Sunset Boulevard.

That night my attorney, Gary Richardson, treated us to dinner at the local Hilton. I feasted on a delicious filet mignon, the best steak I'd ever had. I'd lived on those miserable MREs for weeks, had hardly eaten in prison, and suddenly my ravenous old hunger returned full force. That hunger was my enemy, and I tried to fight it. I was lean, emaciated like a strung-out rocker, and I loved the way I looked. Never in my life had I been so thin, and I wanted to stay that way, as a signal to a hostile world that I was in fighting trim and ready for combat. But that steak was fatal. The wall was breached, and appetite won out. For the following weeks I was hungry all the time and could never feel full. It was my first retreat back into my old mode.

Meanwhile, I had a role to play as witness. David had primed me for the part, and I stepped forward to its first summons.

Gary Richardson, who was my agent as well as my attorney (that's how he hoped his fees would be paid), urged me to give my first interview to the Fox-TV news show *A Current Affair*, which had offered to pay me $25,000. At the same time, Ted Koppel wanted me on *Nightline*, which had a much larger audience but was unpaid. Since *Nightline* had more clout, I had decided to go to New York to see Koppel when Mary Garofalo, the anchor of *A Current Affair*, approached me. She told me she'd been in Waco all the time, had put all her energy into covering the story, and felt she knew more about our ordeal than Koppel, who'd never been near Mount

Carmel. To convince me of her commitment, and her intention to present a balanced view of events, Mary showed me a clip of an interview she'd done with Louis Alaniz on April 19, as part of her program. In that footage Louis talked about David showing him around Mount Carmel two days before the attack, and how happy and healthy the kids were.

Louis also revealed that the FBI had asked him where the children usually hung out, and Louis told them he'd seen many of the kids in the upstairs room over the front door. By informing the feds about this he hoped they would avoid areas where kids concentrated. However, first thing that Monday morning, one of the CEVs deliberately smashed into that very location.

Louis said the feds, duped by their own fantasy that we had antitank weapons, asked him if we had any guns that could take out tanks. "I told them no," Louis asserted. Speaking to the camera a few hours after the conflagration he'd seen on TV, the poor guy was in tears for most of the interview.

Mary's approach and tenacity appealed to me, and I gave her my first interview. On camera I was passionate but fumbling, trying to find my feet as an advocate for my community, attempting to appear to be a rational person, not the gun-toting, Bible-thumping weirdo the public had been led to expect from the Davidian tag. I understood I had to present a personality people could trust and identify with, someone able to leap over the wall of demonization erected by weeks of federal and media propaganda. I also avoided the trap of "Bible babble," knowing any mention of Scripture would immediately turn the audience off. I was just David Thibodeau, a young guy from Bangor, speaking from the heart.

That interview was one of the very few experiences I had with the media in which my words weren't edited and twisted from their original meaning.

It was a stipulation of my release from detention that I had to go directly to Bangor, and on May 5, a week after I left prison, two weeks after the fire, I landed in Maine. My family met me at the airport, including my two grandmothers, my father, and Uncle Bob. In the background were several reporters from local newspapers eager to talk to me, but my mother and I shoved them aside. We'd had enough public exposure for a while, and neither she nor I wanted to destroy the feeling that Bangor was a haven for us, a place to lick our wounds and slowly put our lives back together.

A few days earlier the *Maine Sunday Telegram* had published my disgusting, fat-faced senior-yearbook photo, alongside the "I want shiny cars, dirty money, and lots of rock and roll" quote. The former director of my Bangor High band remembered that, at five-foot-seven and two hundred pounds, I was always busting out of my marching-band uniform. The *Sunday Telegram* encapsulated my odyssey in one neat paragraph. "To many, David Thibodeau will long be known as one of the 'Waco wackos.' But to the people who knew him as he grew up in Portland, South Portland and Bangor, David Thibodeau was just a regular kid who liked heavy-metal music and dreamed of drumming his way to rock 'n' roll fame."

My grandmothers welcomed me home with plenty of food and no questions. My dad, on the other hand, came right at me.

I hadn't spent time alone with my father for years, and he insisted on taking me for a six-hour ride around the countryside. "Why the Bible? Why not Buddha?" he asked me, over and over. Ever since he'd been kicked out of the seminary for smoking, Christianity for him was anathema.

He could, just barely, accept that people had religious impulses—but the Bible, no way. To him, the Old and New Testaments were instruments used to distort impressionable minds. I tried to explain that since, unlike him, I'd never had much exposure to the Bible, its text was as exotic to me as anything Buddha might have said. At times he seemed to be blaming himself for somehow making me vulnerable to a David Koresh, for the absence of a real male role model in my youth. "I'm sorry this happened to you!" he blurted one time, then shut his lips down tight.

"Why the Bible?" The question was also on Balenda's lips. Since she had talked to David on the phone and met people like Julie Martinez, I hoped she'd be more open-minded, and I tried to explain the Seals. "Davey, it's driving me crazy—I can't take it!" she exclaimed, clapping her hands to her ears after a moment or two. "That's David Koresh talking; you sound like a puppet. Why does he still have such a powerful hold over you?"

Her response saddened me. I tried to explain that I was bound to David's teachings, not the man himself, though he'd been my friend. She shook her head impatiently, and I stopped talking. "Look, Mom, we love and respect each other, so let's leave it at that," I said finally. "I really don't need you to understand."

"But I want to understand," she retorted, clearly distressed. "I'm puzzled, you know. Maybe a little jealous—"

I laughed fondly; we hugged each other and let it go at that.

———————

Although I never wanted to see Waco again, I was obliged to return there a few weeks later to testify before the federal grand jury investigating the Mount Carmel events.

Coming back to Texas so soon was bad enough, but the grand jury itself was one of the most miserable experiences of my life. As soon as I saw that collection of Wacoans walk into the large room in the courthouse, I knew our goose was cooked. Adding to the tension was the fact that I was ignorant about the judicial system and didn't realize, until it was too late, that my attorney would not be allowed in the room. I was present only as a material witness, but I felt the other dozen or so members of our community who were paraded before the jury were damned. From the way the jurors' eyes slid right over us without contact, I could see, by and large, that they shared the mind-sets of the FBI and ATF.

Mount Carmel was blamed for giving Waco a bad name. During and after the siege the locals had plainly shown their sympathy for the feds. On the way in from the airport I'd seen large billboards trumpeting the ATF's gratitude for the Wacoans support of "law and order." In the wake of the tragedy, the Waco Red Cross had refused to give people like Sheila Martin and her kids old clothes and furniture, claiming they'd participated in acts of civil disorder and therefore weren't eligible for humanitarian help.

The prosecutors grilled me for two solid hours in front of the grand jury, trying to get me to incriminate others and, possibly, myself. I was well aware that Jaime, Renos, and Graeme Craddock, for example, were damned out of their own mouths, so I had to keep my wits about me. It was obvious that both prosecutors and jurors thought I was an outright liar.

They tried to nail me with abrupt questions like, "Did you have a firearm?" and "Did you start the fire?" Every time I opened my mouth I felt I was lying because I knew I wasn't being believed. At the end of those two hours I staggered out of that courtroom feeling mentally raped.

For a while after that, I was so unnerved I almost convinced myself that I *was* a liar. I wasn't even sure my own attorney trusted me. "They didn't believe me," I exclaimed when I saw Gary. "I told the truth, but they didn't want to hear!" Driving down the street in the big Cadillac Gary had rented, I told him it had been a bad experience, and he immediately changed the subject, as if he didn't want to discuss the veracity of my testimony.

On a deeper level, I felt I hadn't told the true story to the jury because it was too hard to tell.

The "facts" were tricky enough, like who fired the first shots and who set fire to the building. But these issues were easy compared to the wider political and spiritual elements clouding the air. It slowly dawned on me that I might never be able to be a full and true witness to those events. Instead, I might have to select and compose a narrative that would strike people as honest and coherent; a narrative parallel to the whole truth—whatever that was.

The grand jury handed up indictments against eleven of our people. All of them faced serious conspiracy charges. Totally harmless characters like Clive Doyle, Ruth Riddle, and half-blind, almost deaf Bob Kendrick. Jaime Castillo, Renos Avraam, Livingston Fagan, Brad Branch, Kevin Whitecliff, and Norman Allison were also indicted. Even Paul Fatta, who was in Austin when the ATF attacked, was charged. In order to escape the blatant hostility of

Wacoans toward our community, the defendants' attorneys insisted that the trial be moved elsewhere, like San Antonio.

After the grand jury process, I felt impelled to visit the Mount Carmel ruins—with great reluctance. The site was surrounded by a tall chain-link fence; a "Keep Out: This Area Is Quarantined" notice hung on the gate. What I could see was devastated and devastating. "Oh my God, I'm back in hell," I said out loud, and hurried away. After the grand jury debacle, I didn't want to have anything more to do with the place they called Waco.

Back in Bangor, I gave my first press conference, flanked by Balenda and Uncle Bob. Though I was reluctant to speak out so soon, being still unsure of my public role, I felt I had to respond to the made-for-TV movie *In the Line of Duty: Ambush at Waco*, recently shown on NBC. I denounced the movie and pleaded for people to keep their minds open. I deflected personal questions, like why I stayed in Mount Carmel during the siege, fearing my answers might be skewed to represent me as having been brainwashed.

"A lot of people would say to me that David Koresh was guilty of mind control, and I could see why people could say that," I told the press. It was a question that had to be confronted, given the demonization of our community and its leader. I tried to soften the image of a manipulative messiah that had been put out there, accepting that there could be an element of group thinking in any closed society. But my brain hadn't been controlled by anyone, I emphasized. "I'm not that kind of guy. Hell, I'm a Mainer, and no one screws with my stubborn head!"

I felt awkward during the press conference, but afterward people told me that I'd handled myself well in a tricky situation. Maybe I can play this witness role after all, I thought, and not make a fool of myself or let my dead friends down. I hoped, too, that my speaking out would allow the folks in my hometown to live with what I'd done. "We're really proud of you. You've shown us Mainers to be thoughtful," a guy said to me in a bar, which made me feel good.

Not all my experiences with the press were so encouraging, and the media were hard to avoid. Though I resisted calls from national networks, I saw the feds continue to twist the public mind on television so often I felt I had to respond. In quick succession I appeared on several shows such as ABC's *20/20* and NBC's *Prime Time Live*. All of them edited what I'd said to suit their own unsympathetic agendas, taking my quotes out of context to make me appear to confirm their slanted views.

To cap it all, *National Enquirer* concocted a story it untruthfully claimed to be gleaned from interviews with some of my relatives. In the article, a family member was quoted as saying I'd told them that some people in Mount Carmel had been shot by our own side while trying to leave the building during the siege and that I'd admitted that we'd spilled lighter fluid and lantern fluid to set the fire.

I immediately contacted Gary Richardson in Houston, and he said we should sue. In the end, *National Enquirer* settled our suit for $75,000. I wanted to go to court to publicly refute the rag's ugly insinuations, but Gary advised against it on the grounds that his fees would eat up all we might gain.

I tried to shrug off the media's persistent misrepresentations, but they got under my skin all the same, like those Texas chiggers. Once, I was goaded beyond endurance, when Assistant Secretary of the Treasury Ron Noble appeared on television and said: "Our report will show that the Davidians beat their kids and stabbed them to death in a final frenzy at the end." Those old lies made me see red. I jumped out of my chair and started screaming hysterically, totally out of control. My Uncle Bob, who was with me, did an amazing thing. To calm me down, that quiet, serious man started screaming louder than I did. "I was in 'Nam—how can they keep lying!" he shouted at the top of his voice. His fury trumped mine, and I had to laugh.

———

Gradually, I chilled out in peaceful Bangor. To keep myself occupied, I got a job delivering Chinese food for Sing's Restaurant. I lived with my Uncle Bob; it was calmer in his house. Balenda asked too many probing questions, and my grandmother Gloria didn't know what to think. Bob, the one persistent male presence in my childhood, left me alone to sort things out. He gave me a room upstairs where I could sit around in the evenings, playing a keyboard, reading, thinking, mourning, writing songs, trying to get in touch with myself. Once, when a chopper flew over Bob's house, I hit the floor, my heart beating wildly. Often I wandered around town, amazed that people were going about their business as usual.

In June, David's remains were buried at Memorial Park Cemetery in Tyler, Texas, by his mother, Bonnie Haldeman.

Only close family members were there, including his half-brother, Roger Howell, and David's maternal grandmother, Earline Clark. "I didn't get to see the body, and I'm not even positive that is David in there," Bonnie said, standing by the coffin. Whatever was buried that day wasn't David Koresh. Maybe it was the relic of Vernon Howell, "Mr. Retardo," a dumb, abused kid who saw visions.

David's absence was a huge hole in my life. I missed him a lot. He'd come to mean an enormous amount to me, as a person, friend, and spiritual mentor. Now I tried to figure out exactly what my experience at Mount Carmel meant to me and where it had left me.

I was troubled by the loss of my bedrock faith in America and its rule of law, in the essential decency and fair-mindedness of the American people, in their willingness to hear the truth and their ability to resist government and media manipulation. All that seemed to have been trampled underfoot at Mount Carmel. The feds had refused to take any real blame for what they'd done, and the American public had seemingly accepted their gross corruption of our moral and social inheritance.

As the months went by I felt an increasing disjunction between a self-assured public persona, which I knew I had to cultivate as a witness to the memory of my community, and the confused private man I was inside. For two and a half years I'd ridden on David's energy, carried along by his certainties. Now, suddenly, I was thrown back on my own resources, whatever they were. All my life I'd wanted to be special, and for a while I was, sharing David's spirit. Now I'd have to find a way to be special in my own right.

Meanwhile, I floated along, still too numb to come to grips with the shipwreck of my life. I'd lost my natural ease with women, their proximity and promise made me nervous, but I did renew an acquaintance with Paula, one of the sandwich girls I'd worked with at the Pizza Oven before I left for California. An art teacher in a high school, Paula was cheerful, whereas I was moody. She dubbed me "Snapper," like a turtle, when I was grumpy with her, and we passed pleasant hours playing pool at the table Uncle Bob had in his house. She was a real breath of fresh air in my state of mental and emotional exhaustion, but clearly it wasn't going to be simple finding my way back to my sexuality.

I also had to rediscover music. For almost two years, ever since I moved out of Cue Stick, the club back in Waco, I'd let my drumming lapse, except for an occasional jam session with David. I felt I was no longer a professional, that I was back to being the amateur I was before Los Angeles.

To get back in the groove, I started performing with a band I'd played with during the year after high school. We had a few gigs as a cover band playing other musicians' songs, but it was rather desultory. Apart from a few stock routines, my sticks had lost their cunning, and that was a real downer. I felt I wasn't fit for anything anymore, neither sex nor music nor the goddamm human race in general. To try to clear my mind, I bought a motorcycle and roamed the Maine countryside, speeding along country lanes through a green landscape that was, mercifully, utterly different from Texas. The question *What do I do now?* echoed in the wind whistling past my face.

But the real questions were *What* could *I do now? What was I capable of? Did I really have the confidence and kick to go out there and start talking publicly about Mount Carmel? Become the advocate and witness I was meant to be?*

The mere thought of it made my gut churn. It would be like trying to climb an Everest of prejudice and public indifference while weighted down by my own reluctance and inertia. And I was no athlete. Every bone in my body wanted to melt into a dreamy lassitude and float away on the stream of time. When I was really down on myself I felt like a total fuckup. For a few years I'd lifted myself up out of the trough of my weaknesses; now, again, I was nothing. I was, as David said of himself, an empty Dixie cup ready to be thrown away.

———————

In September I got a call from Mark Domangue, the owner of the Brittany Hotel in Waco, about participating in an event with talk-show host Maury Povich. Mark and Povich were planning what they called a "Town Meeting" in Waco in early November, and they wanted Balenda and me to be on the panel.

Still scarred by my earlier encounters with the media, my first reaction was "no way." But Mark assured me that Povich had prom-ised to put a balanced program together, one that would allow us to present our point of view to a national audience. Several other members of our community had agreed to take part, he said, in-cluding Rita Riddle, Catherine Matteson, and Clive Doyle. Marc Breault would also be there, he added, and we could finally con-front the man who'd lit the fuse that had blown up our house.

At the time, Balenda was in Greece, and so Povich offered to fly her to Waco for the show. "I fatuously believed it would be an op-portunity for the survivors and the families of the people in Mount Carmel to express what we felt about it all," she later recalled. We discussed the show on the phone, and she argued that we might have a chance to get our story out there. Povich was an honorable person, she said; but I reminded her about Donahue and Oprah Winfrey, two honorable people who'd done their best to paint us as dupes of David the Demon. Apart from anything else, I hated like hell the prospect of returning to Waco, to speak to an audience of Wacoans, to look at the same faces that had condemned me out of hand during the grand jury proceedings. I remembered all too vividly their cold looks and smug, down-home self-assurance about right and wrong, decency and indecency. To them, I'd hardly been more than a loathsome bug to be squashed underfoot. In the end we agreed on a compromise: We'd both go to Waco, but only she would sit on the panel; I'd stay in the audience.

As it turned out, neither Clive nor any of the others who were under indictment could take part in the panel before their trial, scheduled to begin in San Antonio in January. So Balenda and Mark Domangue became our point people, facing down Marc Breault and others. We agreed that they would concentrate on the way the feds had trampled our right to practice our religion, rather than try to counter the old accusations of child abuse, sexual misconduct, and gun stockpiling that had become the media's stock in trade whenever Mount Carmel was discussed.

Returning to Waco once again was less unpleasant than I'd imagined. To me, now, the boring little town was just another place—not one I much wanted to be in but no longer the place of nightmares. Members of Povich's staff explained that the "Town Meeting" would cover two one-hour episodes of the show but that both would be taped the same day.

We few survivors gathered in the lobby of the Brittany, getting together for the first time since April. The mood was subdued but hopeful. "What can they do to us that they haven't already done?" someone said, and that seemed to sum things up.

On the morning of the taping we were awakened early and then bused out to the studio. As soon as we arrived we had the first indication that we were about to be screwed. The deal had been that the nonparticipants among our group (those who weren't sitting for interviews) would sit in the front row, forming a bloc of support for Mark and Balenda; instead, we were deliberately split up and scattered throughout the audience. Another bad sign was the glimpse I had of Marc Breault going over a script of the show with one of Povich's people. The smell of collusion was in the air.

And, oh, that audience—the very faces in my nightmares.

With my long hair tied in a ponytail, I felt naked amongst that shirt-sleeved, sprayed-hair brigade, sure the knives would soon come out and I and my friends would be cut to ribbons by the

crowd's rampant righteousness. Its mood was cheerfully expectant, like a horde in the Colosseum waiting for the Christians to be
thrown to the lions. They didn't lick their chops openly, but a sort
of obscene glee was plain to see.

The situation turned surreal when a comedian came out to
warm us up. Though this is a standard in all TV shows, I thought
it was totally inappropriate, given the gravity of the topic. But the
people in the audience chortled their heads off.

Amid all this an elderly woman came up and asked for my au-
tograph. "Why?" I asked, taking her program to sign. "You're a celebrity," she said, surprised by my query, and walked off with her
prize. Some celebrity, I thought, watching her go. Looking around,
I noticed Mark Spoons, our former neighbor at Mount Carmel, the
man who'd rented the house by our gate to Robert Rodriguez and
his team.

Povich bounced onto the stage, provoking an outburst of ap-
plause. His gaunt preacher's face seemed at odds with his blow-
dried coiffure and glib tongue—Abraham Lincoln as snake-oil
pitchman. His voice was solemn yet salacious as he introduced the
topic and the panelists, relishing a juicy show.

The juice came early, when poor old Stan Sylvia started sobbing. His seven-year-old son, Joshua, had been placed by the authorities with a family in Massachusetts, and he was fighting to get
the boy back. A New Englander like me, Stan had long been a loyal
follower of David's at Mount Carmel and Palestine. His wife, Rachel, had died in the fire, along with her two-year-old daughter,
Hollywood, one of David's children. Stan refused to believe that
David was Hollywood's father, however, and he'd kind of kept his
distance from the rest of us. During the siege Stan was in Pomona.
Now his short, stocky body heaved with grief at his multiple losses.*

---

* Fifteen children had been taken into state custody during the siege. Ten
had been placed in the Waco Methodist Home before going into foster
care. "What we have here is a beautiful bunch of kids," the Methodist Home
president said at the time. "They're bright. They're doggone bright. You can
see the wheels turning round and round with every new concept." He also
reported that the children while in his custody had many nightmares, panic

"Why didn't they just let the children go?" shouted a redhead sitting right behind me, and the audience cheered her roundly. This person, who pretended to be an audience member, was actually an attendant on Povich's flight to Waco. She, too, had been seen backstage consulting over a script, and all through the taping she leaped to her feet with the same shout—"What about the kids?" Every time Balenda and Mark tried to turn the focus back to the government's actions, the audience started screaming about the children.

"Why didn't you guys come out with a kid under each arm?" Mark Spoons demanded.

"No one wanted to leave," Catherine Matteson explained, but she was hooted down.

Balenda fought like a tigress against the rising tide of malice, refusing to shut up at Povich's command. "Balenda, this is not your show, this is my show," the famous host said testily. She was often booed and rarely applauded by the studio crowd. When Mark tried to say that we should put our raw emotions aside for a moment and dispassionately consider the facts, the audience hissed him into silence. "It was like being eaten alive on television," Balenda said afterward, tears of frustration in her eyes.

During a break, before Marc Breault was introduced, a production assistant told me I should get up and challenge him. She wanted me to ask Marc if he felt responsible for all the deaths. "Get outta my face," I said, shoving her aside. "I'm not going to be part of your damn circus!"

Marc's appearance on the platform was the very first time I'd seen him in the flesh. His lean frame was clothed in black, giving him the look of a shifty undertaker, except for his elaborate, greasy, Elvis-style coif. I remembered David's deep grief over Marc's defection, his frequent tears and occasional fury. Onstage Marc clearly felt ill at ease. His answers were mumbled and unclear, and he was obviously aware of our hostility. I'm sure, too, that he wasn't happy about what had happened. In his book he insisted that Mount Carmel was

attacks, and frightening flashbacks of the initial attack.

one of the most truly religious communities he'd ever encountered.

For me, the truly shattering moment was the testimony of Dr. Crow, who was clearly still very distressed by what he'd seen on his autopsy table. But the good doctor's testimony was lost in the carnival atmosphere, and when the county coroner finished speaking Povich insisted—ignoring Crow's evidence—that the people in Mount Carmel had carried out a mass suicide, echoing President Clinton's declaration that we were a bunch of religious fanatics who'd killed ourselves.

I was furious with the way Povich's show turned out, but I was also glad to have come so nakedly face to face with such hostility. In truth, the experience was bracing. It allowed me to regard the mountain of prejudice in the light of reality. It was a formidable climb no doubt, but I could begin to imagine myself finding a foothold or two on its slopes.

18

CLIMBING THE MOUNTAIN

The trial of eleven members of the Mount Carmel community—charged with conspiracy to murder federal officers, murdering federal officers, and various firearm offenses—commenced in San Antonio in early January 1994. The accused included Norman Allison, Renos Avraam, Brad Branch, Jaime Castillo, Graeme Craddock, Clive Doyle, Livingston Fagan, Paul Fatta, Bob Kendrick, Ruth Riddle, and Kevin Whitecliff. They were represented by thirteen lawyers, including Dick DeGuerin's brother, Mike. I went to San Antonio as a witness for the defense and to show my support for my friends. The trial lasted until February 26, two days short of the first anniversary of the ATF's attack.

Though the trial had been moved from Waco, I was shocked to discover that the judge, Walter Smith Jr., was the same federal magistrate who'd denied David Koresh's right to counsel during the siege. Seeing him up there on the bench made my heart sink. Declaring that "the government is not on trial," Smith had refused defense motions to sever the cases and would not allow defense attorneys to subpoena federal officials who'd helped plan the raid. He arbitrarily cut the jury pool in half before prospective jurors

301

could be questioned, placed the attorneys and jurors under a gag order, and had the jurors escorted into court by armed guards.

I was also appalled to learn that Ray Jahn, the leader of the six U.S. Attorneys assigned to prosecute the case, had been hired as a special counsel to FBI Director William Sessions. Jahn had been involved in planning the use of CS gas to force us out of Mount Carmel, and another prosecutor, Bill Johnston, was one of the people who had organized the ATF's raid.

Johnston's role in the Mount Carmel story was particularly sly. He'd previously tried to suppress a damning Treasury Department internal memo revealing that the ATF had initiated a shooting review on March 1 and had "immediately determined that these stories [of agents who took part in the February 28 raid] did not add up." When he got wind of this, Johnston, in his role as a Justice Department attorney, advised ATF Supervisor Dan Hartnett to stop the review for fear that the ATF was creating evidence that would contradict the prosecution's case.

To cap it all, there was Davy Aguilera, the ATF agent who had authored the original affidavit, seated among the prosecutors. It seemed clear to me that the deck was well and truly stacked.

The Mount Carmel Eleven seemed dazed by the buzz of the attorneys and court officials, the hostile curiosity of the crowd, and the abstractions of the procedure. Jaime caught my eye and smiled, but he looked totally disoriented. He was shuffling, his gaze darting this way and that, as if searching for an escape hatch. I felt so bad that he was up there and I was down among the spectators.

Despite the presumption of innocence guaranteed by the U.S. Constitution, I knew from my grand jury experience that the simple act of entering a courtroom can make one feel guilty, and I imagined how these defendants must have felt. I wasn't allowed to visit Jaime in custody, and the defendants were escorted to and from the court by a motorcade complete with outriders and three police cars in front and behind the prisoners' vans, sirens screaming.

Ray Jahn set the tone with his statement that "the evidence will show that David Koresh's theology was the theology of death." The defendants were accused of being members in a "revolutionary organization," whose core unit was the "Mighty Men." The phrase "the House of David" was given a sinister twist, as if it were a terrorist organization aiming at the violent overthrow of authority.

These accusations reflected the gross distortion of Mount Carmel's image in the mirror of the public mind.

As it turned out, the evidence prosecutors presented was either weakly circumstantial, self-incriminatory, or the testimony of people like Kathy Schroeder, who'd been offered a plea bargain in exchange for testimony. Jaime's attorney, Jeff Kearney, grilled Kathy, but she insisted on identifying eight men with guns, claiming it was her role to hand out the ammunition. She said that Renos Avraam had a .50-caliber machine gun nicknamed the "Bear" and that he'd told her he'd fired shots at the ATF on February 28. (As I mentioned earlier, no such machine gun turned up among the weapons the feds displayed and alleged to have found after April 19.)

In Brad Branch's case, for instance, there was Victorine Hollingsworth's statement that she'd heard Brad say "I got one!" and a contrived argument based on the relative position between Brad and an ATF agent who was killed on February 28. There were no eyewitnesses, and ballistic tests of the bullets in the agent's body did not match any of the guns found in Mount Carmel. Paul Fatta was charged with aiding and abetting the conspiracy, though there was absolutely no evidence that Paul himself had ever converted AR-15s from semiautomatic to automatic. Ruth Riddle was also accused of aiding and abetting because she was supposed to have handed her gun to someone else. Clive Doyle, Jaime, and Graeme Craddock were accused of starting the fire.

Remarking the tenuous nature of such evidence and of the whole case in general, Gerry Morris, Bob Kendrick's attorney, told the jury that the prosecution "made it sound like getting involved in a conspiracy is about like catching a cold."

As the trial wore on it was obvious that the defense team was outmatched by the prosecution team of top Justice Department lawyers. Most of the defense attorneys were acting pro bono, and it showed. They failed to nail down crucial points and let off lightly scores of prosecution witnesses. They also seemed unable to find

a common voice. The only one who struck me as competent was
Clive Doyle's attorney, Dan Cogdell. In preparing for my testimony
he grilled me till I sweated. No prosecutor could break me after
that, I felt. However, I wasn't called to the witness stand. The defense, led by Corpus Christi attorney Douglas Tinker, called few
witnesses and rested early. On the advice of their attorneys, none
of the defendants took the stand.

To me, the defendants' failure to testify was a bad mistake. It
didn't give the jurors a chance to see how essentially harmless most
of the people on trial were—goofy, maybe, to conventional eyes, but
innocuous nonetheless. It also left the prosecution with all the cards,
including that massive display of weaponry. Yet the defense team did
not sufficiently challenge the fact that the government never allowed
an independent inspection of these weapons to verify whether they
had, in fact, been collected from among the ruins of Mount Carmel.

I called lead attorney Douglas Tinker to ask him whether he
thought that resting the defense case early was wise, but he rudely
hung up on me. I called back a second time to make sure we didn't
just get disconnected and he swore at me and then hung up again.

At the close of the trial Judge Smith gave the jury sixty-seven pages
of instructions on how to render a verdict, most of them favoring
the prosecution. However, he did allow an important instruction
offered by the defense: "If a defendant was not an aggressor, and
had reasonable grounds to believe he was in imminent danger of
death or serious bodily harm from which he could save himself
only by using deadly force against his assailants, he had the right to
employ deadly force in order to defend himself."

The jury was a mixed bag, and though I searched the faces
long and hard, I didn't quite know what to make of it. Among the
eight men and four women were housewives, school teachers, civil
servants, and a retired banker. When they left the courtroom to
deliberate on the verdict I felt my friends were likely damned.

But we were all surprised. Four days later the jury found all
eleven defendants not guilty on the murder and conspiracy

charges; Doyle, Allison, and Kendrick were found not guilty on all counts. Seven were found guilty of aiding and abetting in the voluntary manslaughter of federal officials; five of these were also found guilty of carrying a firearm during the commission of a crime of violence. Paul Fatta and Graeme Craddock were also found guilty of other weapons violations.

The jury's comments were interesting. The verdict was a compromise, a few members declared. "Some thought it was outright murder on the part of the Branch Davidians," one juror said. "And some thought it was outrageous murder on the part of the federal government." Another commented that "there were a lot of dirty hands out there that day [February 28], on both sides." Another juror remarked that after seven weeks of testimony, 120 witnesses, and well over a thousand pieces of evidence, "No one had a clue about who had fired the first shot that day." However, they all agreed that none of the defendants deserved life in prison. "When we heard all that testimony, there was no way we could find them guilty of murder," declared one juror. "We felt provocation was pretty evident."

"When I first heard that there was going to be a Branch Davidian trial," jury forewoman Sarah Bain later said, "my first thought was that it was going to be actually a trial of the FBI, or trying to bring some of the FBI people to justice. And I was actually quite amazed to find out that the Branch Davidians were on trial for murdering four ATF agents on February 28."

Bain felt that the jury did not get the complete, truthful picture of the events that occurred during the ATF's initial attack on Mount Carmel. "For example, the question of whether or not the helicopters were firing down on Mount Carmel was a major part of the testimony we received," she declared. "There was so much evidence that there could have been no firing coming from the helicopters, that we pretty much felt forced to believe it. Had we known, as we know now, that there was gunfire from the helicopters, it would have made a strong impression on the jury, and we would have given more consideration to the self-defense argument."

According to Bain, the jury also made a crucial technical error, one that impacted the sentences subsequently handed out by the judge. "Though we found the defendants not guilty of the charges of murder or attempted murder or conspiracy to murder," she explained, "we mistakenly found several of them guilty of the linked charge of using firearms during the commission of a crime—a crime of which they were innocent. That was a totally inconsistent verdict. After the trial was over, Judge Smith came into the jury room and told us that he had no choice but to throw out the firearms conviction on the basis of that inconsistency. However, the prosecution then argued from legal precedent that an inconsistent jury verdict did not necessarily negate that verdict. The judge then reinstated the firearms convictions, and handed out his harsh sentences."

Immediately after the trial Bain wrote to Judge Smith that the defendants, in her view, had indeed fired guns on February 28, but "their actions were rash rather than of murderous intent." Considering time served, none of them should be "facing severe penalties," Bain wrote. "Even five years is too severe a penalty for what we believed to be a minor charge." Most of the defendants, she later said, should be given probation. "If we were to have the trial today, and if I were again the foreman of the jury, with all of the information that has come to light since then, I think the outcome would be very different. Even back then we all felt a little bit blue about our verdicts, which the evidence presented had compelled us to render. We consoled ourselves by saying that the trial of the Davidians was just the first shoe dropping, that the ATF officials who'd formulated the fatal February 28 raid would also be made to face a trial. To me, it's a disappointment and a disgrace that the second shoe has never dropped."

Clive Doyle and Bob Kendrick were immediately set free. Two foreigners, Canadian Ruth Riddle and Briton Norm Allison, were turned over to the INS because they had overstayed their temporary visas. Ruth, however, was rearrested, on Judge Smith's order, on a legal technicality presented by a prosecutor.

The press crowded around us on the courthouse steps as Clive and Bob emerged. Both men shed tears of sheer relief at their release; they also wept for those who were still detained. I gave a few interviews myself, trying to counter the accusations disguised as questions that the reporters flung at me. It was hard to figure out how to reduce all the complex issues to a series of soundbites that would cut through the fog of misconceptions.

David was the ghost hovering over these events, a presence no one could ignore. Without him, none of us—defendants, attorneys, judges, jurors, officials, spectators, media—would have entered that San Antonio courtroom. The next day, Renos and Livingston gave a press conference from prison in which they declared that "David will return in a cloud of glory"; and David's mother, Bonnie, said he'd appeared to her in a series of vivid dreams.

I felt as if he had never left.

———————

Given Sarah Bain's comments, we hoped the sentences of those still in federal custody would be light and that, with good behavior, they'd soon be set free. Then we could concentrate on a future without David's presence and what that would mean to us all.

But on June 17 Judge Smith handed out sentences that flew in the face of the jury's opinion that none of the eight people in custody should face severe penalties. Smith stated that because the defendants had been found guilty of having weapons during the commission of a crime they were in effect guilty of the original charge of conspiracy to commit murder. The supposed conspiracy to kill federal agents was, in Smith's view, "a part of the beliefs of the Branch Davidians, expressed and taught by their leader."

Charging on, Smith declared that we had definitely fired the first shots on February 28 and set Mount Carmel ablaze on April 19. "Finally, by a combination of suicide and murder inflicted by Davidian upon Davidian, all but a handful of the Davidians were killed." It was as if the judge found guilt where the jury had found innocence.

With swift dispatch, Smith handed out stiff sentences. Renos Avraam, Brad Branch, Jaime Castillo, Kevin Whitecliff, and Livingston Fagan were each sentenced to forty years. As a consolation prize for incriminating himself before the grand jury, Graeme

Craddock's sentence was reduced to twenty years. Paul Fatta received fifteen years and Ruth Riddle received five, even though it was clear she hadn't shot at anyone. For her services to the prosecution, Kathy Schroeder received a three-year sentence and has since been released. All eight were heavily fined to compensate the ATF and FBI for their losses in attacking us.

A shocked Livingston declared: "There is no doubt in my mind that the actions that we were forced to take were justified." Paul Fatta told a reporter: "I'm suffering [but] whether I'm out there in the so-called free world, it really doesn't matter. I'm beyond that. The issue to us is relative to what God is doing. . . . Man has already demonstrated his willing incompetence." Jaime told the court: "I just hope that out of this whole situation, I hope it's pricked the conscience of people to realize and to understand."

I wasn't in San Antonio for the sentencing, but I was truly shattered when I learned of its harshness. The terms seemed so vindictive, as if the authorities, not content to have destroyed our community, wanted to grind us down, wipe us out of the collective memory. The thought of quiet, friendly Jaime shut away for forty years made my blood boil.

I wasn't the only one who was upset by Judge Smith's actions.

A few weeks after the sentencing, Sarah Bain wrote a sharp letter to Judge Smith, challenging his criticisms of the jury's verdicts. To a reporter, Bain was even more forthright: "The federal government was absolutely out of control there," she said. "We spoke in the jury room about the fact that the wrong people were on trial, that it should have been the ones that planned the raid and orchestrated it and insisted on carrying out this plan who should have been on trial."

Judge Smith, of course, ignored Bain's plea. A series of appeals was launched, forcing a resentencing hearing in Smith's Waco courtroom on August 4, 1997. There the shackled prisoners once more confronted their nemesis. The defense attorneys argued that in each case no evidence had been introduced to prove that any of the defendants had actually been involved in the crimes for which they'd been convicted. They also reminded Judge Smith that the jury had found no evidence of the conspiracy upon which the judge had based his harsh sentences. Smith listened impatiently, then reconfirmed the sentences he'd handed out three years earlier.

"This nation is supposed to run under laws, not personal feelings," Renos protested. "When you ignore the law you sow the seeds of terrorism."

The seven people who were sentenced were shipped off to different prisons. After several moves, Jaime and Graeme ended up in the Federal Correctional Institution in Oakdale, Louisiana; Kevin and Brad were housed in the federal facility in Beaumont, Texas; Renos in El Reno, Oklahoma; Paul Fatta in Anthony, New Mexico; Ruth Riddle in Danbury, Connecticut (she has since been released, having served out her term). Livingston landed in Leavenworth, Kansas, where he has suffered brutal mistreatment by the guards.

"My salvation remains precarious at best," Livingston wrote in late 1996. In letters given to released fellow inmates, he described being beaten and thrown into a cold open cell, or "cage," in his underwear, without blankets or a mattress, suffering two epileptic seizures as a consequence. "After continuously slamming my head against a concrete, then metal structure, followed by my body against a concrete floor . . . the 300 lb. officer then verbalized his intent to kill me for not cowering to his will." But Livingston's spirits have remained high. "Fear is a cruel master," he wrote early in 1998. "It is not, however, unconquerable."

I didn't know and was at a loss what to do with my feelings of rage at the treatment of my friends, but I didn't want to become the kind of person whose life is powered by fury.

I lingered in San Antonio for a day or two after the original jury verdict, reluctant to return to Bangor. In my hometown I'd been drifting in a daze. My mother, sensing my state of mind, worried over me with anxious phone calls, and I knew my vague answers weren't reassuring.

Then I had one of those chance encounters that seem casual enough yet turn out pivotal. I met Ron Cole, a yuppie kid from Colorado, best described as a Davidian wannabe. Moved by the Mount Carmel catastrophe, he had come to Waco to help the surviving community members trace where our remaining property was before the feds seized it. He wore a "David Koresh/God Rocks" T-shirt and eventually took possession of David's Chevy Camaro.

I wasn't in Waco when Ron arrived, so I hadn't met him till San Antonio. I heard from Clive Doyle that he'd joined the rump group left in Waco and had attended several of the Scripture study sessions. Later, Ron and Clive fell out badly when Ron claimed he'd been "accepted worldwide as a Davidian leader," but at that time they were still friends.

Ron had militia connections, and in 1997 he was arrested and imprisoned in Colorado for possession of illegal weapons, but that was still way down the line when we first met.

Ron said he was going to Florida to give a talk about Mount Carmel, and he suggested I come along for the ride. "We'll do the *Easy Rider* back-roads thing," he said. To me, it seemed a good, wild idea right then, a break from all the heaviness. Ron suggested I address some of the so-called patriot groups he knew in Florida and Louisiana, telling them about Mount Carmel. "Why shut up? Why let them get away with it?" Ron asked, and I had to agree. Silence is a form of consent, and I just couldn't let the evil popular picture of David and our community stand without trying to combat it.

Ron's car had a sound system, and before we set out we visited a music store to buy some CDs to power our ride. Ron favored the songs of a new heavy metal band called Rage Against the Machine, and in my dark mood I liked the sound of the name. As we sped across Texas toward Florida we belted out the lyrics, especially the refrain, *Why stand on a silent platform*. In the verbal violence of the heavy-metal rap I began to find my voice.

The first talk I gave in Florida was at a local school in a small town near the Everglades, home to one of Ron's friends. The spring night was hot and airless and I was sweating as I confronted the rows of faces in the school gym. As Ron introduced me, I silently prayed to God to give me the words to be a true witness, but His attention seemed elsewhere. My throat was dry and my brain felt like a prickly cactus.

Then, suddenly, a gust of wind sprang up, stirring the palm leaves outside, rustling through the auditorium like a cool whisper. I got goosebumps. Rising to my feet at Ron's gesture, I launched into an impassioned description of Mount Carmel's catastrophe, concentrating on the way the feds had trashed our constitutional rights. The audience ate it up, clapping and cheering for several minutes while I sat there, eyes shining, inspired by my own energies.

Is rage truly my kind of inspiration? I wondered afterward, as Ron and I and a few others went to a bar for some beers. The notion was invigorating but scary. Such fury wasn't true to my nature, but it was a way to power my ascent of the mountain. The cost, I dimly began to realize, would be a split between the public and the private man, but at the time that seemed a price worth paying.

What was tricky, though, was the politics of the audiences who most wanted to hear me. They came from the patriot community, a broad, vague label that describes citizens who feel government is all too often guilty of gross abuses of power. Patriots, I began to discover, ranged from average working-class folks—electricians, mail carriers, gas-station attendants, factory workers—to rampant militia members, and all of them were more than ready to view Mount Carmel's fate as a prime example of the feds exceeding their authority.

Early on I encountered the more extreme wing of this loosely organized element of American society. Ron and I were invited to a camp in the Everglades, a place secured by checkpoints manned by armed guards with walkie-talkies. Inside the camp we found several hundred men and women dressed in military fatigues, living in tents while training in survivalist techniques. Their watchword was "preparedness," and I was later invited to several of the survivalists' Preparedness Expos held around the United States.

Before I was called upon to speak, a man named Mark from the Michigan Militia talked about the constitutional right to bear arms. To a chorus of lusty cheers, he damned all "pinko-liberal" advocates of gun control. He was followed by a member of the Florida Militia who described something called "spike training," which I gathered involved a week in the Nevada desert learning how to survive by eating cactus and lizards. *These guys mean business*, I said to myself, and the thought was both chilling and exhilarating.

I was the featured speaker, and I just went for it hammer and tongs. Though I ran on for three solid hours, not a soul in the big marquee moved a muscle. Several hundred eyes were riveted on me, and the electric rush was heady. *What juice there is in words!* I exulted when I finally sat down. It was the kind of power that David possessed, and I saw then how it could electrify the unwary. But on the ride out of camp I began to wonder where I was going with all this amazingly articulate anger.

I knew that those militiamen were right-wing radicals—far too radical for my taste—but they seemed to be the only Americans willing to hear what I had to say. The best of the patriots, I felt, were struggling to rethink their identity as Americans, and like me, they were truly scared by what had happened at Mount Carmel. But Mount Carmel was about Scripture, not politics, and I knew it was a perversion for it to became symbolic for the wrong reasons, for the wrong cause.

What is true patriotism? I asked myself, over and over. Rather than the desperate response of taking up arms against ourselves, it had to be a belief in the inherent decency of America.

In any case, violence was not the answer, and I hoped the main memory of the Mount Carmel community would never become what the feds tried so deviously to imprint on the public mind: that we were a bunch of Bible-spouting wackos armed to the teeth. Most people seemed to have swallowed that story hook, line, and sinker, and I wanted to tell America what happened to us, what we really were about.

After the Everglades experience I spoke frequently to audiences ranging from a dozen to hundreds. Sometimes a family would ask me to come talk in a private home; other times I addressed a group of lawyers concerned with constitutional and civil rights issues. Over and over, people came up to me after I spoke at meetings and said they felt they had been lied to by the government and the media. There seemed to be a considerable and widespread distrust of these forces that shape our society—a healthy distrust, I felt, and I found I could make people weep with my sad tale—or rouse them to anger. Then, I had to suggest they use their anger in positive, not negative, ways.

Altogether, public speaking brought me out of my numb rage and gave me a voice. At times, though, I feared I might be thrown in jail for some of the things I said. All the while, my passion was focused on the memory of all the children who'd died for no good reason.

There was one wonderfully funny moment in my odyssey through the South—in Miami, where I was invited to participate in a TV talk show. A production assistant with a clipboard led me into the studio while an on-camera interview was in progress. To my amazement the man sitting up there with the talk show host was none other than President Clinton!

I was ten feet away from Clinton, who seemed totally unprotected. Looking around, I saw no Secret Service personnel, no guys with brush cuts, lapel mics, and holstered Glocks bulging their jackets. I imagined grabbing Clinton by the lapels, shaking some sense into him, asking him on camera why he'd allowed his attorney general to murder our children. Hell, it was the chance of a lifetime!

"The Clinton look-alike," the assistant said tersely.

"Pity," I muttered, and she laughed.

———

As April approached I planned to return to Waco for a memorial that Clive Doyle and others had organized to mark the first anniversary of Mount Carmel's destruction. The event was named "A Day of Information" to bring people together and remind the public how and by whom our community had been obliterated. When I phoned him, Clive told me he expected several hundred people to attend the ceremony on the site of Mount Carmel's ruin.

Clive also told me that a meeting had been arranged on the day before the event with the core group of survivors and a panel of attorneys led by former U.S. Attorney General Ramsey Clark. Clark and several other attorneys had filed wrongful-death suits totaling millions of dollars against the U.S. government on behalf of the families of people who'd been killed in Mount Carmel, as well as other suits for the survivors collectively.

For the Clark meeting we gathered in a conference room at the Brittany Hotel, where I was staying. There were four other lawyers apart from the former attorney general, but he was the most impressive figure. Tall and serious, he had an air of authority that reinforced his reputation as a former close associate of Robert Kennedy and a dedicated advocate of civil rights cases.

What took place at Mount Carmel, Clark told us, "may be able to tell us more about ourselves as Americans than anything that's happened." There was, he stated bluntly, "absolutely no justification for the fatal acts." His concern in all this, he emphasized, was to defend the free exercise of religion under the First Amendment. "The rights they took away from you they took away from everyone in this country," he declared. Since the federal authorities, abetted by the media, had labeled us a "cult," their actions toward us could only be characterized as religious persecution.

Then Clark added a remark that surprised me. Commenting on the February San Antonio trial (before Judge Smith handed out his harsh sentences) Clark labeled the proceedings "political." I was about to question him on this, when he explained that the government, in his view, could not have afforded to lose that trial in the forum of public opinion. "To my mind, that's what makes this tragedy a political act."

After talking to groups of people in Florida and Louisiana, I knew what he meant. Although mainstream America had apparently made up its essentially indifferent mind about us, the patriot community had adopted Waco as a club to wield against the government. The liberal left, which during the sixties and seventies had itself beaten up on Washington and all it stood for, now seemed to be rallying to the government's defense. I wondered if an old lefty like my mom would have condemned us outright if she hadn't had an inside track on what had really happened at Mount Carmel. She hated guns with a passion, and for one reason or another, the issue of gun control had moved center stage in the controversy over our destruction. If she hadn't known us, the arguments about common Texas practice and the right to defend oneself against excessive force would've washed right over her head.

"Can we get justice, Mr. Clark?" I asked.

"I believe in the possibility of justice," he answered firmly, and his tone encouraged me. Despite my bitter experiences, I didn't want to let go of the notion that America would finally hear us out. Yet sitting in that brightly lit, windowless room in Waco, it seemed to me that the catastrophe at Mount Carmel had ripped an ugly hole in the very fabric of American society.

The attorneys warned us that it could take years before the civil actions came to trial. Clark said he'd been involved in lawsuits arising from the 1970 killing of four Kent State students by the National Guard, and they still were unresolved. But a civil action would allow us to present evidence that Judge Smith had excluded, like the 911 calls Wayne Martin had made to Lieutenant Lynch, as well as a suppressed ATF video that was rumored to prove that the helicopters had fired on us first. The "discovery process" in civil actions, whereby documents can be demanded and must be produced by the parties, would also allow us to dig deeper than the officials who authored the self-justifying reports recently released by the Treasury and Justice Departments.

In concluding his presentation, Clark urged us to consider if we wanted our group to continue as a church. An organized church would help with the lawsuits by presenting a unified community, he said. "I will always consider the community my family," I replied. "We have to go on together."

Privately, though, I wondered what my role might be in the future. My talks in the South had given me some confidence in my ability to be an articulate witness, and I was ready to continue in that capacity, traveling the country, speaking to anyone who'd listen—left, right, or center. I had to keep my spirits up, somehow.

There were encouraging signs that the government had begun to learn some of the lessons of the tragedy at Mount Carmel. The same day we met with Ramsey Clark, FBI Director Louis Freeh announced a new tactics and training program to cope with situations like Mount Carmel and, hopefully, avoid repeating the tragic errors the agency made during the siege. Freeh said the FBI was creating a new position—"special agent in charge of critical incident response" in fed jargon—to provide a more subtle and sophisticated method of dealing with "unusual" groups like ours. However, Freeh still clung to the official line that the whole tragedy was our fault.

John Magaw, the new ATF director, faulted his agency for "intelligence gathering oversights," such as lack of information about our comings and goings. In other words, ATF should have quietly arrested David when he was outside Mount Carmel. The raid was the largest law enforcement action in American history, Magaw said, noting that the ATF would consider changing its dynamic entry strategy. In October 1993 Assistant Secretary of the Treasury Ron Noble told the House Appropriations Committee, "Although we cannot prejudge all future situations, we must be open to the possibility that a dynamic entry, exposing agents, innocent persons and children to gunfire, may simply not be an acceptable policy."

But the frankest admission of fault came from Robert Sanders, former ATF deputy director for enforcement. In 1995 he testified, in the congressional committee hearings, that the agency, at the time of the raid, was "very troubled." The agents in the field thought the assault was "something forced on them by headquarters," Sanders said.

The American Civil Liberties Union (ACLU) had recently appealed to Attorney General Reno and President Clinton for a national commission to review the "policies and practices" of federal law enforcement agencies. The ACLU got no response, according to Gene Guerrero, field director of the ACLU's Washington office: "That illustrates our concern that not only is the Justice Department doing nothing about Waco, it is not adequately addressing the concern for federal law enforcement abuses," Guerrero declared. He went on to compare the official indifference to our fate with the meetings his organization had had with Justice Department officials concerning Rodney King's beating by several Los Angeles policemen.

Other groups planned "Waco Remembrance" demonstrations in Washington, D.C., including one outside the White House. "This has generated more interest than any other case I am aware of," commented one of the attorneys involved in our wrongful-death lawsuits. "I think that is because it is so foreign to what we hold as sacred in this country to see government police surround a place where ninety people live and charge it with tanks." The ACLU's interest in us, though belated, was very welcome. It helped dilute the growing perception that only right-wing zealots sympathized with our pleas for justice.

———————

The patriot community and its more militant extremists had rapidly turned "Waco" into a war cry that was to have its own tragic result in Oklahoma City, which was bombed on the second anniversary of the Mount Carmel fire. Several patriot leaders stated that every federal official who had a part in the assault on our community should be tried, all the way up the chain of command, to Reno and Clinton.

It turned out that Timothy McVeigh had made two visits to Waco, one of them during the siege. During early March 1993 he'd taken part in a libertarian protest meeting held at the Waco Convention Center and had appeared in a video made near Mount Carmel at the time. "A lot of people told me I should be afraid to come down here," he told the camera defiantly. A month earlier, before the siege, McVeigh had visited Paul Fatta's booth at a gun show at Tulsa, Oklahoma, and chatted to him about our community. "I've never seen him madder than when he talks about Waco," a friend of McVeigh's later confirmed.

According to a FBI affidavit based on the interrogation of McVeigh after the bombing of the Alfred P. Murrah Building in

Oklahoma City, which killed 168 and injured some five hundred, McVeigh was "extremely agitated" about the government's assault on Waco. After Oklahoma City, the affidavit stated, "McVeigh's grievance concerning Waco became a matter of national concern."

Mount Carmel's fate, sloganized to "Waco," generated a host of books, pamphlets, and videos put out by radical rightists. In fact, "Waco" became the rallying point for a range of radicals who generally lacked an agreed agenda of reform, apart from being against the feds. "We see Waco as a centralization of power, the central government coming into all areas of our lives," declared Norm Olson, commander of the North Michigan Regional Militia. "Waco was the second shot heard 'round the world." Russel Smith, commander of the Texas Constitutional Militia, said that "Waco woke us up to a very corrupt beast."

When I gave talks after the Oklahoma City bombing, the press often tried to link me to McVeigh, despite my expressed dislike of the man and his actions. After a while I gave up disputing the connection and simply tried to tell what I knew and take whatever heat resulted. But it saddened me that Mount Carmel had become no more than a cork bouncing in the crosscurrents of alien agendas.

The night after the meeting with the attorneys, I ventured alone to Mount Carmel. The area was still fenced off, keeping the curious out and the secrets in. Rows of white wooden crosses had been lined up against the chain-link fence in readiness for the next day's memorial, a small army of ghosts in the moonlight.

As the bullfrogs croaked in the background and as distant cattle moaned in their sleep, I pressed my cheek to the wire and stared at the piles of rubble beyond. All that was left of the bulldozed site was the excavations of the tornado shelter we had never had time to complete and the empty, concrete-lined swimming pool. A stubble of scrub had already reclaimed the site where our building had stood.

The silhouettes of two burned-out buses shared the blighted landscape with twisted rebar, sticking out of lumps of concrete like devil's horns. A dozen or so scorched bathtubs we'd never gotten around to installing were stacked up like giant soap dishes. Charred timbers were strewn among the bluebells, and not far from me I saw a crumpled kid's bike with a busted red frame resting in the grass that had shot up after the spring rain.

In that moment, David's absence was a physical ache. His death had sucked the center from my life, leaving little but a black hole. And though his theology told me he'd fulfilled his purpose on earth, it was no compensation for being deprived of his vivid presence.

Then the thought struck me: *If Mount Carmel hadn't been wiped out, would I have outgrown it? Would I have moved beyond David's teachings yet carried them with me?*

I couldn't imagine having to live in Mount Carmel for too many years. It had been too bleak, and even before we were attacked I was already beginning to feel restless. But the process had been abruptly aborted, leaving me betwixt and between, thrown back on my own resources, whatever they were.

—··—

The next morning was a circus, with some three hundred people packing the site. The crowd milled around the grandstand and under the yellow- and white-striped refreshment tent. Rock music blared from loudspeakers while vendors hawked religious tracts, "David Koresh/God Rocks" T-shirts, tapes of David's teachings and songs and the 911 emergency calls, caps with Branch Davidian logos, bookmarks, and balloons. Amateur photos of the fire were selling for $10 a print.

Several media relay vans were in the background, keeping their distance, aware of the crowd's distrust of their reportage. (At a previous meeting I'd addressed, the audience ejected the media from the auditorium, accusing the reporters of being liars.) Ron Engelman, our friend from KGBS Dallas, was there to "present information the lapdog media doesn't have the courage to report."

There were guided tours of the ruins, bulldozed as a health hazard by McLellan County authorities. The tours were led by a reverend from the God Said Ministry, who unctuously pointed out

the sights. I felt slightly sick watching the minister and his eager
flock of listeners, wondering at our all-too-human ability to turn
tragedy into farce.

There was also a strong "constitutionalist" flavor that I found
distasteful. Patriot groups had helped organize the event, and
their stamp was everywhere—in the books on sale, the ubiquitous
Soldier of Fortune magazines, and the loud voices of their hucksters.
It was they, I suspected, who'd made what should have been a solemn memorial into a carnival.

In his speech, Clive Doyle tried to recapture the seriousness of
the occasion. He surprised me, revealing that this was the first time
he'd visited the site since escaping from the burning building. "I'm
kind of numb," he told the crowd, and people clapped cheerfully,
as if he were paying them a compliment. I made a short speech,
emphasizing Mount Carmel's character as spiritual community. At
the end of the ceremony we read out the names of the dead, tolling
a bell for each one. Then we observed a minute of silence.

After the speeches a group of us went to a restaurant for lunch.
We all felt very emotional, but all the same we weren't sure how to
go forward as a community. Many members had gone away: Oliver Gyarfas to Australia, Rita Riddle to North Carolina to care for
her badly injured daughter, Misty Ferguson. Ten of the surviving
children were back with their parents, and eleven others were with
relatives. No one felt able to actually live on the property, as we
were legally entitled to do. We discussed the need for some kind
of permanent memorial or Mount Carmel museum, but it didn't
get anywhere. (Subsequently, students at Baylor University put together a small exhibit, including a model of Mount Carmel, titled
"The Facts About Mount Carmel," in Waco's Helen Taylor Marie
Museum.)

Clive was clearly the leading light in the small rump group
that had remained in Waco. They were busy fighting a claim on
the property made by Amo Bishop Roden Drake, crazy George
Roden's former common-law wife. For my part, I couldn't handle

living in Waco; just crossing the Texas border oppressed me. But Clive felt Waco was his home.

The sheep were scattering; our cohesion seemed to be weakening. Most of us felt that David's teachings couldn't continue without him, and without David there was no strong, motivating force. He was the heart and soul of our community, and we were the truncated body, helpless to move on.

19

BACK TO THE FUTURE

After the excitement of the past few months, my return to sleepy Bangor was a real downer. My family's attitude toward my experience had hardened into a kind of rough indifference. My two grandmothers' absolute silence about Mount Carmel was deafening, and the mere mention of the word "Bible" turned my dad's mouth sour. My uncle by marriage, who was visiting Bangor, was the only one crude enough to actually put the general feeling into words: "So, did you guys start the fire?" he asked bluntly. Mim snapped at him to shut up, but I knew he'd expressed what they all thought.

My mother was in Greece, but through her letters she told me she was proud that I'd become politically active, like herself. "You have to be willing to fight for your beliefs," she wrote. "In America blind faith is expected as long as the game is maintained."

However, Balenda was still upset that I hadn't been straight with her about my marriage to Michele. "Even if it was not real you both asked me and Gram to acknowledge and accept it in the letters and phone calls," she wrote.

After scolding me, she insisted in her maternal way that Michele, despite the contrivance of our relationship, had really loved me. For Balenda, the basic issue was clear: "Women do not like being treated as tribal entities for God or anyone," she said in the same letter from Andros. "I hope that one day you will understand how un-human that is and that it's not divine either."

As the weeks went by I began to dream about Los Angeles. My feet yearned for the hard pavement of Hollywood Boulevard, my fingers itched for the drumsticks I'd plied when music—and music alone—was the power in my life. Yet the thought of returning to that chaotic, energetic scene bothered me.

Then two things happened, spurring me to take the plane to Los Angeles: I finally received my share of the out-of-court settlement with *National Enquirer,* and I got a call from Ryan, the singer-songwriter in the band I'd abandoned when I followed David to Mount Carmel.

Ryan suggested we put the band together again and take another shot at trying to make it in show business. He didn't ask me a single question about Mount Carmel—about my life there, my survival, what I'd been doing since—and that was a huge relief. I accepted the offer of a couch in his home in Sherman Oaks and said goodbye to my family.

They weren't too sad to see me go. Clearly, they didn't quite know what to do with me, certainly not in my role as the survivor of an embarrassing event. My existence as a musician in Hollywood was something they could live with, even if it led nowhere.

In Los Angeles, Ryan and I connected with Scott, our old lead guitarist, and a bass player, and we put together some demo tapes and got gigs in some of the Sunset Strip clubs like the Whisky and the Roxy. Drumming with the guys made me remember how much I'd missed performing. I rediscovered the sheer exhilaration of being in the music.

In September 1994, I made a trip to Israel at the invitation of professor James Tabor. He met me at Ben Gurion Airport, and we drove straight across Israel to Masada, on the banks of the Dead Sea. In that desolate landscape, looking up at the ruined fortress where the Jews had died after defending their faith against a powerful Roman army, I remembered Mount Carmel and the Texas plains.

Back in Jerusalem, I visited Mount Zion, where David had received his vision in 1985. The walled city was beside me, with the Wailing Wall and the golden dome of the mosque above it, symbolizing the overlay of faiths in this hard land. Maybe, in that context, David's vision hadn't appeared out of the air but rather rose out of a ground alive with inspiration. *Anyone could have visions here,* I thought—*except me.* I was eternally earthbound, a witness but no prophet.

The months drifted by, and just like that it was spring 1995—the second anniversary of the fire.

Nineteen ninety-five was meant to be a significant year. In his 1985 vision David had been set a timeline of ten years before the Apocalypse would occur. However, since he hadn't prophesied his own premature death, no one among us really expected the world to end.

The group that gathered in Waco that year for a rainy-day observance was far smaller than the previous year's throng. The people who made the pilgrimage, huddling under umbrellas as the rain poured down, seemed more sullen, more serious. There were no T-shirt hawkers and balloon hucksters, just survivors and some sympathizers, like Ramsey Clark, attorney Jack Zimmerman, and San Antonio jury forewoman Sarah Bain. The chain-link fence enclosing the property was down, and we dedicated a grove of crepe myrtle trees to those who perished in the flames.

The Northeast Texas Militia had erected a plaque inscribed with the names of the dead, but thankfully the patriot presence was far less forceful than it had been during the first anniversary. True, someone had white-washed a message on one of a cluster of shacks near the gate—"WELCOME HOME MILITIAS, WE KNOW WHO THE GOOD GUYS ARE." I also heard that G. Gordon Liddy, the Watergate defendant and talk-show host, had been invited to broadcast the memorial service from his *Radio Free D.C.* studio in the capital. Fortunately, he'd declined.

In his speech, Jack Zimmerman said he felt the public's interest in us was waning. "There seems to be a slackening off now," the lawyer said. "But we've called for the congressional oversight committee to investigate the Justice Department. Until that happens, I don't think we'll be protected from a repeat."

I'd just finished ringing the replica Liberty Bell, a single chime for each time Clive read out the names of the dead, when the news crew filming us began to ask questions about Oklahoma City. At first we had no idea what they were talking about—then they showed us footage on their monitors of the devastation of the federal building. The journalists told us that an explosion had ripped the building apart just after 9:00 A.M. that morning. A day-care center on the second floor had taken the full force of the blast; nineteen babies were killed.

As we watched televised images of infants being pulled from that pit of devastation, the reporters standing by speculated on a possible link with Mount Carmel. During the first media frenzy the FBI was accusing Islamic terrorists, but some commentators were fingering Waco.

My own reaction was absolute horror at the destruction in Oklahoma City mixed with fury that it should be connected with us. "We know what it's like to lose children," I told a pushy reporter. "Anytime kids die is a tragedy. We're just here to honor our dead. We'll say a prayer for those children, offer our sympathies for the parents who're suffering as we suffered. But to make the assumption that we had anything to do with it is just plain crazy!" However, the insistent linkage between Oklahoma City and Mount Carmel made by the patriot movement has merely served to further pervert the memory of our tragedy.

Back in Los Angeles, most of the people I knew didn't seem to want to talk about any of this, and I was grateful. If people asked me direct questions, I'd answer; otherwise, I kept silent.

However, I did continue giving talks to receptive audiences, at three-month intervals. Mainly I was invited to speak at the regional

Preparedness Expos organized by survivalist groups. These weren't my venues of choice, but in the hardened public perception of Mount Carmel, now linked with Oklahoma City, these were the only people who seemed willing to hear what I had to say. I wanted to break out of the closed circle of patriot sympathizers into a wider pool of listeners, but, apart from the ACLU, liberal groups and organizations shunned us like the plague, leaving us captive to the radical right. For a while I saw myself as an outcast from an America that had always been mine.

Mount Carmel and its fate had become a weight on my spirit. My friends said I'd lost my feeling of fun along with my sense of humor. I'd surely lost touch with the kid in me, that lighthearted side that delighted in toys and cartoons. "As an artist, you have to keep close to your childish stuff," Ryan warned, and he was right.

I kept in contact with other Mount Carmelites. From jail, Renos Avraam wrote that he believed he had his own message to give the world. Livingston Fagan sent letters to all and sundry from his Leavenworth cell. In Waco, Clive Doyle was struggling to hold the frayed threads of our community together. He now lived in a cottage near the site of Mount Carmel, leading a small group of survivors, mainly older women like Catherine Matteson and Tillie Friesen, who had remained in the Waco area. This group included Sheila Martin and her three surviving children.

Some remaining members of our community appeared to believe that David would eventually be resurrected to bring in the final Day of Judgment. They continued to have faith that this would happen.

Jack Zimmerman's hope that a congressional oversight committee would investigate the Mount Carmel tragedy was realized in the summer of 1995. For ten working days, beginning July 19, the Joint Subcommittee of the House Judiciary Committee on Crime and the House Government Reform and Oversight Subcommittee on National Security, Internal Affairs, and Criminal Justice (made up of twenty-eight Republicans, twenty-three Democrats, and one

independent) heard some one hundred witnesses and reviewed
thousands of pages of testimony about the ATF raid on February 28, 1993, and the siege and fire that followed.

But if Jack hoped that any light would come of all this heat, he
had to be sadly disappointed by the outcome. From day one of the
hearings it was clear that David Koresh was on trial, not the Justice
Department or the politicians or the bureaucrats or the mecha-
nisms that made it possible for the federal government to kill innocent Americans. Also, it was soon obvious that the hearings were
essentially a partisan circus in which the Republicans were out to
tarnish the Clinton administration, while the Democrats were determined to defend it.

I was called as a witness the first day, taking my seat in the Capitol hearing room at one of a series of tables facing two raised tiers
of congressmen backed by a large Stars and Stripes. Squatting on
the floor between us were TV cameramen and photographers, set
to capture our expressions as we testified. The high-ceilinged hearing room, with its tall, draped windows and partly paneled walls
decorated with portraits, reflected an architecture of dignity belying the pettiness of the actual proceedings.

For the occasion, I wore a conservative, dark suit, a white shirt,
and a tie. To appear more normal, I pulled my long hair back with
an elastic band. Looking down the row of witnesses, I saw some
familiar faces, including sociologist Stuart Wright, whom I'd met
at an American Academy of Religion conference in Washington on
Thanksgiving 1993, and Henry McMahon, the Waco gun dealer
whom I'd introduced to David in 1990.

Committee co-chair Bill McCollum, a Florida Republican,
banged his gavel and opened the first day's session with a solemn
statement that the hearings were to be solely about constitutional
oversight, not gun control, the militias, or any other issue. He described the siege of Mount Carmel as "the single most fatal episode
in the history of federal law enforcement." However, he showed
his true colors by reading out the names of the four ATF agents
who died during the raid on Mount Carmel, but not those of the
six members of our community whom the ATF had killed, or the

seventy-four others who perished in the fire. "With Waco, Americans got rationalizations instead of accountability," McCollum declared.

No sooner were the words out of his mouth than a dogfight erupted over the National Rifle Association's advisory role to the Republicans. New York Democrat Charles Schumer alleged that the hearings were a plot by the gun-rights group to repeal the Brady gun-control law and the assault-weapon ban and to abolish the ATF. The National Rifle Association, roundly characterized as "rifle rackers in hunting vests," became the hearing's biggest red herring.

The strategy of the Democrats was summed up by presidential press secretary Mike McCurry. "The NRA [National Rifle Association] bought and paid for the congressional investigation that's under way here," he declared. Leon Panetta, White House chief of staff, damned those who supported the hearings as "despicable," and Clinton himself denounced the hearings as nothing short of an ideological "war against police." He added that it was "irresponsible for people in elected positions to suggest that the police are some sort of armed bureaucracy acting on private grudges and hidden agendas."

McCollum's retort to all this was succinct. Such statements were, he said, "plain political hogwash." Through the session and the days following, the hearings degenerated into a scratching match between the dimpled, prissy Republican co-chair and Schumer, a saturnine street fighter. These two pecked at each other as if in a cockfight—a puffed-up hen versus a spur-flashing bantam rooster. The shadow looming over this political pettiness was the recent Oklahoma City bombing. The smoke that still rose from the memory of that catastrophe clouded the issues, reducing the chance that the FBI and ATF would ever be hauled over the coals for their conduct in Waco.

But Schumer's ferocious attitude still floored me. It crystallized the depths of the liberal left's antagonism toward the Mount Carmel community, its absolute lack of sympathy for our fate. Schumer implied that child-abuse allegations alone justified the ATF raid, conveniently ignoring the fact that federal law enforcement had no jurisdiction over child abuse. It staggered me that Democrats like Schumer could have opposed such injustices as the Vietnam War, only to back the brutality of the feds in Waco. As one reporter wrote, "Conservatives defended the counterculturalists while Liberals took a law-and-order stance."

When my time came to testify I was sworn in and questioned by Georgia Republican Bob Barr. Along with Clive Doyle, I was the only survivor who gave testimony at the hearings. While the court reporter beside me tapped at her machine, Barr led me through a series of questions about David's movements in the weeks before the ATF attack, the ATF affidavit, our weapons, and the accusation that we operated a drug lab. I tried to answer calmly and honestly, not claiming to know things I hadn't seen, trying by my sober demeanor to contradict the widely held notion that we were a bunch of religious freaks.

I wanted to read a statement I'd written, but I was allowed only to enter it into the record. It began: "On February 28, 1993, the world witnessed a vulgar display of force set against a community of people living in a large home on the barren prairie lands of Texas," ending with the declaration that this "shows nothing but cowardice and fear, strength in numbers, power in oppression. Not the America I remember."

New York Democrat Louise Slaughter grilled me about the alleged child abuse in Mount Carmel, including the merciless beating of eight-month-old babies. I tried to tell her that I had never seen anything of the sort, but she rolled right over my answers before the words were out of my mouth.

Whatever I had to say about this subject was drowned in the drama of the story told by Kiri Jewell. Accompanied by her father, who sat beside her stroking her back, Kiri repeated her tale of being molested by David in a motel room when she was ten years old. "David took his penis and rubbed it against my vagina," the fourteen-year-old said, reading from her prepared script. Urged on by the maternal Florida Democrat Karen Thurman, Kiri talked about some other young girls whom David had slept with. She said that Michele had told her that her heart was pounding in panic as David penetrated her when she was only twelve years old, a detail that shook me.

When Kiri added the graphic quote she claimed came from David—"Jeannine Bunds had the type of pussy that really hangs onto my dick"—Bill McCollum's prim mouth went into spasm, and he immediately warned the TV audience who might be watching the C-SPAN broadcast to beware.

I was shocked by Kiri's tale. Sitting next to her, watching her flick her long, fair hair from her sweet, girlish face, listening to her teenage lilt, I couldn't easily believe she was lying. "Ever since I was little I've had big ears," the girl said. "This is my truth." After ending her fifteen minutes of testimony, Kiri rested her head on her daddy's strong shoulder. This is not the David I know, I told myself. But maybe I hadn't known him as well as I thought. Or maybe he had changed in the years before I met him.

"We have a very brave young girl here," Congresswoman Thurman murmured, as Kiri dabbed the tears from her eyes, and it was hard not to agree with her. To comfort Kiri, I poured her a glass of water.

It was only later, when I talked to Ruth Mosher, Kiri's grandmother, back in Anaheim, California, that I began to doubt the details of her story. Kiri was also less than convincing when she talked about the plans for mass suicide she said she'd heard in Mount Carmel. She claimed she was told that "the best way to shoot yourself in this battle with Babylon was to put the gun into your mouth back to the soft spot above your throat before pulling the trigger." From my experience in Mount Carmel, ten-year-old children weren't allowed anywhere near a firearm, much less practice any soft-spot-in-the-mouth maneuver. That part of the girl's testimony smacked of manipulation, probably by her father, who'd already exploited Kiri's story by putting her on *Donahue* during the siege and marketing her appearance on a number of TV programs.

With Kiri's testimony, the demonization of David was planted center stage. Brandishing an AR-15, Schumer ranted about "this

evil man," and no one disputed him. California Democrat Charles
Lantos babbled about the "apocalyptic vision of a criminally insane
charismatic cult leader . . . hellbent on bringing about this infernal
nightmare." This amazed me, coming from Lantos, a Hungarian
Jew who had survived the Holocaust.

The witness list had been heavily weighted against us. Of
ninety-four total witnesses, only eight presented our viewpoints.
Webster Hubbell and William Sessions, the now-disgraced duo that
had spurred Reno to make her fatal moves, were there, wagging
their wattles. The forensic experts called to testify about such issues as how the fire started were either current or former government employees or consultants.

However, the issue of automatic weapons allegedly found at the
Mount Carmel site was never resolved. Questioned by Republicans,
officials from the Department of Justice said they could have conducted tests to see if some of the guns allegedly found at Mount
Carmel were, in fact, fully automatic, but they'd decided the tests
were too expensive. To date, no competent authority has been allowed to examine these weapons. To add insult to injury, none of
the witnesses who defended the government's conduct at Waco referred to Mount Carmel's destruction as a tragedy, massacre, or
disaster. To them, it was just the "Waco incident."

The Clinton administration withheld crucial documents and set
up a war room inside the White House to coordinate the media and
the committee Democrats in an attempt to undermine the hearings.
Their efforts were so blatant that Oklahoma Democrat Bill Brewster
publicly complained about pressure from the U.S. Treasury secretary not to embarrass the administration during the hearings.

"Apparently out of fear that revelations in these hearings could
damage the Clinton presidency," Bill McCollum stated, "the White
House, Congressman Schumer, and some at Treasury and Justice set
out this past week to ridicule, trivialize, and discredit these hearings."

But the Republicans really were no better. As nationally syn-
dicated columnist Samuel Francis wrote: "What the Republicans
cared about was trying to pin the whole boondoggle on President
Clinton and thereby chalking up yet another cheap point to score

against him in next year's presidential campaign. By avoiding the real and important issues raised by Waco . . . [the Republicans] not only made themselves look like fools but also may have destroyed the usefulness of Waco as Exhibit No. 1 for what is wrong with federal law enforcement."

Congressman Barr was finally moved to comment that "the tragedy at Waco is, I think, probably without doubt the single most tragic incident in American law enforcement history. We must get to the bottom of the unanswered questions, and take some steps to do everything possible to ensure that this sort of thing does not happen again." He added: "Because I don't believe the American public would stand for another Waco."

I wasn't asked to attend the two-day Senate Judiciary Committee hearing on Waco held at the end of October, but I knew its results would likely be no better than those of the House hearings. Utah Republican Orrin Hatch, the committee chair, declared that the hearings were not out to blame anyone, and Delaware Democrat Joe Biden stated that there was no need for more investigations of what happened at Mount Carmel. Treasury official Ron Noble dismissed the disaster as "a single tragic aberration." This was the closest any government official testifying at either hearing came to referring to the destruction of Mount Carmel as a tragic occurrence rather than a mere "event."

Graeme Craddock, brought inside the Beltway from his prison cell, impressed the senators with his honest, straightforward answers to tricky questions. "If we were deceived [by David Koresh], we were genuinely deceived," he said. Professor James Fyfe of Temple University, a specialist in criminal justice, put his finger on the heart of the matter when he stated that "there is no FBI to investigate the FBI. There is no Justice Department to investigate the Justice Department. There is no independent non-partisan citizen review of incidents like Ruby Ridge and Waco. There should be."

Thus, with barely a whimper, and the hope that time would dim memory, the organs of government digested our terrible experience and excreted a ton of more or less useless paper, which, they hoped, would bury us forever.

"Precisely because there will probably be no meaningful judicial review of any of these constitutional issues in the Waco case, it is all the more imperative in our democracy that we, the people, think critically about what the government did at Waco," professor Edward Gaffney wrote, "lest the raid on the Davidians becomes by our silence or our complicity a precedent for doing it again to some other marginalized religious group of which the government disapproves."

20

THE DOUBLE HELIX

During the return flight to Los Angeles following the congressional hearings, I was more depressed and confused than I'd been in a long time. Some of the things I'd heard in Washington disturbed me deeply, especially the accusations about David. Kiri Jewell had said David told her the biblical King David had taken young women to warm his blood, and the image of Michele's twelve-year-old heart pounding wildly as David took her virginity burned a hole in my mind. I knew that if Michele had been my sister I would have considered what he did with her as very evil and very wrong.

Did I still believe in everything David had taught me? I wondered. I realized I hadn't opened a Bible in months; and when I did, my eyes glazed over. David had said, quoting Scripture: *If inspiration is cut off, what are the saints to do?* At that moment, I didn't have a clue. Riding above the clouds, I realized I'd come halfway back through the fence dividing belief from disbelief. I was caught in an act of retreat, and that made me feel very weak.

When I'd been with David, I shared his strength, his spiritual awareness. Now that that had been taken, I was left to fend for myself. But his legacy was imprinted on my mind and spirit, making my native sensuality a source of guilt. The spiritual and the sensual threads of my character were unraveled, the strands floating loose

335

like a disconnected double helix. *Would I ever be able to weave them together into an integrated pattern? Use my spirituality to refine my sensuality, my sensuality to ground my soul? Make a whole life out of a pair of uncoupled spirals?*

"I'm not going to kill myself over who I am," I muttered, drawing a curious look from the man in the seat beside me.

I was truly depressed by the futility of the procedures I'd been part of inside the Capitol. Their main aim seemed to be to grind down the harsh realities of our pain and loss so that they could be swallowed and forgotten. But thinking it over, I began to comprehend that maybe that was how it had to work. Perhaps, despite the politicking, manipulation, and ass-covering—or maybe because of them—the ground of opinion had begun a slow seismic shift.

At the hearings, even earlier, it had been tacitly recognized that the attitudes and tactics displayed by the FBI and ATF during the siege and raid were badly out of whack. Sure, there'd been no outright apologies for the feds' appalling actions; and with the reinstatement of ATF raid leaders Charles Sarabyn and Philip Chojnacki, no government official had ever really been punished for those actions. Certainly, none had been indicted, as David had demanded during the siege; and Janet Reno, who'd made such ill-informed and devastating decisions, was still in office.

This enraged me. However, in a calmer frame of mind, I came to see that even though bureaucracies protect their own they inevitably feel social pressure and slowly shift the basis of their methods. I began to hope that the ATF and FBI would act very differently next time they focused on an "alternative" community like ours.

Still, I had to wonder what might have happened if only Janet Reno had shown some contrition; if only she could have brought herself to admit that what she had allowed to happen in Mount Carmel was a terrible mistake. If she had, the true healing process over this American tragedy might have finally begun. Without that generous admission, the public conscience has remained in limbo, strung out between guilt and outrage.

David Koresh's own actions, both positive and negative, certainly contributed to the Mount Carmel disaster. However he justified his sexual relationships with young girls, he was guilty of the crime of statutory rape, and he had to know that would eventually provoke the authorities to investigate the community, as indeed it did. This issue opened us up to all kinds of hostility that might well have been avoided, given that the community had peacefully coexisted with locals for fifty years before David arrived in Waco.

More subtly, David failed to actively respond to the ominous signs that law enforcement officials were focusing attention on Mount Carmel for months before the February 28 attack. If he'd been more savvy, he might have hired an attorney to challenge the authorities on the issue of stockpiling illegal weapons, which they used as the prime wedge against us. The ATF would then have been forced to show its hand publicly, preempting the agency's devious intentions. Wayne Martin once advised David to do just that, but he'd ignored this wise counsel.

Maybe David was half in love with Armageddon. Or perhaps he feared that this strategy would have brought everything out into the open, including his own criminal culpability in having sex with underage girls. This, indeed, was the worm in the apple of our collective innocence.

Yet the very fact that the hearings had been held showed that America couldn't quite forget Mount Carmel. Its brutal fate truly was a rip in society's fabric, and I had to believe that a slow mending would eventually work a change in the pattern of our culture. Such belief in the capacity of America to repair its errors, I realized, might be the truest kind of patriotism. It was certainly more profound than the paranoia of the patriot community and the militias' penchant for violent action.

The tension between the strands of institutional inertia and natural justice was another kind of double helix. Like my own, its spirals were also rather frayed. But I had to believe that, in both cases, the threads would come together. I had to believe in America and in myself. Frankly, I had nowhere else to go. I'd crossed back through the fence far enough to know that I could not exist

under the shadow of doom David had predicted. For him, his belief in Armageddon was an affirmation; for me, it was a crusher.
Right now, all I could do was live for myself, play music, remember.

As I stared out the plane's window, the world below seemed to
drop away into a bottomless pit.

———————

Failure met me early on my return to Los Angeles.

In the L.A. music scene you have to work twice as hard as anywhere else to make anything happen. You have to want it a hundred
percent and more, because there are hordes of others pressing
around you who do. The blunt fact was that our band wasn't going
anywhere, and eventually it just faded away. The band's demise hit
me hard, a personal as well as a professional failure. The songs
were world class, but divided we fall, and not everyone in the band
seemed willing to put in one hundred percent.

Then there was my ambiguous, post–Mount Carmel attitude
toward sex. Surprisingly, given my long celibacy, I didn't go crazy
with women for a few years after I left Waco. I missed female company, but I was just too busy trying to rediscover who on earth I
was. Also, I seemed to have lost my taste for casual sex. Women
often came up to me after I gave a talk, seemingly turned on by my
public soul-baring. We went out for dinner or a drink, but mostly I
let the moment slide. I wasn't yet ready for a serious relationship, either. Clearly, my erotic energies were dulled, and that worried me.

However, my dilemmas seemed petty when I'd receive one of
Jaime's letters from jail. Often they were written in faint pencil, as
if each printed letter had been carefully considered:

Dear Dave,

*I had intentions of calling you, but, do [sic] to an unavoidable fight, I
now find myself in the hole. I've been in here 25 days with another 14
to go! I don't know how Livingston can endure this kind of shit. . . .*

*Since I've been in segregation, I've just about spanned my whole
life. I've thought about my childhood years, teenage days, high school*

and the beginning of my spiritual quest. And although the present is a
bitter experience, I have no regrets that I am where I am.

Though we all as individuals still share the same experience of
what we went through, that's something we'll all have to deal with on
our own. All of us have the responsibility to remain faithful to what
we perceived was the truth.

Keep rockin' and HANG IN THERE! Oh ya, don't go by your
feelings! Just fucken with you!

Anyway bro, take care of yourself and keep the faith.
Love,
Your friend,
Jaime

Reading this, I was stricken with a strange envy. How simple it
would have been if I'd been sent to jail, along with Jaime and the
others. Prison routine would've neatly continued the discipline of
Mount Carmel. Now, out here in the world, I was trying to structure my own days, but it wasn't going well.

———·•·———

I attended the annual memorial events at the Mount Carmel site
in 1996 and 1997. The gatherings, held on the windy plain, were
muted and ritualized. We gave speeches, and Clive Doyle and I appeared on national television, mostly to field questions about the
connection between Mount Carmel and Oklahoma City. "I am not
a member of militias," Clive emphatically told the media. "I don't
speak to militias."

At the 1994 memorial I met Greta Stephens, a beautiful young
woman with a chiseled face and startling blue eyes. I was drawn to
her seriousness, her spiritual awareness. Greta joined me in Los
Angeles in 1996. We hadn't meant to have an affair, but she was too
desirable to resist. Later, she got pregnant, and we decided to get
married. Our daughter, Dylan, was born in December 1997.

Inside Mount Carmel I was close to the kids, but I didn't know
what it was like to have a child of my own. It changed everything,

challenging my sense of myself. I'm crazy about that little girl, and I want to watch her grow up. There's nothing as joyful as holding Dylan in my arms.

Sometimes I wonder what my life might have been like if I hadn't met David that day on Sunset Boulevard back in 1990.

A friend once said to me, "What if, at the moment you met David, Mick Jagger had come up to you and offered you a spot with the Stones?" My answer was that I would surely have chosen the Stones. However, if the choice had occurred after I'd spent a few months inside Mount Carmel, I would've chosen David.

Though it was utterly different from anything I'd ever imagined, the time with David changed something crucial in me. His God wasn't the God I'd ever thought I wanted. In fact, before I knew David, I hadn't known I needed to experience a spiritual opening. My mother and family, and maybe many friends, feel that my meeting David knocked me off my perch, maybe permanently, leaving me confused and disoriented. Sometimes I even think that myself, but I know it's not really so.

So, all I can say in the end is that everything that happened to me in Waco sprang from the fact that I became a believer, a man of religion, like millions of other Americans. (A recent *Time* poll reported that almost a quarter of the American population believes in the literal truth of the Bible, and an overwhelming majority follows some kind of faith.) Belief can't really be explained to those who don't have it, but that doesn't make it invalid, and my religious commitment is essentially no different from that of the many people who attend regular churches, synagogues, mosques, and temples. My teacher, David Koresh, had his own vision of biblical truth, but that was his God-given right and his privilege as a U.S. citizen—mine, too.

My interrupted time in Mount Carmel has made me more guarded, less spontaneous; more thoughtful, less impulsive; more cautious, less careless. The tension between my soul and my flesh is a hard struggle, but it is also very valid and worthwhile. I believe in Scripture, though I often don't act as if I still do. In the words of an old hymn, I was blind and now I see—but seeing ain't easy. I'm still making mistakes, but I'm not going to let those errors destroy my self-respect. While striving to knit up the loose strands of my nature, I go on drumming and witnessing, doing what I can to honor the hard truths David Koresh, my friend and teacher, and the community he created gave me as a gift.

AN EPILOGUE TO THE PAPERBACK EDITION

Even though nearly twenty-five years have passed since the horrific events at Waco, it still stands out as the seminal experience of my life. I try not to think of the siege too much because my life has moved on and when I dwell on what happened and why, I feel that familiar emotion of anger. One memory will never be erased, though, or even fade, and that's the memory of Serenity, the daughter of Michele, the woman I was most close to in Waco. I remember the sweet little pout on her face, her wide blue eyes, and the way she had of making you feel important and loved when she looked at you in her trusting way. I imagine her telling me all the good things that have happened to her in the intervening years. We even discuss today's current events and the changes that have taken place in the world since that fateful day on the Texas plains, April 19, 1993.

Who would she be today? Where would she be today? Even at such a young age, Serenity was an inspiration to anyone who had the good fortune to have known her. She was a bright light walking around Mt. Carmel, and the thought of her going up in flames is unbearable.

I think of her particularly when I see my daughter, Nova, who is now nineteen years old. She's a delightful woman, stubborn like her father, beautiful like her mother. But little Serenity never had the opportunity to grow up. She perished at the age of three in the conflagration of Mt. Carmel, along with her mother, two siblings, and twenty-one other children all under the age of fifteen. Like the others who burned or suffocated to death, she was completely innocent.

Looking back, I see those events as so needless, so unjustified, and so horrific. Seventy-six people perished on that day, a day that could have been avoided had the federal government acted with compassion and restraint. If only they would have allowed David Koresh to finish writing out the Seven Seals manuscript as had been negotiated. But the government, for many different reasons, chose to attack rather than let him complete his writing. Apart from not acting with compassion and restraint, the FBI—with the government's collusion—acted out of ignorance and a lack of any sense of psychological insight. The situation could easily have been defused, but instead the FBI literally lit the fuse, hurled it into the building, and incinerated most of its inhabitants.

I now realize that David Koresh made huge mistakes. He was guilty of statutory rape and slept with a number of women, among them Michele, who was fourteen at the time. (Serenity was one of David's children.) It should be noted that the age of consent in Texas at that time was fourteen (with parental permission) and although David's actions might have been legal at the time, they were morally reprehensible, as well as bigamous. Also, he should have allowed the children to leave before the end result and for that he will have to answer to God.

David, along with other Davidians, went regularly to gun shows in Waco to buy and sell guns, which was perfectly legal. I'll never be able to understand why the feds couldn't have picked him up on one of those numerous trips when he left the compound. The fact is, there was only one man on that warrant and they could have picked him up at any time away from the group. That would have been such an easy, logical, and sensible thing to do. But the government was crazed with power and wanted to get a big bust at any cost. What if they had actually done their research and realized they were dealing with a man who really believed in the Bible? Even at this late date, it astonishes me to realize how many mistakes were made by the leaders of the ATF and by the commanders on the ground. They didn't even listen to their own agent, whom they'd sent in that fateful morning to talk to David. Although the tragic and ignorant mistakes that were made have already been covered in this book, they are important to emphasize.

So many of the Davidians have been demonized by the media. As one of a handful of survivors, I felt it my duty to tell the true story of a group of people who were trying to live according to their religious beliefs and the teachings of a man they all considered divinely inspired. I don't take the Bible literally but I do believe that David Koresh, despite his many failings, knew the Bible better than anyone I've ever met. Not that I'm a typical follower of Scripture. In fact, I was raised in a household of nonbelievers or, at the very least, agnostics. I watched cartoons as a kid, ate Cap'n Crunch cereal, laughed at Archie Bunker's antics with my father, and obsessed about girls at school, hoping that someday I would be cool enough to talk to them. I also grew up loving music and wanting to be a drummer, and it was this ambition, more than any spiritual yearning, that first led me to Mt. Carmel.

Whatever my expectations when I arrived at Mt. Carmel, I ended up sharing an experience that made history, an experience that has been misrepresented at almost every turn. Both the ATF and the FBI were so good at lying about the government's role that I decided the most effective balance to these webs of distortions and outright lies was to publish my own words as an eyewitness. I have never cared if they call me a liar or a cultist or otherwise try to discredit me.

After the traumatic events of Waco, I would have been happy just going back to my music. The tragedy seemed at the time—and still seems—unreal, as if this part of my life was a work of fiction written by some unseen hand. But so many overt lies and cover-ups have threatened to obscure the true story of Waco that even now, twenty-five years later, I feel a strong sense of responsibility to tell it as honestly as possible. In these pages I wanted to honor each and every one of the people who died, as well as those who survived, and this was a daunting task. Apart from all the complexities of the Davidians and their individual stories, no one can really understand Waco without having a knowledge of the Scripture that David taught, but I'm not a preacher. Interpreting Scripture is neither my calling nor my job, which is why I tried to keep my book as political as possible. Even writing my own story may have been beyond my capabilities, but it turns out that one thing I'm good at is finding the right team to help me make this book a reality. I was introduced to Leon Whiteson through my agent, Charlotte Gusay. In Leon, I found the perfect partner to bounce ideas off and be inspired by. He was a gifted writer, and I was deeply saddened that in 2013 at the age of eighty-two, he died of cancer.

Not until four years ago, when I was approached by filmmakers John Erick Dowdle and Drew Dowdle about making a movie, did I feel a similar level of trust. I had been approached frequently by so many people but, to tell the truth, I never wanted a film to be made. Every other Waco film had been absolute crap, with the exception of the 1997 documentary *Waco: The Rules of Engagement* (directed by William Gazecki, written by William Gazecki, Dan Gifford, and Mike McNulty). The Dowdle brothers had done so much research and had so much material they ended up deciding to make a six-part series with the Weinstein Company and Spike TV. I knew they could achieve so much more in that format than in a two-hour movie, so that came as a relief. John and Drew flew to my home in Bangor, Maine, and we hung out and talked for hours. I appreciated where they were coming from and started to see the vision they had. After so many previous disappointments, and because they wanted me to be on set as a story consultant, I began to hope that this version would get the facts straight and even help those in charge avoid repeating their fatal mistakes. Maybe it could even change the way people thought of those who died at Mt. Carmel, because no matter what you think of David Koresh, his followers died needlessly for their faith.

When I finally arrived in Santa Fe, I spent the first day on the set in stunned silence. I was shown into the office of Karyn Walker, who was responsible for all the costumes and clothing of the era. She had photos of everyone she could find up on the walls, and I stared in fascination at pictures of every individual I had known at Mt. Carmel. There was Julie Martinez and her two sons Joseph and Isaiah; Greg Summers, Jaime Castillo, Steve Schneider, and Wayne Martin; the Henrys; Perry and Mary Bell Jones; and of course, Michele and my little Serenity. That was a heavy day, but also a joyful one. Seeing those faces again was like going back in time, which was both unsettling and exciting. But nothing could compare to the day we drove a car out of town to the area where Mt. Carmel had been rebuilt. The location was amazing! They had managed to find a place that was flat for miles around just like Mt. Carmel. Across the street was an old building that looked similar to the ATF house where Robert Rodriguez had stayed with his fellow agents. There it was—a complete re-creation of the area.

The most intense experience, though, was seeing the film's full reproduction of Mt. Carmel. The set was perfect down to the tiniest detail. They even had a flagpole with a Star of David fluttering from the top and a re-created Seraph flag, which had been designed by David Koresh and Cliff Sellers, the group's artist. Some details were changed—time sequences for example—but I was reassured by the fact that some of the people I knew and was close to were represented and honored appropriately. It was an even greater surprise when I walked into the set of the chapel area to see a double bass Pearl drum set just like the first drum set I had owned. I sat on the stage feeling completely at home. That's when Taylor Kitsch, the actor playing David Koresh, walked in. "Man," he said, "It's so cool to see you sitting on that stage. I spend a lot of time in here alone trying to get into the head of my character."

One of the great pleasures of being on the set was talking to the filmmakers themselves, from the actors to the writers and producers. Every single one of them told me that reading my book and the subsequent film script had been an eye-opener. Paul Sparks, the actor who plays Steve Schneider, said that when he first heard about the events at Waco, he fell right in line with the propaganda that portrayed Waco as being a really bad situation headed for a really bad end. Having worked on the film and read the book, he still felt Waco was a bad situation headed for a bad ending, but for vastly different reasons.

Like Paul Sparks, Sal Stabile, who was the executive producer and main script writer, told me that until he'd read my book, he believed what he had heard in the media—that there was an imminent danger from this heavily armed doomsday cult who were torturing children. "For the first time in my life, I was shocked that so little true information had been given out. What shocked me most, though, was that these people had negotiated a deal to come out of the compound but were never given the chance. I thought I lived in a country where you were presumed innocent until you were found guilty in a court of law. If this could happen to a group of Christians living in Texas, it could happen to a group of Muslims in a mosque or any group at all. We're living in a time where it's hard to find the truth and Waco serves as an example of how the truth isn't always what we're presented with. If we were really interested in the truth, we need to do our own due diligence. It's twenty-five years too late, but I think all those families should be given a proper apology." His sentiments were echoed again and again by both cast and crew. As Taylor Kitsch remarked, "Now that I've been exposed to countless events and personal accounts, I've changed my views on Waco entirely. It's disappointing we haven't learned from the tragedy that was Waco. Just maybe we'll be able to open ourselves up to multiple viewpoints."

For John Dowdle, the experience of working on this film series had been like peeling the layers of an onion in order to uncover the truth about the events of 1993. "I found it shocking to discover the humanity of the people of Mt. Carmel. That alone changed a lot of what I thought I knew. When you know people better, it truly humanizes them. It becomes harder to write them off and it hurts to see their pain and suffering."

On my drive back from the set in New Mexico to my home in Maine, I stopped over to visit with some of the survivors of Mt. Carmel. Clive Doyle and Sheila Martin are still living in Waco. Both of them had been in the church even before David Koresh came on the scene. Clive told me that most of his life is devoted to serving God but he was reluctant to talk about the events in Waco. Even though he lived at the Mt. Carmel property for many years after the fire, so many people came to see where it had all happened and asked so many questions, he became overwhelmed. He now lives a quiet life in the town of Waco and has written a book about his experiences called *A Journey to Waco*.

While visiting Clive, I asked him what had happened to Brad Branch since I had not been able to find a trace of him through my research. Brad was released from prison in 2006 with the remaining survivors. I found out that another survivor, British subject Renos Avraam, claimed to have received a message from God. He had a vision that revealed to him that America was going to be destroyed and that Central America was the only safe place. Brad Branch and Kevin Whitecliff ended up following him there and are all now awaiting the end. I have to admit I didn't see this turn of events coming for my old friends.

Another survivor, Kathy Schroeder, lives in Tampa, Florida. She turned state's evidence after the siege, because she wanted to protect her children, and has spent the last twenty-five years rebuilding her life. Asked why Waco is important today, she said that part of David's teachings involved people paying more attention to avoiding a herd mentality. "We follow in the steps of the person in front of us without really thinking about what we're doing. We should love our parents but we should not live their lives. We must do what's right for us." She still talks about how important the Seventh Seal is to her. "When I first learned the Seventh Seal, it was utterly and totally amazing for me to be at that point. It taught me that I knew nothing, that everything we had learned is like an atom compared to God's universe and what He has in store for us. My relationship with God is about me believing and following. I regret nothing and would do everything again exactly the same way."

I found that most of the survivors continue to serve God in some fashion, whether this includes leading a prayer group, working in a soup kitchen or food bank, or serving the poor and handicapped. Livingston Fagan, who now lives in the UK, works with the elderly and is still very involved in studying Scripture. He is probably the best biblical scholar of any of the survivors. I was particularly shocked when I found that my closest friend and ally at Mt. Carmel, Jaime Castillo, died at the age of forty of liver failure brought on by hepatitis C. He was sentenced to forty years in prison on a weapons and manslaughter charge. Later his sentence was reduced by the Supreme Court and he was released in 2006. I wish I'd had the opportunity to reunite with him before he died.

Looking back, I can see that I learned a huge amount from my time in Mt. Carmel, but that now, unlike some of the other survivors, I feel "messaged out." I'm happy to live my life in the best way I can and honor those who were cheated of theirs. Waco has left a stain on American history that will never be erased, and we ignore its lessons at our peril. John Dowdle's reply to my question about why Waco is both relevant and important today sums it up perfectly. "I feel as if we have a very 'us versus them' mentality. Everything has grown so politicized that it's hard to find common ground even on simple issues. There is a rush to judgment and condemnation that I feel is really hurting our ability to effect positive change. Waco, for me, is a story of force versus understanding. When attempts were made to listen to and understand one another, things got better. Conversely, attempts at force never brought positive results. At this moment in time, I feel as if that's an important lesson to remember. When we listen to one another, we heal and learn. When we condemn and vilify one another, at best we lose the ability to grow; at worst, people get hurt."

It's hard to believe that almost a quarter of a century has passed since I emerged from the hell of that final day. I'll be forever a changed man, but I still believe life is a wonderful thing, even in dark times. Someone once told me that, after Waco, the rest of my life would be gravy. Well, it wasn't quite gravy. There were times early on when being a survivor became too much to handle. I would pray to God to allow me to go nuts and lose touch with reality so I wouldn't have to face all the negativity and hate. Fortunately, I kept my faculties intact, but the emotion of anger is always with me. It comes from living this long and seeing the utter lack of justice for the children and adults of

Waco. These feelings linger and will never go away. Overall, though, I'm happy. I love to laugh and enjoy my family and bandmates. People on the film set kept telling me how normal and well adjusted I seem considering everything I've been through. I may not share their opinion, because I have to live with myself. I know the anger that comes from having been in a helpless situation, but I also have a lot of hope that this generation will do the right things for the right reasons.

I have one last wish. I often think of the children who survived Waco, the ones who lost mothers, fathers, brothers, uncles, grandparents. I have not been in touch with any of them, except for Kevin Jones. He is a fine young man who would have made his father proud. To those I have not been in touch with, especially David's children, I want to tell them I'm available whenever they want to reach out. They may not want to be reminded of the trauma of those days, but with so much demonization, I want to assure them that they were and are loved. Their parents were not evil and they were not robots. They had personalities and dreams like everyone else. To these children, I say:

If you should ever feel alone, I promise that I and many others think of you fondly and hope that you can go on to show the world you are strong and unstoppable. Much love to you and to everyone I share this planet with.

—*David Thibodeau, September 2017*

SPECIAL THANKS AND ACKNOWLEDGMENTS

First I wish to thank the Father and Mother of all creation for the experience and guidance that has been given to me throughout my life, especially during the stubborn times when I felt I had no guidance at all. Thanks to David for giving me the knowledge of the Scripture, showing me the importance of the Book in this generation and for showing me the depths of the eternity it represents. I wish to thank my wife and daughter for their patience and support during the course of creating this book and for warming my heart during the coldest of times. Thanks to my mother, Balenda, for always believing in me and being behind me, no matter what. Thanks to my father for giving me a love of history, as well as words of wisdom. I would like to thank my uncle, Bob, for all his help and support, and my grandmothers, Gloria and Flo (Mim), for teaching me values that are rarely found in this generation.

This book would not have been possible if it weren't for my literary agent Charlotte Gusay, who had the courage, belief, and tenacity to take on and promote such a controversial story, and Leon Whiteson, who helped me to reach deep within and open up the darkest chapters of my life, spending countless hours putting it all into written form. Leon's charming wife, Aviva, was an expert editor and friend. A very, very special thanks to Geoff Shandler and the team at PublicAffairs for taking on this book and many other books that are of paramount importance to this nation.

Thanks to my friends in Maine: Leonard Smith III, for being my best friend and always being there for me; James Brown; Sherry, for being there for me when no one else was. Thanks to my dear friend Stacy Hanna, who excelled in my high school drama class, danced like an angel, and was destined to become a shining star on the world stage, R.I.P. Your memory gave me much hope and confidence, and you are greatly missed. Thank you so much, Mr. Pike, for bringing out the best in me.

I would like to thank my early roommates and dear friends Brian (thanks for calling the studio) Paris and Ryan Azevedo. Who could forget Bam Bam? Thanks to Ryan Martin, Scott Gephart, Tobias Kroon, and Torbjorn Anderson for the ymi! years. Thanks to the guys in Stirling Brig. My hat's off to John McKane for his part in the story you've just read and for letting me crash on his couch (the house-guest turned roommate, again!) and to his bandmates. Best of luck, guys—see you at the Rainbow!

At the end of this book there is a list of all those who have died, those who are in prison, and those who are free to tell the tale. I would like to thank some of those who have been directly involved and some who have been like family to me throughout the last five years: Clive and Edna Doyle, Sheila Martin, Jaime Castillo, Misty Ferguson, Derek Lovelock, Ruth Riddle, Rita Riddle, Catherine Matteson, the Haldeman family, Mary Belle Jones, Ofelia Santoyo, Livingston Fagan, Brad Branch, Paul Fatta, Kalani Fatta, Kevin Whitecliff, Ruth Mosher, and the two theologians Philip Arnold and James Tabor. I have seen the best and the worst in people throughout my ordeal, and one of the best is Dr. Rodney Crow. I would like to thank three people who uncovered vital information: James Pate, for investigating and finding the truth; Mike McNulty for digging deep and finding the facts to prove the impossible, and who made the unbelievable believable; and Ron Engelman (last, but certainly not least), for standing up for our rights when many others wouldn't.

I would also like to thank Dan and Amy Summer Gifford for having the courage to produce the documentary *Waco: The Rules of Engagement*. You have both helped to increase awareness of what happened to my community and to the world at large. Thanks to William Gazecki for all the hard work and long hours he spent editing *The Rules of Engagement*, and also for allowing me to come and view it while it was being put together. William's efforts have made the documentary a world-class film. Special thanks to Dan Chittock and the entire team at Preparedness Expos. Thanks to Richard Mosely.

My thanks to all the individuals that I may have forgotten to mention personally in the acknowledgments. All of the people who sponsored me and let me into their homes while I gave talks about my experience, and the hundreds of people who asked me to write this book—you have all shown me by example that an open mind and a charitable outlook are truly the road to the divine. You have demonstrated the best of humanity.

Many thanks to Dick Reavis for writing the book *Ashes of Waco* and for all of his extensive research and effort to get to the truth. And a special thanks to James Tabor for the book *Why Waco?* and for attempting to research and explain the spiritual dimension of our community. And to Phil Arnold of the Reunion Institute, thanks for being one of the first to listen to us.

In closing I would like to thank the people of the press, especially the editors who have helped to create history to fit their own agenda. These people have helped to make me stronger and more determined to overcome obstacles, reveal the truth, and set the record straight.

APPENDIX

The Mount Carmel Community: The Living and the Dead

In February, 1993, before the ATF assault, the community had around 130 members, including 45 women and 43 children.

During the ATF assault, and in the final conflagration, 80 community members died: 33 women, 26 men, and 21 children.

5 men and 1 woman died on February 28.

35 exited during the siege: 9 women, 5 men, and 21 children;

83 people remained inside to the end: 35 women, 21 children, and 27 men.

32 women, 21 men, and 21 children—a total of 74—died on April 19 (plus two stillborn fetuses).

9 people survived the April 19 fire: 6 men and 3 women.

9 others were outside Mount Carmel itself on February 28, including Michael Schroeder, who was killed that day.

DIED FEBRUARY 28, 1993:
Winston Blake, British, 28, black.
Peter Gent, Australian, 24, white.
Peter Hipsman, 28, American, white.
Perry Jones, 64, American, white.
Michael Schroeder, 29, American, white.
Jaydean Wendell, 34, American, Hawaiian.

DIED APRIL 19, 1993:

Adults:

Katherine Andrade, 24, American, white.

Jennifer Andrade, 20, American, white.

Alrick George Bennett, 35, British, black.

Susan Benta, 31, British, black.

Mary Jean Borst, 49, American, white.

Pablo Cohen, 28, Israeli, white.

Abedowalo Davis, 30, British, black.

Shari Doyle, 18, American, white.

Beverly Elliot, 31, British, black.

Doris Fagan, 60, British, black.

Evette Fagan, 30, British, black.

Lisa Marie Farris, 24, American, white.

Raymond Friesen, 76, Canadian, white.

Sandra Hardial, 27, British, black.

Zilla Henry, 55, British, black.

Vanessa Henry, 19, British, black.

Phillip Henry, 22, British, black.

Paulina Henry, 24, British, black.

Stephen Henry, 26, British, black.

Diana Henry, 28, British, black.

Novellette Hipsman, 36, Canadian, black.

Floyd Houtman, 61, American, black.

Sherri Jewell, 43, American, white.

David Jones, 38, American, white.

David Koresh, 33, American, white.

Rachel Koresh, 23, American, white.

Jeffery Little, 32, American, white.

Nicole Gent Little, 24, Australian, white
     (and her stillborn child).

Livingston Malcolm, 26, British, black.

Diane Martin, 41, British, black.

Wayne Martin Sr., 42, American, black.

Anita Martin, 18, American, black.

Wayne Martin Jr., 20, American, black.

Juliet Martinez, 30, American, Hispanic.

John-Mark McBean, 27, British, black.

Bernadette Monbelly, 31, British, black.

Rosemary Morrison, 29, British, black.

Sonia Murray, 29, American, black.

Theresa Nobrega, 48, British, black.

James Riddle, 32, American, white.

Rebecca Saipaia, 24, Filipino, Asian.

Steve Schneider, 43, American, white.

Judy Schneider, 41, American, white.

Clifford Sellors, 33, British, white.

Scott Kojiro Sonobe, 35, American, Asian.

Floracita Sonobe, 34, Filipino, Asian.

Gregory Summers, 28, American, white.

Aisha Gyarfas Summers, 17, Australian, white
     (and her stillborn child).

Lorraine Sylvia, 40, American, white.

Michele Jones Thibodeau, 18, American, white.

Neal Vaega, 37, New Zealander, Samoan.

Margarida Joann Vaega, 47, New Zealander, Asian.

Mark H. Wendell, 40, American, Asian.

Children 15 and under:

Chanel Andrade, 14 months, American, white.

Paige Gent, 1, American, white.

Dayland Gent, 3, American, white.

Serenity Sea Jones, 4, American, white.

Chica Jones, 22 months, American, white.

Little One Jones, 22 months, American, white.

Cyrus Koresh, 8, American, white.

Star Koresh, 6, American, white.

Bobbie Lane Koresh, 2, American, white.

Lisa Martin, 13, American, black.

Sheila Martin Jr., 15, American, black.

Crystal Martinez, 3, American, Hispanic.

Isaiah Martinez, 4, American, Hispanic.

Joseph Martinez, 8, American, Hispanic.

Abigail Martinez, 11, American, Hispanic.

Audrey Martinez, 13, American, Hispanic.

Melissa Morrison, 6, British, black.

Mayanah Schneider, 2, American, white.

Startle Summers, 1, American, white.

Rachel Sylvia, 12, American, white.

Hollywood Sylvia, 1, American, white.

LEFT MOUNT CARMEL DURING SIEGE:

Brad Branch, 34, American, white.

Livingston Fagan, 34, British, black.

Nehara Fagan, 4, British, black.

Renea Fagan, 7, British, black.

Oliver Gyarfas, 19, British, black.

Victorine Hollingsworth, 58, British, black.

Heather Jones, 10, American, white.

Kevin Jones, 11, American, white.

Mark Jones, 3, American, white.

Margaret Lawson, 75, American, Asian.

James Lawten, 70, American, white.

Christyn Mabb, 8, American, white.

Jacob Mabb, 10, American, white.

Scott Mabb, 12, American, white.

Daniel Martin, 6, American, black.

James Martin, 11, American black.

Kimberly Martin, 4, American black.

Sheila Martin, 46, American, black.

Catherine Matteson, 77, American, white.

Natalie Nobrega, 11, British, black.

Gladys Ottman, 67, American, white.

Annetta Richards, 64, Jamaican, black.

Rita Fay Riddle, 35, American, white.

Ofelia Santoyo, 62, American, Hispanic.

Bryan Schroeder, 3, American, white.

Kathryn Schroeder, 34, American, white.

Angelica Sonobe, 6, American, Asian.

Crystal Sonobe, 3, American, Asian.

Joshua Sylvia, 7, American, white.

Joann Vaega, 7, New Zealander, Asian.

Juanessa Wendell, 6, American, Hawaiian.

Tamara Wendell, 5, American, Hawaiian.

Landon Wendell, 4, American, Hawaiian.

Patron Wendell, 1, American, Hawaiian.

Kevin Whitecliff, 31, American, white.

SURVIVORS, APRIL 19, 1993:

Renos Avraam, 32, British, white.

Jaime Castillo, 27, American, white.

Graeme Craddock, 35, Australian, white.

Clive Doyle, 52, Australian, white.

Misty Ferguson, 17, American, white.

Derek Lovelock, 37, British, black.

Ruth Riddle, 32, Canadian, white.

David Thibodeau, 24, American, white.

Marjorie Thomas, 30, British, black.

OUTSIDE MOUNT CARMEL ON FEBRUARY 28:

Norman Allison, 28, British, black.

Donald Bunds, 55, American, white.

Paul Fatta, 35, American, Hawaiian.

Kalani Fatta, 14, Amcrican, Hawaiian.

Janet Kendrick, 34, American, white.

Woodrow Kendrick, 62, American, white.

Janet McBean, 25, British, black.

Stan Sylvia, 50, American, whitc.

INDEX